COLUMBO
UNDER GLASS:

A critical analysis of the
cases, clues and character of
the Good Lieutenant

Sheldon Catz

Columbo Under Glass

© 2016. Sheldon Catz. All rights reserved.

Published in the USA by:
BearManor Media
P O Box 71426
Albany, Georgia 31708
www.bearmanormedia.com

Printed in the United States of America

ISBN   978-1-59393-956-4 (paperback)

Book & cover design and layout by Darlene Swanson • www.van-garde.com

Contents

Contents

Contents

Foreword by Mark Dawidziak

Well, it's about time. I've been waiting for this book for almost thirty years. Not this particular book, you understand, but some book-length study that would build on the foundation I tried to establish with *The Columbo Phile*. Let me explain. When *The Columbo Phile*, my look at the forty-five original *Columbo* mysteries, was published in 1989, I fully expected it would be followed by lively and insightful tomes addressing all sorts of elements and aspects of the classic series that I neglected. You see, I didn't view *The Columbo Phile* as THE book on the good Lieutenant. I viewed it as merely A book on the beloved television character played so brilliantly by Peter Falk. Book-wise, this was meant to be the first word on the subject, never the last. Columbo's trademark line was, of course, "Oh, just one more thing." *The Columbo Phile* didn't leave just one more thing to say about the character and the series. It left lots and lots of things to explore, examine, and investigate. Look at how many books have been written about Sherlock Holmes. Consider how many volumes have charted the *Star Trek* universe. Certainly *Columbo* merited at least a few more book-length treatments. I was the first to realize how much more there was to say about the deceptive detective in the raincoat. So after *The Columbo Phile* was published by the Mysterious Press, I sat back and waited for another *Columbo* phile to pick up the cigar and run with it. And I waited. And I waited. Year after year, I wondered when that book would make its appearance.

It has been like that long early stretch in most *Columbo* mysteries where you're waiting for our disheveled hero to make his entrance. Okay, where is he, already? It typically turns out that the wait makes his delayed appearance all the more welcome, delicious, and delightful. The same might be said of the book you now hold in your hands. It was more than worth the wait.

At this point, that's kind of the point. It had to be worth the wait. It couldn't just be a book about *Columbo*. It had to be something special. And this one is. That's because the job fell into the capable hands of Sheldon Catz, who kept on the job with a dogged determination and bulldog perseverance that Columbo himself would have admired. This has been a long and challenging quest for Sheldon, and he has more than earned the observation the first *Columbo* murderer, Dr. Ray Fleming (Gene Barry), made about the scruffy sleuth: "You're the most persistent creature I ever met, but likable."

A great deal has happened on the *Columbo* front since the publication of *The Columbo Phile*. As that book was going to print, new *Columbo* mysteries were in production for ABC's revival of the character – a revival that would net Peter Falk yet another Emmy. There ultimately would be twenty-four *Columbo* capers on the Alphabet Network, bringing the Lieutenant's total of TV mysteries to sixty-nine. A seventieth had been developed, but Universal couldn't get ABC to commit to it. There were other developments, on screen and off, but I'll let Sheldon tell you all about that, and many other "one more" things. The evidence is overwhelming. This book had to be written, and thank goodness it was written by Sheldon.

Another phrase *Columbo* was known to utter was, "I'll be a son of a gun." Even with my familiarity with all things *Columbo*, I was left saying this over and over again as Sheldon found insights and intriguing clues in episode after episode. That applies just as much to the original forty-five mysteries as it does to the twenty-four new ones.

Peter's foreword to *The Columbo Phile* contained this passage: "Now I know what it feels like to be one of the murder victims on *Columbo* – stretched out on an autopsy table with an expert going over you piece by piece. Mark Dawidziak has done a first-rate job dissecting the whole *Columbo* series, not only the Lieutenant himself but every character, clue, guest star, you name it. After reading his book I really think he knows more about the damn show than I do." The time has come to pass along that *Columbo* compliment to someone who has picked up where *The Columbo Phile* left off and run in all kinds of fascinating directions. I know that Peter would second this, probably adding a "I'll be a son of gun" that was dripping with admiration.

It's about time. And it's about time you got started on this splendid trip. You'll be traveling in a wheezy Peugeot with a lieutenant named Columbo, a dog named Dog, and a *Columbo* phile named Catz. You couldn't ask for better company.

Introduction

This book had its genesis back in 1989, when three remarkable events coincided. First, I bought a copy of a recently published book, Mark Dawidziak's *The Columbo Phile: A Casebook* (Mysterious Press, New York), to date the best reference work on the series (and the only one that exists, at least in English). For the first time, I had the ability to read about my favorite episodes, answer those pesky questions I had always wondered about, get a sense of the series as a whole and learn what the writers, actors, directors and producers had to say about the show.

Second, it was at this same time that ABC, after a ten-year hiatus, brought the good Lieutenant back to life, first as part of a mystery wheel and then on his own, ultimately resulting in twenty-four new mysteries. This gave *Columbo* fans something to talk about, some new material to appreciate and something to look forward to. Although these new entries have not, for the most part, matched the quality of the two pilot movies and forty-three episodes produced between 1971 and 1978, many of them are very enjoyable and a few have been outstanding.

Third, and on a personal note, it was just about then that I finally managed to see all of those "original" forty-three episodes. I came to the series somewhat late in its first run (having been born in 1965, I wasn't really able to appreciate the show when it premiered) and I watched some episodes chopped to pieces on *CBS Late Night* in the early 1980s. While at school in Boston, I found a local station that aired all of the episodes on weekend afternoons, and I watched them regularly, many times each. With the help of Mark's book, I came to appreciate the entire package and I wrote to him to discuss it. Being the gracious individual he is, he wrote back and we corresponded for a while. One day, I asked if there was a newsletter or fan club out there so that we could chat with others who shared our interest. He said not yet, and challenged me to do something about it.

So I did. In late 1991, I put together the first issue of *The Columbo Newsletter*. Over the next ten years, I had the pleasure of editing this quarterly publication, in which I included my reviews of the episodes from the 1970s (presented chronologically), along with comments from other fans, interviews, articles and so on. Meanwhile, the new *Columbo*s were being aired, so we discussed those as well. A cadre of regular contributors sent articles in every quarter and provided some different points of view.

For me, one of the most enjoyable aspects of putting out the newsletter was the ability it gave me to discuss the show from the perspective of someone who had seen all of the episodes. Whether they realized it or not, the writers had created a template with a number of fascinating variations. I made note of and named some of these recurring features, such as the "final clue" (the piece of evidence or trick, etc. by which Columbo arrests the murderer at the end), the "first clues" (those initial observations that lead him to suspect that the scenario is a false one and to begin his series of one-on-one dialogues with the individual we know to be the murderer) and so on. Best of all, I love to compare the episodes to each other and rank them.

When I approached "The Conspirators" (#43), the last episode from the 1970s, it was late in 2001 and I faced a choice: to continue with the newsletter for another five years or so (one episode review per issue, four issues per year twenty-four new episodes) or write a book. I chose the latter option, for the following reasons. First, I figured that the twenty-four episodes formed a small enough unit that they could be contained within a single book, so that everyone could read about them without waiting five years to see the end. Second, there was so much other news to discuss (*Columbo* episodes then became available for purchase from Columbia House Video, what William Link had been doing, etc.) that I wanted to put all of that out at once.

But time passed, things happened and I changed course. I eventually decided to use this book to discuss the series as a whole, but life (in various aspects, good and bad) kept getting in the way. Indeed, it was Peter Falk's death on June 23, 2011, that finally gave me the push I needed to finish this opus.

In the seventh season episode "Columbo Under Glass" (#40), the clever title manages to refer to both food (as in "pheasant under glass") and the magnifying glass that has been a symbol of the classic detective. I call this book *Columbo Under Glass* because my goal is to put everything I think about the show in one book, to celebrate the show and all that I love about it as well as to point out where it fails to hit the mark. The purpose of this book is not so much to talk about any one episode of the show as it is to discuss all of them simultaneously, to compare them to and contrast them with each other, to find themes and to probe the character and all of the changes that have been made to him. I hope that it is half as fun to look through as it was for me to compile and that it answers most (if not all) of the questions you ever had about *Columbo*.

Before I forget, let me answer some questions I've been asked on occasion: why all the discussion? Can't you just enjoy the show without picking it apart? The answer is simple: I enjoy it all the more because I can take it apart and put it back together again (very few shows lend themselves to this kind of in-depth analysis) and, just like some sports fans love to review every play of a game they've seen, I love to dissect *Columbo*. What can I say? If you don't enjoy the discussion, then this is not the book for you.

Another question I expect is, "If you love the show, why is there criticism in this book?" Yes, I do, and that's why I think it's fair to praise the show when it hits all the right notes and to point out when it doesn't. I don't expect everyone to agree with me, but that's what makes it all the more fun.

Assuming you're still with me, let me explain how the book works. In Part

I, there are summaries of every episode of *Columbo* (identified by full name and chronological number, such as "Murder By the Book" (#1)), including the two pilot movies (*Prescription: Murder* (pilot A) and *Ransom for a Dead Man* (pilot B)) and even the play (*Prescription: Murder*) and live show ("Enough Rope") that preceded them (they are in the Prologue). This constitutes Chapters 1 through 14, the first thirteen corresponding to seasons and the last five TV movies are in Chapter 14. The epilogue discusses William Link's 2007 play, *Columbo Takes the Rap*, and his 2010 book of new short stories, *The Columbo Collection*. Following the epilogue is a table of the major production information, although the full production information is included in each season.

Each capsule lists the "guest murderer," victim(s) and other significant characters, explains what the scenario is supposed to look like (a robbery, suicide, etc.) and provides the motive. Then I give the "Final Clue," that last piece of information that Columbo uses to arrest the murderer. Following the plot description is a quick review of the episode, its best points and its not-so-good ones. Finally, I give my ranking for each episode (on a scale of 1 to 10, with 10 being the best); the complete ranking list is contained in Appendix I. Appendix II is *Columbo* by the numbers: a complete list of facts and figures about the show, such as who wrote the most episodes (Jackson Gillis, who wrote eleven stories and/or screenplays) or which episode has the most victims ("A Bird in the Hand" (#59) has three).

Here's where it gets interesting, and the name of the game is cross-reference. Throughout these summaries are cross-references to essays that are contained in Part II. These essays (some of which first appeared in *The Columbo Newsletter*; others are new for this book) break the show down and compare and contrast various elements to one another. If you want to know more about "Confession Endings," just open the book to the essay about them and each episode that employs one is so noted in the summaries.

The essays are grouped together by topic. Chapter 15 is called Let's Talk Columbo, containing discussions of "Why I Love Columbo," "Recurring Problems" and the infamous "Bloating Problem" that at least occasionally accompanied the show's expansion to two hours in 1972. Chapter 16 describes the plot structure, Chapter 17 explores all the different kinds of *Columbo* endings, Chapter 18 outlines variations and "non-*Columbos*." Chapter 19 contains essays about "Motive, Method and Appearance" (with three corresponding tables), Chapter 20 discusses the various kinds of Columbo-murderer relationships, and Chapter 21 contains More About the Character (including "The Developing Character," "Peter Falk as Columbo," two essays about Columbo's morality, a little side bar on "Does He Exist?" and a piece on Columbo's first name, "You Can Call Him Lieutenant." Chapter 22 talks about Other Actors and Characters (including actors who repeated their performance as murderers, "The Supporting Cast" of regulars, "Bert, Barney and Dog" and "Colleagues and Sidekicks") and Chapter 23 discusses titles, music, continuity and Columbo's accolades. Finally, Chapter 24, called "Columbo Everywhere," contains additional information, including news about how to purchase the episodes, a list of *Columbo* books and a discussion of *Columbo*'s "offspring" and *Columbo* on the Web.

The book also provides me with an opportunity to debunk some "myths" I have seen out there on the Internet. Maybe as time has passed, people have forgotten the details of the show, but I've been somewhat surprised by some of the ideas people share. So here, in no particular order, are the five most common misunderstandings about *Columbo*:

1) His wife doesn't exist. Actually, she does—people are getting the little shtick he does about having a relative for every occasion confused with the fact that he has a real, honest-to-goodness wife at home (it's just that she's kept hidden from the audience). See "Does Columbo Exist?" for more on this one.

2) Columbo just magically "knows" whodunit when he first arrives at the scene of the crime. Not so—as explained in "First Clues" there are usually two clues he spots, one indicating that the setup left by the murderer is false and another pointing toward the guilty party.

3) The show is a devious "up-with-the-proletariat" social commentary in which a middle-class cop takes down a wealthy and haughty murderer. Well, it's true that Peter Falk's New York accent and Columbo's sloppy appearance contrast nicely with wealthy, vain murderers, but Levinson and Link explained a long time ago that they were not trying to make a societal point. Moreover, it's easy to demonstrate that this is not a necessary premise of the show. Just check out "Swan Song" (#22), in which famed country western singer Johnny Cash plays a version of himself, a down-home guy who calls Columbo "little buddy" and is anything but haughty and superior.

4) Columbo usually tricks the murderer into making a dumb move or a confession. The way I count them, most episodes end with Columbo finding a piece of evidence that ties the murderer to the scene of the crime (24), busts the alibi they've relied on (5) or the scenario they've created (7), or shows them that it's all been for naught (2). That adds up to thirty-eight. Of the other twenty-nine episodes, eighteen rely on trick endings, eight are confessions and three utilize the "Kill Columbo Ending." See the chapter on "Final Clues" for more details.

5) All of Columbo's business about little details bothering him and being forgetful is just an act; he's really a brilliant guy who lulls the murderer into a false sense of security. Well, I agree that Columbo is smarter than he lets on and he certainly uses that to his advantage. But as for being forgetful, that was in the original live TV program "Enough Rope" (he says his wife gives him a new pencil every morning because he loses the one from the day before) and what's wrong with that? When it's important he remembers the details, whether it's by writing them down, putting them on a tape recorder (as he does in "Mind Over Mayhem" (#21)) or taping little notes to his shaving mirror (as he does in "Double Exposure" (#19)). As for those little details, there's a great scene in "Negative Reaction" (#25) in which he tells Captain Sampson about a point that bothered him (an alleged kidnapper riding around in cabs) and how he put it all together.

A note on style: as mentioned above, episodes are always listed by their full titles, with initial capitals and the chronological number ("Blueprint for Murder" (#7)), TV shows are in italics (*Columbo*)—as are books (*Just One More Thing*) —but characters are not (Columbo). Essays are in quotes ("First Clues"), music is in quotes ("This Old Man") and plays are in italics (*Columbo Takes the Rap*).

So, here's what I have not done in this book. You will not find anything in here about visual continuity errors; you know, when a scene shows different amounts of ash on Columbo's cigar or the show employs two different styles of helicopters in the same scene in "A Friend in Deed" (#23). That kind of thing is hard to discuss in a book, and it's not really of much interest to me anyway. I suggest The Ultimate Columbo website (see "*Columbo* on the Web").

Nor does this book talk about Peter Falk's other TV appearances, movies or plays. It isn't that I don't like his other work (I enjoy much of it), but that's outside the scope of this book. I suggest the Internet Movie Data Base (www.imdb.com), an excellent resource I refer to frequently.

This book would not have been possible without Mark Dawidziak's prior work, his advice and constant support. I cannot thank him enough.

I also owe a huge debt of gratitude to my wife (that's "Mrs. Catz"), who not only put up with all the time I spent working on the book, but who also served as my first and last editor. Finally, a quick word about my daughter, who wasn't even born when I began working on the book, but who now (at age 12) watches an episode of *Columbo* with me faithfully every Sunday morning and who is responsible for several observations about the show. It has been a wonderful opportunity to watch the episodes again and share them with her.

Part I: The Episodes

Prologue:
Pre-Columbian Columbo

Before *Columbo* premiered on *The NBC Mystery Movie* on September 15, 1971, the character was first on television, then in a play and then again on TV. Here's a brief history.

Richard Levinson and William Link met in junior high school in Philadelphia and began a writing partnership that lasted for forty-one years until Levinson's untimely death on March 12, 1987, at age fifty-two. They wrote tons of mystery stories, one of which was published in *Alfred Hitchcock's Mystery Magazine* under the name "Dear Corpus Delecti." It ended with a knock on the door; had the cop entered, he would have been Columbo. During a writer's strike in 1960, they turned the story into a one-hour installment of *The Chevy Mystery Show*, a summer replacement for *The Dinah Shore Chevy Show* on NBC. It was directed by Don Richardson. On Sunday, July 31, 1960, host Walter Slezak introduced the following story:

"Enough Rope"

Psychologist Dr. Roy Fleming (Richard Carlson) strangles his wife Claire (Barbara Stuart) in their New York City apartment the night she thinks they are leaving for a second honeymoon in Toronto. Then his patient and lover, Susan Hudson (Joan O'Brien) arrives. Dressed in Claire's clothes, she accompanies Fleming to the airport where they stage a fight and she storms off the plane, so it will look like Claire went home and was attacked by a burglar.

Fleming returns several days later. Lieutenant Columbo (Bert Freed), who smokes a cigar and wears a hat, is suspicious of the scenario, particularly the fact that Fleming's luggage is nine pounds lighter on return (a result of him having disposed of the items the burglar "stole" from them). Fleming is nervous, but he comes up with answers to Columbo's "loose ends." Columbo has Fleming listen to a man named Tommy (Thomas Nello) confess to the crime, but Fleming doesn't fall for the trap (for one thing, his suitcase doesn't have his initials on it, so Tommy couldn't have seen them). Eventually, Fleming asks his friend from the district attorney's office, Dave Gordon (Duncan McLeod), to have Columbo taken off the case. Columbo comes to Fleming's office and asks to be taken on as a patient, but Fleming throws him out. In the end, the wily Lieutenant returns to the luggage issue. He recreates Fleming's list of stolen items and amazingly they add up to the nine-pound weight difference. Susan is brought in and asks how they found the stuff. Columbo announces that he intends to dredge the lake near the cabin where Fleming stayed to find the real "stolen" items. Fade to black.

Additional cast: Harry (Frank Behrens), Miss Petrie (Mimi Walters)

Production Information

Executive supervisor: Norman Lessing. Producer: Himan Brown. Executive producer: Henry Jaffe. Unit manager: Don Van Atta. Art director: Robert Kelly. Associate director: Tom Foulkes. Costumes: Grady Hunt. Make-up: J. Manning Smith. Technical director: Clair McCoy. Lighting: Joe Viera. Audio: Bill Cole. Senior video: Ray Olsen. Music coordinator: Phebe Haas. Production assistant: Jean Messerschmidt.

The show did well enough that Levinson and Link converted it into a full-length stage play, which they titled *Prescription: Murder*. It opened at the Curran Theatre in San Francisco on January 20, 1962, and played across the country, but not in New York. Levinson and Link wanted to make changes to it and threatened to sue. Every time it played, however, the same thing happened: the main character was supposed to be the murdering doctor, but the Columbo character got the biggest applause. The plot follows that of "Enough Rope" with these changes:

Prescription: Murder (the play)

Psychiatrist Dr. Roy Flemming (Joseph Cotten) [note the change in profession and the spelling of his last name] tells his wife Claire (Agnes Moorehead) that they will take a trip to a lodge in upstate New York, then strangles her and is assisted by his patient and lover Susan Hudson (Patricia Medina) as described above. Columbo (Thomas Mitchell), who smokes a cigar and wears an ash-covered topcoat, notices that Flemming doesn't call to his wife upon returning. Claire is in a coma, but revives only enough to say Flemming's name before she dies. The Lieutenant mentions but does not pursue the luggage weight discrepancy clue. Tommy's confession is mentioned, but not used to trick Flemming. Columbo and Flemming have a scene in Flemming's office in which he describes Columbo as a "perfect example of compensation" (that is, he is smarter than he looks, so he plays dumb to lull people into a false sense of security) and the Lieutenant responds "you got me pegged, Doc." They also discuss a "hypothetical murderer" who plans every detail and Flemming says he cannot catch someone like that. Columbo seems to take Flemming's advice and focuses on Hudson, the weak link in the plan. He grills her severely and she nearly breaks down, but rallies and he lets her go. But the following morning, he comes to Flemming's office and expresses his regret—he must have pushed Hudson too far and she committed suicide. After confirming this fact with Dave Gordon (Howard Wierum) from the D.A.'s office, Flemming turns himself in because his plan has all been for naught. After the men leave, Hudson (who had been driven around by a policeman while the calls went back and forth) comes into Flemming's office and smiles as she opens a gift he left for her. Curtain.

Additional cast: Miss Petrie (Lucille Fenton), dry cleaner delivery boy (Raleigh Davidson.)

The play also did well and, several years later when Levinson and Link heard that Universal Studios was looking for TV movie projects, they submitted it and it was accepted. Richard Irving, a seasoned director, producer and studio executive, was assigned to direct it. With the writers' permission, he changed the setting from New York to Los Angeles to save on production costs. Thomas Mitchell had died in December 1962 (an understudy took over for the duration of the production of the play, see "Prescription: Mitchell" for more) and Levinson and Link's initial choices of Lee J. Cobb and Bing Crosby did not work out. A young actor named Peter Falk, whom they knew socially, had seen the script and wanted the part. Irving convinced them to give him a try. The movie was filmed and it aired on NBC on Tuesday, February 20, 1968. The plot follows that of the play, with these changes:

Prescription: Murder (pilot A)

Psychiatrist Dr. Ray Flemming [note the change in first name] (Gene Barry) would gladly divorce his wife Carol [note the change in first name] (Nina Foch), but she has announced that she would make a scandal of it and take everything from him. So he convinces her that they're leaving for a trip to Mexico, then strangles her and is assisted by his patient and lover, Joan Hudson [note the change in first name] (Katherine Justice), as outlined above. Columbo (Peter Falk), who mostly carries around his raincoat, notes that Flemming does not call out to his wife upon returning. Carol is in a coma, but by the time Flemming pulls some strings at the hospital to get to see her, she has said his name and died. Columbo mentions but does not pursue the luggage weight discrepancy. Flemming is very cool and has answers to all of the questions posed by Columbo, but he also asks his friend from the D.A.'s office, Burt Gordon [note the change in first name] (William Windom), to have the Lieutenant taken off the case. Tommy (Anthony James) confesses to the crime, but Flemming says he's lying. Flemming compliments Columbo on being a textbook example of compensation and they discuss the hypothetical murderer who Flemming says cannot be caught. Columbo interrogates Hudson, but she withstands it. In the end, Hudson doesn't show up for an appointment, so Flemming goes to her house, where he and Columbo watch as her body is removed from the pool. Columbo asks Flemming to confess, seeing as how he killed his wife to be with Hudson and now he can't. But Flemming laughs—he (that is, the hypothetical murderer they discussed in his office) just needed "the girl" to pull off the crime and he eventually would have gotten rid of her, too. Hudson, who has been listening from another room, comes out and agrees to testify against him. This movie contains some of the sharpest Columbo/murderer dialogue ever heard on the show, excellent acting and direction. But the "First Clue" is a behavioral one (that Flemming doesn't call out to his wife when he enters), which is not very strong and presents something of a prescience problem (see "Recurring Problems"). The ending is a little difficult to believe, because Hudson is very much in love with and dependent on Flemming and the groundwork is not laid for her to turn on him in this fashion (see "The Three Cs" and "Accomplices, Blackmailers and Schlimazels"). The scene in which Columbo badgers Hudson seems out of place with the character as later developed, but the movie does introduce his droll manner and forgetfulness (he loses the pencil his wife gives him every morning). See "Columbo Gets Angry" and "The Developing Character."

Additional cast: Miss Petrie (Virginia Gregg), Cynthia Gordon (Andrea King), blonde (Susanne Benton), nurse (Ena Hartman), air hostess (Sherry Boucher)

Production Information

Director & Producer: Richard Irving. Associate producer: Jerrold Freedman. Music: Dave Grusin. Director of photography: Ray Rennahan. Art director: Russell Kimball. Film editor: Richard G. Wray. Unit manager: Edward K.

Dodds. Assistant director: George Bisk. Set decorations: John McCarthy & James S. Redd. Sound: James T. Porter. Color coordinator: Robert Brower. Editorial supervision: Richard Belding. Musical supervision: Stanley Wilson. Costumes: Burton Miller. Makeup: Bud Westmore. Hair stylist: Larry Germain.

The movie did very well and NBC proposed a series, but Falk (who had a bad experience playing the lead in *The Trials of O'Brien* from 1965 to 1966) was wary. In 1971, Universal and NBC came up with an idea to make the series more palatable to Falk—it would rotate with two other series in a Mystery Movie package (the idea had already succeeded with a show called *Name of the Game* (NBC 1968-71), in which Gene Barry, Tony Franciosa and Robert Stack were each featured in discrete episodes; and *McCloud*, which would shortly rotate with *Columbo* and other shows, had already premiered as one of *Four in One*—the shows aired consecutively in the 1970-71 season and did not rotate with one another). He could make six shows per year rather than twenty-four.

Nevertheless, the network also asked for another pilot, just to make sure the concept would work. Levinson and Link sketched out an idea, which was fleshed out by Dean Hargrove, and Richard Irving again directed. The TV movie aired on Monday, March 1, 1971.

Ransom for a Dead Man (pilot B)

Attorney Leslie Williams (Lee Grant) shoots her husband Paul (Harlan Warde) and makes it looks like he was killed after she pays the ransom to his kidnappers. Columbo tricks Williams into believing that her annoying stepdaughter Margaret (Patricia Mattick) will go away if she is paid off and Williams uses the marked ransom money. This second pilot is not as sharp as the first one, and it contains a lot of behavioral clues (including the "First Clue" that she didn't inquire about her husband) and a not very nice comment by Columbo about a man working for a woman (see "Recurring Problems"). Also, the plot is driven far too much by Margaret. However, the trick ending is solid (see "The Three Cs"), Falk and Grant are excellent, as is Harold Gould as FBI agent Carlson. The movie introduces the audience to some more aspects of the Columbo character—his fear of flying, kind nature (witness his gentle treatment of Margaret), love of chili and the game of pool and the character of his friend Bert (Timothy Carey) at Barney's Beanery (see "Bert, Barney and Dog"). See "The Developing Character" for more.

Additional cast: Michael (John Fink), Hammond (Paul Carr), Phil (Jed Allan), Richard (Charles Macaulay), attorney (Henry Brandt), Pat (Jeane Byron), Perkins (Richard Roat), Celia (Norma Connolly), Crowell (Bill Walker), judge (Judson Morgan), priest (Richard O'Brien), Gloria (Celeste Yarnell), Nancy (Lisa Moore), waitress (Lois Battle), mechanic (Reginald Fenderson)

Production Information

Music: Billy Goldenberg. Director of photography: Lionel Lindon. Art director: John J. Lloyd. Film editor: Edward M. Abroms. Set decorations: Bert F. Allan. Unit manager: Don Gold. Assistant director: George Bisk. Sound: Robert Bertrand. Editorial supervision: Richard Belding. Costumes: Burton Miller. Aerial sequences by Tallmantz Aviation, Inc.

Chapter 1:
The First Season (1971-72)
(Episodes 1-7)

A s explained in the Prologue, NBC and Universal Studios convinced
Peter Falk to star in *Columbo* as part of a "mystery wheel" so that it
would rotate with two other shows and they would only have to make six
episodes. Between March and September 1971, the team wrote, directed
and produced six shows; then they were asked for a seventh and they fin-
ished it, too. The other spokes of the wheel were *McCloud,* starring Dennis
Weaver as Marshal Sam McCloud, who is visiting New York City from Taos,
New Mexico, to "learn big-city techniques" but mostly winds up annoying
Chief of Detectives Peter B. Clifford (J.D. Cannon); and *McMillan and Wife,*
starring Rock Hudson as Stewart "Mac" McMillan, Police Commissioner in
San Francisco, Susan St. James as his slightly ditzy wife Sally, John Schuck as
Mac's assistant, Sergeant Enright, and Nancy Walker as the maid, Mildred.
The three series rotated as the *NBC Mystery Movie* on Wednesday nights be-
ginning in the fall of 1971 (in the second year, the whole package would
move to Sunday night and remain there for its duration).

Some of us remember the terrific opening sequence (if not, you can
watch it on YouTube): a man approaches from the background as twilight
descends, he swings a flashlight which comes to rest on each of the rotating elements, and a beautiful score by Henry Mancini plays. Indeed, since

Columbo was the only program not to have its own music, some people mistakenly think the Mancini music is the "*Columbo* theme." During this season, there were seven episodes each of *Columbo*, *McCloud* and *McMillan and Wife*, each ninety minutes long.

(#1) Murder By the Book

Written by Steven Bochco. Directed by Steven Spielberg. Music by Billy Goldenberg. Airdate: 9/15/71.

Ken Franklin (Jack Cassidy in the first of his three appearances, see "Multiple Murderers") does not want his mystery writing partner James Ferris (Martin Milner) to break up their relationship, particularly because people will discover that Ferris did all the writing. In addition, by killing Ferris, Franklin can collect on an insurance policy. Franklin shoots Ferris after tricking him into telling his wife Joanna (Rosemary Forsyth) that he's working late at the office when he's actually at Franklin's cabin in San Diego. Later, storeowner Lilly La Sanka (Barbara Colby), who can place Ferris and Franklin together on the day of Ferris's murder, tries to blackmail Franklin. She winds up a "drowning victim" (see "Accomplices, Blackmailers and Schlimazels"). Columbo arrests Franklin when he discovers that Ferris's death matches a plot idea that Ferris jotted down some time ago (ironically, it was Franklin's, the only good one he ever had). Although this episode has a fantastic pedigree—terrific acting by Falk and Cassidy, a clever plot by Bochco, excellent direction by Spielberg and some solid clues—the ending is disappointing (see "Busting Alibis, Busting Scenarios"), particularly when a better alternative (the sequence of telephone calls) already exists (see "Intermediate Clues"). The "First Clue" is a behavioral one and the "Final Clue" presents a right answer/wrong means situation (see "Recurring Problems"). The car is introduced here (see "The Developing Character"), as is "scene two" in which Columbo gathers his "First Clues" (see "Columbo Deconstructed"). Ranking: fair (6.5).

Additional cast: Interviewer Gloria Jr. (Lynnette Mettey), Mike Tucker

(Bernie Kuby), Sergeant (Hoke Howell), second reporter (Haven Earle Haley) [note: Marcia Wallace is listed in the credits as "woman" but she actually appears in "Lady in Waiting" (#5)]

(#2) Death Lends a Hand

Written by Richard Levinson & William Link. Directed by Bernard Kowalski. Music by Gil Mellé. Airdate: 10/6/71.

Arthur Kennicut (Ray Milland) hires private investigator Mr. Brimmer (Robert Culp in the first of his three appearances, see "Multiple Murderers") when he suspects his wife Lenore (Patricia Crowley) of having an affair. When Brimmer finds this to be true, he lies to Kennicut and tries to blackmail Lenore, realizing that she can provide him with information regarding her husband's powerful business connections. Lenore threatens to turn him in, and Brimmer strikes out in anger and her head hits a glass coffee table, with fatal results. Columbo believes that Brimmer transported Lenore's body in the trunk of his car, so he convinces Brimmer that Lenore's missing contact lens is still there. When Brimmer breaks into a garage to retrieve the lens, the Lieutenant is waiting for him. This episode had a good premise and solid acting by Milland. The planted contact lens allows Brimmer to cry frame-up (see "The Three Cs") and sets an unfortunate precedent for Columbo's morality (see "The Morality of Columbo II"). The opportunity exists for a showdown between Columbo and the private investigator, but it is lost because Brimmer simply plays a defensive game. Culp's acting is rather wooden. The episode introduces the fact that Columbo doesn't carry a gun (see "The Developing Character"). Ranking: poor (5.35).

Additional cast: Ken Archer (Brett Halsey), Denning (Eric James), medical examiner (Don Keefer), Captain of Detectives (Len Wayland), Ceil Gentry (Lieux Dressler), Brimmer's secretary (Barbara Baldavin)

(#3) Dead Weight

Written by John T. Dugan. Directed by Jack Smight. Music by Gil Mellé. Airdate: 10/27/71.

Major General Martin J. Hollister (Eddie Albert) hears from Colonel Roger Dutton (John Kerr) that the Inspector General is investigating Hollister's military contracts and Dutton intends to flee the country. But Hollister is concerned that Dutton will spill the beans if caught, so he shoots him, an act witnessed by Helen Stewart (Suzanne Pleshette), as she attempts to control her boat on a nearby lake. When Columbo searches the house, the body is nowhere to be found. Hollister woos Helen and she eventually comes to doubt what she saw. Nonetheless, the Lieutenant arrests the Major General because the weapon Hollister used was none other than his famous pearl-handled pistol, the gun that is hiding in plain sight at the exhibit established by his alma mater, the Marine Military Institute. The interaction between Falk, Albert and Pleshette is interesting and Kate Reid is enjoyable as Pleshette's mother (Mrs. Walters), but this episode has dull clues (including the "Final Clue," conclusive as it is, plus it doesn't make sense because when did Hollister decide to claim that his gun disappeared?) and it works only as a one-time limited idea. Nice touch in having the "Final Clue" be suggested by Bert (Timothy Carey, see "Bert, Barney and Dog"). First appearance by Val Avery, as boat renter Harry Barnes (see "The Supporting Cast"). Introduces Columbo's seasickness and explores his Italian heritage a bit (see "The Developing Character") and has one of the two scenes where the name on his badge can be read (see "You Can Call Him Lieutenant"). Ranking: poor (5.1).

Additional cast: TV newsman (Clete Roberts), Officer Sanchez (Ron Castro), first officer (Glen Vernon), second officer (Jimmy Pelham), first marine cadet (Jim Halferty)

(#4) Suitable for Framing

Written by Jackson Gillis. Directed by Hy Averback. Music by Billy Goldenberg. Airdate: 11/17/71.

Art critic Dale Kingston (Ross Martin) shoots his uncle Rudy Mathews (Robert Shayne) and makes it look like a robbery. Art student Tracy O'Connor (Rosanna Huffman) assists him by staying with the body, removing an electric blanket that's keeping it warm and firing a shot into the air so a security guard will hear it while Kingston attends an art show. A few days later, Kingston knocks her over the head with a rock and sends her off the road in her car (see "Accomplices, Blackmailers and Schlimazels"). Mathews has recently changed his will, leaving his art collection to his ex-wife, Kingston's Aunt Edna (Kim Hunter). Kingston tries to frame Edna for the murder by planting the stolen paintings in her house. While the paintings are in Kingston's possession, Columbo touches them, leaving fingerprints that are later used to catch Kingston. Many people love this episode, but the way Columbo gets his prints on the paintings is implausible (see "Busting Alibis, Busting Scenarios"), Martin's portrayal of an art critic is silly and the premise of framing daffy Aunt Edna is not credible. Nice work by Don Ameche as family lawyer Frank Simpson. Introduces Columbo's shyness about the topic of sex (see "The Developing Character"). Ranking: poor (5.9).

Additional cast: Sam Franklin (Vic Tayback), Mitilda (Joan Shawlee), Captain Tyler (Barney Phillips), landlady (Mary Wickes), matron (Sandra Gould), Evans (Curt Conway), policeman (Claude Johnson), parking boy Joe (Dennis Rucker)

(#5) Lady in Waiting

Written by Steven Bochco (story by Barney Slater & Ted Leighton). Directed by Norman Lloyd. Music by Billy Goldenberg. Airdate: 12/15/71.

Beth Chadwick (Susan Clark) is fed up with living under the control of her brother Bryce (Richard Anderson) and when he announces that he is firing her fiancé, Peter Hamilton (Leslie Nielsen), it's the last straw. She plots to shoot Bryce, intending to make his death appear accidental. Having lost his house key, Bryce will "break into her bedroom" and set off the alarm. But the plan goes awry when Bryce comes in through the front door because he knows where a spare key was hidden. Beth is caught when Hamilton admits that, as he was approaching the house that night, he heard the shots *before* the alarm went off. While Falk, Clark, Nielsen (in his pre-parody days) and Jessie Royce Landis (as Beth's mother) give strong performances, every clue Columbo gathers is a result of an error in Beth's plan (Bryce's unknown spare key), yielding a very weak episode (see "Busting Alibis, Busting Scenarios"). Columbo and Beth do not have a "Sympathetic Murderer Relationship," particularly when she assumes Bryce's place as head of the family-owned advertising business and when her response to Columbo coming to arrest her is to pull a gun on him. First appearance by Fred Draper, as the cab driver (see "The Supporting Cast"). Ranking: bad (4.9).

Additional cast: Charles (Joel Fluellen), second detective (Richard Bull), first detective (Garry Walberg), hostess (Barbara Rhoades), hearing officer (Jon Lormer), Fred (Frank Baxter), waitress (Susan Barrister) [and Marcia Wallace as the chatty woman talking to Columbo at the coroner's inquest]

(#6) Short Fuse

Written by Jackson Gillis (story by Gillis and Lester and Tina Pine). Directed by Edward M. Abroms. Music by Gil Mellé. Airdate: 1/19/72.

Clever but immature scientist Roger Stanford (Roddy McDowall) cannot allow his evil uncle David Buckner (James Gregory) to sell the family chemical company to a conglomerate. He plants a bomb in Buckner's cigar box, thereby blowing up both Buckner and his chauffeur/legman Quincy [identified in the credits as "Murphy"] (Lawrence Cook) as they drive to a cabin in the mountains. But Columbo tricks Stanford into thinking that the car actually crashed in the rain and Stanford incriminates himself when he tries to get rid of what he thinks is the real bomb while trapped with Columbo and VP Everett Chambers (William Windom) on a tram over a steep ravine. Although this episode is a bit choppy because it was prepared at the last minute when the network asked for one more, it is still a strong installment with a solid ending (see "The Three Cs") and good acting by McDowall, Windom, Ida Lupino (as Aunt Doris), and Anne Francis (as Betty Bishop). But Stanford's motive is a confused mess (see "The Sympathetic Murderer Relationship"), the "First Clue" is a behavioral one (see "Recurring Problems") and there are not enough other clues. Introduces Columbo's fear of heights (see "The Developing Character"). Ranking: fair (6.7).

Additional cast: Sergeant (Steve Gravers), Nancy (Rosalind Miles), Farrell (Lew Brown), policeman (Jason Wingreen), Ferguson (Eddie Quillan), pinstripe (Stuart Nisbet), girl (Annette Molen), plainclothesman (Jim Neumarker), man (George Sawaya)

(#7) Blueprint for Murder

Written by Steven Bochco (story by William Kelley & Ted Leighton). Directed by Peter Falk. Music by Gil Mellé. Airdate: 2/9/72.

Architect Elliott Markham (Patrick O'Neal) has a good thing going when young impressionable Jennifer Williamson (Pamela Austin) is willing to fund his plans for Williamson City, a building complex, supposedly in honor of her wealthy but gruff husband. But when Beau Williamson (Forrest Tucker) returns to town unexpectedly, he slaps Markham and says he's shutting the project down. Markham shoots the Texan and hides the body. Columbo and the architect play a game of finesse, with the Lieutenant appearing to fall for Markham's hint that the body is beneath the building foundation (he digs it up at great cost to the city). That night, when Markham returns to the site to put the body in the hole before concrete is re-poured, he's met by Columbo. Although Falk was allegedly given this toughie to quash his interest in directing, he does a good job. Also, the episode has a nice trick ending (see "The Three Cs"), clever clues and great acting by Falk, O'Neal and Janis Paige as Beau's first wife, Goldie. First appearance by John Finnegan, as construction chief Carl (see "The Supporting Cast"). First time Columbo tries to quit smoking (see "The Developing Character"). Ranking: very good (8.8).

Additional cast: Miss Sherman (Bettye Ackerman), Dr. Moss (John Fiedler), guard (Nick Dennis), clerk (Robert Gibbons), Officer Wilson (Cliff Carnell), workman (Jimmy Joyce)

Production Information

Producers: Richard Levinson & William Link (#1, 2, 4, 6, 7); Everett Chambers (#3, 5). Executive producers: Richard Levinson & William Link (#3, 5). Associate producer: Robert F. O'Neill. Director of photography: Russell L. Metty (#1, 2, 3, 4, 5); Harry Wolf (#6); Lloyd Ahern (#7). Film editor: John Kaufman (#1, 6); Edward M. Abroms (#2, 5); Richard Sprague (#3); Budd Small (#4); Robert L. Kimble & Chris Kaeselau (#7). Art director: Arch Bacon. Set decorations: Richard Friedman (#1, 2, 3, 4, 5); Charles S. Thompson (#6,7). Unit manager: Henry Kline. Assistant director: Ralph Ferrin (#1, 5); Jack Barry (#2, 3); Gil Mandelik (#4); Kevin Donnelly (#6); William Hole (#7). Sound: David H. Moriarty (#1, 2, 3, 5); James R. Alexander (#4); Melvin M. Metcalfe, Sr. (#6); Roger A. Parish (#7). Costumes: Burton Miller. Editorial supervisor: Richard Belding. NBC Mystery Movie theme: Henry Mancini. Story editor: Steven Bochco. Main title design: Attila de Lado (#1); Wayne Fitzgerald (#2, 3, 4, 5, 6, 7). Titles and optical effects: Universal Title. Special photographic effects: Albert Whitlock (#6).

Chapter 2:
The Second Season (1972-73) (Episodes 8-15)

The *NBC Mystery Movie* did so well that it was moved to Sunday night and replaced with a *Wednesday Mystery Movie* wheel that did not quite measure up. Meanwhile, the network started trying to come up with a fourth element for the wheel, and the first entry was *Hec Ramsey*, with Richard Boone (Paladin from *Have Gun, Will Travel*) as a deputy sheriff just as the century turned to 1900, exploring new ideas like fingerprints. The other major change was an expansion of the *NBC Sunday Mystery Movie* to sometimes run two hours, rather than ninety minutes (see "The Bloating Problem" for a more detailed discussion). During this season, there were eight episodes of *Columbo*, five of *McCloud*, seven of *McMillan and Wife* and five of *Hec Ramsey* on *The NBC Sunday Mystery Movie*.

(#8) Etude in Black
Written by Steven Bochco (story by Richard Levinson & William Link). Directed by: Nicholas Colasanto. Music by Dick de Benedictis. Airdate: 9/17/72. 2 hrs.

While he is supposedly taking a nap before a big concert, symphony conductor Alex Benedict (John Cassavetes) visits his lover, pianist Jenifer Welles (Anjanette Comer), hits her over the head and turns on the gas when she threatens to reveal their affair unless he leaves his wife Janice (Blythe Danner). Columbo doesn't buy the suicide scenario and Benedict is caught when his lapel boutonniere, which he dropped at the scene of the crime and picked up later that night, is visible in a TV news clip of him leaving her house, but not on the earlier concert tape. The secondary story of Janice's growing independence from Benedict (and her domineering mother Lizzi Fielding, played by Myrna Loy) is fascinating, and this is the episode that introduces Dog (see "The Developing Character" and "Bert, Barney and Dog"). But the clues at the beginning and end don't measure up. Columbo relies on behavioral clues to conclude that the suicide setup is false, there is a prescience problem in him arriving at the garage the next morning in time to check the odometer and the dropped flower is a sloppy gift clue that just keeps on giving: if it's the reason he suspects Benedict, it makes for a poor "First Clue" and as a "Final Clue" it is telegraphed to the audience two hours in advance (see "Recurring Problems"). Some of Benedict's behavior at the end just doesn't fit (see "The All-in-the-Game Relationship"). The two-hour format introduced here also brings with it "The Bloating Problem"). Ranking: bad (5.0).

Additional cast: Paul Rifkin (James Olson), Billy (James McEachin), Mike Alexander (Don Knight), house boy (Pat Morita), Dr. Benson (Michael Fox), Audrey (Dawn Frame), Durkee (Charles Macaulay), Everett (George Gaynes), TV director (Wallace Chadwell) [note: Michael Pataki is listed in the credits as "Sam" but doesn't appear in the episode]

(#9) The Greenhouse Jungle

Written by Jonathan Latimer. Directed by Boris Sagal. Music by Oliver Nelson. Airdate: 10/15/72. 90 min.

Orchid grower Jarvis Goodland (Ray Milland) plots with his nephew Tony (Bradford Dillman) to fake a ransom scenario in order to circumvent a trust fund's restrictions, but he then shoots Tony to keep the money for himself. Columbo catches Goodland when he discovers that a bullet, fired about a year before at a burglar in the man's greenhouse, matches the bullet from Tony's body even though Goodland has planted the gun on Tony's wife, Cathy (Sandra Smith). There are some nifty clues in this episode which introduces Bob Dishy, as Sergeant Wilson—he will appear again in "Now You See Him" (#34) (see "Colleagues and Sidekicks"), albeit with a different first name (see "Hello, Continuity Department?"), and demonstrates that Columbo is adept at pool (see "The Developing Character"). But there's a clue delayed (see "Intermediate Clues") and Milland's bellowing and further bad acting by Sandra Smith and Bill Smith (as Cathy's lover Ken Nichols) take away from what could have been a better result. Ranking: fair (6.8).

Additional cast: Gloria West (Arlene Martel), Grover (Robert Karnes), driver (Milton Frome), woman (Peggy Mondo), officer (Richard Annis), sound man (Larry Watson).

(#10) The Most Crucial Game

Written by John T. Dugan. Directed by Jeremy Kagen. Music by Dick de Benedictis. Airdate: 11/5/72. 90 min.

Paul Hanlon (Robert Culp in the second of his three appearances, see "Multiple Murderers") manages sports teams for his wealthy boss, Eric Wagner (Dean Stockwell), but he decides to knock Wagner over the head with a piece of ice so that he drowns in his pool. Columbo destroys Hanlon's alibi by demonstrating that he could not have been in the owner's box when he spoke with Wagner on the phone. The clock in the owner's box would have chimed during the call yet there is no chime heard on a tape of the conversation. This is an odd little episode that doesn't make sense on several levels: the "First Clue" is weak and presents a prescience problem of why Columbo knew to check the water on the pool deck (see "Recurring Problems"), the motive is never revealed, the lack of chimes on the tape could be explained away easily (see "Busting Alibis, Busting Scenarios") and the acting by Culp, Dean Jagger (as Walter Cannell) and Valerie Harper (as prostitute Eve Babcock) leaves a lot to be desired. Nice work by Val Avery as PI Ralph Dobbs (see "The Supporting Cast"). Ranking: poor (5.5).

Additional cast: Coach Larry Rizzo (James Gregory), Shirley Wagner (Susan Howard), Miss Johnson (Kathryn Kelly Wiget), Mr. Freemont (Richard Stahl), deputy coroner (Don Keefer), plainclothesman (Cliff Carnell), box attendant Jimmy (Joe Renteria), Sgt. Hernandez (Ivan Naranjo), Los Angeles Rockets (Los Angeles Lakers)

(#11) Dagger of the Mind

Written by Jackson Gillis (story by Richard Levinson & William Link). Directed by Richard Quine. Music by Dick de Benedictis. Airdate: 11/26/72. 2 hrs.

Columbo is in London, getting a tour from Scotland Yard Detective Chief Superintendent Durk (Bernard Fox), when ham actors Nicholas Frame (Richard Basehart) and his wife Lillian Stanhope (Honor Blackman) accidentally kill Sir Roger Haversham (John Williams) by hitting him in the head with a cold cream jar after he threatens to stop funding their stage productions. Later, when Haversham's butler Tanner (Wilfrid Hyde-White) tries to blackmail the couple, they kill him and plant evidence that he murdered his master and then hanged himself (see "Accomplices, Blackmailers and Schlimazels"). The duo take their final bow when Columbo convinces them that a bead from Stanhope's necklace, which was broken during the fight, wound up in Haversham's umbrella. Frame falls apart and Stanhope confesses. It is a lot of fun watching Columbo away from home and enjoying the sights with Durk (see "Colleagues and Sidekicks"), but the actual mystery features really bad acting (and not just in the show-within-a-show of *Macbeth*), a disappointing ending (see "Confession Endings" and "Get 'Em for the First Murder") and mundane clues, including gift ones that Columbo receives because the murder is not preplanned (see "Recurring Problems"). Ranking: poor (5.15).

Additional cast: Joe Fenwick (Arthur Malet), Det. Sgt. O'Keefe (John Fraser), Diver the pathologist (Richard Pearson), director (Harvey Jason), Mr. Jones (Ronald Long), customs man (Hedley Mattingly), PC Charlie

Fatheringham (John Orchard), constable (Peter Church), gardener (Walker Edmiston), Inspector Smythe (Gerald S. Peter), Miss Dudley (Sharon Johansen)

(#12) Requiem for a Falling Star

Written by Jackson Gillis. Directed by Richard Quine. Airdate: 1/21/73. 90 min.

Fading movie actress Nora Chandler (Anne Baxter) appears to make a mistake when, in attempting to blow up gossip columnist Jerry Parks (Mel Ferrer) by lighting a fire under his car, she mistakenly kills her own assistant, Jean Davis (Pippa Scott). Columbo discovers in the end that Davis was the intended victim because she was the only one who knew that Chandler had killed her husband Al Cumberland years ago and buried the body on the studio lot under a fountain. Chandler was afraid that Davis would reveal her secret to Parks. This is the first of the "Variations on a Theme by Jackson Gillis," here toying with who the intended victim is. But it doesn't add up, because either way Chandler is in the spotlight. Also, the trick ending doesn't go far enough (see "The Three Cs" and "Get 'Em for the First Murder") and there's way too much ham acting all around. Ranking: bad (4.6).

Additional cast: Dr. Frank Simmons (Kevin McCarthy), Mr. Fallon (Frank Converse), Edith Head (herself), director (Sid Miller), Sgt. Jeffries (William Bryant), Paul (John Archer), gate guard (Jack Griffin), Joe (Robert E. Meredith), Sgt. Fields (Bart Burns)

(#13) A Stitch in Crime

Written by Shirl Hendryx. Directed by Hy Averback. Music by Billy Goldenberg. Airdate: 2/11/73. 90 min.

Heart surgeon Barry Mayfield (Leonard Nimoy) is frustrated when his boss, Dr. Edmund Heideman (Will Geer), wants to do more testing before announcing their new transplant anti-rejection drug. When Heideman requires a heart valve operation, Mayfield performs the surgery using dissolving suture, meaning the old man will die in a few days. But nurse Sharon Martin (Anne Francis) suspects something is wrong, and he has to get rid of her first (which he accomplishes with a tire iron), planting evidence that she was killed for drugs by her old friend Harry Alexander (Jared Martin). When Columbo doesn't buy this scenario, Mayfield gives Alexander an overdose of drugs and kills him, too (see "Accomplices, Blackmailers and Schlimazels"). Then Columbo, who has put the pieces together, threatens to perform an autopsy on Heideman if he dies, and Mayfield sets up a second operation to remove the dissolving suture, but the Lieutenant is waiting for him. This episode features a clever plot, wonderful clues, terrific acting and the first of a very few scenes where Columbo actually loses his cool (see "Columbo Gets Angry"). But it looks like Mayfield can only be arrested for the attempted murder of Heideman (see "Get 'Em for the First Murder") and observation about Mayfield resetting his desk clock is an odd behavioral clue (see "Recurring Problems"). Introduces Columbo's fear of needles and the sight of blood, as well as his hard-boiled egg for breakfast routine (see "The Developing Character"). Ranking: very good (8.7).

Additional cast: Marsha Dalton (Nita Talbot), Nurse Morgan (Aneta Corsaut), Det. Flores (Victor Millan), Paul (Kenneth Sansom), Dr. Simpson (Murray MacLeod), Dr. Michaelson (Leonard Simon), Tom (Ron Stokes), cleaning woman (Patsy Garrett)

(#14) The Most Dangerous Match

Written by Jackson Gillis (story by Gillis, Richard Levinson & William Link). Directed by Edward M. Abroms. Music by Dick de Benedictis. Airdate: 3/4/73. 90 min.

When chess master Emmet Clayton (Laurence Harvey) plays a secret game with his rival Tomlin Dudek (Jack Kruschen) the night before the big match, he learns he has no chance against the old man, so he pushes him into a trash compactor in the hotel basement. That doesn't finish Dudek off, so Clayton switches the drugs Dudek will receive in the hospital. Columbo demonstrates that the murderer had to be Clayton, a deaf man whose hearing aid was broken when he pushed Dudek, because otherwise he would have heard the machine shut off and would have turned it back on. This is a very interesting episode, with solid clues (except for the one about the game at the French restaurant, see "Intermediate Clues"), excellent acting by Falk, Harvey and Kruschen and some nice moments with John Finnegan as the workman (see "The Supporting Cast"), including the first time Dog helps solve a case (see "Bert, Barney and Dog"). But the Lieutenant's proof that it wasn't an accident (Dudek's bag contains someone else's toothbrush) is not convincing. Lloyd Bochner is a bit over the top as Mazoor Berozski, Dudek's "coach." Ranking: very good (8.6).

Additional cast: Linda Robinson (Heidi Bruhl), Sgt. Douglas (Paul Jenkins), Dr. Benson (Michael Fox), proprietor of French restaurant (Oscar Beregi), Anton (Mathias Reitz), first reporter (Drout Miller), second reporter (Manuel Depina), Dr. Sullivan (Stuart Nisbet), nurse (Abigail Shelton)

(#15) Double Shock

Written by Steven Bochco & Peter Allan Fields (story by Jackson Gillis, Richard Levinson & William Link). Directed by Robert Butler. Music by Dick de Benedictis. Airdate: 3/25/73. 90 min.

Dexter Paris (Martin Landau), host of a TV cooking show, does not want his uncle Clifford (Paul Stewart) to marry his youthful fiancée Lisa Chambers (Julie Newmar), so he tosses a mixer into Clifford's bathtub while Clifford is in it and electrocutes him. Later, when family lawyer Michael Hathaway (Tim O'Connor) shows Dexter Clifford's new will that leaves everything to Chambers anyway, Dexter pushes her off a balcony and frames Hathaway for the crime (see "Accomplices, Blackmailers and Schlimazels"). Or perhaps both murders were committed by Dexter's identical twin brother Norman (also Martin Landau), a bank manager with gambling debts. In the end, Columbo returns with Detective Murray (Dabney Coleman, see "Colleagues and Sidekicks") and proves it took both men to do it and, despite their façade of hating each other, they cooperated in this deadly endeavor. Not only does the plot twist not work (see "Busting Alibis, Busting Scenarios" and "Variations on a Theme by Jackson Gillis"), but the "First Clue" is problematic, the mixers present a right answer/wrong means issue (see "Recurring Problems"), and there is too much silliness in the scene with Newmar, in the ad-libbed cooking show scene (see "The Bloating Problem") and in three scenes in which the sloppy Lieutenant upsets fussy housekeeper Mrs. Peck (Jeanette Nolan) (see "Peter Falk as Columbo"). Ranking: bad (4.1).

Additional cast: Mrs. Johnson (Kate Hawley), young lawyer (Michael Richardson), second detective (Robert Rothwell), older lawyer (Gregory Morton), Stickman (Tony Cristino)

Production Information

Producer: Dean Hargrove. Associate producer: Edward K. Dodds. Director of photography: Harry Wolf (all, plus Geoffrey Unsworth for #11). Film editor: Budd Small (#8, 12); Sam E. Waxman (#9); J. Terry Williams (#10); Ronald LaVine (#11); Robert L. Kimble (#13); Larry Lester (#14, 15). Art director: Arch Bacon. Set decorations: John McCarthy. Unit manager: Henry Kline (#8, 9, 10, 12, 13, 15); Henry Kline & Kenny Williams (#11); Kenny Williams (#14). Assistant director: Brad Aronson (#8, 10, 15); Foster H. Phinney (#9, 13); David Dowell (#11, 12, 14). Sound: Edwin S. Hall. Costumes: Grady Hunt. Editorial supervisor: Richard Belding. NBC Mystery Movie theme: Henry Mancini. Music supervisor: Hal Mooney. Main title design: Wayne Fitzgerald. Executive story consultant: Jackson Gillis. Special photographic effects: Albert Whitlock (#8, 11). Technical advisor: Charles Clement (#14). Titles and optical effects: Universal Title.

Chapter 3:
The Third Season (1973-74)
(Episodes 16-23)

*T*he *NBC Sunday Mystery Movie* continued, with eight episodes of *Columbo*, five of *McCloud*, six of *McMillan and Wife* and five of *Hec Ramsey*.

(#16) Lovely But Lethal

Written by Jackson Gillis (story by Myrna Bercovici). Directed by Jeannot Szwarc. Music by Dick de Benedictis. Airdate: 9/23/73. 90 min.

When Viveca Scott (Vera Miles), head of the cosmetics firm Beauty Mark, learns that her chemist and former lover Karl Lessing (Martin Sheen) has stolen the formula for wrinkle-removing cream and intends to sell it to her rival David Lang (Vincent Price), she tries everything to get it back from him. He humiliates her and in anger she hits him over the head with a microscope, killing him. Later, when her confidante, Lang's secretary Shirley Blaine (Sian Barbara Allen), starts making too many demands, Scott gives her a poisoned cigarette, causing Blaine to drive her car off the road (see "Accomplices, Blackmailers and Schlimazels"). Columbo catches Scott when he discovers that both of them have poison ivy that they contracted by touching the broken microscope slide in Lessing's house. This episode has a lot of talent going for it and a very clever second murder (see "Get 'Em for the First Murder"). But it never clarifies what Scott's attitude is toward Columbo and because the murder is not preplanned and she takes no steps to cover it up, there are gift clues, missing clues and pieces of evidence, and the Lieutenant does not treat her very well (see "Recurring Problems"). Price, Sheen and Allen are solid, but Fred Draper's Dr. Murcheson is completely unbelievable (see "The Supporting Cast" for this and the first appearance by Bruce Kirby, here as the crusty janitor). John Finnegan appears as an unnamed sergeant (see "Colleagues and Sidekicks"). Ranking: good (7.8).

Additional cast: Ferdy (Gino Conforti), Burton (Dick Stahl), fingerprint man (Marc Hannibal), policeman (David Toma), fashion moderator (Layne Matthess)

(#17) Any Old Port in a Storm

Written by Stanley Ralph Ross (story by Larry Cohen). Directed by Leo Penn. Music by Dick de Benedictis. Airdate: 10/7/73. 2 hrs.

Snobby winemaker Adrian Carsini (Donald Pleasance) is infuriated when his half-brother Ric (Gary Conway) announces that he's selling the winery's land to a big company. Carsini hits Ric over the head, but Ric is not dead, so Carsini ties him up in the wine cellar and turns off the air conditioning, leaving him to suffocate. A week later, Carsini dresses him in scuba gear and throws his body into the ocean. Columbo demonstrates that, ironically, Carsini also destroyed his beloved collection of rare wines by turning off the air conditioning during a week that saw an unusual heat wave, and Carsini turns himself in. This is the series' first excellent episode, featuring outstanding clues and a number of firsts—the introduction of "The Sympathetic Murderer Relationship," the first and best use of the "Metaclue Ending," the first real exploration of the Lieutenant's Italian heritage (see "The Developing Character"), the first time he is shown in his office, the first time he talks to his wife on the phone (see "Does Columbo Exist?") and the first time he hums "This Old Man." It also features the first appearance by Vito Scotti, as the maitre d' (see "The Supporting Cast"). In addition, there is a wonderful second story involving Carsini's secretary Karen Fielding

(Julie Harris), who uses the opportunity to form a partnership with Carsini that he just can't deal with. Ranking: excellent (9.7).

Additional cast: Joan Stacey (Joyce Jillson), Falcon (Dana Elcar), drunk (Robert Donner), Stein (Robert Ellenstein), Billy Fine (Robert Walden), Lewis (Regis J. Cordic), Andy Stevens (Reid Smith), officer (John McCann), Frenchman wine expert (George Gaynes), steward (Monty Landis), auctioneer (Walker Edmiston), Cassie Marlowe (Pamela Campbell)

(#18) Candidate for Crime

Written by Irving Pearlberg, Alvin R. Friedman, Roland Kibbee & Dean Hargrove (story by Larry Cohen). Directed by Boris Sagal. Music by Dick de Benedictis. Airdate: 11/4/73. 2 hrs.

Nelson Hayward (Jackie Cooper), who is running for senator, and his unscrupulous campaign manager Harry Stone (Ken Swofford) have manufactured stories about death threats and Hayward has been given police protection. When Stone orders Hayward to end his affair with campaign worker Linda Johnson (Tisha Sterling) and pretend to be happily married to his wife Victoria (Joanne Linville), who spends most of her time drinking, Hayward uses the opportunity to get rid of Stone. He persuades Stone to switch clothes with him, and after Stone leads the police on a chase, he arrives at Hayward's beach house to be greeted by a bullet. Columbo doesn't buy the scenario that killers mistook Stone for Hayward, so the candidate decides to convince him. On election day, he fires a bullet into the wall behind his desk, then gets rid of the gun and, several hours later, sets off a squib to make it look as if a gunman aimed at him from the window. But Columbo has removed the bullet from the wall while Hayward was gone, and he is caught. Although this episode has solid acting from Falk, Cooper, Vito Scotti as Mr. Chadwick (see "The Supporting Cast") and Robert Karnes as Sergeant Vernon (see "Colleagues and Sidekicks"), the clues seem forced and the murderer essentially plays a trick on himself with no input from Columbo (see "The Three Cs"). There is a "Bloating Problem" in the scene when Columbo's car is stopped. Bad attempt at humor when Columbo's dentist, Dr. Perenchio (Mario Gallo), complains about Mafia stereotypes. Ranking: poor (5.4).

Additional cast: Sgt. Rojas (Jay Varela), deputy commissioner (Regis J. Cordic), Harris (Sandy Kenyon), director (Jack Riley), highway patrolman (Jude Farese), TV anchorman (Clete Roberts), first detective (Angelo Grisanti), second detective (Lew Brown), Larry (Don Diamond), Shelly (James G. Richardson), campaign manager (Bill Andes), Lucy (Lucille Meredith), secretary (Katie Sagal), newsman (Larry Burrell)

(#19) Double Exposure

Written by Stephen J. Cannell. Directed by Richard Quine. Music by Dick de Benedictis. Airdate: 12/16/73. 90 min.

Motivational expert Dr. Bart Kepple (Robert Culp in the third of his three appearances, see "Multiple Murderers") turns to murder when his plan of blackmailing Victor Norris (Robert Middleton) with revealing photographs doesn't work and Norris threatens to expose him. He makes a screening room warm and inserts subliminal cuts of a cold drink into a film to induce Norris to leave the room for a drink of water, and Kepple is waiting in the hall to shoot him. Later, projectionist Roger White (Chuck McCann) tries to blackmail Kepple and he also gets shot (see "Accomplices, Blackmailers and Schlimazels"). Columbo uses Kepple's own technique to catch him, inserting subliminal cuts of him searching Kepple's office into the film. Kepple runs to his office to make sure that the calibration converter he hid in a lamp is safe, and Columbo is waiting for him. This episode has a great trick ending (see "The Three Cs"), neat clues, solid acting, and also introduces the "All-in-the-Game Relationship" with juicy scenes of Kepple and Columbo going at it in the man's office and on the golf course. Ranking: very good (8.1).

Additional cast: Mrs. Norris (Louise Latham), press photographer (Denny Goldman), first detective (John Milford), film editor (George

Wyner), ballistics man (Richard Stahl), Patterson (Francis Desales), housekeeper (Alma Beltran), Det. Marley (Dennis Robertson), second detective
(Harry Hickox), Mrs. Halstead (Ann Driscoll), Norbert (E.A. Sirianni),
first detective (Manuel Depina), technician (Thomas Bellin), narrator (Peter
Walker), receptionist (Mary Beth Sikorski) [note: Arlene Martel is listed in
the credits as "Tanya Baker" but does not actually appear in the episode]

(#20) Publish or Perish

Written by Peter S. Fischer. Directed by Robert Butler. Music by Billy
Goldenberg. Airdate: 1/13/74. 90 min.

Unethical publisher Riley Greenleaf (Jack Cassidy in the second of his
three appearances, see "Multiple Murderers") has no intention of allowing writer Allen Mallory (Mickey Spillane) to take his work to rival Jeffrey
Neal (Jacques Aubuchon), so he hires psychotic veteran Eddie Kane (John
Chandler) to shoot Mallory for him. Greenleaf makes it look as if Kane
was framing him for the crime, and he completes the plan by planting an
outline of the book Mallory was writing in Kane's filing cabinet and blowing Kane up with one of the man's own homemade bombs. Columbo busts
the scenario (that Kane killed Mallory and framed Greenleaf for it because
they stole his book idea) by demonstrating that Kane could not have written
an outline nine months ago featuring an ending that Mallory's agent Eileen
McRae (Mariette Hartley) just came up with last week. This is a very complicated episode by Peter Fischer, who would go on to write some of the
series' finest installments. On this first outing, his script just won't fit into
the ninety minutes it was given (see "The Bloating Problem"), and he sets
for himself the almost impossible task of busting the scenario (see "Busting
Alibis, Busting Scenarios") rather than proving that Greenleaf killed Eddie
Kane (see "Get 'Em for the First Murder"). Columbo telling Greenleaf that
the key left at the scene didn't fit the lock is disturbing, not only because it
seems to go somewhere and then doesn't, but also because Columbo should
not be helping to set up a situation in which Greenleaf will do away with

his accomplice (see "Accomplices, Blackmailers and Schlimazels.") Still, the episode has neat clues and fine acting all around. Ranking: good (7.2).

Additional cast: Lou D'Allesandro (Gregory Sierra), David Chase (Alan Fudge), Sgt. Young (Paul Shenar), Norman Wolpert (Jack Bender), security guard (Ted Gehring), restaurant owner (Vern Rowe), lab technician (Lew Palter), Mr. Black the locksmith (George Brenlin), Palmer (J.S. Johnson), Charles the waiter (Maurice Marsac), Ralph Morgan (James Millhollin), Mrs. Morgan (Margesther Denver), Kramer (Davis Roberts), parking attendant (Rocky Frier) [and James B. Sikking as the cop who finds the gun]

(#21) Mind Over Mayhem

Written by Steven Bochco, Dean Hargrove & Roland Kibbee (story by Robert Specht). Directed by Alf Kjellin. Music by Dick de Benedictis. Airdate: 2/10/74. 90 min.

Marshall Cahill (Jose Ferrer), head of the Cybernetics Research Institute, is delighted to hear that his son Neil (Robert Walker) has won the Scientist of the Year Award. When chemist Howard Nicholson (Lew Ayers) reveals that Neil stole the work from the files of a late colleague and threatens to expose the young man as a fraud, Cahill runs Nicholson over in his driveway and makes it look like he was killed by drug users who were after the heroin he kept in his garage. Columbo gathers enough real evidence and adds some fake touches—cleverly tapping into the fact that Neil is attracted to his therapist, Nicholson's much younger wife Margaret (Jessica Walter)—to convince Cahill that he can build a case against Neil. Thus, the father who killed to protect his son has to confess to save him from a false arrest. This example of a "Confession Ending" works well, and the episode features some nifty clues, including the "First Clue" about the burned match that Columbo knows from smoking cigars (see "The Developing Character"). Also, there are some nice moments when Columbo and Dog team up with MM-7 ("Robby the Robot" from Forbidden Planet) and his creator, "boy genius" Steven Spelberg (Lee H. Montgomery) (see "Bert, Barney and Dog").

However, the methods the Lieutenant uses here are problematic (see "The Morality of Columbo II"). Ranking: good (7.25).

Additional cast: Ross (Lou Wagner), Murph (Art Batanides), motel manager (Darrell Zwerling), Farnsworth (Charles Macaulay), coroner (John Zaremba), Fields (William Bryant), Mr. Whitehead (Bert Holland), plainclothesman (Ed Fury), Jeff (Jefferson Kibbee), lady scientist (Dianne Turley), receptionist (Deidre Hall), first reporter (Dennis Robertson), officer (Luis Moreno) [note: a William Christopher is listed in the credits as "male scientist" but it is not the actor best known for playing Father Mulcahy on *M*A*S*H*]

(#22) Swan Song

Written by David Rayfiel (story by Stanley Ralph Ross). Directed by Nicholas Colasanto. Music by Dick de Benedictis. Airdate: 3/3/74. 2 hrs.

Singer Tommy Brown (Johnny Cash) doesn't mind lending his talent to the Lost Soul Crusade, but he wants to keep some of the money for himself instead of putting it all into escrow to build a tabernacle. His manipulative wife Edna (Ida Lupino) refuses to yield, and she holds over Brown the knowledge that he checked into motels with young crusader Maryann Cobb (Bonnie Van Dyke) when she was under sixteen. So, while flying the two women from Bakersfield to Los Angeles, Brown drugs them and leaps out of the small plane with a homemade parachute, breaking his leg on impact. Columbo tricks Brown into going back to the site to recover the parachute, where the Lieutenant is waiting for him. This solid episode has wonderful clue progression (see "Intermediate Clues") and a "Sympathetic Murderer Relationship" as well as an interesting collaboration between the Lieutenant and National Transportation Safety Board investigator Roland Pangborn (John Dehner) (see "Colleagues and Sidekicks"), plus some great music from Cash. Nice work by Vito Scotti as Grindell (see "The Supporting Cast"). Ranking: good (8.0).

Additional cast: Luke Basket (William McKinney), J.J. Stringer

(Sorrell Booke), Tina (Janit Baldwin), Air Force colonel (John Randolph), seamstress (Lucille Meredith), Bennett (Richard Caine), Phil (Donald Mantooth), Frank (Jefferson Kibbee), Jeff (Doug Dirkson), TV reporter (Larry Burrell), TV cameraman (Mike Edward Lally), police pilot (Tom McFadden), manager (Harry Harvey, Sr.)

(#23) A Friend in Deed

Written by Peter S. Fischer. Directed by Ben Gazzara. Music by Billy Goldenberg & Dick de Benedictis. Airdate: 5/5/74. 2 hrs.

When Hugh Caldwell (Michael McGuire) strangles his wife Janice in a fight, he turns to his friend Mark Halperin (Richard Kiley) for help and Halperin makes it look like the work of the Bel Air Burglar. Then, using the opportunity to his advantage, Halperin, who is a Deputy Police Commissioner, drowns his own wife Margaret (Rosemary Murphy) in the bathtub and employs Caldwell to make it look like the burglar came after her to keep her from identifying him and threw her in the swimming pool. Columbo locates the real Bel Air Burglar, Artie Jessup (Val Avery, see "The Supporting Cast"), and has him contact Caldwell with a blackmail scheme. Halperin plants the jewelry "stolen" from the Caldwell house at the address listed for Jessup in his police file. But Columbo has altered the file and the room where they find the jewels has been rented by the Lieutenant himself. The only person who saw this false information was Halperin. This episode has very clever clues (Caldwell did not dress his wife in a nightgown because there was one under her pillow which he knew about, but Halperin did not), terrific acting by Falk, Kiley, McGuire, Avery and John Finnegan as Lieutenant Duffy [identified in the credits as "Lieutenant Dryer"] (see "Colleagues and Sidekicks") and a superb trick ending (see "The Three Cs"). The Halperin/Caldwell relationship features an interesting use of an accomplice (see "Accomplices, Blackmailers and Schlimazels"). Ranking: excellent (9.2).

Additional cast: Bruno Wexler (Eric Christmas), Jessup's "wife" Thelma (Eleanor Zee), jewelry store salesgirl (Arlene Martel), Doyle

(Victor Campos), Dr. MacMurray (Joshua Bryant), Charlie Shoup (John Calvin), Amos Lawrence (Byron Morrow), Sharkey the fence (James V. Christy), Mrs. Fernandez (Alma Beltran), Al Como (Albert Popwell), Sgt. Ned Randall (Ben Marino), Charles (Judson Morgan), policeman (Tom Castronova), Pete Haley the police pilot (Paul Sorensen), Nathan Flowers (Bernie Kuby), second bartender (Mike Lally), first patrolman (Richard Lance), photographer (Eldon Burke), limousine driver (Jack Krupnick)

Production Information

Producer: Douglas Benton (#16); Robert F. O'Neill (#17); Dean Hargrove & Roland Kibbee (#18, 19, 20, 21); Edward K. Dodds (#22, 23). Associate producer: Robert F. O'Neill (#16); Edward K. Dodds (#18, 19, 20, 21). Executive producers: Dean Hargrove & Roland Kibbee (#16, 17). Director of photography: Harry Wolf (#16, 17); William Cronjager (#18, 19, 20, 21, 22, 23). Film editor: Larry Lester (#16); Larry Lester & Budd Small (#17); Robert L. Kimble (#18, 20, 23); Ronald LaVine (#19, 21); Bob Kagey (#22). Art director: Loyd S. Papez (#16); Arch Bacon (#17); John Wm. Corso (#18, 19, 20, 21, 22, 23). Set decorations: George Gaines (#16); John Dwyer (#17); William J. McLaughlin (#18, 19, 20, 21, 22, 23). Unit manager: Kenny Williams (#16); Wilbert Mosier (#17); Brad Aronson (#18, 19, 20, 21, 22, 23). Assistant director: Jack Doran (#16); Joe Boston (#17); Walt Gilmore (#18, 20); Phillip Cook (#19, 21, 22, 23). Sound: Terry Kellum (#16); David H. Moriarty (#17); Edwin S. Hall (#18); Wallace Bearden (#19, 20, 21, 22, 23). Costumes: Grady Hunt. Editorial supervisor: Richard Belding. NBC Mystery Movie theme: Henry Mancini. Music supervisor: Hal Mooney. Main title design: Wayne Fitzgerald. Titles and optical effects: Universal Title. Executive story consultant: Jackson Gillis. Robot furnished by Bill Malone (#21).

Chapter 4:
The Fourth Season (1974-75) (Episodes 24-29)

On *The NBC Sunday Mystery Movie, Hec Ramsey* was replaced with *Amy Prentiss*, a progressive show with Jessica Walter (Margaret Nicholson from "Mind Over Mayhem" (#21)) as the first female Chief of Detectives in San Francisco, but it didn't last long. In all, there were eight episodes of *Columbo*, nine of *McCloud*, six of *McMillan and Wife* and only three of *Amy Prentiss*.

(#24) An Exercise in Fatality
Written by Peter S. Fischer (story by Larry Cohen). Directed by Bernard Kowalski. Music by Dick de Benedictis. Airdate: 9/15/74. 2 hrs.

Milo Janus (Robert Conrad) owns a chain of health spas and is ripping off his franchisees by making them buy his products at inflated prices. When Gene Stafford (Philip Bruns) uncovers the scheme, Janus strangles him and makes it look like a barbell fell on his windpipe while he was exercising alone. Janus swears that he had a phone conversation with Stafford after Stafford changed into his gym clothes, but Columbo demonstrates that someone else dressed Stafford based on the loops of his shoelaces. This episode has some good ideas, including the story of Stafford's widow Ruth (Collin Wilcox), who is almost destroyed by Janus herself, leading to a rare scene where "Columbo Gets Angry." It also features solid acting by Conrad, Falk, Wilcox and Gretchen Corbett as Janus's secretary Jessica Conroy. Great phone call between Columbo and his wife (see "Does Columbo Exist?") and the jingle for the Milo Janus spas is terrific (see "This Old Man"). But the ending is not quite strong enough—the shoelace clue is a rare example of "Morris the Explainer" (see "Recurring Problems"), is more of an "Intermediate Clue" than a "Final Clue" and would require Janus to pull off the victim's dress shoes which would leave his prints on them. In addition, by then, Janus had already told Columbo to talk to his lawyer, so there would be no reason for him to concede the point. The scene with the computer printing goes on way too long (see "The Bloating Problem"). Ranking: very good (8.9).

Additional cast: Buddy Castle (Pat Harrington), Al Murphy (Jude Farese), Lewis Lacey (Darrell Zwerling), Jerry (Dennis Robertson), Sgt. Rickets (Raymond O'Keefe), medical examiner (Victor Izay), Fred (Eric Mason), Harry Lassiter (J.R. Clark), Dr. Freeman (Mel Stevens), photographer (Manuel Depina), nurse (Kathleen O'Malley), Doberman (Don Nagel), Rose (Susan Jacoby)

(#25) Negative Reaction

Written by Peter S. Fischer. Directed by Alf Kjellin. Music by Bernardo Segall. Airdate: 10/6/74. 2 hrs.

Photographer Paul Galesko (Dick Van Dyke) shoots his wife Frances (Antoinette Bower) and makes it look like a kidnapping by recently released felon Alvin Deschler (Don Gordon), whom he then shoots in "self-defense" to complete the scenario (see "Accomplices, Blackmailers and Schlimazels"). Columbo tricks Galesko into incriminating himself by identifying the camera that contains the negative of the ransom photo of Frances. Writer Peter Fischer achieves excellence with this episode, with a great trick ending (see "The Three Cs") and many fine little clues (see "Intermediate Clues"). Van Dyke gives a fantastic serious performance, plus there are humorous touches by Vito Scotti (as the wino Thomas Dolan, see "The Supporting Cast" for this and the appearance of Fred Draper as the fingerprint man),

Joyce Van Patten (as the Sister of Mercy who thinks Columbo is a bum) and Larry Storch (as Mr. Weekly, the driving instructor who is convinced the Lieutenant is a menace on the road—although this scene should have been moved earlier in the episode, when its humor would not interrupt the flow leading up to the ending). Michael Strong is excellent as Sergeant Hoffman (see "Colleagues and Sidekicks"). The motive is clearly to get rid of Frances so that Galesko can spend more time with his assistant, Lorna McGrath (Joanna Cameron), but the episode never explains why he can't simply file for divorce. Ranking: excellent (9.5).

Additional cast: Ray (David Sheiner), Mrs. Mayland (Alice Backes), Harry Lewis (Harvey Gold), Capt. Sampson (Bill Zuckert), Dept. of Motor Vehicles clerk (Adrian Ricard), hotel manager Charles Victor (Thom Carney), doctor (Tom Signorelli), real estate man Calvin MacGruder (John Ashton), minister (Edward Colmans), Mrs. Charleswort (Irene Tedrow), first policeman (Mike Santiago), second policeman (Edward Cross)

(#26) By Dawn's Early Light

Written by Howard Berk. Directed by Harvey Hart. Music by Bernardo Segall. Airdate: 10/27/74. 2hrs.

Colonel Lyle Rumford (Patrick McGoohan in the first of his four appearances, see "Multiple Murderers"), commandant of Haynes Military Academy, cannot allow Chairman of the Board William Haynes (Tom Simcox) to turn the academy into a coed junior college, so he tricks Haynes into firing the cannon on Founder's Day after having rigged it to explode. Columbo places Rumford at the scene of the crime when he demonstrates that the only time the Colonel could have seen the cider some cadets were fermenting in a window was when he was stuffing a rag down the barrel of the cannon early that morning. This is the best episode of the series, with outstanding clues, a fascinating "Sympathetic Murderer Relationship," great acting (McGoohan deservedly received an Emmy for his performance), nice character touches (this is where the Lieutenant is asked if he has a first name, see "You Can Call Him Lieutenant") and good interaction with cadets Roy Springer (Mark Wheeler) and Morgan (Bruno Kirby). Bruce Kirby introduces the character of Sergeant Kramer (see "Colleagues and Sidekicks"). Ranking: excellent (10.0).

Additional cast: Capt. Loomis (Burr DeBenning), Susan Gerard (Karen Lamm), Miss Brady (Madeleine Thornton-Sherwood), Officer Corso (Sidney Armus), boodle boy Jonathan B. Miller (Robert Clotworthy)

(#27) Troubled Waters

Written by William Driskill (story by Jackson Gillis). Directed by Ben Gazzara. Music by Dick de Benedictis. Airdate: 2/9/75. 2 hrs.

Columbo and his wife (who is always delightfully just off camera, see "Does Columbo Exist?") take a three-day cruise to Mexico, but the Lieutenant is called to duty when Rosanna Welles (Poupée Bocar), the singer on board, is found murdered in her cabin. The evidence of the shooting points toward band member Lloyd Harrington (Dean Stockwell), whose advances she rejected. But Columbo believes the evidence has been planted by Hayden Danziger (Robert Vaughn), a used auto mogul who needed to stop Welles from revealing their affair to his wife Sylvia (Jane Greer). Danziger has faked a heart attack and slips out of the ship's hospital between bed checks to shoot Welles. Columbo comments to Danziger that he just doesn't have enough evidence against Harrington without the glove worn by the murderer, so Danziger tries to complete the frame-up by firing a pistol so as to leave powder burns on the outside of a glove. But the surgical glove incriminates Danziger because his fingerprints are on the inside of it. This delightful episode has Columbo investigating the crime without the assistance of the "lab boys" (he uses graphite from a pencil to check fingerprints, and fires the gun into a mattress to do a ballistics check) and fun moments such as seeing Columbo enjoy himself while relaxing in a tropical atmosphere. The trick ending employed is credible (see "The Three Cs") and there is solid acting by Vaughn, Greer, Stockwell, Patrick Macnee (as Captain Gibbon, see

"Colleagues and Sidekicks"), Bernard Fox (as the purser, Preston Watkins) and Robert Douglas (as the doctor, Frank Pierce). The music is appropriately upbeat and fun (see "This Old Man"). Ranking: good (7.9).

Additional cast: Melissa the nurse (Susan Damante), band leader Artie Podell (Peter Maloney), the magician (Curtis Credel)

(#28) Playback

Written by David P. Lewis & Booker T. Bradshaw. Directed by Bernard Kowalski. Music by Bernardo Segall. Airdate: 3/2/75. 90 min.

Harold Van Wyck (Oskar Werner), president of Midas Electronics, is about to be ousted by his mother-in-law Margaret Midas (Martha Scott), so he shoots her. He makes it look like a robbery by using the camera equipment in his gadget-filled house to record the incident and then play it back later for the security guard. Columbo uses Van Wyck's own technology to undo him. He discovers on the tape that, on the table above the body is the very invitation that Van Wyck would take with him that night to the art gallery. A powerful albeit tense episode (it could have used more time, see "The Bloating Problem"), with clues Van Wyck does not expect (especially the door that opened when he fired the actual shot), and great performances by Falk, Werner and Gena Rowlands as Van Wyck's wife Elizabeth, who bonds with Dog (see "Bert, Barney and Dog"). Features the only time Columbo fires a gun, into a box of sand (see "The Developing Character"). Ranking: excellent (9.3).

Additional cast: Arthur Midas (Robert Brown), Francine (Patricia Barry), Baxter (Herb Jefferson, Jr.), Marcy (Trisha Noble), Thompson (Bart Burns), policeman (Steven Marlo), attendant (Joe O'Har)

(#29) A Deadly State of Mind

Written by Peter S. Fischer. Directed by Harvey Hart. Music by Bernardo Segall. Airdate: 4/27/75. 90 min.

Psychiatrist Marcus Collier (George Hamilton in the first of his two appearances, see "Multiple Murderers") is having an affair with his patient

Nadia Donner (Lesley Ann Warren) and administering drugs to deepen her hypnotic state to further research a book he's writing. When Nadia's husband Karl (Stephen Elliott) attacks them at the Donners' beach house, Collier hits him with a poker and kills him. He tries to set up a robbery scenario, but Nadia is too weak a link in the chain and Columbo knows it. So Collier murders Nadia in a remarkable remote-control way, giving her a post-hypnotic suggestion to leap off her apartment balcony into a pool upon receiving code words from him via phone. Columbo can't prove the second murder (see "Get 'Em for the First Murder"), but he cleverly puts Collier at the scene of Karl's murder by having a man come in and identify him. Collier, who knows that he almost ran over a blind man on the way out of the Donners' driveway, retorts that the man is blind, but he's wrong. This is the brother of the man he actually saw and the witness who puts Collier at the head of the driveway at the time of the murder is none other than Collier himself. This episode is deceptively clever—it takes what might not have worked and turns it into an excellent installment with a two-level investigation, an ending that fits like a glove (see "The Three Cs"), good acting and fine touches such as the Lieutenant's real anger when Nadia has been killed while on his watch (see "Columbo Gets Angry"). Collier solves the accomplice problem (see "Accomplices, Blackmailers and Schlimazels"). Bruce Kirby appears as Sergeant Kramer (see "Colleagues and Sidekicks") and Fred Draper is quite effective as David Morris, brother of the blind man (see "The Supporting Cast"). Ranking: excellent (9.4).

Additional cast: Dr. Anita Borden (Karen Machon), Dr. Hunt (William Wintersole), Charles Whelan (Ryan MacDonald), Daniel Morris (Jack Manning), Brenda (Glorie Kaufman), Arnold (Redmond Gleeson), Officer Hendryx (Vance Davis), Gary Keppler (Danny Wells), lab man (Morris Buchanan), second receptionist (Kathy Speirs)

Production Information

Producer: Edward K. Dodds (#24); Everett Chambers (#25, 26, 27, 28, 29). Executive producers: Dean Hargrove & Roland Kibbee. Associate producer: Edward K. Dodds (#25, 26, 27, 28, 29). Director of photography: William Cronjager (#24, 25, 27); Jack Priestley (#26); Richard C. Glouner (#28); Earl Rath (#29). Film editor: Bob Kagey (#24, 26); Ronald LaVine (#25, 28, 29); Robert L. Kimble (#27). Art director: John Wm. Corso (#24, 25); Michael Baugh (#26, 27, 28, 29). Set decorations: William J. McLaughlin (#24, 25, 26); Jerry Adams (#27, 28, 29). Unit manager: Maurie M. Suess (#24); Ray Taylor (#25, 26, 27, 29); Carter DeHaven Jr. (#28). Assistant director: Ray Taylor (#24); Phillip Cook (#25); G. Warren Smith (#26); Kevin Donnelly (#27, 28, 29). Sound: John Kean (#24); Robert Miller (#25); Donald F. Johnson (#26); Jerry E. Smith (#27, 29); Frank Wilkinson (#28). Costumes: Grady Hunt. Editorial supervisor: Richard Belding. NBC Mystery Movie theme: Henry Mancini. Music supervisor: Hal Mooney. Main title design: Wayne Fitzgerald. Titles and optical effects: Universal Title.

Chapter 5:
The Fifth Season (1975-76)
(Episodes 30-35)

The fourth element of *The NBC Sunday Mystery Movie* was changed to *McCoy*, with Tony Curtis as a con man who stole from rich criminals and returned most of the money, keeping some for himself. There were six episodes of *Columbo*, seven of *McCloud*, seven of *McMillan and Wife* and five of *McCoy*.

(#30) Forgotten Lady

Written by William Driskill. Directed by Harvey Hart. Music by Jeff Alexander. Airdate: 9/14/75. 2 hrs.

Former dancer Grace Wheeler (Janet Leigh) wants to revive her career, but her wealthy husband, retired physician Henry Willis (Sam Jaffe), inexplicably refuses to provide the finances. So Wheeler drugs him and shoots him, making it look like he committed suicide. Columbo hounds Wheeler as she prepares for her new show, much to the consternation of her former partner and long-time love, Ned Diamond (John Payne). In the series' most unusual finale, the Lieutenant explains to Diamond that Willis knew that his wife has an inoperable brain aneurysm that could burst at any moment and he did not want the strain of dancing to hasten her death. The condition has resulted in extreme short-term memory loss and Columbo does not believe

Wheeler even remembers having shot her husband. Before the Lieutenant can arrest Wheeler, Diamond "confesses" to the crime, making sure that Columbo agrees to take "a few months" (all the time she has left) to break his story. This is a fascinating episode with neat little clues (Willis didn't dog-ear the page of the book he was reading the night of his death), an ending that works in the circumstances (see "Busting Alibis Busting Scenarios"), an incredibly "Sympathetic Murder Relationship" that all makes sense in the end and wonderful acting by Falk, Leigh, Payne and Maurice Evans as Wheeler's butler Raymond, who follows Columbo around with an ashtray (see "Peter Falk as Columbo"). Cute interactions with Dog (see "Bert, Barney and Dog"). However, the ending is problematic (see "The Morality of Columbo I") and the supposedly humorous side story of Columbo avoiding his gun practice requirements raises real problems (see "Does Columbo Exist?"). Ranking: very good (8.3).

Additional cast: Dr. Lansberg (Ross Elliott), Dr. Westrum (Robert F. Simon), Army Archerd (himself), Alma (Linda Scott), Sgt. Leftkowitz (Francine York), Harris (Jerome Guardino), bookstore clerk (Danny Wells), deputy coroner Henderson (Harvey Gold)

(#31) A Case of Immunity

Written by Lou Shaw (story by James Menzies). Directed by Ted Post. Music by Bernardo Segall. Airdate: 10/12/75. 90 min.

Hassan Salah (Hector Elizondo), First Secretary of the Suarian Legation in Los Angeles, kills security chief Youseff Alafa (Andre Lawrence) by striking him over the head with a tire iron. He is assisted by impressionable code clerk Rahmin Habib (Sal Mineo), and later knocks him out and sends him over a cliff in his car to wrap up the case. When Columbo becomes too annoying, Salah calls upon the U.S. State Department to invoke diplomatic immunity. Columbo shakes Salah's hand for having beaten him and Salah accepts the compliment, not knowing that his country's king (Barry Robins) is hiding in the next room. Rather than face execution at home, Salah waives his diplomatic immunity and confesses to the crime. This solid episode contains some very good clues, a believable "Confession Ending," a clever second murder (see "Accomplices, Blackmailers and Schlimazels"), excellent acting by Falk, Elizondo and Xenia Gratsos (as Zena) and nice touches of humor, as when Salah silently moves priceless objects out of Columbo's reach (see "The Developing Character" and "Peter Falk as Columbo"). But its refusal to explain the motive is frustrating and its portrayal of Arabs as good guys only when they "act Western" is very stereotyped (see "Recurring Problems"). Ranking: good (7.5).

Additional cast: Police Commissioner (Kenneth Tobey), Kermit Morgan (Dick Dinman), Kura (George Skaff), Hakim (Nate Esformes), Capt. August (Bill Zuckert), second picketer (Bart Braverman), coroner (Harvey Gold), Capt. Ortega (Jay Varela)

(#32) Identity Crisis

Written by William Driskill. Directed by Patrick McGoohan. Music by Bernardo Segall. Airdate: 11/2/75. 2 hrs.

Nelson Brenner, head of the West Coast branch of the CIA and code named "Colorado" (Patrick McGoohan in the second of his four appearances, see "Multiple Murderers"), has to get rid of an old colleague who resurfaces, a spy with the code name "Geronimo" (Leslie Nielsen) who knows Brenner is a double agent. So Brenner brains Geronimo with a tire iron under the Santa Monica pier, making it look like a robbery committed by Lawrence Melville (Otis Young) or perhaps the work of the shadowy figure known as Steinmetz (Brenner himself in disguise). Columbo breaks the alibi Brenner has constructed by demonstrating that he could not have dictated a speech during the night of the murder but must have done so the next morning because he included information from the morning's news (namely that the Chinese were pulling out of the Olympics). This unfortunate episode does not work, because as a spy Brenner could be lying about his alibi for any reason (see "Busting Alibis, Busting Scenarios").

Also the "All-in-the-Game" motif is too heavily applied, Brenner seems to turn himself in because it's the end of the episode, McGoohan's acting is way over the top and David White (as Phil Corrigan) does not make a credible agency director. Significant roles for Vito Scotti as Salvatore DeFonte, Val Avery as Louie the bartender (see "The Supporting Cast") and Bruce Kirby as Sergeant Kramer (see "Colleagues and Sidekicks"). First time Columbo speaks Italian (see "The Developing Character"). Ranking: bad (4.3).

Additional cast: Joyce (Barbara Rhoades), gallery attendant (William Mims), Don the photo shop man (Cliff Carnell), executive (Edward Bach), Parsons (Paul Gleason), Ruth (Angela May), Della (Betty McGuire), bell-boy (Kelly Flynn), kid (Alicia Chambers)

(#33) A Matter of Honor

Written by Brad Radnitz (story by Radnitz & Larry Cohen). Directed by Ted Post. Music by Bernardo Segall. Airdate: 2/1/76. 90 min.

Retired matador Luis Montoya (Ricardo Montalban) inexplicably lures his old friend Hector Rangel (Robert Carricart) into the ring, where he drugs him and leaves him to be killed by a bull named Marinero. Columbo, who is visiting Mexico when his beloved car is impounded after a fender-bender, suggests to his colleague Comandante Emilio Sanchez (Pedro Armendariz, Jr.) that foul play is afoot. In the end, the Lieutenant uses Rangel's son Curro (A Martinez) to demonstrate that Montoya killed Rangel to keep a secret—when Marinero broke loose a few days before, it was Rangel who kept the bull at bay while Montoya froze in his tracks. The matador hands Columbo his cape and sword. This episode works like "Troubled Waters" (#27) with the Lieutenant making small observations away from the lab (he finds a piece of Hector's lance in the ring, notices the mark left by the dart by which Montoya administered the chloral hydrate and realizes it didn't rain because there are no water marks on the cape). Columbo has a nice relationship with Sanchez (see "Colleagues and Sidekicks") and the supporting cast is very good. But Montalban's Montoya is a bit too stiff and the episode tries to include a traditional final clue that doesn't fit (see "The Metaclue Ending"). Second time the name on Columbo's badge is legible (see "You Can Call Him Lieutenant") Ranking: very good (8.5).

Additional cast: Nina Montoya (Maria Grimm), Jaime Delgado the foreman (Enrique Lucero), Miguel Fernandez (Emilio Fernandez), housekeeper (Evita Muñoz Chachita), Carlos (Jorge Rivero)

(#34) Now You See Him

Written by Michael Sloan. Directed by Harvey Hart. Music by Bernardo Segall. Airdate: 2/29/74. 2 hrs.

The magician known as The Great Santini (Jack Cassidy in the third of his three appearances, see "Multiple Murderers") is hiding quite a bit up his sleeve: he's actually a former Nazi named Stephan Mueller. When Jesse Jerome (Nehemiah Persoff), owner of the club where Santini performs, threatens to reveal his secret if the magician doesn't cough up more profits to him, Santini shoots Jerome while he is performing his water tank illusion. Columbo teams up again with Sergeant Wilson (Bob Dishy) (introduced in "The Greenhouse Jungle" (#9); see "Colleagues and Sidekicks"), who has oddly changed his first name (see "Hello, Continuity Department?"). They uncover what's really going on when they discover that Jerome was typing a letter to the Immigration Service with a one-use carbon ribbon. This brilliant episode uses Santini's profession to layer the levels of deception (he's in the water tank, no he's in the basement, no he's in Jerome's office) and it features great performances by Falk, Dishy and Cassidy, in his last role for the show. Signature role for character actor Michael Lally (see "The Thirty-One Hats of Michael Lally"), and great scene in which Columbo gets a major clue from him, but doesn't overemphasize it (see "Peter Falk as Columbo"). Good support from Robert Loggia (as Harry Blandford) and Thayer David (as the magic shop proprietor). Delightful comic touch in having Columbo's wife give him a stiff new raincoat that he keeps trying to lose, but Wilson helpfully finds it for him each time. Fantastic music (see "This Old Man"). One tiny mistake in giving Santini a daughter (Cynthia Sykes) who has to be written out of the show halfway through (see "Intermediate Clues"). Ranking: excellent (9.6).

Additional cast: Danny Green (Patrick Culliton), Thackery (George Sperdakos), George Thomas (Redmond Gleeson), Lassiter the locksmith (Victor Izay), Rogers (Robert Gibbons), Jefferson (Michael Payne)

(#35) Last Salute to the Commodore

Written by Jackson Gillis. Directed by Patrick McGoohan. Music by Bernardo Segall. Airdate: 5/2/76. 2 hrs.

Crusty old shipbuilder Otis "the Commodore" Swanson (John Dehner) announces that he has no use for his drunken daughter Joanna Clay (Diane Baker), her greedy husband Charles (Robert Vaughn), his nephew "Swanny" Swanson (Fred Draper) or anyone else around him except shipyard foreman Wayne Taylor (Joshua Bryant). It looks as if Charles Clay knocks the old man over the head with a belaying pin and dumps the body at sea, but later the audience learns that he only disposed of the body when he found it and thought his wife had committed the deed. Clay himself is found dead just as Columbo and his team come to arrest him and they have to reevaluate the situation. In the end, with the suspects gathered as in a traditional drawing-room mystery, Columbo tricks Swanny into saying that the item pressed to his ear "t'isn't" the Commodore's watch, which it isn't because he smashed it and it should not have been ticking. This very bad episode alters the format by keeping the murderer hidden from the audience (see "Variations on a Theme by Jackson Gillis") and does a poor job of it. Also, it has no real clues to speak of and a sad excuse for an ending (see "The Three Cs"). Finally, there is far too much "comic relief" with ham acting from Falk (see "Peter Falk as Columbo"), Draper (see "The Supporting Cast"), Bruce Kirby (Sgt. Kramer, see "Colleagues and Sidekicks") and Dennis Dugan (Theodore "Mac" Albinsky). Vaughn plays it straight, and John Finnegan does his usual solid job, here as the gate guard (see "The Supporting Cast"). Columbo again tries to quit smoking (see "The Developing Character") and "This Old Man" plays at the end. Ranking: bad (4.0).

Additional cast: Kittering (Wilfrid Hyde-White), Lisa King (Susan Foster), Coast Guard officer (Rod McCary), shop foreman (Joseph Roman), woman (Hanna Hertelendy), watchman (Jerry Crews), sailor (Fred Porter), handwriting expert (Jimmy Joyce), bartender (Tom Williams)

Production Information

Producer: Everett Chambers. Associate producer: Edward K. Dodds (#31, 34). Director of photography: Charles Correll (#30); Richard C. Glouner (#31, 32, 35); Gabriel Torres (#33); William Cronjager (#35). Film editor: Jamie Caylor (#30, 34); Ronald LaVine (#31, 32, 33); Robert L. Kimble (#35). Art director: John Wm. Corso (#20, 31, 32, 33, 34); Seymour Klate (#35). Set decorations: Jerry Adams (#30, 31, 32, 34); Rafael Suarez (#33); Joseph J. Stone (#35). Unit manager: Frank Losee (#30, 32); Fred R. Simpson (#31, 34); Frederico Serrano (#33); Ralph Sariego (#35). Assistant director: Sam Freedle (#30, 34); Kevin Donnelly (#31, 33, 35); Reuben Watt (#32). Sound: Jerry E. Smith. Costumes: Burton Miller (#30, 31, 32, 34, 35); Rudy Nava Luna (#33). Editorial supervisor: Richard Belding. NBC Mystery Movie theme: Henry Mancini. Music supervisor: Hal Mooney. Main title design: Wayne Fitzgerald. Titles and optical effects: Universal Title. Executive story consultant: Bill Driskill & Peter S. Fischer (#30, 32, 33, 34, 35); Peter S. Fischer (#31). Choreographer: Miriam Nelson (#30). Magic sequences by Mark J. Wilson (#34). Second assistant camera: Louis Niemeyer (#32, 34). Music editor: James D. Young (#34).

Chapter 6:
The Sixth Season (1976-77) (Episodes 36-38)

The sixth season of *Columbo* was the last season for the mystery wheel. Ironically, NBC finally found a show that worked (*Quincy, M.E.* with Jack Klugman as the crusading coroner), so well in fact that it was made into its own series in the spring and was replaced by *Lanigan's Rabbi*, a series based on the novels of Harry Kemelman about a small-town rabbi (Bruce Solomon) who helps the police chief (Art Carney) solve crimes. Also, *McMillan and Wife* was renamed *McMillan* after Susan St. James left and her character was killed off, leaving "Mac" free for romantic pursuits. In all, there were three episodes of *Columbo*, six of *McCloud*, six of *McMillan*, four of *Quincy, M.E.* and four of *Lanigan's Rabbi*. One team produced the first two *Columbo* episodes. The third one, not aired until the following May, was produced by an entirely new team led by Richard Alan Simmons (see "Columbo Deconstructed" and "The Developing Character" for his changes to the show).

(#36) Fade in to Murder

Written by Lou Shaw & Peter Feibleman (story by Henry Garson). Directed by Bernard L. Kowalski. Music by Bernardo Segall. Airdate: 10/10/76. 90 min.

Ward Fowler (William Shatner in the first of his two appearances, see "Multiple Murderers"), star of the popular TV show *Lieutenant Lucerne*, shoots his producer Claire Daley (Lola Albright) who has been blackmailing him, and makes it look like a robbery. The actor, in his Lucerne persona, engages in an odd collaboration with Columbo in which he often seems to be accusing himself of the crime, although he also attempts to frame Daley's husband Sid (Alan Manson). In the end, the real Lieutenant solves the case by demonstrating that Fowler, who used a gun from the studio prop department to commit the crime, left his fingerprints on the bullets. This is a confused episode, with too much of the plot driven by the "All-in-the-Game Relationship" and Fowler's bizarre habit of pointing the finger at himself (see "First Clues"). Also, a good idea like using a VCR to create an alibi is wasted when Fowler simply shows the device to Columbo. Good work by Manson and Bert Remsen (as Fowler's gofer, Mark Davis), but Shatner is miscast as a dandy. The episode contains another appearance by John Finnegan (as the assistant director who tells Columbo he's ruining the scene), marks the last appearance of Fred Draper (as the actor who flubs his line as "Joseph" on the fictional show) and features the debut of Shera Danese, as Sid's girlfriend Molly (see "The Supporting Cast"). Ranking: poor (5.8).

Additional cast: Sgt. Morella ["Johnson" in the credits] (Walter Koenig), director (Danny Dayton), Tony (Timothy Agoglia Carey), Conroy (Victor Izay), camera operator (Jimmy Joyce), Walter Gray (Frank Emmett Baxter)

(#37) Old Fashioned Murder

Written by Peter S. Feibleman (story by Lawrence Vail). Directed by Robert Douglas. Music by Dick de Benedictis. Airdate: 11/28/76. 90 min.

Ruth Lytton (Joyce Van Patten) cannot allow her brother Edward (Tim O'Connor) to sell the family museum that has become her whole life, so she shoots him. She also shoots Milton Schaeffer (Peter S. Feibleman, who wrote the episode), a shifty security guard hired by her niece Janie (Jeannie Berlin) and makes it look like Edward interrupted Schaeffer robbing the museum (see "Accomplices, Blackmailers and Schlimazels"). Columbo finds an inventory tape made by Edward that lists an item (gold-plated belt buckle) that Ruth later plants on Janie in an attempt to frame her (meaning it wasn't stolen in the robbery). However, Ruth essentially confesses in exchange for Columbo's promise to withdraw his accusation that she murdered Janie's father years ago. Talk about confusion! In this episode Ruth goes from trying to save the museum for Janie to framing her for the crime to confessing to save her from hearing other bad news (see "Confession Endings"). The attempted "Sympathetic Murderer Relationship" is also a mess. In addition, there is overacting by Berlin and by Celeste Holm as Janie's mother, Phyllis Brandt, and bad attempts at comedy such as Columbo submitting to a haircut in order to interview the hair stylist (see "The Developing Character" and "The Bloating Problem"). Ranking: bad (4.8).

Additional cast: Dr. Tim Schaeffer (Jess Osuna), Sgt. Miller (Jon Miller), Darryl the hairstylist (Anthony Holland), Elise (Lucy Saroyan), watch salesman (Gary Krawford), maid (Eloise Hardt), second detective (Morris Buchanan), photographer (Giles Douglas)

(#38) The Bye-Bye Sky High IQ Murder Case

Written by Robert Malcolm Young. Directed by Sam Wanamaker. Music by Bob Prince. Airdate: 5/22/77. 90 min.

Accountant Oliver Brandt (Theodore Bikel) reluctantly murders his partner Bertie Hastings (Sorrell Booke) to keep him from revealing that Brandt has been stealing from their clients. Brandt shoots Hastings in the library at the Sigma Society, the club for geniuses to which they both belong. He rigs a Rube Goldberg-type device to make the club members think Hastings was shot by a robber a few minutes later while they are all downstairs. Columbo recreates the scenario, which involves attaching alligator clips to a record player's tone arm so that, as the arm swings, it hits certain contact points and squibs hidden in Brandt's umbrella in the chimney go off. The Lieutenant leaves out a crucial piece of the puzzle (how the sound of the body falling was created) and tricks Brandt into supplying this information (a marker was knocked off the record player and hit an unabridged dictionary balanced so that it would fall to the floor), thereby incriminating himself. There are a lot of clever ideas in this "All-in-the-Game" episode, including a clever trick ending (see "The Three Cs") which is a forerunner to the "Kill Columbo Ending" to be introduced shortly, but the power going off for dramatic effect but coming back on just when Columbo needs it is too big a coincidence. Brandt is not a worthy adversary for the Lieutenant, and the other characters—his wife Vivian (Samantha Eggar), Jason Danziger, president of the club (Basil Hoffman) and Miss Eisenback (Dorrie Thomson)—are ridiculous spoofs. Cute bit with Jamie Lee Curtis as the grumpy waitress. No plan should depend on the murderer being able to come back to the scene the next day and remove evidence, nor should Columbo be taking umbrellas from people's houses (see "The Morality of Columbo II"). First of two fascinating speeches by Columbo about himself, this one focusing on how he had to work harder to keep up with "all the smart people" (see "The Developing Character"). Introduces the character of Sergeant Burke (played by Todd Martin, see "Colleagues and Sidekicks"). First time Columbo makes a more formidable entrance meeting the murderer in "scene two" rather than gathering his "First Clues" (see "Columbo Deconstructed") Ranking: good (7.6).

Additional cast: Mike Marks (Kenneth Mars), George Camponella (Howard McGillin), Mr. Wagner (George Sperdakos), Caroline Treynor (Carol Jones), Amy (Carlene Watkins), Angela (Fay Dewitt), Suzy (Kathleen King), receptionist (Mitzi Rogers)

Production Information

Producer: Everett Chambers (#36, 37); Richard Alan Simmons (#38). Associate producer: Joseph D'Agosta. Director of photography: Milton R. Krasner (#36); Irving I. Lippman (#37); Ted Voigtländer (#38). Film editor: Ronald LaVine (#36); Stanley Frazen (#37); Jerry Dronsky (#38). Art director: Michael Baugh (#36, 37); Howard E. Johnson (#38). Set decorations: Peg Cummings (#36, 37); Richard B. Goddard (#38). Unit manager:

Robert Anderson (#36, 37); D. Jack Stubbs (#38). Assistant director: Mark Sandrich (#36); Charles Walker (#37); Ray Taylor (#38). Sound: Jerry E. Smith (#36, 37); Edwin J. Somers, Jr. (#38). Sound effects editor: Brian Courcier. Costumes: George R. Whittaker. NBC Mystery Movie theme: Henry Mancini. Titles and optical effects: Universal Title. Music editor: Robert Mayer (#36); James D. Young (#37); Al Teeter (#38). Executive story consultant: Bill Driskill. Second assistant director: Robert Latham Brown (#38).

Chapter 7:
The Seventh Season (1977-78)
(Episodes 39-43)

For its seventh season, *Columbo* was presented as five TV movies, on different nights of the week. Richard Alan Simmons continued as executive producer and he introduced structural and several stylistic departures (see "Columbo Deconstructed" and "The Developing Character" for more).

(#39) Try and Catch Me

Written by Gene Thompson & Paul Tuckahoe (story by Thompson). Directed by James Frawley. Music by Pat Williams. Airdate: 11/21/77 (Monday). 90 min.

Mystery writer Abigail Mitchell (Ruth Gordon) does not intend to stand idly by and allow Edmund Galvin (Charles Frank) to get away with killing her beloved niece Phyllis (his wife), so she tricks Galvin into entering her soundproof safe and locks him inside to suffocate. Columbo discovers that Galvin left deathbed testimony implicating Mitchell—he used a match to scratch out the first two words from her last novel so that the book's title page, which he hides in a burned-out light bulb socket, reads "I Was Murdered by Abigail Mitchell." This is a brilliant episode with a terrific two-part ending that raises interesting morality questions (see "The Morality of Columbo I"). It also features a wonderful "Sympathetic Murderer

Relationship," a lot of exploration of Columbo's characteristics (see "The Developing Character") and that incomparable scene at the Ladies' Club where he gives a speech that summarizes his character (or at least the character he's become). Terrific acting is provided by Falk, Gordon and Mariette Hartley as Mitchell's secretary, Veronica Bryce. It could have used a few more clues (see "The Bloating Problem") and the paint under the fingernails is a clue delayed (see "Intermediate Clues"). Sergeant Burke returns (now played by Jerome Guardino) and Dog has a great scene looking at the sea, which "makes him frisky" (see "Bert, Barney and Dog"). Delightful theme music creates a leitmotif each time Mitchell takes action (see "This Old Man"). Ranking: excellent (9.8).

Additional cast: Martin Hammond (G.D. Spradlin), Annie the maid (Mary Jackson), dance instructor (Marie Silva-Alexander)

(#40) Murder Under Glass

Written by Robert Van Scoyk. Directed by Jonathan Demme. Music by Jonathan Tunick. Airdate: 1/30/78 (Monday). 90 min.

Smarmy food critic Paul Gerard (Louis Jourdan) somehow manages to kill restaurant owner Vittorio Rossi (Michael V. Gazzo) to prevent him from revealing Gerard's blackmailing, but how? Rossi was alone when he was poisoned. In the final scene with Gerard, Columbo cooks scaloppine while explaining how Gerard switched Rossi's compressed-air wine bottle opener for an identical one after he put fugu poison in the tip, causing Rossi to poison his own wine. Of course, the Lieutenant has no proof of this until Gerard tries the same trick on him, but Columbo has switched the wineglasses and Gerard is caught. This is a delightfully fun episode to watch, and it contains a clever murder plot and great "All-in-the-Game" interaction between Gerard and Columbo, but the critic's plan leaves behind too many witnesses, including Rossi's nephew Mario Deluca (Antony Alda) and Gerard's dimwitted assistant Eve Plummer (Shera Danese, see "The Supporting Cast" and "Accomplices, Blackmailers and Schlimazels"). The "Kill Columbo

Ending" introduced here raises as many questions as it answers. Columbo's investigation of the bottle opener is odd (see "Intermediate Clues") and it's not quite fair to keep hidden the scene in which Gerard returns to switch openers again. Great acting is supplied by Falk, Jourdan, Danese, Mako (as Mr. Ozu) and Larry Mann (as Chef Albert), but Gazzo and Alda are annoying and Richard Dysart and France Nuyen (as restaurant owners Max Duvall and Mary Choy) are not given enough to do. Nice exploration of Columbo's Italian heritage (see "The Developing Character") and best use of "This Old Man" music at the Restaurant Writers' Banquet. Sergeant Burke (rotatingly played by Todd Martin here) returns (see "Colleagues and Sidekicks"). Ranking: very good (8.4).

Additional cast: Crawford (Fred Holliday), Chef Louis (Alberto Morin), Charlie (Jim Murphy), Claire the bank cashier (Carolyn Martin), first geisha (Miyako Kurata), second geisha (Mieko Kobavashi)

(#41) Make Me a Perfect Murder

Written by Robert Blees. Directed by James Frawley. Music by Patrick Williams. Airdate: 2/25/78 (Saturday). 2 hrs.

TV producer Kay Freestone (Trish Van Devere) cannot believe it when her lover and boss Mark McAndrews (Laurence Luckinbill) is promoted but won't take her with him or allow her to have his old job. She shoots him while she is supposedly in a projection room screening a film for studio head Frank Flanagan (Patrick O'Neal) and makes it look like the work of some whacko. Columbo tricks Freestone into thinking that the gun, which she had hidden in the panel above an elevator, has jiggled loose and she disposes of a planted weapon. Not only are the "First Clue" and final clue disappointing (finding the gun in the elevator was inevitable; see "The Three Cs") but the Lieutenant's silly behavior with his neck brace and his participation in the episode's misogyny (see "Recurring Problems" and "Peter Falk as Columbo") make it very uncomfortable to watch. The scene in which Columbo plays with the test patterns presents a "Bloating Problem." Bruce

Kirby returns, not as Sergeant Kramer but as a TV repairman (see "The Supporting Cast"). Jerome Guardino takes another turn as Sgt. Burke (see "Colleagues and Sidekicks") Ranking: bad (4.4).

Additional cast: Valerie Kirk (Lainie Kazan), Walter Mearhead (James McEachin), Luther (Ron Rifkin), Jonathan (Kenneth Gilman), dubbing chief (Milt Kogan), Madge (Dee Timberlake), Pete Cockrum (Don Eitner), Ames (Morgan Upton), Al Staley (Joe Warfield), the producer (George Skaff), Wendy (Susan Krebs), Angela (Susan Bredhoff), masseur (H.B. Haggerty), guard (Buck Young), Roark (James Frawley), Nancy (Socorro Swan)

(#42) How to Dial a Murder

Written by Tom Lazarus (story by Anthony Lawrence). Directed by James Frawley. Music by Patrick Williams. Airdate: 4/15/78 (Saturday). 90 min.

Dr. Eric Mason (Nicol Williamson), Director of the Institute for Life Control, discovered that his wife Lorraine and best friend Charles Hunter (Joel Fabiani) were having an affair. Six months ago, he killed Lorraine (in an apparent auto accident), and he has a grisly fate in store for Charlie—he has trained his two Dobermans (Laurel and Hardy) to kill upon receiving a two-part signal, a ringing telephone and the word "Rosebud." He asks Charlie to wait for him at his house and a phone call takes care of the rest. Columbo pulls the clues out of pockets on Mason's pool table and Mason decides to give him the "whole picture." He calls out the kill command, but Columbo has already discovered it and the dogs have been reprogrammed to kiss, rather than kill, upon hearing it. This is an intense and powerfully drawn "All-in-the-Game" episode, with great clues, and a "Kill Columbo Ending" that actually answers many questions about the wisdom of using such a device. As usual, the Lieutenant makes no attempt to solve the past murder (see "Get 'Em for the First Murder") The "First Clue" here may be unique in proving too much. Falk and Williamson are terrific, and look for a solid early performance by Kim Cattrall as Joanne Nichols. Dog has some nice moments, but could have been better used (see "Bert, Barney and Dog"). Ranking: very good (8.2).

Additional cast: Miss Cochrane (Tricia O'Neil), Dr. Garrison (Frank Aletter), Officer Stein (Ed Begley, Jr.), technician (Fred J. Gordon)

(#43) The Conspirators

Written by Howard Berk (idea by Pat Robison). Directed by Leo Penn. Music by Patrick Williams. Airdate: 5/13/78 (Saturday). 2 hrs.

Irish poet Joe Devlin (Clive Revill) is secretly negotiating to buy guns to send to Northern Ireland. When arms dealer Vincent Pauley (Albert Paulsen) forces him to pay $50,000 more to get the guns aboard the ship on time, Devlin shoots Pauley and marks the killing as just deserts by putting a bottle of his favorite whiskey (Full's Irish Dew) with its slogan "Let Each Man Be Paid in Full" next to the body. Columbo uses this bottle to place Devlin at the scene of the crime, because the poet followed his usual practice of marking on it the level to which he intended to drink with his distinctive diamond ring. And the Lieutenant realizes that the guns are on the tugboat pulling the ship when he notices that the house flag on the tug is that of Devlin's friends, the O'Connell family. This is another "All-in-the-Game" episode with some neat clues and a double mystery. This time the fun goes a bit too far as Columbo gets major clues (including the bottle) from spending so much time cavorting with Devlin (see "The Developing Character" and "Peter Falk as Columbo"). Despite the title, Kate and George O'Connell (Jeanette Nolan and Bernard Behrens) have little to do with the murder or the cover-up (see "Accomplices, Blackmailers and Schlimazels"). The Irish conflict is not explored (see "Recurring Problems"). Nice work by L.Q. Jones as RV salesman and arms dealer Chuck Jensen. Ranking: good (7.3).

Additional cast: Kerry Malone (Michael Horton), Angela (Deborah White), captain (Sean McClory), Michael Moore (Michael Prince), Leach (Donn White), tow truck driver (Johnny Silver), interviewer Carole Hemingway (herself), Harry (Tony Giorgio), Brandon (John McCann), barmaid (Doreen Murphy), customs officer (Kedric Wolfe)

Production Information

Producer: Richard Alan Simmons. Associate producer: Anthony Kiser (#40, 41, 42, 43). Director of photography: Ted Voigtländer (#39); Duke Callaghan (#40, 41); Isidore Mankofsky (#42, 43). Film editor: Howard S. Deane (#39, 41, 43); Gene Ranney (#40); Robert Watts (#42). Art director: Howard E. Johnson . Set decorations: Richard B. Goddard. Unit manager: D. Jack Stubbs (#39); Jack P. Cunningham (#40, 41, 42, 43); . Assistant director: Dodie Foster (#39); David O. Sosna (#40, 42); Mark Sandrich (#41); Phil Ball (#43). Sound: Harold Lewis (#39); James Pilcher (#40, 42, 43); Leroy Joseph (#41). Sound effects editor: William Wistrom. Supervising sound editor: William Wistrom (#42, 43). Costumes: George R. Whittaker. Titles and optical effects: Universal Title. Music editor: James D. Young. Second assistant director: Charles Norton (#42). Leadman: Bruce Wayne Mecchi (#40, 43). Casting: Bill Kenney (#43). Lamp operator: Gary Stark (#43). Special technical consultants: Jean Brady & Connie Burdick (#40).

Chapter 8:
The Eighth Season (1989)
(Episodes 44-47)

L ate in the spring of 1988, it was announced that *Columbo* was coming back in a new mystery wheel on ABC. Unfortunately, a screenwriters' strike delayed the entire season, and the new shows did not premiere until spring 1989. The other two elements that rotated with *Columbo* were *B.L. Stryker*, with Burt Reynolds as a private detective in Florida, and *Gideon Oliver*, with Louis Gossett, Jr. as the anthropological sleuth based on the novels by Aaron J. Elkins. All shows were two hours long and they aired on Monday nights in place of *Monday Night Football*. Replacing the wonderful "man-with-flashlight" visual and Henry Mancini music from the 1970s (see Season 1 for a description) was a new visual (a bunch of mystery clichés such as a swinging light bulb, a black cat and a knife blade opening) and some odd jazzy music by Mike Post. In all, there were four episodes of *Columbo*, five of *B.L. Stryker* and five of *Gideon Oliver*. William Link served as supervising executive producer for the mystery wheel, and Richard Alan Simmons returned as executive producer of *Columbo* (as he had been in the seventh season ten years earlier).

(#44) Columbo Goes to the Guillotine

Written by William Read Woodfield. Directed by Leo Penn. Music by John Cacavas. Airdate: 2/6/89.

Phony psychic Eliot Blake (Anthony Andrews) gets help from noted debunker Max Dyson (Anthony Zerbe) in fooling the government into thinking he's the Real McCoy when he demonstrates "seeing at a distance" (drawing pictures of buildings seen by military men in various parts of the city, but not shown to him), but he still beheads Dyson with his own guillotine in revenge for Dyson having left him to rot in a Ugandan prison. Columbo tells Blake he intends to keep hounding him and sticks his neck into the guillotine, and Blake tries to eliminate the good Lieutenant, but he has already switched the labels on the collar. Although the trick Blake pulls on the government and Columbo's solution to it are very neat, the whole thing is only tangentially related to the motive. There's no real "First Clue" pointing toward Blake as the killer and the screwdriver is a clue delayed (see "Intermediate Clues"). The "Kill Columbo Ending" really doesn't work (merely because Blake knows how to use the guillotine doesn't mean he used it on Dyson). Columbo forgets that he was shown a trick guillotine before in "Now You See Him" (#34) (see "Hello, Continuity Department?"). Blake gives Columbo a gift clue (see "Recurring Problems") by palming the cartridge when he returns to the scene. Very poor ending of Columbo sticking a fake gun in Blake's face (see "The Developing Character"). Return of "scene two" in which Columbo gathers his "First Clues" (see "Columbo Deconstructed"). All in all, a very disappointing return for the series. Ranking: bad (4.2.)

Additional cast: Paula Hull (Karen Austin), Bert Spindler (James Greene), Sgt. Russo (Robert Costanzo), Harrow (Alan Fudge), Tommy (Michael Bacall), Dori (Dana Anderson), Col. Eckhardt (Charles Howerton), medical examiner (Milt Kogan), clergyman (Tony Amendola), young man (Rob Garrison), polygraph operator (Frank Simons), Eddie (Lenny Hicks), Kevin (Ben Yudell), locksmith (Nick Demauro), detective (Peter Noel Duhamel), Lt. Bravo (Steve Zettler), Capt. Alpha

(Andrew Philpot), Maj. Charlie (Charles Champion), magicians at funeral (Christopher Hart, Dan Birch), magician (Jillian Gotlib)

(#45) Murder, Smoke and Shadows

Written by Richard Alan Simmons. Directed by James Frawley. Music by Patrick Williams. Airdate: 2/27/89.

Brilliant young movie director Alex Brady (Fisher Stevens) is confronted by his old friend Len Fisher (Jeff Perry) with evidence that Brady was involved in the death of Fisher's sister years ago. Brady has the studio street wet down and backs Fisher into an iron gate, electrocuting him. He then renders the body unrecognizable. Columbo gets Brady's secretary Rose Walker (Nan Martin) to blackmail him and has the conversation overheard in bits and pieces by undercover detectives and Brady's former girlfriend, Ruth Jernigan (Molly Hagan). This episode needed a major rewrite. There are problems both large and small. Columbo (who is afraid of heights) should not be eager to hop on Brady's swinging crane; the director should insist on it so that he can continue working and then have fun making the Lieutenant turn green as it moves around. Brady should not bring up Jenny Fisher's death; let Columbo raise the topic. Most significantly, the ending is backwards: it should start with the feeble ticket clue (which Columbo tries to use to place the victim in Brady's playroom, but then drops when Brady appropriately refers to it as "claptrap") and then the clue about Brady's attempted blackmail of Rose (see "The Three Cs"), without the silly curtain calls and having Columbo appear in Brady's mind in a ringmaster's outfit (see "The Developing Character" and "Does Columbo Exist?"). After Columbo admits he can't nail Brady for Lenny Fisher's death, he should then explain that he wondered what Lenny had on the director and end with the powerful film of Jenny's motorcycle accident, which makes for a decent clue as to the motive for Lenny's murder, but a powerful "Final Clue" insofar as Jenny's death is concerned (see "Get 'Em for the First Murder").

Good work by Stevens as the Spielberg-like director and clever idea of having the body identity obscured, but a disappointing trick ending (see "The Three Cs"), poor acting by the supporting players and too much silliness, including having Columbo appear in Brady's mind in a ringmaster's outfit (see "The Developing Character" and "Does Columbo Exist?), take away from this episode. Dog makes his first re-appearance (see "Bert, Barney and Dog") and Sgt. Burke (Jerome Guardino) returns (see "Colleagues and Sidekicks"). Ranking: poor (5.6.)

Additional cast: Marosco (Steven Hill), Phil Crossette (Al Pugliese), Fran "the nurse" (Elizabeth Ruscio), Stan (Time Winters), Lisa "the bridesmaid" (Gayle Harbor), Archie Sewell (Stewart J. Zully), Kardarsian (Avner Garbi), tour guide (Meg Jones), waitress (Lisa Barnes), waiter/cop (Robert Madrid), gate guard (William "Scotty" McGlynn)

(#46) *Sex and the Married Detective*

Written by Jerry Ludwig. Directed by James Frawley. Music by Patrick Williams. Airdate: 4/3/89.

Sex therapist Dr. Joan Allenby (Lindsay Crouse) is devastated to learn that her lover and partner David Kincaid (Stephen Macht) is fooling around with her assistant Cindy Galt (Julia Montgomery), so she dresses up as a courtesan named Lisa and lures him to the clinic's therapy boudoir, where she shoots him. Columbo eventually locates the store in Chicago where Allenby bought the Lisa clothes. Crouse is excellent and she creates a wonderful "Sympathetic Murderer Relationship" with Columbo, but the clues are lackluster, especially the "Final Clue," and the business with the keys makes for a poor "Intermediate Clue." Ham acting by supporting cast, especially the stereotyped sex therapists, Dr. Simon Ward (Peter Jurasik) and Dr. Walter Neff (Ken Lerner). A bizarre scene in which Columbo plays the tuba for a group of children does not help the matter, but it was nice to see him turn red when Allenby asks him about his sex life (see "The Developing Character"). Sergeant Burke (now played by Stewart J. Zully) makes his last appearance (see "Colleagues and Sidekicks"). Ranking: poor (5.7.)

Additional cast: Helen Hendrix (Marge Redmond), Norm Lentz (Dave Florek), Charlie (Harry Johnson), tuba player (Pierrino Mascarino), maid (Leeza Vinnichenko), Madge (Susan Gibney), Ozzie (Peter Wise), airline clerk (Michele Lamar Richards), first bartender (Doug Machugh), Jill (Janet Julian), men in bar (Gary Berner, Peter J. Saputo), women in bar (Heather James, Locky Lambert)

(#47) Grand Deceptions

Written by Sy Salkowitz. Directed by Sam Wanamaker. Music by John Cacavas. Airdate: 5/1/89.

Colonel Frank Brailie (Robert Foxworth) needs to keep the true nature of his Special Projects Fund secret, so he knifes Lester Keegan (Andy Romano), the investigator sent after him by General Jack Padget (Stephen Elliott), and makes it look like an accident during war games. Keegan also has discovered that Brailie is having an affair with the General's young wife, Jennie (Janet Eilber), and Columbo uncovers this truth as well. Columbo busts the alibi Brailie has set up by showing that he wasn't setting up Civil War soldiers for the General's birthday party, he was tossing books on a shelf. Unique among final clues, this one simply doesn't work (see "Busting Alibis, Busting Scenarios"). Columbo brings up a behavioral clue that Brailie is too arrogant to clean up the mud and is handed two gift clues, the chatty friend at the funeral and the secretary who mixes up the reports and allows him to walk off with the incriminating one (see "Recurring Problems"). Odd treatment of the Columbo character in the scene in which he finds the flashlight (see "Peter Falk as Columbo"), when he insults Brailie and when he appears as a figurine on the Civil War board at the end (see "Does Columbo Exist?" and "The Developing Character"). The I-Ching sticks come off as a failed attempt at an "All-in-the-Game Relationship." Foxworth's acting is wooden and the eccentrics at the paramilitary camp are stereotyped. Dog has a brief appearance (see "Bert, Barney and Dog"). Ranking: bad (4.7.)

Additional cast: Sgt. Sidney Winnick (James Lashley), Marcia Bennett

(Lynn Clark), Sgt. Marty Tanzer (Michael McManus), Corp. Warren (Bennett Liss), paramilitary men nos. 1-4 (Christopher Titus, John William Gibson, Lee Arenberg, Stephen Quadros), medical examiner (Milt Kogan), police officer (Rick Marzan), Mr. Martinson (George J. Peters), Mrs. Martinson (Norma MacMillan), major's wife (Carolyn Carradine), I-Ching scholar (Charles Gideon Davis), mercenary (Randy Lee Troyer)

Production Information

Executive producer: Richard Alan Simmons. Co-executive producer: Peter Falk. Producer: Stanley Kallis. Associate producer: John A. Martinelli (#44, 45, 46); Todd London (#47). Supervising producer: Philip Saltzman. Coordinating producer: Abby Singer. Co-producer: Peter V. Ware. Director of photography: Robert Seaman. Film editor: John A. Martinelli (#44); John A. Martinelli & Jay Scherberth (#45); Jay Scherberth (#46); Jay Scherberth, Leslie Dennis Bracken & Ellen Ring Jacobson (#47). Production design: Arch Bacon (#44); Bill Ross (#46, 47). Art director: Cameron Birnie (#44, 45); Arch Bacon & Hugo Santiago (#46); Hugo Santiago (#47). Set decorations: Richard B. Goddard (#44, 45); Mary Ann Good (#46, 47). Costume design: Brienne (#44, 45, 46); Jacqueline Saint Anne (#47). Hairstylist: Carolyn Elias. Makeup artist: Greg LaCava. Unit production manager: Abby Singer (#44, 45, 46); Ted Schilz (#47). Sound mixer: Jim Alexander (#44, 45); Dean S. Vernon (#46, 47). Sound editor: Deni King (#44); Paul Clay (#45, 46, 47). Casting: Darlene Kaplan. Costume supervisor: Michael Long. Supervising music editor: Laurie L. Higgins. ABC Mystery Movie theme: Mike Post. Executive story consultant: Jackson Gillis. Special magic technical advisor: Bruce Sinclair (#44). Special consultant: R.J. Visciglia. First assistant director: Daniel Dugan (#45, 47); Richard A. Wells (#46). Second assistant director: Brenda Kalosh (#45, 46, 47).

Chapter 9:
The Ninth Season (1989-90) (Episodes 48-53)

In the fall of 1989, the mystery wheel was moved to Saturday night, the originally planned time slot. William Link continued as supervising executive producer of the mystery wheel. *Gideon Oliver* was gone, replaced by another returning classic . . . Telly Savalas as *Kojak* (now an inspector with the NYPD, with the legwork left to his assistant, played by Andre Braugher). In addition, ABC added a fourth show, *Christine Cromwell,* with Jaclyn Smith as a high-priced lawyer whose clients inexplicably were accused of murder. In all, there were six episodes of *Columbo,* five of *Kojak,* four of *Christine Cromwell* and seven of *B.L. Stryker.* At the end of the season, *The ABC Saturday Mystery Movie* was cancelled.

On *Columbo,* after the first episode (which had been filmed but not aired the prior spring), Richard Alan Simmons left and Jon Epstein became the executive producer. He toned down some of the elements introduced by Simmons and the season includes some good entries.

(#48) Murder: A Self Portrait
Written by Robert Sherman. Directed by James Frawley. Music by Patrick Williams. Airdate: 11/25/89.

Artist Max Barsini (Patrick Bauchau) has an unusual personal life: he lives with his wife/business manager Vanessa (Shera Danese) and Julie (Isabel Lorca), a model he paints and sleeps with, while his ex-wife Louise (Fionnula Flanagan) lives next door and prepares the meals. When he discovers that Louise plans to move away to live with her former therapist, Sidney Hammer (George Coe), Barsini is worried that she will reveal an old secret, so he drowns her while he is supposedly painting a picture of Vito's Bar. The investigation proceeds in a unique way, as Barsini paints Columbo's portrait while the Lieutenant plays tapes made by Louise of her nightmares (and the dreams are brought to life in stylized black-and-white scenes). Columbo interprets the dream language to mean that Louise was repressing her memory of how Barsini killed his first art dealer, Harry Chudnow, and buried him in the basement of Vito's, where they lived years ago. Of course, Columbo can't use dreams as evidence, but he places Barsini at the scene of Louise's drowning by proving that the smudge on her lip is actually his famous "Barsini red" paint that was on the rag he used to knock her unconscious. Some people don't like the dream sequences, but I think at least the first two are effective. Nevertheless, the structure delays all of the "Intermediate Clues" to the end, where they lose their impact. Also, there's no real "First Clue" pointing toward Barsini as the killer. The "All-in-the-Game" relationship is interesting, but Columbo should not be taking evidence such as the cleaning rag without a warrant (see "The Morality of Columbo II"). Touching final appearance by Vito Scotti as Vito and nice work by Flanagan and Danese (see "The Supporting Cast") and cute moments with Dog (see "Bert, Barney and Dog") particularly at the Bassett Hound Picnic. Ranking: fair (6.4.)

Additional cast: Ralph (David Byrd), customer at Vito's (Don Bovingloh), morgue attendant (Lenny Hicks), lifeguard (Danny Hassel), night visitor (Roger Etienne), officer (Frank L. Wiltse), bystander at beach (Don Schneider), Harry Chudnow (Harold Harris)

(#49) Columbo Cries Wolf

Written by William Read Woodfield. Directed by Daryl Duke. Music by Dennis Dreith. Airdate: 1/20/90.

All of the evidence points toward Sean Brantley (Ian Buchanan), co-owner of the men's magazine *Bachelor's World*, when his partner Dian Hunter (Deidre Hall) disappears on her way to London to sell controlling interest to media mogul Sir Harry Matthews (Alan Scarfe). Columbo believes that Dian was shot on her way to the airport and replaced by a double, probably Brantley's latest "nymph" Tina (Rebecca Staab) and he has no choice but to tear apart The Chateau looking for her body. He finds nothing . . . because she shows up alive. It was all a publicity stunt, but also a prelude to the real thing. Dian raises the price, Matthews accepts and tells Brantley to pack up his nymphs, Brantley goes up to Dian's room and breaks her neck and then Tina (dressed as Dian) waves to the security camera as she drives away. The next morning, Columbo races to the scene and congratulates Brantley; why, he can't even dig up The Chateau again because he "cried wolf." But he does ask if he can make a phone call . . . and he and Brantley hear a beeping sound which they follow into Dian's bathroom, where workmen are replacing some tiles. Columbo uses a crowbar to remove the drywall and uncover Dian's body underneath. Brantley and Dian wear matching pager bracelets and hers is still on the body. "I got the number from the mobile phone company," says Columbo, "and you just saw me dial in my message." He opens the pager to reveal: Gotcha! Excellent episode, with a powerful ending and little clues that are worthy of the show even if they were planted as part of the stunt (the "double" puts cream in her coffee at the airport, something Dian never does). Very interesting use of accomplices, whether defined as Tina, Dian or even Columbo (see "Accomplices, Blackmailers and Schlimazels"). Fine acting by Falk, Buchanan, Hall and Mark Margolis as Dian's driver, Cosner. Bruce Kirby has a cameo as the officer who announces to the Chief (played by John Finnegan) that Hunter is missing a second time (see "Colleagues and Sidekicks"). Nice touch in remembering Chief Superintendent Durk (see "Dagger of the Mind" (#11)) when Dian disappears on the way to London (see "Hello, Continuity Department?"). Columbo modestly comments only that the models "sure have their health" (see "The Developing Character"). Ranking: excellent (9.9.)

Additional cast: Mayor (David Huddleston), Jeanne Wolf (herself), Dian's secretary Helen Robinson (Gigi Rice), Mayor's aide (Peter Zapp), Wilson (Morgan Jones), factotum (Darrell Kunitomi), art director (Rainelle Saunders), guest (Matt Flynn), chief of detectives (Tom Moses), security guard (Mike Masters), security man (James Willett), helicopter pilot (Craig Hosking), police official (Farrell Mayer), policeman (Bill Edward Rogers), city employee (Luis Delgado), tile man (George Chavez), reporters (Gil Newsome, BeeBe Smith, Jimmy Ortega, Primo Lopez, Laurance Grant), next Nymph of the Month (Daphne Cheung), Southern nymph (Kendra Booth), nymph at pool (Paula Trickey), other nymphs (Sandra Wild, Alicia Gilbert, Cameron)

(#50) Agenda for Murder

Written by Jeffrey Bloom. Directed by Patrick McGoohan. Music by David Michael Frank. Airdate: 2/10/90.

Oscar Finch (Patrick McGoohan in the third of his four appearances, see "Multiple Murderers") is the right-hand man to Senator Paul Mackey (Dennis Arndt), who has just become a vice-presidential candidate, and Finch imagines himself as the next Attorney General. But then he gets a call from Frank Staplin (Louis Zorich), a shady character who will reveal an old "favor" Finch did for him if he doesn't help make an imminent indictment go away. Finch shoots Staplin and makes it look like a suicide. Columbo notices Finch munching all the time and places him at the scene of the crime with bite mark evidence, specifically a piece of cheese he nibbled. A solid ending (though hardly novel—it had been used on *Quincy, M.E.* years before) and other clues (the blood that dried before the gun hit the floor, the single dry parking spot in Finch's parking lot) elevate this episode. Nice twist in using Mackey as an accomplice after the fact, although it's left unresolved what will happen to him, or his campaign (see "Accomplices, Blackmailers and Schlimazels"). Falk, McGoohan, Arndt and Anne Haney (as Finch's secretary, Louise) are excellent, but Arthur Hill is wasted as the presidential candidate, Governor James Montgomery, and the show needed to have more details about what the candidates stood for. A reference or two to the prior political episode, "Candidate for Crime" (#18), would have been appropriate (see "Hello, Continuity Department?"). Bruce Kirby returns as a sergeant, as yet unnamed (see "Colleagues and Sidekicks"). Ranking: good (7.15.)

Additional cast: Mrs. Finch (Penny Fuller), Tim (Steven Ford), Rebecca Christy (Annie Stewart), Toby (Stanley Kamel), laundry truck driver (Michael Goldfinger), Amir (Shaun Toub), Diane (Carol Barbee), security men (Peter Allas, Bryan Montgomery), police technician (Kirk Thornton), coroner's man (Doug Franklin), staffer (Rande Leaman), gal (Eva Charney), D.A. (Jake Jacobs), man (Huey Redwine), radio announcer (Jim Carson)

(#51) Rest in Peace, Mrs. Columbo

Written by Peter S. Fischer. Directed by Vincent McEveety. Music by Richard Markowitz. Airdate: 3/31/90.

The episode opens on a rainy day and a funeral . . . the funeral of Mrs. Columbo. But a series of flashbacks fill us in on the typical story. Real estate agent Vivian Dimitri (Helen Shaver) shoots her boss, Charleton Chambers (Ed Winter), the man who ratted out her husband Pete to the police years ago (Pete was involved in a financial scandal and killed a client in a panic; after he died in prison she moved back to L.A.). She suggests that Chambers died much later than when she shot him by obtaining cash at an ATM using his card, provides herself with an alibi for that later time of being in bed with Leland St. John (Ian McShane) and drops the gun at an abandoned lot of a housing development to pin the blame on a hothead who lives there who had threatened Chambers. But she has bigger plans in store—she intends to take revenge on Columbo (who arrested Pete) and to do it by killing his wife. Columbo politely puts off her attempts at meeting the missus, but Dimitri sees her chance when he comments that his wife would enjoy some lemon marmalade Dimitri is eating. She gives him a jar to pass along to his wife . . . and the next thing you know we're at the funeral. Afterward, they go to Columbo's house, where he finds the open jar of marmalade and eats some. Now Dimitri has to confess what she's done, just as her psychiatrist, Dr. Steadman (Roscoe Lee Browne) told Columbo she would feel compelled to do. But the Lieutenant is just faking the dying act. What's more, they're at the house of Sergeant Brady (Tom Isbell) because his wife is home with the flu. After Dimitri is taken away, the Lieutenant calls his wife and tells her not to worry that she missed an episode of her soap opera. The "Confession Ending" here works on a technical level, but the episode as a whole suffers because Dimitri is not a worthy *Columbo* villain. The episode contains five serious problems when both Dimitri and Columbo fail to make common-sense observations (see "Recurring Problems" for details). The flashbacks from the funeral not only become tiresome, but they actually don't make sense because some of the scenes were not witnessed by the person supposedly remembering them. Falk, McShane, Browne and Isbell (see "Colleagues and Sidekicks") do a nice job, but Shaver is sometimes way over the top. Fischer does recall some Columbo traits not seen in a long time (see "The Developing Character") and, after taunting us with the possibility of killing off the beloved Mrs. Columbo, treats us to a rare Columbo call with his wife at the end (see "Does Columbo Exist?"). Ranking: bad (4.5.)

Additional cast: Didi Perkins (Teresa Ganzel), Mitchell Connelly (Michael Alldredge), priest (Hugh Gillin), Mrs. Thornwood (Rosanna Huffman), Mr. Thornwood (George Buck), Rudy (Don Calfa), Liz Cooper (Peggy Walton Walker), Joe the bookie (Joe Bellan), Jerry (Robert Balderson), Abe Lusko (Julius Branca), Theo Kellerman (Roger Hampton), waiter (Robin Bach), maitre d' (Jean-Paul Vignon), plainclothesman (Ed McCready), Gracie (LaRue Stanley), landscaper (Michael Bandoni), uniformed policemen (Rob Narita, Bill Edward Rogers), ambulance attendant (Ken Bryan), Bennie (Dafidd McCracken), hooker (Susan Bachli), valet (Lenny Citrano)

(#52) Uneasy Lies the Crown

Written by Steven Bochco. Directed by Alan J. Levi. Music by James di Pasquale. Airdate: 4/28/90.

Dentist Wesley Corman (James Read) is in practice with his father-in-law, Horace Sherwin (Paul Burke), but he'd much rather be at the track. He needs Sherwin's money, so he devises a way to put the family in his debt. Corman knows that his wife Lydia (Jo Anderson), who has a heart condition, is having an affair with actor Adam Evans (Marshall Teague), so he puts some of her digitalis mixed with dissolving gel in Evans's crown and, hours later when Evans is making love to Lydia, he has a heart attack. Corman rushes to the scene and plants clues suggesting that Lydia unintentionally gave Evans some of her heart medicine, then enlists her brother David (Mark Arnott) into helping him put Evans's body in his car and pushing it over a cliff. Columbo follows the false trail Corman has set for him, but quickly comes to suspect the truth. In the end, he summons Corman to the morgue where he "demonstrates" that digitalis stains teeth blue, and before Sherwin can extract Evans's tooth, Corman confesses. After he leaves, Dr. Johnson (Steven Gilborn, see "The Supporting Cast") observes that Columbo actually used laundry bluing. This episode, rewritten from a Steven Bochco script that was first used on the final season of McMillan, has some solid clues (the reprogramming of the 911 button on the phone, the amount of digitalis Corman put in the blender) and an unusual employment of an "almost accomplice" who doesn't know what is really going on (see "Accomplices, Blackmailers and Schlimazels" for this and a discussion of Adam Evans, a schlimazel who's killed as part of a plan and not for anything he has done). But the "Confession Ending" is a big letdown and it does not work as a "Metaclue Ending" either. Good work by Read and nice touch in having Nancy Walker, Dick Sargent and Ron Cey play themselves, but the mimic at the poker game (John Roarke) went a little too far. John Finnegan returns, this time as the sneezing waiter (see "The Supporting Cast"). Weird moment when Columbo takes cream in his coffee, something he's never done before (see "Hello, Continuity Department?"). Ranking: good (7.4.)

Additional cast: Sgt. Macauley (James A. Watson, Jr.), Frances (Lynne Marta), lab technician (Morgan Jones), Dr. Rosetti (Raymond Singer), John Valentine (Victor Bevine), woman at track (Mimi Cozzens), men (John Bowman, Eugene Dauls), maitre d' (Khin-Kyaw Maung), bartenders (Daniel Bryan Cartmell, John Idakitis), Wesley's friend (Randall James Jeffries), blonde (Melissa Young), policemen (Steve Kelso, James Landi), spectator (Henry A. Crowell, Jr.), paramedic (Edward Talbot "Chip" Matthews)

(#53) *Murder in Malibu*

Written by Jackson Gillis. Directed by Walter Grauman. Music by Patrick Williams. Airdate: 5/14/90.

Wayne Jennings (Andrew Stevens) has many female companions but he intends to marry romance novelist Theresa Goren (Janet Margolin), so when she calls him in the middle of the night to break off the engagement, he races to Malibu and shoots her so he can collect on an insurance policy. About halfway through the episode, Columbo has enough evidence to arrest Jennings, but then the preliminary coroner's report reveals that Theresa was already dead when he shot her, so they have to let him go. In the end, Columbo explains that Jennings fired the first shot too, then (trapped at the scene by some men working on the cable TV), he adopted Plan B. Jennings must have been the shooter, because he dressed the body in knee socks (knowing she was to leave town that day) but mistakenly put her underwear on backwards. Another of the "Variations on a Theme by Jackson Gillis," this is one is uninspired. Stevens's acting is poor, Brenda Vaccaro is way over the top as Theresa's excitable sister, Jess McCurdy, and Floyd Levine's portrayal of Lieutenant Schultz (see "Colleagues and Sidekicks") is heavy-handed and not funny. Ranking: poor (6.0.)

Additional cast: Helen Ashcroft (Laurie Walters), Mrs. Rocca (Sondra Currie), TV host (Tom Dreesen), truck driver (Charles Walker), coroner (Ben Slack), Rosa (Yolanda Lloyd), McGee (Efrain Figueroa), Mavis Thompson (Mary Margaret Lewis), Shorts (Robin Gordon), spinster's father (Bill Zuckert), middle-aged spinster (Judy Jean Berns), receptionist (Connie Danese), plainclothesmen (Michael G. Hawkins, John Petlock, Joe Staton), Mrs. Gompertz (Louise Fitch), Charlie Fisher (Peter Jolly), waitress (Jill Beeber), nurse's aide (Marr Nealon), usher (Janna Brown), policewoman (Liddy Roley), women at TV show in order (Maggie Mellin, Linda Burroughs, Annie Waterman, Virginia Bingham, Michele Bernath, Sandra Giles), photographer (Larry Grant), saleswoman (Kathy Lukather)

Production Information

Executive producer: Richard Alan Simmons (#48); Jon Epstein (#49, 50, 52, 53); Peter S. Fischer (#51). Co-executive producer: Peter Falk. Producer: Stanley Kallis (#48); Penny Adams (#49, 50, 52, 53). Associate producer: Todd London. Supervising producer: Philip Saltzman (#48); Robert F. O'Neill (#51). Co-producer: Peter V. Ware. Director of photography: Robert Seaman (#48, 49); David Michael Frank (#50); Jack Priestley (#51, 52, 53). Film editor: Jay Scherberth (#48, 49); Richard Bracken (#50, 52); Edward M. Abroms (#51); Bill Parker (#53). Production design: Bill Ross. Art director: Hugo Santiago. Set decorations: Mary Ann Good. Costume design: Jacqueline Saint Anne. Hairstylist: Donna Turner Culver (#48); Janice Brandow (#49); Danne D. Long (#50, 52); Charlene Rossi (#53). Makeup artist: Greg LaCava (#48); Dee Manges (#49, 50, 51, 52, 53). Unit production manager: Christopher Seiter (#48, 49, 51, 53); Henry Kline (#50, 52). Sound mixer: Dean S. Vernon (#48); Thomas E. Allan, Sr. (#49, 50, 51, 52, 53). Supervising sound editor: Paul Clay. Casting: Darlene

Kaplan (#48, 49, 50, 51, 52); Ron Stephenson (#53). Costume supervisor: Michael J. Long. Supervising music editor: Laurie Higgins Tobias. ABC Mystery Movie theme: Mike Post. Executive story editor: Jackson Gillis. Executive story consultant: William Read Woodfield (#49, 50, 51, 52, 53). Special consultant: R.J. Visciglia, Jr. First assistant director: Daniel Dugan (#48, 51, 53); Bill Lukather (#49); Janet Davidson (#50); Patrick McKee (#52). Second assistant director: Brenda Kalosh (#48); Patrick McKee (#49, 50); Katy Garrestson (#51, 52, 53). DGA trainee: Jason Saville. Painter: Jaroslav Gebr (#48). Ladies' costumes: Karen Bellamy (#49, 50, 51, 52, 53). Men's costumes: Steve Ellsworth (#49, 50, 51, 52, 53). Creative consultant: Bill Driskill (#49, 50, 51, 52, 53). Foley artist: Tim Chilton (#51). Driver: Chris Haynes (#51, 53).

Chapter 10:
The Tenth Season (1990-91) (Episodes 54-56)

Without a mystery wheel, *Columbo* was again produced and aired less frequently and on different nights of the week (see individual episodes and Production Table for details), as had occurred in 1977-78. Executive producer Jon Epstein died just about the time the first episode aired and his duties were probably taken over by supervising producer Alan J. Levi.

(#54) Columbo Goes to College

Written by Jeffrey Bloom (story by Bloom & Frederick King Keller). Directed by E.W. Swackhamer. Music by James di Pasquale. Airdate: 12/9/90 (Sunday).

Freemont College frat boys Justin Rowe (Stephen Caffrey) and Cooper Redman (Gary Hershberger) kill their criminology professor, D.E. Rusk (James Sutorius) before he can fail or expel them for stealing answers to a test. While Columbo is giving his first guest lecture to their class, the boys use a camera and remote-controlled gun hidden in their truck to blow Rusk's brains out in the garage below. The boys suggest various suspects, but when Justin's father, university lawyer Jordan Rowe (Robert Culp), tells Columbo that Rusk was preparing to write a book about organized crime, they decide to frame Dominic Doyle (William Lucking), ex-con brother of school security guard Joe Doyle (Jim Antonio), which makes sense since they stole Joe's gun to commit the crime. When they hear Columbo receive a description of Dominic's car from a colleague on the phone, they put the murder weapon in it. But it isn't Dominic's car, it's Mrs. Columbo's, and the boys are the only ones who heard the phony information. The murder plot is very clever (but how did these guys come up with it?) and it was a great idea to have Columbo teach a class and interact with the students. But the frat boys make unworthy opponents (they put themselves in the spotlight too much and don't even realize Columbo is after them), and the use of the information Columbo reveals only to the murderer does not work as well here as in "A Friend in Deed" (#23) (see "The Three C's"). A better ending might have gone farther with the locking mechanism and video (perhaps the sound of the door unlocking is on the tape). And it was a poor choice to have the episode end with Justin suggesting his father will get them off. Steven Gilborn returns as Dr. Johnson, the medical examiner (see "The Supporting Cast"). Strange choice to have the class ask Columbo about "the Devlin case" only to have him say that he can't remember it (neither can we, see "Hello, Continuity Department?"). Ranking: good (7.7.)

Additional cast: June Clark (Katherine Cannon), Mrs. Rusk (Bridget Hanley), Mr. Redman (Alan Fudge), Mrs. Rowe (Maree Cheatham), Malloy (Les Lannom), Sarah (Elizabeth Swackhamer), Ollie Sachs (Karl Wiedergott), John (James Ingersoll), janitor (Dick Balduzzi), maitre d' (Robin Bach), Todd (Greg Rogen), crime lab man (Morgan Jones), producer (Jane Alden), detective (Noel Conlon), professors (Frank Farmer, Alfred Powers), Dean Howard Gillespie (Laurence Haddon), news anchor (Larry McCormick), officer (George C. Simms), policeman (Aaron Seville), newswoman (Shauna Steiner), Toby (Jerry McCollum), Cary (Troy Shire), crewman (David Cowgill), Norm (Robert R. Ross Jr.), Charles (Tony Beninati), reporters (Mary Angela Shea, Casey Van Patten), valet (Darren Scott), Latin maid (Mary Maldonado)

(#55) Caution: Murder Can Be Hazardous to Your Health

Written by Sonia Wolf, Patricia Ford & April Raynell. Directed by Daryl Duke. Music by John Cacavas. Airdate: 2/20/91 (Wednesday).

Wade Anders (George Hamilton in the second of his two appearances, see "Multiple Murderers") is the host of *Crime Alert*, a crime re-creation show similar to *America's Most Wanted*. News anchor Budd Clark (Peter Haskell) is furious that he was passed over for the job and he has the means to blackmail Anders to quit—a porno movie Anders made years ago. Anders murders Clark by putting drops of nicotine sulfate into Clark's cigarettes. Columbo places Anders at the scene of the crime by proving that Clark's dog, with her distinctive missing claw, scratched Anders's car the night of the murder. Hamilton's acting is wooden, Haskell's character annoying and the rest of the cast is forgettable. There's no real "First Clue" pointing toward Anders as the killer. Redundant clues are used to prove that someone else was with Clark when he died. The episode suffers from "The Bloating Problem" with lots of wasted time (particularly the crime show reenactments) and forced set-ups for Columbo to talk to Anders at different locations (TV awards, a black-tie dinner). The scratch-mark clue was utilized much better in "The Conspirators" (#43), and it takes Columbo far too long to put the pieces together (see "The Developing Character"), although his knowledge about smoking comes in handy and Dog's help was a nice touch (see "Bert, Barney and Dog"). Third appearance of Steven Gilborn as the medical examiner (see "The Supporting Cast"). Ranking: fair (6.9.)

Additional cast: Maxine Jarrett (Penny Johnson), Arnie (Robert Donner), Henry Santos (Rick Najera), Lisa (Marie Chambers), Sgt. Lewis (Dennis Bailey), Melanie (Patricia Allison), John (Jack Tate), Jack (Paul Ganus), "Barbara Baylor" (Linda Dona), "Duke Dimarco" (Michael Russo), technician (Louis Herthum), Linda (Emily Kuroda), hairdresser Maurice (Guerin Barry), Randy (Barry O'Neill), Al Morrow (Seth Foster), production assistant (Jim Jarrett), Sgt. Fitzwater (Mary Ingersoll), Judy (Lisa Marie Russell), Wanda (Mimi Monaco), Tisha (Marabina James), customer (Mark Daneri), redhead (Brenda Isaacs), officer (Lawrence Scott Maki), S.W.A.T. officer (Gary Kernick), young Wade (Aristides Priakos), porno actress (Nicole Grey), phone girl (Leesa Bryte), choreographer (Joanne DiVito), woman (Jan Hoag), Detective Frank (Raymond Lynch), real Duke (Timothy Moran), real Barbara (Tricia Long), male voice (John Paul Ahearn), female voice (Jennifer Asch), second female voice (Barbara D'Altair).

(#56) Columbo and the Murder of a Rock Star

Written by William Read Woodfield. Directed by Alan J. Levi. Music by Steve Dorff. Airdate: 4/29/91 (Monday).

When famous criminal defense lawyer Hugh Creighton (Dabney Coleman) discovers that his lover, rock star Marcy Edwards (Cheryl Paris) is having an affair with her drummer, Neddy Malcolm (Julian Stone), he tries to throw her out, but she wants palimony and knows about the skeletons in his closet. Creighton breaks her neck at the beach house and frames Malcolm for the crime. Later, we learn that Creighton used his assistant Trish Fairbanks (Shera Danese) to unwittingly fake an alibi for him by speeding down a street in Pasadena wearing a mask of his face at the time of the crime, so that an automatic camera would snap "his" picture for a ticket. Trish demands to be made his partner and wife and states that if anything happens to her an envelope will appear on Columbo's desk. In the end, Columbo destroys the alibi (there is no shadow under Creighton's nose in the photo because it's a flat mask) and claims to place Creighton (who was driving Trish's car) at the scene of the crime by finding berries in the car's window well that fall only on a particular street in West L.A. at this time of year. The episode is strong for the first three-quarters, but then it gets bogged down in Columbo's investigation into how Creighton faked the ticket photo (and how exactly could anyone drive a car when the mask has no eyeholes?) The "Final Clue" about the berries is just not credible.

Interesting use of an accomplice, at first without her knowledge. Then she makes sure she protects herself against any reprisals by the murderer (see "Accomplices, Blackmailers and Schlimazels"). Danese does a nice job, as does John Finnegan as Chief Quentin Corbett and Steven Gilborn as the medical examiner (see "The Supporting Cast"), but Coleman appears to be phoning in his performance (he fidgets, but neither gets angry nor has any snappy comebacks). It was refreshing to see Columbo have a female assistant in Sgt. Hubach (Sondra Currie, see "Colleagues and Sidekicks"), but having her kick down doors and chase suspects is out of character for the show. Cute guest visit by Little Richard and nice "music video" at the end with Columbo singing along with Danese, who supplied the vocals (see "This Old Man"). Big mistake to have Columbo say it's his first time taking the top of his car down (see "Hello, Continuity Department?"). Ranking: fair (7.0.)

Additional cast: Sam Marlowe (John Martin), Ando Miaki (Tad Horino), housekeeper (Deborah Rose), prosecutor (Joseph Chapman), judge (Ann Weldon), decorator "Vito" (B.J. Turner), defendant (Steve Tschudy), Darlene Glinski (Susie Singer), contractor (Terrence Beasor), policeman (Terry G. Warren), kid (Chad A. Bell), sergeant (Mark Voland), receptionist (Carolyn Carradine), Chief's secretary (Dorothy Constantine), Jerry the photographer (Robert Terry Lee), D.A. Everett (Robert Trumbull), second technician (Bruce Marchiano), bartender (Michael Leopard), waiter (Loren Blackwell), lawyer from Idaho (Joe Faust), reporter #1 (Regina Leeds), reporter #2 (Curt Booker), client (William Chalmers)

Production Information

Executive producer: Jon Epstein. Co-executive producer: Peter Falk. Co-producer: Todd London. Supervising producer: Alan J. Levi. Director of photography: George Koblasa. Film editor: Bill Parker (#54); Richard Bracken (#55, 56). Production design: Bill Ross. Art director: Cosmas

Demetriou. Set decorations: Mary Ann Good. Costume design: Jacqueline Saint Anne. Hairstylist: Danne D. Long (#50, 52). Makeup artist: Dorinda Carey. Unit production manager: Norman Henry (#54, 56); Henry Kline (#55). Sound mixer: Thomas E. Allan, Sr. (#54, 55); Patrick Mitchell (#56). Supervising sound editor: Paul Clay. Casting: Donna Dockstader (#54); Ron Stephenson (#55, 56). Costume supervisor: Michael J. Long (#54, 55); Karen Bellamy (#56). Supervising music editor: Laurie Higgins Tobias. ABC Mystery Movie theme: Mike Post. Executive story editor: Jackson Gillis. Executive story consultant: William Read Woodfield. First assistant director: Mary Ellen Canniff (#54, 56); Patrick McKee (#55). Second assistant director: Barbara Bruno. Ladies' costumes: Karen Bellamy (#54, 56); Jill Sheridan (#56). Men's costumes: Steve Ellsworth (#54, 55); Robert Bush (#56). Leadman: Bruce Wayne Mecchi (#56). Sound effects editor: Rick Bozeat & Susan Kurtz (#56). Sound re-recording mixer: Peter Reale (#56). Sound editor: Cathie Speakman (#56). Set lighting technician: Joseph T. Terranova (#56).

Chapter 11:
The Eleventh Season (1991-92) (Episodes 57-58)

Although only two new episodes aired during the 1991-92 season, ABC also aired seventeen repeats, regularly on Thursday nights, including all of the episodes that had been produced since 1988 and the two original pilots, *Prescription: Murder* and *Ransom for a Dead Man*. For many people, this was the first opportunity to see these movies in many years. On the other hand, ABC also aired "WordGames" the 2-hour pilot to the ill-conceived *Mrs. Columbo*, the ridiculous attempt to cash in on *Columbo* after it shut down in 1978. Peter Falk assumed the role of executive producer for *Columbo*.

(#57) Death Hits the Jackpot
Written by Jeffrey Bloom. Directed by Vincent McEveety. Music by Steve Dorff. Airdate: 12/15/91 (Sunday)

While watching TV, photographer Freddy Brower (Gary Kroeger) discovers he has just won a $30 million lottery prize, but doesn't want his wife Nancy (Jamie Rose) to find out before their divorce is finalized or she'll get half the winnings. He confides in his uncle, jewelry store owner Leon Lamarr (Rip Torn), who comes up with a scheme to claim he won the money and secretly give it to Freddy. But on Halloween night, Lamarr, dressed in a

King George III costume, comes to Freddy's apartment, knocks him out and drowns him in his tub. Nancy arrives and kisses Lamarr; she stays around to phone Lamarr at home at 8:00 (pretending to be Freddy) and provides him with an alibi. In the end, Columbo places Lamarr at Freddy's on the night of the murder with a fingerprint . . . not his, but that of a chimpanzee that was there at the time. The chimp is attracted to shiny objects (like Columbo's badge) and it grabbed the medallion around Lamarr's neck. When Columbo thanks Nancy for "all of her help," Lamarr reveals her part in the murder and she is arrested too. This episode looks like a combination of "Suitable for Framing" (#4) (fingerprints other than those of the murderer connecting him to the crime and using an accomplice to delay the time of death), "The Greenhouse Jungle" (#9) (uncle and nephew scheme to make a fortune, then uncle kills nephew and keeps it all himself) and "Candidate for Crime" (#18) (smashed watch provides fake time of death, but Columbo notices it doesn't fit with the rest of the scene), but these parts don't add up. The use of an accomplice here raises multiple problems (see "Accomplices, Blackmailers and Schlimazels") and Nancy's behavior draws attention to her, as even Lamarr realizes. Columbo never explains why he thinks it's murder rather than an accident, even at the end, and it's very frustrating (no real "First Clue" pointing toward Lamarr either). The acting is very poor and the supporting cast consists of a bunch of bad stereotypes: Trish the ditzy flower child (Britt Lind), Meyer McGinty the colorful Irishman (Shane McCabe), the fussy old Italian lady (Penny Santon). There's a huge "Bloating Problem." Sad excuse for a second story involving Columbo's search for his wife's 25th wedding anniversary present (see "The Developing Character" for this and the bizarre scene in which Columbo speaks Italian to the little old lady), which is never resolved, but is supposed to be played for laughs with Detective Jack Stroller (Warren Berlinger) (see "Colleagues and Sidekicks"). The scene also confuses the question of whose car is older, Columbo's or his wife's (see "Hello, Continuity Department?"). Poor version of "This Old Man" is employed and it's oddly placed at the beginning of the episode, before Columbo even appears. Ranking: poor (5.3.)

Additional cast: Martha Lamarr (Betsy Palmer), Gregory Lopiccolo (Anthony Ponzini), Jody (Marilyn Tokuda), Det. Laneer (Robert Alan Browne), Det. Braverman (Daniel Trout), auctioneer (Donald Craig), Otto (Peter Schreiner), Leda (Elizabeth Lambert), Shari (Victoria Boa), Mr. Weatherford (Michael Prince), Mrs. Weatherford (Anita Dangler), Master of Ceremonies (Dick Patterson), security guard (Ed McCready), Greta (Dianne Turley Travis), minister (Robert Rothwell), saleswoman in jewelry store (Margaret Howell), first woman (Kathryn White), second woman (Marjorie Stapp), third woman (Charner Wallis), John (Larry Randolph), car salesman (Webster Williams), staff person (Michael Halpin), patrolman (Gerry Okuneff), lady at auction (Marte Boyle Slout), man at auction (Allen Rice), second model (Dona Speir)

(#58) No Time to Die

Written by Robert Van Scoyk (from the Ed McBain novel *So Long As You Both Shall Live*). Directed by Alan J. Levi. Music by Patrick Williams. Airdate: 3/15/92 (Sunday)

Columbo's nephew, Andy Parma (Thomas Calabro), is a cop who has just married Melissa Hayes (Joanna Going), but she is abducted from their hotel room that night by Rudolf Strassa (Daniel McDonald), a psychopath who wants to "marry" and then kill her. The police race to find her in time. In the end, just as Strassa prepares to "consummate" his "marriage" to Melissa, Columbo, Andy and other cops kick in the door and blow Strassa away. Sound like an episode of *Columbo*? Well, it isn't, except in name. As explained in detail in "No Time for Columbo, No Place for McBain," this was the first of two attempts to "adapt" Ed McBain police procedurals into episodes of *Columbo*, and the idea was a terrible one. Here, the violence is uncomfortable to watch, the tension unbearable (with no humor to lighten it) and the plot makes little sense. Falk tries to insert some Columbo manner-isms in, but the format just won't allow for it (see "Peter Falk as Columbo"). Donald Moffat brings some dignity to the role of Melissa's father, Sheldon Hayes, and Dan Butler is solid as Sergeant Goodman, but most of the char-acters are forgettable, including Andy, and Melissa comes off as weird when she talks to herself while trying to escape. Ironically, despite discarding most of the format of the show (see "Hello, Continuity Department?"), this episode maintains the "rule" that Columbo's first name is not revealed, but that makes for awkward moments when Andy should call him "Uncle [first name]" (see "You Can Call Him Lieutenant"). And it keeps the jolly tune "This Old Man," odd as it seems at the end of this tense and violent show. Ranking: not Columbo (3.0.)

Additional cast: Alex Varick (Daniel Davis), Det. Mulrooney (Doug Savant), Bill Bailey (David Byrd), Tubby Comfort (Cliff Emmich), Eileen Hacker (Juliet Mills), Louise Hays (Patricia Huston), Albert Wagner (Don Swayze), Cindy (Beth Chamberlin), Samantha (Siobhan McCafferty), President Loren Jefferson (Stack Pierce), Janet (Yvonne Farrow), Abdul (Richard Assad), bartender (Jose Rey), Sandy (Mark Alan Kaufman), tech-nicians (Tom Marvich, Gary Hollis, Darnell Harrison)

Production Information

Executive producer: Peter Falk. Co-executive producer: Alan J. Levi (#58). Co-producer: Todd London (#57, 58). Producer: Christopher Seiter. Director of photography: George Koblasa. Film editor: Michael J. Lynch (#57); Richard Bracken (#58). Production design: Bill Ross. Art director: Cosmas Demetriou (#57); Peg McClellan (#58). Set decorations: Mary Ann Good. Costume design: Jacqueline Saint Anne. Hairstylist: Paula Griffin. Makeup artist: Lisa Pharren (#57); James Scribner (#58). Unit production manager: Christopher Seiter. Sound mixer: Thomas E. Allan, Sr. (#57); Mark Hopkins McNabb (#58). Supervising sound editor: Paul

Clay. Casting: Ron Stephenson. Costume supervisor: Robert Bush & Jill Sheridan (#57); Jill Sheridan & Alice Daniels (#58). Supervising music editor: Laurie Higgins Tobias. Executive story consultant: William Read Woodfield. First assistant director: Joseph Ingraffia. Second assistant director: David O'Vidio (#57); Brad Michaelson (#58). Assistant location manager: Joshua Silverman (#57).

Chapter 12:
The Twelfth Season (1992) (Episode 59)

After "No Time to Die" (#58), there was some outcry from *Columbo* fans that this was not the show they wanted. Perhaps Falk heard and considered this criticism. In any event, he went back and picked up an old script by Jackson Gillis that had previously been submitted and put on the shelf. Only one episode aired during the 1992 season.

(#59) A Bird in the Hand
Written by Jackson Gillis. Directed by Vincent McEveety. Music by Dick de Benedictis. Airdate: 11/22/92 (Sunday)

Gambler Harold McCain (Greg Evigan) plans to blow up his uncle, "Big Fred" McCain (Steve Forrest) with a bomb underneath Big Fred's Rolls Royce, but Big Fred is killed in a hit-and-run and his hapless gardener Fernando (Leon Singer) gets blown up when he goes to move the car. Harold is having an affair with Fred's drunken wife Dolores (Tyne Daly) and he intends to maneuver control of Big Fred's football team, the Stallions, away from her, but she proves to be tougher than he thought. In fact, it turns out that she killed Big Fred and when Harold threatens to reveal some information he has about this, she shoots him and makes it look like a he was killed for not paying his gambling debts, probably by the guy named

Hacker (Michael Gregory) who has been after him for this very reason (see "Accomplices, Blackmailers and Schlimazels" for more on Harold and poor Fernando, a schlimazel who is killed by mistake). Columbo nabs Dolores when she leaves Harold's hat at her place and it has tiny hairs in it from the haircut he just got. In this last of the "Variations on a Theme by Jackson Gillis," the trick is announced right in the title—Columbo does not follow the unwritten rule that he must "Get 'Em for the First Murder" and instead arrests Dolores for killing Harold. But the "First Clue" is wanting, the three small mysteries in this episode don't add up to one good one, Gillis keeps one card hidden at all times and the acting by Daly (way over the top as a drunk) and Evigan (he just yells at Columbo) is not up to *Columbo* standards. Frank McRae plays it straight as Lieutenant John Robertson (see "Colleagues and Sidekicks"). Ranking: poor (5.25.)

Additional cast: Bertie Selkowitz (Don S. Davis), casino manager (Stephen Liska), salesman (G.F. Smith), casino waitress (Carol Swarbrick), Ed (Ed McCready), medical examiner (John Petlock), Clyde (Joel Beeson), Honey (Kay Perry), Sgt. Nancy Duran (Joanne Sanchez), policeman (Bebe Louie), barber (Lenny Citrano), serviceman (Elven Havard), dealer (Gerry Okuneff), detective at Harold's (Dick Baker), policemen (Cody Glenn, Vincent J. McEveety), policeman at stadium (Robert Deery), traffic policeman (Ron Tron), bystander at accident (David Alan Graf), signing football player (Geoff Koch), football player at wake (Jeff Hochendoner), football player at stadium (Lonnie Johnson), guests at wake (Rodha Lawrence, Buck Young), girl at wake (Kyle Fredericks), policeman on P.A. (Buddy Joe Hooker)

Production Information

Executive producer: Peter Falk. Producer: Christopher Seiter. Associate Producer: Jack Horger. Co-associate producer: Lisa Tygett. Director of photography: George Koblasa. Film editor: Bill Parker. Production design: Bill Ross. Art director: Hugo Santiago. Set decorations: Mary Ann Good. Costume design: Jacqueline Saint Anne. Hairstylist: Paula Griffin. Makeup artist: Rita Sabatini. Unit production manager: Christopher Seiter. Sound mixer: Thomas E. Allan, Sr. Supervising sound editor: Paul Clay. Casting: Ron Stephenson. Costume supervisor: Jill Sheridan. Supervising music editor: Laurie Higgins Tobias. Executive story consultant: William Read Woodfield. First assistant director: Joseph Ingraffia. Second assistant director: Brad Michaelson.

Chapter 13:
The Thirteenth Season (1993-94) (Episodes 60-62)

S eason 13 included two traditional *Columbos*, one written by Peter Falk himself ("It's All in the Game" (#60) and the other by veteran Peter S. Fischer ("Butterfly in Shades of Grey" (#61)). The other episode (sadly) was the second experimental Ed McBain adaptation, "Undercover" (#62).

(#60) It's All in the Game
Written by Peter Falk. Directed by Vincent McEveety. Music by Dick de Benedictis. Airdate: 10/31/93 (Sunday).

Socialite Lauren Staton (Faye Dunaway) shoots Nick Franco (Armando Pucci) and her young assistant Lisa Fiore (Claudia Christian) stays with the body, keeps it warm under an electric blanket and fires a shot into the air hours later just as Staton and Franco's landlord, Mr. Ruddick (Bill Macy) are walking down the hall to his apartment. The motive appears to be revenge, because Staton and Lisa have discovered that Franco was secretly dating both of them. But in the end we learn that Franco was an evil man who met Lisa in Rome, learned about her wealthy mother (Staton) in L.A. and dated them both on the sly, then sliced Lisa's neck and threatened to kill her if she interfered with his plan to marry Staton. Columbo, who becomes Staton's latest object of attraction from the moment they meet, allows

Lisa to leave in return for Staton's confessing to the crime and she claims she was assisted by a male accomplice whom she refuses to name. Writer Peter Falk has several neat clues (the water in the fridge resulting from it being on the same turned-off circuit that controlled the lights, the fact that Staton has a circulation problem and absent-mindedly turned on the heat while waiting for Franco to return, the antique chair in the background of two pictures that connects Staton and Lisa), but he relies on them too much and has Columbo decide early on that he must obtain a "Confession Ending" instead of exploring other possibilities. The plot looks a lot like that of "Suitable for Framing" (#4). It's not at all clear why Lisa has to remain hidden after Franco's death, since she is in fact Staton's daughter, which makes the entire business of Columbo finding her (not all that clever, he just traces her through Franco's telephone bills) seem pointless. Dunaway is luminous in her Emmy-winning role, and Falk plays nicely off her, but Staton's only response to Columbo's questions is to flirt with him. Moreover, both Columbo's ends (letting the accomplice go, see "Accomplices, Blackmailers and Schlimazels" and "The Morality of Columbo I") and his means (engaging in the bizarre flirting game with Staton but then disavowing it (see "The Morality of Columbo II") are very questionable here. The "Sympathetic Murderer" relationship goes way too far (despite the title and some of the behavior, at the end it is clear that this is not an "all-in-the-game" episode). Dog plays an important role and Barney of Barney's Beanery (well-played by John Finnegan, see "Bert, Barney and Dog") makes some very insightful comments here, but Columbo makes light of them. Riley (Doug Sheehan) is an assistant who gets annoyed with Columbo's meandering investigation (see "Colleagues and Sidekicks"). Ranking: fair (6.2.)

Additional cast: Nick's maid (Shelley Morrison), fingerprint man (Tom Henschel), investigators (Jack Shearer, Shashawnee Hall, Stewart J. Zully), medical examiner (Bruce E. Morrow), photo clerk (Heath Kizzier), detectives (Daniel T. Trent, Ed McCready), telephone company clerk (Talya Ferro), Eddie (Johnny Gardella), cashier (Michele Bernath), first drunk

(Art Kassul), close friend (Lorna Scott), second female guest (Catherine Battistone), pianist (Sammy Goldstein), singing lady (Ann Whitney), policeman (Frank Di Elsi), butler (Douglas Fisher), male guest (John Petlock), TV announcer (Ron Olsen), plainclothes detective (Gerry Okuneff), other policemen (Jeff McGrail, Joe Banks, Vincent J. McEveety), kid (Jeff Bollow), second drunk (Al Benner), maid (June Saruwatari), female guest (Maura Spencer-Reed), second woman (Jessica Devlin)

(#61) Butterfly in Shades of Grey

Written by Peter S. Fischer. Directed by Dennis Dugan. Music by Dick de Benedictis. Airdate: 1/10/94 (Monday)

Reactionary talk-show host Fielding Chase (William Shatner in the second of his two appearances, see "Multiple Murderers") is furious when his foster daughter Victoria (Molly Hagan) announces that she plans to leave his radio show and pursue a writing career, as suggested by her friend (and Chase's researcher) Jerry Winters (Jack Laufer). Winters calls Chase at home, not knowing that Chase is actually in Winters's den. Chase picks up the phone and shoots Winters in the back, then calls out "Jerry, what happened?" and, after leaving the scene, he calls 911 from his car and reports the shooting. Chase attempts to frame Winters's recent lover, soap opera actor Ted Malloy (Mark Lonow), by leaving a handkerchief with pancake on it near the scene of the crime, but once Columbo discovers that Malloy has an alibi, the clue essentially implicates Chase as one of the few people who knew about this relationship. Columbo busts the scenario Chase has created and/or busts his alibi (see "Busting Alibis, Busting Scenarios") by demonstrating that Chase could not have called 911 from the road near his house, a mansion in the hills of Malibu where he has to have satellite TV because no signal can be obtained. As noted, this is a very clever ending and the episode also contains some other interesting clues, but the answering machine business does not work (see "Recurring Problems"). There are not enough clues to fill the time and instead way too much time is spent on Chase's destruction of the senator, which is not very interesting (see "The Bloating Problem"). Shatner does a good riff on Rush Limbaugh, and Hagan is convincing, but the rest of the cast is dull. Winters's implication that Chase's interest in his daughter is "not exactly fatherly" is an ugly accusation that is never proved or dispelled. Nice use of the fact that Columbo does not carry a gun (see "The Developing Character"). Ranking: fair (6.6.)

Additional cast: Lou Cayton (Richard Kline), station manager (Yorgo Constantine), Howard Sperling (Brian Markinson), Dierdre Ross (Beverly Leech), Senator Gordon Madison (Robin Clarke), Marian Burke (Christopher Templeton), Officer Davis (John C. Anders), Martha (Denice Kumagi), second biker (Deryl Caitlyn), engineer (Glenn Taranto), Fritz the maitre d' (Wayne Dvorak), chairman (Douglas Stark), Allison Montgomery (Francesca Cappucci), P.A. (Ann Noel), first biker (Carolyn Carradine), soap opera director (Eric Poppick)

(#62) Undercover

Written by Gerry Day (from the Ed McBain novel *Jigsaw*). Directed by Vincent McEveety. Music by Dick de Benedictis. Airdate: 5/2/94 (Monday)

Two low-lifes kill each other while fighting over a scrap of paper that turns out to be a piece of a puzzle that, when assembled, will reveal the location of $4 million in money missing from a bank robbery. Insurance investigator Irving Krutch (Ed Begley, Jr.) asks the police to help him find the other pieces and solve the puzzle, and Columbo and Sergeant Arthur Brown (Harrison Page) take up the challenge. Along the way, the Lieutenant dons a number of disguises, banters with Geraldine Ferguson (Shera Danese) and Dorthea McNally (Tyne Daly), disarms Mo Weinberg (Burt Young) and gets pistol-whipped by Bramley Kahn (Edward Hibbert). More seriously, Ferguson and Weinberg are killed and the police suspect Krutch, whose alibi for both murders is that he was in bed with his girlfriend, Suzie Endicott (Kristin Bauer). But Columbo's friend from the parking authority, Zeke Rivers (Robert Donner), busts this alibi when he finds a coin with Krutch's prints on it that must have been put there during one of the murders and Suzie admits he left for several hours. The police finally assemble the puzzle and retrieve the money, but Columbo says he's had enough of this case and that he's taking Dog for a walk. Second unfortunate attempt to adapt an Ed McBain novel (see "No Time for Columbo, No Place for McBain"), this one succeeds only in being somewhat less jarring to watch than "No Time to Die" (#58). The story of the puzzle pieces is so convoluted that I had to read the McBain novel (*Jigsaw*) to understand it and it wasn't worth the effort. The disguises are not funny, and the mobster one further compromises the character when Lucia (Penny Santon), the old Italian lady tells him it's an honor to meet a member of "that family" (see "Peter Falk as Columbo," "The Developing Character" and "Does Columbo Exist?"). Begley, Hibbert and Danese (see "The Supporting Cast") are good, but the rest of the supporting cast is forgettable and Tyne Daly is back playing another drunk. Falk injects a bit more of the Columbo character here and the ending suggests (prophetically as it turned out) that this would be the last of the McBain police procedurals. Thank goodness. Ranking: not Columbo (3.5.)

Additional cast: Det. McKittrick (Albie Selznick), Mercer (Joe Chrest), Capt. Landau (Hank Garrett), Sheila Byrnes (Marla Adams), Nurse Hilda (Marianne Muellerleile), woman down the hall (Ora Frosh), medical examiner (Jeff Michalski), patient (Alexander Folk), man in pajamas (John William Young), front desk nurse (Kay Yamamoto), photographer (John Dunbar), J.J. Dillinger (Jon Beshara)

Production Information

Executive producer: Peter Falk. Producers: Christopher Seiter (#60, 61); Seiter & Vincent McEveety (#62). Associate Producer: Jack Horger. Co-associate producer: Lisa Tygett. Director of photography: George Koblasa. Film editor: Dayle Mustain & Bill Parker (#60); Bill Parker (#61, 62). Production design: Bill Ross. Art director: Peg McClellan (#62). Set decorations: Mary Ann Good. Costume design: Jacqueline Saint Anne. Hairstylist: Carolyn Elias (#60); Paula Griffin (#61, 62). Makeup artist: Lori Benson & Deborah Huss (#60); Lori Benson & Rita Sabatini (#61); Lori Benson (#62). Unit production manager: Ron Graw (#60); Jimmy Simons (#61); Christopher Seiter (#62). Sound mixer: Thomas E. Allan, Sr. Supervising sound editor: Paul Clay. Casting: Ron Stephenson. Costume supervisor: Brenda Cooper & Jill Sheridan (#60); Jill Sheridan (#61); Alice Daniels & Bob Iannaccone (#62). Supervising music editor: Laurie Higgins Tobias. First assistant director: Joseph Ingraffia. Second assistant director: Brad Michaelson

Chapter 14:
TV Movies (1995-2003)
(Episodes 63-67)

After the three episodes of the 1993-94 season, *Columbo* became a very sporadic and infrequent show. For this reason, I have decided to describe the five final episodes that aired between 1995 and 2003 in one chapter, but without a corresponding season. What is a season of a television show and why draw the line here? Well, there were a few other possibilities, but this one made the most sense.

First, I could have stopped counting seasons after the cancellation of ABC's *Mystery Movie* in 1990. But *Columbo* is still *Columbo*, with or without a mystery wheel on which to rotate. The next possibility was to stop counting seasons somewhere during 1992. There are two reasons that would support such a decision. First, there were only two episodes produced during the 1991-92 television season, and only one during the 1992-93 season. One episode hardly constitutes a "season." Second, after "No Time to Die" (#58) aired in March 1992, I seriously questioned whether what I had seen was actually an episode of *Columbo*. As explained in "No Time for Columbo, No Place for McBain," I rank it as "Not Columbo."

If that had been the way things continued, I would probably have stopped numbering seasons (and maybe stopped reviewing the show completely) at that point. But the program returned to its normal format the following season, and the year after that we were treated to three new episodes. So, I've concluded that the two episodes in 1991-92 constitute *Columbo*'s eleventh season, "A Bird in the Hand" (#59) represents in its entirety the show's twelfth season, and the three episodes aired during the 1993-94 season make up the thirteenth season.

However, once we reach 1994, there really is no option of referring to seasons anymore. "Strange Bedfellows" (#63) would not air until May 1995, and "A Trace of Murder" (#64) would not appear until two years later. Then came "Ashes to Ashes" (#65) in 1998, but "Murder With Too Many Notes" (#66) did not air until 2001 (although it was filmed in 1999) and "Columbo Likes the Nightlife" (#67) appeared in 2003 (again, it was filmed earlier). Calling each one of these episodes a separate season does not help us keep track of them, particularly as they aired in non-consecutive years. They also aired on various nights of the week. See individual episode information and Table 1 following the Epilogue at the end of Part I of this book for details.

(#63) Strange Bedfellows

Written by Lawrence Vail. Directed by Vincent McEveety. Music by Dick de Benedictis. Airdate: 5/8/95 (Monday)

Horse farm owner Graham McVeigh (George Wendt) is fed up with having to cover the gambling debts racked up by his younger brother Teddy (Jeff Yagher), so he shoots Teddy and pins the murder on Bruno Romano (Jay Acovone), a restaurateur with mob connections whom he then kills in "self-defense" (see "Accomplices, Blackmailers and Schlimazels"). Columbo doesn't get very far in his investigation before he is grabbed and brought to the home of Vincenzo Fortelli (Rod Steiger), a Mafia don who claims he is retired, but insists that Columbo solve the case quickly or he'll have to handle it "his way." The episode then alternates awkwardly between traditional scenes in which McVeigh becomes increasingly annoyed with Columbo (culminating in his order for the Lieutenant to leave and the assertion that "there is no 'just one more thing'") and bizarre scenes in which

McVeigh is threatened by Fortelli and seeks Columbo's help. In the end, Columbo and McVeigh find themselves trapped at Fortelli's restaurant, The Bay Leaf, where they are roughed up (!) and brought before the don. Fortelli announces that Columbo's investigation is over and now he is the judge, jury and executioner. He suggests the Lieutenant walk away . . . or else. Columbo apologizes that "they don't pay me enough for this stuff" and heads for the door. A desperate McVeigh confesses and even tells Columbo where to find Romano's gun, which Columbo confirms by calling his assistant, and Fortelli agrees to allow the system to work. Columbo and Fortelli exchange a "thumbs up," but after McVeigh is taken away, the Lieutenant politely declines Fortelli's offer of a drink, saying, "I'm a cream soda kind of guy, and you're not." Well, the "Confession Ending" works here, but having Columbo team up with the Mafia to solve the crime is not inspired and raises uncomfortable questions about "The Morality of Columbo II: How Far Will He Go?" It's not very clever of McVeigh to frame Romano and he seems genuinely surprised when he has bigger problems than the police on his hands. The violence in this episode (albeit much of it faked) is atypical (see "Recurring Problems"), but accepting the premise, all of the Mafia threat scenes should be placed *after* the regular investigation, except for the car chase, which should be removed entirely. The "First Clue" is very contrived (cigarette ash in the victim's car). Steiger has fun with the mob boss role, but Wendt just rumbles around and his disguise is not credible. Bruce Kirby's character is finally given a name, Sergeant Phil Brindle (see "Colleagues and Sidekicks") and we get another visit to Barney's with John Finnegan (see "Bert, Barney and Dog"). Columbo's decision to turn down a drink with Fortelli and his pretending that he doesn't speak Italian are just right, but his upset stomach from eating clams is too gross (see "The Developing Character"). Decent version of "This Old Man" plays at the end. Columbo strangely says he's been on the job for twenty-five years (see "Hello, Continuity Department?"). Ranking: poor (5.2.)

Additional cast: Lorraine Buchinski (Linda Gehringer), Randall Thurston

(William Bogert), Rudy (Don Calfa), Pat O'Connor (Gerry Gibson), Gwen (Shani Wallis), Lt. Albert Schiffer (Justin Lord), pawnbroker (Alex Henteloff), Tiffany Keene (Karen Mayo-Chandler), thug (Richard Epcar), Bayleaf hostess (Kate Benton), fingerprint man (Frantz Turner), man in bar (Ed McCready), waiter (David Sobel), Bay Leaf waiter (Mark Helm), patrolman Kallohar (Jim Bockelman), deputy (Marshall J. Nord), Ruth (Nancy Ragan), waiter Sterling (Gerry Okuneff), Emilio (Johnny Carabajal)

(#64) A Trace of Murder

Written by Charles Kipps. Directed by Vincent McEveety. Music by Dick de Benedictis. Airdate: 5/15/97 (Thursday)

Cathleen Calvert (Shera Danese) is married to boorish but wealthy businessman Clifford Calvert (Barry Corbin), but is having an affair with the more genteel Patrick Kinsley (David Rasche). She wants to murder Clifford, but Kinsley warns that suspicion would immediately fall on her. Instead, they come up with a devious plan: they will kill Howard Seltzer (Raye Birk), a man who is suing Clifford over some bad financial advice, and use Kinsley's skills as a police forensic scientist to frame Clifford for the crime. So Kinsley shoots Seltzer, leaves an end from one of Clifford's cigars and vacuums up carpet fibers and cat hair which Cathleen rubs on Clifford's suit. Columbo follows the false trail, but eventually comes to suspect Cathleen and then Kinsley. In the end, he separates the conspirators and convinces Cathleen that Kinsley is about to turn state's evidence and she rushes to the D.A. to be first. As Columbo explains to Barney (John Finnegan, see "Bert, Barney and Dog") and his busboy John at the end, the key to this case was the Lieutenant's realization that Cathleen and Kinsley know each other. He cleverly deduces this when he sees Kinsley passing Cathleen artificial sweetener rather than sugar and opening the rear door of a police car for her (because he knows she gets carsick riding in the front). These are great clues, but not the "Final Clue." Besides, why does Columbo take Kinsley along to meet Cathleen before he has reason to believe they knew each other? In addition, the ending is a bit too much of "Morris the Explainer" (see "Recurring Problems") and it would have made more sense for Columbo to explain what happened to Clifford. The frame has just the right touch (not too heavy) and some of the clues are good (the cigar end doesn't match Clifford's wedge cutter, he stopped for cough drops after the murder but in the wrong direction from the wedding he was headed to, Columbo finds a picture of Clifford at the wedding with no fibers on his back before he dances with his wife), but the episode struggles to find a conclusion. First, Columbo suggests that maybe Kinsley's knife has microscopic fibers which would match up with Clifford's cigars, but we never learn if this is true. Then the Lieutenant makes some effort to poke holes in the frame-up the murderers have created by pointing out that Clifford's suit doesn't have cat hair and carpet fibers on it until he dances with Cathleen at the wedding, the implication being that she planted them on him (see "Busting Alibis, Busting Scenarios" for more on this aspect of the ending). But the 'Final Clue' is disappointing. Tricking a murderer into believing that a conspirator is about to go to the police could be done in many episodes and is not very inspired here (see "The Three Cs" and "Accomplices, Blackmailers and Schlimazels" for more on the Kinsley/Cathleen relationship and poor Seltzer, the ultimate schlimazel). But as noted, the writers clearly feel that the most interesting part (held until the end) is the revelation of how Columbo concluded that Kinsley and Cathleen knew each other, which is very odd. Corbin has some good lines as Clifford, but neither Danese (see "The Supporting Cast") nor Rasche are evil enough for the roles. The Columbo character slips into parody as he tosses fruit around and announces to Officer Will (Will Nye, see "Colleagues and Sidekicks") that a cat is a witness to a crime and tells Kinsley that "three eyes are better than one" (see "The Developing Character"), although his knowledge of smoking is put to good use. Ranking: fair (6.3.)

Additional cast: Harry Jenkins (Franklin Cover), Harriet Jenkins (Alice Backes), Stuart March (Dion Anderson), Tracy Rose (Donna Bullock),

Doherty (John F. O'Donohue), Bobbi Colenari (Dyana Ortelli), District Attorney (Kymberly S. Newberry), store clerk (Maury Sterling), Kurtz (Jeffrey King), busboy (Vincent J. McEveety), newscaster (Richard Saxton), receptionist (Cady Hoffman), maid (Roma Alvarez), bartender (Jim Almenzar)

(#65) Ashes to Ashes

Written by Jeffrey Hatcher. Directed by Patrick McGoohan. Music by Dick de Benedicts. Airdate: 10/8/98 (Thursday)

Funeral home director Eric Prince (Patrick McGoohan in his record-breaking fourth appearance, see "Multiple Murderers") is confronted by gossip monger Verity Chandler (Rue McClanahan) with a story she intends to air accusing him of stealing diamonds off a corpse years ago. He strikes her over the head with a trocar and cremates the body before anyone notices she is missing. In order to do so—and because the oven breaks—he must "double up" former Western movie star Chuck Huston with dweeb Mel Lerby and Columbo catches him by finding Huston's famous piece of shrapnel in Lerby's urn. This episode has a very clever murder plot and an interesting idea for an ending, but it doesn't go far enough (see "Busting Alibis, Busting Scenarios"). Columbo should find a solid piece of evidence relating to Chandler, such as a piece of her pager, in "Huston's" ashes. This would require re-writing the story so that Huston's widow Liz (Sally Kellerman) doesn't dump his ashes over the Hollywood sign, but that's not an important part of the storyline and it would make for a far better ending. Too much time is spent (see "The Bloating Problem") on the musical and dance numbers. McGoohan is excellent as is his daughter Catherine (as Rita, Prince's assistant), Richard Riehle is fine as Sergeant Degarmo (see "Colleagues and Sidekicks") and Spencer Garrett adds humor as Chandler's assistant, Roger Gambles. Some of the scenes are odd, as when Columbo and Prince stand on opposite sides of a room and yell at each other and Falk and McGoohan allow their personal relationship to be visible through the characters (see "Peter Falk as Columbo" and "The All-in-the-Game Relationship"). Strange scene in which Columbo reveals that he's lying when he makes one of his famous relative references (see "The Morality of Columbo II: How Far Will He Go?" and "The Developing Character"). Dog has a nice role (see "Bert, Barney and Dog"). The version of "This Old Man" that plays is forgettable and Columbo again tells a murderer he's been on the job for only twenty-five years (see "Hello, Continuity Department?"). Ranking: good (7.05.)

Additional cast: Mrs. Lerby (Edie McClurg), Eddie (Ron Masak), Sheik Yerami (Richard Libertini), Fred the minister (Aubrey Morris), Henry Chalfont (Conrad Bachman), singer (Ken Weiler), driver (Sid Burton), Gerald (Scott N. Stevens), morticians (Ted Rooney, Charlie Dell), tap dancer (Arthur Duncan), colleague (David Doty), bartender (Roberta Hanlen), guards (Roy Kerry, Marco Khonlian), anchorwoman (Karissa Corday)

(#66) Murder With Too Many Notes

Written by Jeffrey Cava & Patrick McGoohan (story by Cava). Directed by Patrick McGoohan. Music by Dick de Benedictis. Airdate: 3/12/01 (Monday)

Findlay Crawford (Billy Connolly) is a famous composer, who works for movie director Sidney Ritter (Charles Cioffi), but a lot of his recent work was actually written by his young protégé, Gabriel McEnery (Chad Willett). When McEnery threatens to tell Ritter the truth, Crawford drugs him and puts the body on the roof, where McEnery is known to conduct in time to Crawford below. Crawford uses an old elevator to rise and open up just as he is beginning a concert, tossing the body off the roof. Columbo demonstrates that the reason McEnery didn't hear the elevator approaching is because he was unconscious—he shows that McEnery was given secobarbital (it dissipated in his system, but he cut his hand and that spot retained the drug). And Columbo points out that McEnery didn't put on his own shoes, because he never wore dress shoes and the ones on his feet are the wrong size. But Columbo doesn't really have a "Final Clue" here; all he does is sum up the clues he's gathered and arrests Crawford, which makes him "Morris the Explainer" (see "Recurring Problems" and "Busting Alibis, Busting Scenarios"). Some of the clues are very good (the secobarbital, the baton that falls to the bottom of the elevator shaft), but the "Intermediate Clues" are unnecessarily delayed to the end, where they lose impact. There are also "Recurring Problems" of a gift clue based on the way the shoe clue is executed, and uncharacteristic violence, not in the murder itself, but in the repeated movie stabbing scene. Connolly is a good actor, but the writers never decide what his character's attitude toward Columbo is (sometimes angry, sometimes having fun in an "All-in-the-Game Relationship" way that is not fulfilled) and there is a "Bloating Problem" with the lengthy (supposedly humorous) scene in which Columbo and Crawford drive back to the conductor's house. Richard Riehle returns as Sergeant Degarmo (see "Colleagues and Sidekicks") and there are some very nice moments with Hillary Danner as Rebecca, McEnery's girl-friend. Parody comes calling when the orchestra makes fun of Columbo (see "The Developing Character") and there are major inconsistencies when he demonstrates no fear of heights (see "Hello, Continuity Department?") and when he states that "This Old Man" is *Mrs.* Columbo's favorite tune and that he needs help playing it, since he demonstrated he knew how in "Try and Catch Me" (#39). Ranking: good (7.1.)

Additional cast: Marcia (Anne McGoohan), Tony (Scott Atkinson), Nathaniel (Obi Ndefo), Joshua (Randy Ogelsby), Antonio (Luis Avalos), Fitch (Harry Danner), Schwartz (Michael P. Byrne), photographer (Van Epperson), Angela (Joanna Lara), stalker (Rob Elk), Priestly (Hershel Sparber), Thorne (Steve O'Connor), woman victim (Susan Edwards), young actor (Douglas Callan), young actress (Jennifer Fobos)

(#67) Columbo Likes the Nightlife

Written by Michael Alaimo. Directed by Jeffrey Reiner. Music by Ken Jordan & Jim Latham. Airdate: 1/30/03 (Thursday)

Justin Price (Matthew Rhys) is about to open a dance club called The Bait, but he needs an infusion of capital to do it, and he's about to get it from Tony Galper (Carmine Giovinazzo). Unfortunately, Tony has a temper and when he goes to visit his ex-wife, actress Vanessa Farrow (Jennifer Sky), he spots her in a picture with Justin and explodes. Vanessa pushes him away, but his head strikes a coffee table and he is dead. Vanessa calls Justin, who decides that Tony needs to remain "alive" for thirty-six hours until the money is wired into his bank account. Justin creates the scenario that Tony left his hotel room, but then he is contacted by Linwood Coben (Douglas Roberts), a tabloid photographer who has incriminating photos of Justin and Vanessa standing over Tony's body. Justin arranges to pay Linwood for the negatives, but then attempts to strangle him and make it look like a suicide. Even that doesn't quite work as Linwood revives, but Justin pushes him out the window and the man's weight pulls the radiator to which the rope is tied out the window after him, and it follows him four flights down. Columbo investigates Linwood's death and eventually hears about Tony's disappearance. Indeed, he learns that Tony's father is head of a New York Mafia family and the family sends a messenger named Freddy (Steve R. Schirripa) to offer to lend a hand. But Columbo solves this case on his own when he concludes that Tony has been buried under the fish tanks at The Bait, which he demonstrates with "Brown penetrating radar." Columbo returns Freddy's card. The plot has a lot of twists and turns and the two murders give Columbo much to work with, so there is no "Bloating Problem." Some of the clues are good, including the "Final Clue," the "First Clue" (Linwood used mouthwash and clipped his nails, so he probably wasn't planning suicide) and the means by which he finds Vanessa: Sean Jarvis—played by John Finnegan in his last appearance on the show, see "The Supporting Cast"—allowed Linwood to use a tree in his backyard to spy on her. But Tony's murder looks a lot like the murder of Lenore Kennicut in "Death Lends a Hand" (#2), and the setup of an accidental murder in which the perpetrator calls on a friend for help and that person commits a second more heinous murder was used to better effect in "A Friend in Deed" (#23). See "Get 'Em for the First Murder" and "Accomplices, Blackmailers and Schlimazels." Even the hide-the-body trick has been handled better before, in both "Blueprint for Murder" (#7) and

"Columbo Cries Wolf" (#49). In addition, there was a coarseness to this episode that made it uncomfortable to watch, including the violent murder of Linwood (see "Recurring Problems"), Columbo sticking his hand into a toilet to find the nail clippings and the "bathroom" clue involving Tony "missing the bowl" (see "The Developing Character"). Vanessa just gets nervous when Columbo calls and Justin alternates between disdain and some odd "All-in-the-Game Relationship" behavior (sending him the funky shirt) that doesn't fit. It was good to see Columbo turn down the offer of help from the Mafia (see "The Morality of Columbo II") unlike his bizarre partnership in "Strange Bedfellows" (#63). Ranking: good (7.125.)

Additional cast: Sgt. Harkins (Julius Carry), Julius (Jorge Garcia), Officer Rogers (Patrick Cupo), pink feather boa (Eve Kagan), print guy (Jamison Yang), maid (Karen Maruyama), paramedic (Ariel Llinas), police officer (Iris Bohr), attendant (Audrey Wasilewski), hotel assistant manager (Katie O'Rourke), messenger (Brian Patrick Farrell)

Production Information

Executive producer: Peter Falk. Producers: Christopher Seiter & Vincent McEveety (#63, 64, 65, 66); John Whitman (#67). Associate Producer: Jack Horger. Co-associate producer: Lisa Tygett (#63). Director of photography: George Koblasa (#63); Fred V. Murphy (#64, 65); Jiggs Garcia (#6); Feliks Parnell (#67). Film editor: Bill Parker (#63, 64, 65, 66); Carter DeHaven IV (#67). Production design: Bill Ross (#63); Hub Braden (#64, 65, 66); Pam Warner (#67). Art director: Lauren Cory (#63); Mary Dodson (#64, 65, 66); Michael Paul Clausen (#67). Set decorations: Mary Ann Good (#63); Bill Gregory (#64); Don Remacle (#65, 66); Donald Elmblad (#67). Costume design: Jacqueline Saint Anne (#63, 64); Faye Sloon (#65, 66); Kristen Anacker (#67). Hairstylist: Paula Griffin (#63, 64, 65, 66); Joy Zapata (#67). Makeup artist: Kevin Westmore (#63, 65); Lori Benson (#64); Kandace Westmore (#66, 67). Unit production manager: Christopher Seiter

(#63, 64, 65, 66); John Whitman (#67). Sound mixer: Thomas E. Allan, Sr. (#63, 64, 65, 66); Ray Czmoszinski (#67). Supervising sound editor: Paul Clay (#63, 64); Kevin Spears (#65, 66); Jason George (#67). Casting: Ron Stephenson (#63); Eddie Dunlop (#64); Eddie Dunlop & Reuben Cannon (#65, 66); Nelia Morago (#67). Costume supervisor: Alice Daniels & Bob Iannaccone (#63); Alice Daniels & Tom Cummins (#64); Nancy Renard (#65); Kathleen Brodbeck (#66); George W. Ward (#67). Supervising music editor: Laurie Higgins Tobias. First assistant director: Joseph Ingraffia (#63); Kevin Corcoran (#64); Nick Smirnoff (#65); Bruce A. Simon (#66); Liz Ryan (#67). Second assistant director: Brad I. Michaelson (#63); Marty Mericka (#64); Bruce A. Simon (#65); Robert Papazian, Jr. (#66); Rick Clark (#67). Post-production supervisor: Bruce Gorman (#64); Lisa Tygett (#67); Additional editor: Dale Mustain (#64). Script supervisor: Betty A. Griffin (#65, 66); Helen Caldwell (#67). Property master: Michael Milgrom (#67). On-set dresser: Greg Wyszynski (#67). Music editor: Adam Kay (#67). General foreman: Brian Berkel (#67). Location manager: Lisa Blok-Linson (#67). Production coordinator: Greg Pallini (#67).

Epilogue

In 2007, William Link wrote an all-new *Columbo* play, titled *Columbo Takes the Rap*. In it, the Lieutenant faces off against a famous record producer who kills one of his young rap stars. The show played in various regional theaters across the United States but, just as was the case with *Prescription: Murder* in 1962, never quite made it to Broadway. Chicago actor Norm Boucher played Columbo, although there was some discussion about Levar Burton taking on the role. And speaking of the first Columbo play, it was resurrected and toured the United Kingdom in 2010.

In 2010, Link wrote a new book, *The Columbo Collection* (Crippen & Landru Publishers, Norfolk, Virginia). See "*Columbo* in Print" for more details.

Table 1: *Columbo* Episode Major Production Information

#	Title	Air Date		Network*	Length (min)
	Enough Rope	Sun	7/31/60	NBC	60
A	*Prescription: Murder*	Tue	2/20/68	NBC	120
B	*Ransom for a Dead Man*	Mon	3/1/71	NBC	120
1	*Murder by the Book*	Wed	9/15/71	NBC	90
2	*Death Lends a Hand*	Wed	10/6/71	NBC	90
3	*Dead Weight*	Wed	10/27/71	NBC	90
4	*Suitable for Framing*	Wed	11/17/71	NBC	90
5	*Lady in Waiting*	Wed	12/15/71	NBC	90
6	*Short Fuse*	Wed	1/9/72	NBC	90
7	*Blueprint for Murder*	Wed	2/9/72	NBC	90
8	*Etude in Black*	Sun	9/17/72	NBC	120
9	*The Greenhouse Jungle*	Sun	10/15/72	NBC	90
10	*The Most Crucial Game*	Sun	11/5/72	NBC	90
11	*Dagger of the Mind*	Sun	11/26/72	NBC	120
12	*Requiem for a Falling Star*	Sun	1/21/73	NBC	90
13	*A Stitch in Crime*	Sun	2/11/73	NBC	90
14	*The Most Dangerous Match*	Sun	3/4/73	NBC	90
15	*Double Shock*	Sun	3/25/73	NBC	90
16	*Lovely But Lethal*	Sun	9/23/73	NBC	90
17	*Any Old Port in a Storm*	Sun	10/7/73	NBC	120
18	*Candidate for Crime*	Sun	11/4/73	NBC	120
19	*Double Exposure*	Sun	12/16/73	NBC	90
20	*Publish or Perish*	Sun	1/13/74	NBC	90

Writer (screenplay)	Writer (story)	Director	Music
Levinson/Link	N/A	Don Richardson	N/A
Levinson/Link	N/A	Richard Irving	Dave Grusin
Dean Hargrove	Levinson/Link	Richard Irving	Billy Goldenberg
Steven Bochco	N/A	Steven Spielberg	Billy Goldenberg
Levinson/Link	N/A	Bernard Kowalski	Gil Mellé
John T. Dugan	N/A	Jack Smight	Gil Mellé
Jackson Gillis	N/A	Hy Averback	Billy Goldenberg
Steven Bochco	N/A	Norman Lloyd	Billy Goldenberg
Steven Bochco	N/A	Edward Abroms	Gil Mellé
Steven Bochco	N/A	Peter Falk	Gil Mellé
Steven Bochco	Levinson/Link	Nicholas Colasanto	Dick de Benedictis
Jonathan Latimer	N/A	Boris Sagal	Oliver Nelson
John T. Dugan	N/A	Jeremy Kagan	Dick de Benedictis
Jackson Gillis	Levinson/Link	Richard Quine	Dick de Benedictis
Jackson Gillis	N/A	Richard Quine	N/A
Shirl Hendryx	N/A	Hy Averback	Billy Goldenberg
Jackson Gillis	Gillis, Levinson/Link	Edward Abroms	Dick de Benedictis
Steven Bochco, Peter Allen Fields	Levinson/Link, Jackson Gillis	Robert Butler	Dick de Benedictis
Jackson Gillis	Myrna Bercovici	Jeannot Szwarc	Dick de Benedictis
Stanley Ralph Ross	Larry Cohen	Leo Penn	Dick de Benedictis
Irving Pearlberg, Alvin Friedman, Roland Kibbee, Dean Hargrove	Larry Cohen	Boris Sagal	Dick de Benedictis
Stephen J. Cannell	N/A	Richard Quine	Dick de Benedictis
Peter S. Fischer	N/A	Robert Butler	Billy Goldenberg

#	Title		Air Date	Network*	Length (min)
21	Mind Over Mayhem	Sun	2/10/74	NBC	90
22	Swan Song	Sun	3/3/74	NBC	120
23	A Friend in Deed	Sun	5/5/74	NBC	120
24	An Exercise in Fatality	Sun	9/15/74	NBC	120
25	Negative Reaction	Sun	10/6/74	NBC	120
26	By Dawn's Early Light	Sun	10/27/74	NBC	120
27	Troubled Waters	Sun	2/9/75	NBC	120
28	Playback	Sun	3/2/75	NBC	90
29	A Deadly State of Mind	Sun	4/27/75	NBC	90
30	Forgotten Lady	Sun	9/14/75	NBC	120
31	A Case of Immunity	Sun	10/12/75	NBC	90
32	Identity Crisis	Sun	11/2/75	NBC	120
33	A Matter of Honor	Sun	2/1/76	NBC	90
34	Now You See Him	Sun	2/29/76	NBC	120
35	Last Salute to the Commodore	Sun	5/2/76	NBC	120
36	Fade in to Murder	Sun	10/10/76	NBC	90
37	Old Fashioned Murder	Sun	11/28/76	NBC	90
38	The Bye-Bye Sky High IQ Murder Case	Sun	5/22/77	NBC	90
39	Try and Catch Me	Mon	11/21/77	NBC	90
40	Murder Under Glass	Mon	1/30/78	NBC	90
41	Make Me a Perfect Murder	Sat	2/25/78	NBC	120
42	How to Dial a Murder	Sat	4/15/78	NBC	90
43	The Conspirators	Sat	5/13/78	NBC	120

Table 1: *Columbo* Episode Major Production Information

Writer (screenplay)	Writer (story)	Director	Music
Steven Bochco, Dean Hargrove, Roland Kibbee	Robert Specht	Alf Kjellin	Dick de Benedictis
David Rayfiel	Stanley Ralph Ross	Nicholas Colasanto	Dick de Benedictis
Peter S. Fischer	N/A	Ben Gazzara	Billy Goldenberg, Dick de Benedictis
Peter S. Fischer	Larry Cohen	Bernard Kowalski	Dick de Benedictis
Peter S. Fischer	N/A	Alf Kjellin	Bernardo Segall
Howard Berk	N/A	Harvey Hart	Bernardo Segall
William Driskill	Jackson Gillis	Ben Gazzara	Dick de Benedictis
David P. Lewis, Booker T. Bradshaw	N/A	Bernard Kowalski	Bernardo Segall
Peter S. Fischer	N/A	Harvey Hart	Bernardo Segall
William Driskill	N/A	Harvey Hart	Jeff Alexander
Lou Shaw	James Menzies	Ted Post	Bernardo Segall
William Driskill	N/A	Patrick McGoohan	Bernardo Segall
Brad Radnitz	Brad Radnitz, Larry Cohen	Ted Post	Bernardo Segall
Michael Sloan	N/A	Harvey Hart	Bernardo Segall
Jackson Gillis	N/A	Patrick McGoohan	Bernardo Segall
Lou Shaw, Peter Feibleman	Henry Garson	Bernard Kowalski	Bernardo Segall
Peter Feibleman	Lawrence Vail	Robert Douglas	Dick de Benedictis
Robert Malcolm Young	N/A	Sam Wanamaker	Bob Prince
Gene Thompson, Paul Tuckahoe	Gene Thompson	James Frawley	Patrick Williams
Robert Van Scoyk	N/A	Jonathan Demme	Jonathan Tunick
Robert Blees	N/A	James Frawley	Patrick Williams
Tom Lazarus	Anthony Lawrence	James Frawley	Patrick Williams
Howard Berk	Pat Robison	Leo Penn	Patrick Williams

#	Title	Air Date		Network*	Length (min)
44	Columbo Goes to the Guillotine	Mon	2/6/89	**ABC**	120
45	Murder, Smoke and Shadows	Mon	2/27/89	**ABC**	120
46	Sex and the Married Detective	Mon	4/3/89	**ABC**	120
47	Grand Deceptions	Mon	5/1/89	**ABC**	120
48	Murder: A Self Portrait	Sat	11/25/89	**ABC**	120
49	Columbo Cries Wolf	Sat	1/20/90	**ABC**	120
50	Agenda for Murder	Sat	2/10/90	**ABC**	120
51	Rest in Peace, Mrs. Columbo	Sat	3/31/90	**ABC**	120
52	Uneasy Lies the Crown	Sat	4/28/90	**ABC**	120
53	Murder in Malibu	Mon	5/14/90	**ABC**	120
54	Columbo Goes to College	Sun	12/9/90	ABC	120
55	Caution: Murder Can Be Hazardous to Your Health	Wed	2/20/91	ABC	120
56	Columbo and the Murder of a Rock Star	Mon	4/29/91	ABC	120
57	Death Hits the Jackpot	Sun	12/15/91	ABC	120
58	No Time to Die	Sun	3/15/92	ABC	120
59	A Bird in the Hand	Sun	11/22/92	ABC	120
60	It's All in the Game	Sun	10/31/93	ABC	120
61	Butterfly in Shades of Grey	Mon	1/10/94	ABC	120
62	Undercover	Mon	5/2/94	ABC	120
63	Strange Bedfellows	Mon	5/8/95	ABC	120
64	A Trace of Murder	Thu	5/15/97	ABC	120
65	Ashes to Ashes	Thu	10/8/98	ABC	120
66	Murder With Too Many Notes	Mon	3/12/01	ABC	120
67	Columbo Likes the Nightlife	Thu	1/30/03	ABC	120

*bold for mystery wheel

Table 1: *Columbo* Episode Major Production Information

Writer (screenplay)	Writer (story)	Director	Music
William Read Woodfield	N/A	Leo Penn	John Cacavas
Richard Alan Simmons	N/A	James Frawley	Patrick Williams
Jerry Ludwig	N/A	James Frawley	Patrick Williams
Sy Salkowitz	N/A	Sam Wanamaker	John Cacavas
Robert Sherman	N/A	James Frawley	Patrick Williams
Woodfield	N/A	Daryl Duke	Dennis Dreith
Jeffrey Bloom	N/A	Patrick McGoohan	David Michael Frank
Peter S. Fischer	N/A	Vincent McEveety	Richard Markowitz
Steven Bochco	N/A	Alan J. Levi	James di Pasquale
Jackson Gillis	N/A	Walter Grauman	Patrick Williams
Jeffrey Bloom	Bloom, Frederick King Keller	E.W. Swackhamer	James di Pasquale
Sonia Wolf, April Raynell, Patricia Ford	N/A	Daryl Duke	John Cacavas
Woodfield	N/A	Alan J. Levi	Steve Dorff
Jeffrey Bloom	N/A	Vincent McEveety	Steve Dorff
Robert Van Scoyk	Ed McBain	Alan J. Levi	Patrick Williams
Jackson Gillis	N/A	Vincent McEveety	Dick de Benedictis
Peter Falk	N/A	Vincent McEveety	Dick de Benedictis
Peter S. Fischer	N/A	Dennis Dugan	Dick de Benedictis
Gerry Day	Ed McBain	Vincent McEveety	Dick de Benedictis
Lawrence Vail	N/A	Vincent McEveety	Dick de Benedictis
Charles Kipps	N/A	Vincent McEveety	Dick de Benedictis
Jeffrey Hatcher	N/A	Patrick McGoohan	Dick de Benedictis
Jeffrey Cava, Patrick McGoohan	Jeffrey Cava	Patrick McGoohan	Dick de Benedictis
Michael Alaimo	N/A	Jeffrey Reiner	Ken Jordan, Jim Latham

Part II: The Essays

Chapter 15:
Let's Talk About Columbo

Why I Love *Columbo*

It goes without saying that TV mysteries were preceded by the mystery novel and they're often better. The ability to reconsider clues before writing them down in final form lends itself to more carefully crafted mysteries. This is not to say that mystery books always achieve this goal. However, it does explain why television mysteries do not, in general, enjoy the following of great mystery novels written by Sir Arthur Conan Doyle, Agatha Christie and Rex Stout. When the works of such writers are dramatized on television, the program benefits from the carefully laid out plot in the book (although sometimes so much of this is chopped up to make the program fit a time slot that the essence is lost). Mysteries that are written specifically for television often display a careless disregard for the importance of good clues, character traits and other elements that make books readable time and again. What is unusual about *Columbo* is that it often has clever plots, fascinating character traits, excellent music and other factors that make episodes re-watchable. I will offer a brief list of those particular elements that I believe make the program outstanding in its genre.

1. Great Clues. *Columbo* has some of the best clues ever seen on television. Because of the inverted format (see below), the "Final Clue," the means by which Columbo catches the murderer, has to be (and in many cases is) conclusive, clever, and outstanding.

The show also has neat "First Clues," the means by which Columbo sees through the setup the murderer has constructed and realizes who is behind this deception. Finally, there are "Intermediate Clues" that keep the investigation going. All of these elements are detailed further in the essays that follow.

2.   Inverted Structure Format. Levinson and Link did not create the inverted structure format, in which the audience witnesses the murder and is therefore several steps ahead of the detective (a British author named R. Austin Freeman did, in the 1912 book *The Singing Bone*), but they did put it to excellent use. Because television is primarily a visual medium, having the murder occur at the beginning allows the audience to track the action as it unfolds in a way that would simply not be as practical in a book format. This has a twofold benefit: we know when Columbo has arrived at the proper conclusion (because we witnessed the murder) and we can follow how he got there. This makes it all the more satisfying when Columbo arrests the murderer at the end.

3.   Relationship with the Murderer. In the typical TV mystery, the detective takes a tough stance with all the suspects (without the inverted structure, neither we nor the detective knows who did it), sometimes reminding them of what will happen if they go to trial, occasionally using physical force to get information. This strikes many people as the way it should be—after all, no one likes being questioned, whether by a policeman or a private detective. The complaint often heard about *Columbo* is that by presenting a dialogue between the murderer and the detective, the program violates reality and makes it impossible to "willfully suspend disbelief." There are two responses to this. First, the idea that the murderer tries to steer Columbo astray is not as preposterous as it might seem. It is a well-known fact in the legal community that people have an extraordinary habit of talking to the police, even when it's not in their best interests (that's why defense lawyers fight so hard for the courts to keep a

strong Miranda rule—if people kept quiet, there would be no need for it). Truly innocent people proclaim their innocence (they feel they have nothing to hide, resent being unfairly accused, and think they can best help their situation by answering all questions asked by the police) and guilty individuals, believe it or not, actually think they can talk their way out of precarious situations. Add to this the fiction that the murders are extremely clever (sometimes including a cover-up to the murder as well as the crime itself) and you can see why the murderer would want to ensure that Columbo sees things the way he or she wants them to be seen. Second, the program is fiction, and as such is allowed a measure of flexibility, often called artistic license, to bend reality to make it more interesting to watch. Yes, the murderer could simply say "I don't know" for two hours, but the result would be unbearably boring (see "Murder, Smoke and Shadows" (#45) for an example of what happens when the writers do just that).

4. Lack of violence and sex. An often-heard complaint about television in general is that is contains too much violence and sex, too many scenes of reckless car chases, gory maimings, scantily clad women and lurid behavior. What is perhaps more disturbing than the pervasiveness of these scenes is the belief that "that's what people want to see." Now, in some measure, there is truth in this—concerned individuals and groups may complain but the offending programs do well in the ratings, demonstrating that some appreciable percentage of people out there enjoy that sort of thing. On the other hand, when an occasional program appears that does not rely on these tired formula attractions, such as *Columbo* or *Murder, She Wrote*, networks are often surprised to discover that more than a few people tune them in. What is significant about *Columbo* is that it operates on a minimum of action. Usually the only violence is the original murder itself, and that is often only suggested or shown in a stylized fashion. Then the detective enters and the rest is a series of dialogues, with escalating

tension as each additional clue brings him one step closer to putting the murderer away. And, surprise of surprises, we don't need any car chases, shoot outs or fist fights to enjoy the program; in fact, they would get in the way if they were inserted (I squirm each time I watch Columbo get pistol-whipped in "Undercover" (#62)).

5. Columbo's self-effacing attitude, references to his family and background, and other intangible elements. These points do not operate by themselves, of course, but in concert with each other. That is to say, consider that we spend a lot of time with the murderer (it might even be said that we observe much of the episode from the murderer's point of view, although there are occasional scenes between Columbo and other witnesses and police). Therefore, there is a great tendency to root for if not empathize with him or her (particularly if the motive is a sympathetic one). Thus, it makes sense that, in order for the detective to be at all likeable, he must not appear too arrogant. It's all very well for Sherlock Holmes or Hercule Poirot to be egocentric, because we spend all the time with them and not the murderer and this serves to humanize the detectives. But imagine if we spent most of the time observing Colonel Rumford in "By Dawn's Early Light" (#26) carefully executing his plan while trying desperately to stay out of the grasp of the police, only to have an arrogant detective come in and start cavalierly tossing around accusations and threats. Who would want to watch such a program week after week? By making Columbo a truly likeable character, the writers avoid having the audience root too much for the murderer and despise the detective. As for the comments about his wife, family, dog, car and so forth, these help to make Columbo's character full-fledged and believable. Little characteristics often speak louder than grand ones, and any touch that sets a character apart from the original mold is a welcome addition. That is why, in my view, Columbo got better as it went along (to a point). Every additional characteristic served to further define the man. First, there was the car, added in "Murder By

the Book" (#1). Then came the dog, added in "Etude in Black" (#8). Then the song "This Old Man," added in "Any Old Port in a Storm" (#17). See "The Developing Character" for a complete list. Oh, and one more thing. Not showing his wife was a brilliant idea. As has often been said, leaving unseen characters to the audience's imagination makes them more three-dimensional than showing them, because everyone has a picture in his or her mind of what Mrs. Columbo looks like (this was used effectively in *M*A*S*H*, where each character had unseen relatives stateside). I know I'm not alone on this one—the negative reaction from the public to a program showing Columbo's wife got the idea canceled after a very short run. See "Does Columbo Exist?" for more on this topic.

6. In-depth study of the murderer's profession. In some of the best episodes, Columbo spends a lot of time learning about the murderer's profession, which means that we learn as well. In addition to being interesting in its own right, this has the advantage of allowing Columbo to better understand the murderer's motive, means and modus operandi. This is particularly effective when the writers have the murderer commit a crime that is connected in some way with his or her profession, such as cosmetics mogul Viveca Scott causing a victim to drive off the road by using inserting a chemical to poison her cigarette in "Lovely But Lethal" (#16), winemaker Adrian Carsini killing his half-brother by not allowing him to breathe in "Any Old Port in a Storm" (#17), and health club owner Milo Janus strangling his victim and making it look as if the man's barbell slipped and struck his windpipe in "An Exercise in Fatality" (#24).

7. Unusual aspects of the program's format, such as the longer running time, lack of regularized music or credits. Simply put, *Columbo* has better mystery stories because the writers have more time to write fewer of them, between three and eight ninety-minute or two-hour episodes instead of twenty two one-hour installments per season. The longer running time allows the mystery more freedom to develop. One of the complaints

made about *Murder, She Wrote* was that it has no sooner built up an excellent plot when the one-hour time constraint forces a hasty resolution, usually by having Jessica catch the murderer in a verbal slip ("but you could only have known that if you were there...."). Because the episodes begin in the middle of the murder or the planning of it, opening music would be inappropriate, so the credits simply run as the action proceeds. This works very well. For one thing, the 1970s episodes were already preceded by one of the best themes on television—Henry Mancini's *Mystery Movie* theme (in reruns, local stations often play this as they announce that *Columbo* is about to be shown; it has in effect become the *Columbo* theme because the other programs all had their own individual themes by which they are remembered). Beyond that, the lack of regular music leaves the episodes free to develop their own particularized music. This seemed to occur more often as the program continued—the first two seasons ended with one of several nondescript themes, but in the third season and following, the end music is often individualized and memorable (for particularly outstanding examples, see "An Exercise in Fatality" (#24), "Now You See Him" (#34) and "Try and Catch Me" (#39)). See "This Old Man" for more on this topic. By contrast, the creativity that went into the endings of the episodes seemed to go down as the years went by: for the first three seasons, the final credits (the ones after the commercial; I call the ones before that the end credits) were shown as the camera focused in and out of various scenes from the episode, a highly distinctive style that made the program stand out from the crowd even more; beginning with the fourth season, the final credits were shown over the flashlight shot of Columbo's face from the *Mystery Movie* introduction (even though this shows less creativity, I still like it because it's now the only way to be visually reminded of the stylistic opening); in the seventh season, the credits played over a single shot from the episode, not necessarily the last one, but a representative one; in most of the new episodes, the cheapest method is used—a single shot of whatever appeared on screen last, no matter how silly or pointless. The titles are often used as an expression for the writers' creativity, connecting the murderer's occupation to the serious crime committed (best examples include "By Dawn's Early Light" (#26), "Now You See Him" (#34), and "Candidate for Crime" (#18)). Because mysteries always have titles and because this was a mystery movie (and movies always have titles), the writers may have felt a particular need to title *Columbo* episodes. Whatever the reason, I'm glad they did. For one thing, it allows for easy reference when discussing the episodes. See "Creative Columbo Titles" for more on this topic.

Recurring Problems

Just as there are definable characteristics that make the program better than its peers, there are also aspects of individual episodes that can detract from the program's good qualities. Let's look at these recurring problems.

1. Prescience Problem. As stated in "Why I Love Columbo," the value of the inverted format is that we can admire how Columbo gets to the clues when it's done well, but it's glaringly obvious when he knows things for no apparent reason. A good detective has intuitions, but it would help if the writers would always give him something to go on, as they often do so well. This is particularly important with respect to the "First Clue"; it's something of a let-down to have the murderer's carefully constructed plan come crashing down—without even knowing how it happened. Examples: *Prescription: Murder* (pilot A) (how does Columbo know that he should be hiding at Flemming's place to see how the doctor reacts when he comes in?); "Etude in Black" (#8) (how does he know to check the odometer the next morning? If it's because of the dropped flower, then that presents a gift clue, see below); "The Most Crucial Game" (#10) (what makes Columbo think to check the water on the pool deck to see if it's chlorinated?).

2. Right Answer/Wrong Means Problem or Eating Your Cake and Having it, Too. Sometimes Columbo arrives at the right solution, but we're not

supposed to notice that it was by pure luck because the path he was following shouldn't have led where it did. This is playing fast and loose with
the idea that his deductions are thoughtful. It's okay if the writers have
him go down the wrong path occasionally (he does so several times in "By
Dawn's Early Light" (#26), that's how carefully layered the plot is), but his
solution must make sense. Examples: "Murder By the Book" (#1) (he
proves it was a planned murder by finding the plot written out in detail in
Ferris's notes, but then Franklin says it was his only good idea— so there's
no reason why it would be among Ferris's notes); "Double Shock" (#15)
(he says Dexter just bought two new mixers, leading us to believe he's uncovered the murder weapon, but then Dexter shows him the mixers, still
wrapped up, in a closet).

3. Gift Clues. The idea is supposed to be that these are carefully planned
    and executed murders, but sometimes major clues fall into Columbo's
    lap because the murderer has made a serious mistake, which means the
    writers had the murderer make this major error to facilitate the solu-
    tion. It's fair to expect better, particularly because we get it often enough
    to demonstrate that they know how to do it better. Examples: "Etude
    in Black" (#8) (dropping the flower is dropping the ball; it's a serious
    mistake that not only raises Columbo's suspicions against Benedict but
    then comes back to nail him at the end as the "Final Clue"); "Make Me a
    Perfect Murder" (#41) (the closed building dooms the plan from the be-
    ginning, and it's only a matter of time before Columbo finds the gun Kay
    Freestone has hidden in the diffuser panel above the elevator light); "The
    Conspirators" (#43) (Columbo goes bar-hopping with Joe Devlin, which
    is a lot of fun to watch, but incredibly dumb on Devlin's part, as it leads
    to the Lieutenant observing how Devlin marks his whiskey bottles at the
    level where he intends to stop drinking and that leads to the final clue, the
    bottle from the scene of the crime); "Columbo Goes to the Guillotine"
    (#44) (Eliot Blake, called back to the scene of the crime by Columbo,

spots the cartridge he left there the other day and palms it; very sloppy); "Grand Deceptions" (#47) (Columbo gets two gift clues when the victim's friend decides to confide in the Lieutenant about the Special Projects Fund and when the murderer's secretary gets so confused about which report to shred that she doesn't see him walking off with the incriminating version); "Murder With Too Many Notes" (#66) (it's convenient for Columbo that the tux shop guy puts dress shoes in the victim's bag and that the victim doesn't say "no shoes" as he did the last time he rented a tux). I also think the show takes a misstep when it has the murder occur in the heat of the moment rather than being preplanned, because then the murderer simply cannot anticipate what will happen and gift clues arise as a result. Examples: "Dagger of the Mind" (#11) (Nicholas Frame and Lillian Stanhope would not have planned to get into a fight with Sir Roger Haversham in her dressing room, but because they do, a necklace is broken and beads scatter everywhere, beads which Columbo will use to catch the couple by suggesting they wound up in Haversham's umbrella); "Lovely But Lethal" (#16) (Viveca Scott wouldn't have planned to hit Karl Lessing over the head with a microscope, and had she not done so, the broken slide with poison ivy wouldn't have been there for her or Columbo to touch).

4. Behavioral Clues. Particularly in the earliest episodes, Columbo makes an observation about the way the murderer has behaved or failed to behave. The presumption behind this clue is supposed to be that "everyone does X," but the problem is this simply isn't true. This often results in Columbo's "First Clue," but behavioral clues don't make very strong ones. Examples: *Prescription: Murder* (pilot A) (Columbo finds it odd that Flemming doesn't call out to his wife when he arrives home, but as Burt Gordon responds, maybe he doesn't do that or maybe he was still angry about the fight they had on the plane); *Ransom for a Dead Man* (pilot B) (everything Leslie Williams does in this episode seems to rub Columbo

the wrong way—she doesn't ask how her husband is doing when he calls with the ransom information, she faints when informed of his death even though she's been controlled up to that point and she doesn't ask how he died; I agree that it's odd that she asks "when?" in the gap she left on the tape after Paul says how much money the kidnappers want, but his other observations are too definite about subjective human behavior); "Murder By the Book" (#1) (I can accept his observation that it's odd that Ken Franklin drove back from San Diego rather than flying—although I do like Franklin's answer that it's not that much faster when you consider all the time spent traveling to the airport—but Columbo makes way too much of Franklin's act of opening the mail, not just because he could have done it after he called the police and was waiting for their arrival, but also because it goes too far to say no one would do that); "Short Fuse" (#6) (Columbo seems to suspect Stanford because he keeps checking his watch during the phone call, afraid the bomb will go off before Buckner hangs up, but that's sloppy behavior on Stanford's part); "A Stitch in Crime" (#13) (same point regarding Barry Mayfield's act of resetting his desk clock while being told of his nurse's death—as a surgeon he probably can split his concentration like that); "Grand Deceptions" (#47) (Columbo claims that Colonel Brailie is "too arrogant" to clean up mud, so it must be that he thought he left it there while committing the murder).

5. Ignoring Reality or the Case of the Missing Clues. Occasionally, instead of having Columbo uncover subtle clues which even the most clever criminal would not notice, the writers seem to ignore reality by going for subtle observations (or none at all) when the most glaring points are present. The reason is no doubt that the obvious clues would prove too much too soon, but that's no excuse for sloppy writing. Examples: "Rest in Peace, Mrs. Columbo" (#51) (there are five non-clues in this disastrous episode: 1) the marmalade jar would have had a pop-up lid to prevent tampering; 2) ATM machines have cameras in them and Dimitri's photo would be on tape

for the time when Chambers supposedly withdrew cash; 3) Dimitri calls the police station to see if Columbo is back from vacation, but she cannot possibly ensure that he will be assigned the Chambers case; 4) the police record incoming calls and Dimitri's voice would be on tape as having called claiming to be Columbo's dentist; and 5) Dr. Steadman is wrong, because doctor-patient privilege does not apply when a patient makes a specific threat against a recognizable victim and after Dimitri carried out part one of her plan (killing Chambers) he had a duty to warn the next potential victims, (the Columbos); "Butterfly in Shades of Grey" (#61) (in the scenario, Chase picks up his phone after his answering machine starts recording, but that would mean the machine would shut off, yet he really picks up the extension in the victim's den and that's why it does not shut off).

6. Changes to the format. If it ain't broke, don't fix it. See "Variations on a Theme by Jackson Gillis" and "No Time for Columbo, No Place for McBain" for what happens when the writers tweak—and sometimes even abandon—the wonderful structure of the show.

7. Violence. On a few of the later episodes, the show's usual lack of violence is cast aside. See "No Time for Columbo, No Place for McBain" for how "No Time to Die" (#58) and "Undercover" (#62) have un-Columbo-like scenes of violence. In addition, "Columbo Likes the Nightlife" (#67) has a very violent second murder, in which the victim is strangled, then (when that didn't take) pushed out of a window and his weight causes a radiator to be pulled out after him and he and the radiator plummet to a nasty impact with the ground. "Strange Bedfellows" (#63) features the series' only (and unnecessary) car chase and several violent scenes of the Mafia beating up the murderer and even Columbo, albeit much of this is faked to convince the murderer to confess. Finally, "Murder With Too Many Notes" (#66) features a violent murder, but not the murder of the episode. The scene opens on the final scene of a movie for which murderer Findlay Crawford (Billy Connolly) has written the music: a man with a

knife hunts down and stabs a woman. Then the scene is repeated without the music for greater effect, but watching this violent scene twice runs contrary to the premise of *Columbo*.

8. Morris the Explainer. This is an old film term that refers to a character whose job is to come in and explain the plot to other characters and the audience. For the most part, *Columbo* avoids this practice (for a great example of a non-Morris ending, check out "Columbo Cries Wolf" (#49), where the Lieutenant uncovers the hidden body and points to the beeper on the victim on which is written the single word "Gotcha!"). But every once in a while . . . Examples: "An Exercise in Fatality" (#24) (Columbo gets murderer Milo Janus to say that he spoke to the victim after he changed into his gym clothes, then goes on a really long tangent to explain how the victim's shoelaces indicate that he didn't tie his own shoes, at which point Janus says anybody could have done it, having forgotten what he said at the beginning of this scene!); "A Trace of Murder" (#64) (Columbo has the co-conspirators on either side of a street and goes back and forth trying to get them to turn on each other, then the episode concludes with another "Morris" scene as Columbo tells Barney of Barney's Beanery how he figured out that they knew each other); "Murder With Too Many Notes" (#66) (Columbo doesn't actually have a "Final Clue" here, so instead he summarizes all the clues, some of which he never told the murderer about, and then places him under arrest).

9. Falk's Hamming and Other Changes to the Character. See "Peter Falk as Columbo" for occasions when the actor goes a bit too far. See "The Developing Character" for more on the character. And see "No Time for Columbo, No Place for McBain" for how the character is compromised in "No Time to Die" (#58) and "Undercover" (#62).

10. Misogyny. Columbo can be very compassionate, and he demonstrates
    kindness to "Sympathetic Murderers" such as Grace Wheeler in "Forgotten
    Lady" (#30), Abigail Mitchell in "Try and Catch Me" (#39), Joan Allenby
    in "Sex and the Married Detective" (#46) and Lauren Staton in "It's All in
    the Game" (#60). But sometimes the good Lieutenant and the show come
    off as women-bashing. In *Ransom for a Dead Man* (pilot B), Columbo tells
    Leslie Williams's associate (who happens to be a man) "I don't know how
    you can work for a woman." In "Lovely But Lethal" (#16), Columbo is
    particularly tough on Viveca Scott. Recall that Karl Lessing has stolen the
    formula for vanishing cream from her lab and intends to sell it to her com-
    petitor. Her first reaction is to call her lawyer, but he's out, so she goes to
    Lessing's place and tries everything to get it back from him—bartering,
    pleading, threats. When he humiliates her, she strikes out in anger, acci-
    dentally killing him (she never would have done so on purpose, because
    she needs the formula and only he knows it). Despite these facts, Columbo
    hounds her mercilessly, even refusing her pleas at the fat farm to come back
    later when he has no real questions to ask and he's acceded to similar re-
    quests from other murderers. But none of this can compare to the show's
    treatment of Kay Freestone, the murderer in "Make Me a Perfect Murder"
    (#41): she's insulted by everyone from the technical director to the studio
    head (who accuses her of "leaping so quickly behind a dead man's desk")
    and Columbo rejects the idea that she killed for "just a job" (actually, she
    did) and lectures her about not telling him the truth (as though none of the
    other murderers did that). Even the show itself seems to torture her, as she
    struggles to get the gun she thinks has jiggled loose from its hiding place
    above an elevator diffuser.

11. Social Commentary. *Columbo* is a murder mystery, and when it strays
    beyond that genre into the realm of social commentary, it fails and regret-
    table results ensue. In particular, when international issues arise, the show
    falls flat. In "A Case of Immunity" (#31), Hassan Salah is the bad guy and

the Suarian king the good guy. No problem there, but note how stark the contrast is—Salah wears an Arab robe, eats Suarian food and wants to preserve his country's traditions, while the king dresses in Western (military) garb, eats French food and keeps talking about changing with the times. In other words, Arabs are okay, so long as they dress and act like us. And in "The Conspirators" (#43), the show doesn't even try to explore the conflict in Northern Ireland. Of course, there can be no justification for the violence, but as is pointed out, it exists on both sides.

The Bloating Problem

NBC expanded *Columbo* (along with the other spokes on its mystery wheel, *McCloud* and *McMillan and Wife*) from ninety minutes to two full hours beginning with the 1972-73 season, and from then on the series would bounce back and forth between the two time spans. The reason was simple: it gave the network an additional thirty minutes of program for which commercial time could be sold and with an expensive show like *Columbo*, the more NBC could get in return, the better. When ABC returned *Columbo* to the airwaves in 1989, all twenty-four new episodes were two hours long.

Just about everybody thinks it was bad for the show. Levinson and Link described it as a "creative disaster" in their book *Stay Tuned*, while Steven Bochco, Dean Hargrove and Peter Falk all agree that the extra time made the show inflated and indulgent (*The Columbo Phile*, p. 95). For his part, *The Columbo Phile* author Mark Dawidziak reports that "even though Columbo was a natural ninety-minute series, the two-hour experiments were not all failures. After all, Hargrove had demonstrated in *Ransom for a Dead Man* that the format could be sustained over two hours. And some of the longer Columbo episodes, certainly "Any Old Port" and "Troubled Waters," rank with the series' best efforts." (*Ibid.*)

I'm not sure I agree with these pronouncements. That is, I agree with the premise that it is more difficult to sustain a show for two hours than for ninety minutes. It requires writing another thirty minutes of quality script, with more clues, more interaction between Columbo and the murderer, more details about Columbo's life and the murderer's profession, and more scenes of the Lieutenant remembering "just one more thing" or fishing through his pockets for that seemingly lost piece of paper. At a certain point, the writers run out of material, the right amount of this mixture becomes too much and the infamous "bloating" occurs. I should mention that I would recommend having a clue in every scene, but I must admit that some scenes without one, but which contain character development, can be very enjoyable, such as the scene in Flemming's office in *Prescription: Murder* (pilot A) where he and Columbo discuss the "hypothetical" murderer who calculates every detail of the crime and would be impossible to catch.

But I would not say that all, or even most of the ninety-minutes episodes are great while most of the two-hour variety are poor. Yes, it's true that some of the two-hour episodes have scenes that the program could easily do without, such as Columbo's gushing praise about Alex Benedict's house the morning after the murder without asking a single question in "Etude in Black" (#8) (he finally admits that he's come for an autograph), or the roadside stop in "Candidate for Crime" (#18) in which Columbo demonstrates how bad a shape his car is in. "An Exercise in Fatality" (#24) has a scene in which Columbo waits for a computer to finish printing out Lewis Lacey's address and it drags on forever. "Make Me a Perfect Murder" (#41), which has many problems, also is bloated with an extra scene of Columbo playing with the test patterns.

Some of the newer episodes also have long stretches of time with pointless filler. "Caution: Murder Can Be Hazardous to Your Health" (#55) shows the audience Wade Anders at work on his crime re-enactment show, including scenes of the perpetrators being caught. "Death Hits the Jackpot" (#57) takes a full thirty minutes for the crime to unfold, then another fifteen for Columbo to survey the scene and contact Leon Lamarr to tell him his nephew is dead. It also wastes time at the nephew's funeral, at a wake held by his friends, in having Lamarr's accomplice Nancy call Lamarr and repeat what she just told Columbo and in Columbo's continuing search for his wife's anniversary present. "Butterfly in Shades of Grey" (#61) spends a lot of time on Fielding Chase's plan to destroy a particular senator on his radio show, as well as the actual destruction itself. "Ashes to Ashes" (#65), which has some very good clues, suffers because it has three scenes that have no clues in them: a singer entertains the crowd before Eric Prince receives the Funeral Director of the Year Award, a tap dancer performs at Dan Riley's funeral and we have to sit through the Chuck Huston funeral led by Fred the minister. In "Murder With Too Many Notes" (#66), Columbo and Findlay Crawford spend a lot of time, first in separate cars and then in one, traveling back to Crawford's house on the night of the murder. There is also a bizarre scene in which the orchestra joins Crawford in making fun of Columbo's apparent lack of musical knowledge (see "The Developing Character").

But many of the two-hour episodes from the 1970s (some of the best of the series) and some of the newer ones do not have unnecessary scenes and fully deserve the two hours they have been given. What should be removed from "By Dawn's Early Light" (#26), "Any Old Port in a Storm" (#17), "Now You See Him" (#34) or "Negative Reaction" (#25)? There's no fat in "Columbo Cries Wolf" (#49). In other words, two hours can seem to drag on, but it doesn't have to be that way.

On the other hand, one of the biggest time wasters during the show occurs during the ninety-minute episode "Double Shock" (#15), in which Peter Falk and Martin Landau ad lib a cooking show. Not only does Columbo not ask any questions of the murderer, but in addition the Lieutenant's stumbling performance in the kitchen undermines the notion (first suggested in "Murder By the Book" (#1) and later expanded upon in "Murder Under Glass" (#40)) that he knows how to cook. Plus, it contrasts with the lack of discomfort he shows in front of an audience in "Now You See Him" (#34) and "Try and Catch Me" (#39). "Publish or Perish" (#20) could have used another thirty minutes to sort out its convoluted story, instead of splitting the screen three ways and leaving the audience completely confused. In addition, in "Old Fashioned Murder" (#37), Columbo almost fails to get a hair dresser to talk to him until he agrees to have his hair styled while he talks. Personally, I've never found these scenes very humorous, but that's not to say others may not. I prefer to watch a scene and enjoy it for its humor or if I don't think it's very funny I can always fast forward through it.

Obviously, how people feel about the "bloating" problem depends in part on what they think is important to making a good episode of *Columbo*. "Taut pacing" has never been high on my list of criteria. In fact, much of the show is spent on extended scenes: if the Lieutenant would just ask all of his questions and go, no doubt the episode could be finished in less time, but think of what we'd lose. As my episode reviews and Appendix I indicate, I look first and foremost to the clues to determine if an episode is of good quality. Now, more doesn't necessarily mean better (on the whole, the newer episodes have fewer and less interesting clues in two hours than the old ones had in ninety minutes), but sometimes ninety minutes' worth just isn't enough. That's why, as much as I admire "Try and Catch Me" (#39) and "Playback" (#28) , I can't raise them as high as I could if only they'd been given more clues (the Ruth Gordon episode has only four: the fact that the alarm was on when the victim was found inside the safe, the victim's missing keys, the torn piece of paper and the paint under the victim's fingernails). "Playback" could definitely spend more time on developing the characters; Columbo never even investigates the motive. And even the bloating problem adherents have to admit that "Publish or Perish" (#20), with its three-way split screen and last-minute second murder, could easily have benefited from more time to tell the story. In the end, I'll admit that some of the old (and many of the new) two-hour episodes are padded with excess material, but it really doesn't bother me as I'm watching the show, or even as I'm evaluating it. Nor does it make the difference between a good episode and a bad one—would "Columbo Goes to the Guillotine" (#44) and "Grand Deceptions" (#47) be better episodes at ninety minutes, or would they just be shorter?

Chapter 16:
The Plot Structure

Columbo Deconstructed

Although it may not appear obvious on the surface, the plot of an episode of *Columbo* is actually rather complicated. In this introduction, I will provide my version of the show's structure, which will then be explored in greater depth in the essays that follow. I should note at the beginning that not everyone enjoys deconstructing the show in this manner. Some people feel that it is most enjoyable when viewed as a whole and that picking it apart detracts from this enjoyment. All I can say in response is to each his (or her) own. I love watching the show, but I also love talking about it in depth in all its little parts. For me, this process demonstrates just how much there is to enjoy in each episode. Just as some sports fans love to review every detail of a game their team won or lost, so too I find that examining the details actually enhances my enjoyment of the whole.

As everyone who has seen a *Columbo* knows, every episode (except the two Ed McBain "adaptations" "No Time to Die" (#58) and "Undercover" (#62)) begins with the murder. This is called inverted structure or open mystery. We the audience see the crime and we watch as the detective puts the pieces together. As has been noted elsewhere, Richard Levinson and William Link did not invent this literary device (see "Why I Love Columbo), but they were probably among the first to apply it in a television mystery and they certainly made excellent use of it. If we consider a television program in segments (between the commercials), we can see that "scene one" of a *Columbo* consists of our introduction to the murderer and witnessing of the crime.

In "scene two," enter the detective. Now here comes a bit of variation. In some episodes, the second segment consists of Columbo meeting the murderer. That is certainly true in the two pilot movies. In *Prescription: Murder*, the first thing that happens after the break is that Ray Flemming walks back into his apartment and is confronted by the Lieutenant. And in *Ransom for a Dead Man*, Leslie Williams has a house full of FBI agents when the doorbell rings and she encounters Columbo looking for his lost pen. However, beginning with the first episode of the series, "Murder By the Book" (#1), scene two consists of Columbo making his first examination of the scene of the crime. It is at this point that the Lieutenant obtains his "first clues" (see the next essay for more on this topic) that lead him to believe that something is not as it seems and send him in the direction of the individual the audience already knows committed the crime. Thus, in these cases, the detective and criminal do not actually meet until "scene three."

Interestingly, the show would return to having Columbo meet the villain in scene two during the 1977-78 season when Richard Alan Simmons took over as executive producer of the program. In *The Columbo Phile*, Mark Dawidziak recounts that Simmons wanted to "shake up and improve" the *Columbo* formula. Accordingly, his episodes (actually beginning with the last episode of the 1976-77 season, "The Bye-Bye Sky High IQ Murder Case" (#38)) can be distinguished by three stylistic departures: 1) Columbo makes a more formidable entrance; 2) we get more involved in the murderer's background and emotional makeup; and 3) we learn more about the Lieutenant's background. *The Columbo Phile* (p. 282.) I would expand on Mark's first point in this regard. In a Simmons's era episode, Columbo does make a formidable entrance in the second scene and part of what makes it more dramatic is that he meets the murderer right there and then. For example, in "The Bye-Bye Sky High IQ Murder Case" (#38), Oliver Brandt is left waiting in the library (where he discovers that he has soot on his forehead from the handkerchief he used and he frantically removes it) when he is confronted by Columbo. Similarly, in "Try and Catch Me" (#39), Abigail Mitchell returns home and is conducted to her study, where Columbo comes bursting out of the soundproof safe where she left Edmund to suffocate.

This is not to suggest that Columbo has no reason to suspect the murderers until he happens to meet them. On the contrary, he has already been on the scene collecting clues; it's just that we have not been witnesses to it. Thus, for example, he has already noticed that the alarm was found on when the victim was in the safe in Try and Catch Me (#39) and he will ask Mitchell about it as soon as he meets her. Or in "The Conspirators" (#43), he goes to Joe Devlin's house because he found an autographed copy of the poet's book in the victim's coat pocket.

In yet a further twist, when the show returned in 1989 after a ten-year hiatus, the second segment in which Columbo examines the murder scene before meeting the villain had been restored, even though Simmons was once again the executive producer. It may be that, because the episodes had to be two hours in length, this scene had to be kept in the format.

In any event, after Columbo and the murderer meet, the following scenes (two or three to five in a ninety-minute episode, two or three to seven in a two-hour installment) consist of a series of one-on-one dialogues between the Lieutenant and the villain. Columbo keeps tracking down the killer in different locations and keeps asking "one more thing" that is bothering him. He finds "intermediate" level clues that support his suspicions and further the investigation. In addition, he meets with other folks who can provide him with some information about the events or the murderer. Occasionally, the murderer engages in a second murder to get rid of an accomplice or witness. In these cases, Columbo makes some investigation into the second crime, but almost always arrests the murderer for the first one (see "Accomplices, Blackmailers and Schlimazels" and "Get 'Em for the First Murder").

This brings us to the conclusion and what I have called the "Final Clue." I refer here to the last scene of the show in which Columbo arrests the murderer. The method by which he does so can take one of several different forms: he can produce a piece of evidence that places the murderer at the scene of the crime, trick the villain into making an incriminating act, maneuver the killer into confessing, or poke holes in the criminal's apparently airtight alibi or in the scenario that has been constructed. All of these endings (as well as several other special cases) are explored in greater depth in the next chapter, in the essays on Columbo Final Clues.

First Clues

As I previously described, during the second scene of a *Columbo* episode, the Lieutenant spots the "first clue" that causes him to disbelieve the scenario that the murderer has set up (suicide, accident, etc.). Let's call this the First Clue that the Setup is false or FCS for short. What is fascinating to observe is that in more than half of the episodes, there is also another distinct first clue, which serves to point the Lieutenant in the direction of the murderer. Let's call it the First Clue as to who the Murderer is, or FCM for short. As we shall see, in some instances only the FCS is present (sometimes that's enough, sometimes arguably it really isn't) and in other instances only the FCM is present, but in many episodes, I can point to two definite clues, one to explain why the case is premeditated murder and the other to explain why Columbo's hot on the trail of the guest murderer.

The pattern, although not followed in every instance, is this: first the Lieutenant spots the FCS—usually during his first inspection of the location of the murder or the body in the show's second scene—and this gets him looking not only for more clues but for some indication of whodunit. Then he encounters the FCM and is on his way. The opposite would not make much sense narratively, since after discovering evidence that a particular person may be a murderer, the detective has no need for a clue suggesting that the death was premeditated (of course, any clue that does more than suggest is always welcome).

Sometimes Columbo does not even mention the first clues at the time, but he brings the point home to the murderer in the last scene. He tells Marshall Cahill at the conclusion of "Mind Over Mayhem" (#21) that he incriminated himself when he pulled out a cigar. The match in the victim's house was burned from top to bottom, meaning it had been used to light a cigar (the FCS was the victim's pipe: when Columbo found it in the driveway it meant that the scenario that the victim was killed by drug crazies raiding his house was staged). In a second example, Columbo tells Nelson Brenner at the end of "Identity Crisis" (#32) that he suspected him once he saw that the victim's coat was removed, something muggers don't need to do. Since the victim was a CIA operative, his coat had to be removed so Brenner could take off his shoulder holster (he knew Brenner was involved once he found him in a photo with the victim at an amusement park the day before he was killed). And Columbo tells Paul Gerard at the end of "Murder Under Glass" (#40) that his act of coming right away after being told that he had eaten dinner with a poisoned man was the "damndest act of good citizenship I've ever seen" (Columbo knows something is up based on the description of the victim's state of mind).

Two first clues appear in forty-three out of the sixty-seven episodes and movies (not counting the Ed McBain "adaptations"). Sometimes, an FCM is present even when it would not have been necessary. For example, in "The Bye-Bye Sky High IQ Murder Case" (#38), if it wasn't a robbery but a preplanned murder (and the angle of the shots raise this as an issue), then Oliver Brandt is a fairly obvious suspect, but the episode nonetheless provides us with the FCM of the record cuing.

The first season contains only three episodes with the full complement of two first clues and "Dead Weight" (#3) is something of a stretch because it uses Helen Stewart's witnessing of a shooting twice, both to show that the murdered man isn't simply missing and again to suggest that General Hollister is responsible for it. In "Death Lends a Hand" (#2), the FCS is the distinctive cut on the victim's face, meaning she was struck by a left-handed individual wearing a particular kind of ring. Columbo pursues this idea by taking palm readings, first of her husband and then of Mr. Brimmer, who has the right kind of ring, and the Lieutenant has his FCM. I have said that Columbo is indeed lucky that this strategy works on his second try and I wonder about his apparent vast knowledge of palmistry, which does not seem in keeping with his character. The best usage of two first clues occurs in "Blueprint for Murder" (#7). It's easy to spot the "first clue" of the classical music heard on the radio, which proves that someone other than country music-loving Beau Williamson was driving the car. But chronologically, that is the second clue. The first one is Goldie's fears. Elliot Markham's plan was for Beau simply to disappear, with no questions asked for at least a month. But Goldie, Beau's first wife, knows that he was in town and that he wouldn't have left again without letting her know, a habit preserved from their marriage. She thus gets the Lieutenant on the case far faster than Markham ever anticipated. And the music on the radio is the FCM, the one that points toward Markham (after the Lieutenant sees all the classical music records in his office, of course) because Goldie already has him looking for evidence of foul play. That is, the mix of music would suggest nothing if foul play weren't already suspected (Beau could like both). Notice that the clues may not always be clever or even prove very much; all they have to do is get Columbo on the case and on the trail of the real murderer.

At the end of this essay is a table containing all of the episodes that employ both an FCS and an FCM. What follows is a discussion of the episodes that are not in the table, for various reasons.

I have excluded a few episodes from this analysis because their structure of delaying certain revelations until late in the story complicates the issue of what a first clue would be. In "Suitable for Framing" (#4), the early "clues" about the sound of high heels being heard on the back steps and the questionably picked lock may be insightful observations by Columbo, or they might be planted clues left by Dale Kingston as part of his scheme to frame his Aunt Edna for the murder, a scheme that will only become evident much later in the episode. In "Uneasy Lies the Crown" (#52), early clues about matches in the victim's shirt pocket and the car being in neutral were left by Wesley Corman to lead the Lieutenant toward the frame-up of Corman's wife Lydia, which is his slowly revealed plan (although Lydia's missing pills eventually point the Lieutenant toward Corman as the real killer). And in "Columbo Cries Wolf" (#49), all the clues except those observed during the last twenty minutes turn out to be fakes, dropped by Sean Brantely to lure the Lieutenant into believing that Dian Hunter has been murdered and is buried at The Chateau. I also am excluding "Requiem for a Falling Star" (#12) and "Publish or Perish" (#20). In both cases, there are first clues of a kind (the flat tire in "Requiem," the key that doesn't fit the lock in "Publish"), but the scenarios in those episodes are for Columbo to suspect the murderers at first before they rule themselves out: Nora Chandler tries to show that she had no motive to kill the apparently intended victim, and Riley Greenleaf makes it look like someone else was framing him for the crime. I'm also excluding the non-*Columbo* format episodes "No Time to Die" (#58) and "Undercover" (#62) from this analysis.

Of course, not every episode has both clues. In many cases, we get only the FCS (something is wrong with the situation as set up by the murderer), and no specific clue points toward the specific guest star as the culprit. But, in half of these twelve episodes, there is no need for another clue because the murderer has put him or herself so far into the spotlight that, if it isn't a suicide, accident or robbery but a preplanned murder, it takes no leap of the imagination to guess who's responsible. In "Lady in Waiting" (#5), there are only two possibilities: either Beth Chadwick shot her brother by accident or she did it deliberately, and the newspaper in the front hall (the FCS) suggests that Bryce didn't enter through her window at all, but came in the front door. Similarly, if campaign manager Harry Stone wasn't shot by crazies who thought they had caught up with candidate Nelson Hayward in "Candidate for Crime" (#18) (and the cold car and broken street light suggest that the scenario is a false one), then someone must have been gunning for Stone himself, and the only one who knew that he and Hayward had exchanged clothes was Hayward. If Alvin Deschler wasn't responsible for the elaborate kidnapping of Paul Galesko's wife and the shooting of Galesko in "Negative Reaction" (#25) (and the powder burns and testimony of the wino suggest otherwise) then Galesko must have engineered this entire scenario himself, and killed both his wife and Deschler. In "Forgotten Lady" (#30), if Henry Willis didn't shoot himself (and the sleeping pill and lack of dirt on his slippers suggest otherwise) then his wife is the only real suspect. In "Try and Catch Me" (#39), if Edmund Galvin didn't get locked in Abigail Mitchell's safe by accident (and the fact that the alarm was on when he was found inside raises this as a possibility), then Abby herself is the most likely suspect. And in "How to Dial a Murder" (#42), if the dogs attacked Charlie not by chance (and the telephone dangling off the hook with a tone meaning Charlie was talking to someone when the dogs attacked indicates something else was going on), then their owner Eric Mason is the only one who could have trained them to attack. Indeed, this clue may go a little too far, because the way Columbo describes it, Mason is about the only person who could have been on the line, although there is a possibility that Charlie ended the call before the dogs attacked, or perhaps it was a wrong number and thus even if the caller heard the screams, he couldn't say who was on the other end.

Unfortunately, sometimes when we get only the FCS it really isn't enough to point Columbo toward the murderer. In "Fade in to Murder" (#36), the bullet hole suggests that the killing was not part of a robbery (because the victim had her hands up at the time) but nothing, except for Ward Fowler's bizarre and inexplicable behavior of accusing himself through his Lieutenant Lucerne character, specifically points toward him as the murderer. In "Make Me a Perfect Murder" (#41), the fact that the victim's glasses were on his head may show that he recognized his killer, but why does that indicate Kay Freestone when the building has lots of other people he knew in it? In "Columbo Goes to the Guillotine" (#44), the wrong screwdriver in the victim's hand gets the Lieutenant thinking his beheading wasn't an accident, but what points toward Eliot Blake as the killer? In "Murder: A Self Portrait" (#48), the fact that the victim had one contact lens in and one out may suggest murder rather than drowning, but what points toward her ex-husband as the killer? In "Caution: Murder Can Be Hazardous to Your Health" (#55), the unsmoked cigarettes suggest that foul play was at work, but why is Wade Anders the target of the investigation (yes, he had seen the victim before his death, but it was several days before)? It would have made more sense to have Columbo find about the porno film and then go after Anders. Finally, in "Death Hits the Jackpot" (#57), the fact that the victim would not have worn the watch into the tub questions the accidental drowning scenario, but why is his uncle Leon Lamarr the prime suspect?

These situations, although a minority among the total number of episodes, provide grist for the mill of those people who like to take potshots at the show. I have often heard their claim that it's a terrible flaw that Columbo miraculously "knows" who to pursue moments after arriving on the scene. In most instances, I reply that there is a definite clue sending him in the right direction, but occasionally there isn't, and these episodes are it. Now, I'm not suggesting that the program has to counter all the criticisms of these armchair experts, but as a mystery fan and devotee of the show, I think it works better with both clues. Once again, it shows how much complicated structure exists beneath the seemingly simple format.

Sometimes the FCS just doesn't hold water. In "Etude in Black" (#8), there are many unusual items that could make the suicide of Jenifer Welles suspicious: the fact that someone who knew her well (Paul Rifkin) says she wasn't depressed and would never commit suicide, the fact that her beloved pet cockatoo Chopin was killed by the gas also, the fact that the suicide note was typed and that it was then removed from the typewriter and replaced. The problem is that, before we get to any of these items, Columbo sits in Welles's house and notices other things, such as "her eyes" not looking like the eyes of someone who would commit suicide (whatever that means) and the pictures in her scrapbook missing "something," which he says must be a man. These observations about human behavior are unnatural and unnecessary, particularly when there is so much in the manner of real clues to utilize (see "Recurring Problems"). Then, the only thing that seems to lead Columbo to suspect Alex Benedict is the flower that he picks up at Welles's piano (he claims to have just dropped it, but we know he did so hours earlier when he killed her). And it's no small matter, because Columbo has to suspect maestro Alex Benedict the first night or he would have no reason to beat him to the repair shop and get the odometer reading the next morning.

Finally, there are those rare occasions when we get a clue that can only be characterized as an FCM without a corresponding FCS. The two pilot movies fall into this category, as do the episodes "Murder By the Book" (#1), "Short Fuse" (#6), "A Bird in the Hand" (#59) and "Strange Bedfellows" (#63). Of these, Murder By the Book can be excused because, since Ken Franklin has made it look like a mob killing and since there's really no way to prove that the mob didn't do it, any clue pointing toward anyone is sufficient, here the fact that he drives back from San Diego to L.A. But in *Prescription: Murder* (pilot A), the first clue is that Ray Flemming didn't call out to his wife, clearly a clue pointing toward the killer. Nothing shows that it wasn't a robbery and I believe there's something of a prescience problem in explaining why Columbo is in the bedroom just when Flemming comes in. It might have worked a little better if something had been wrong about the setup and that led Columbo to wait for Flemming to come home. Similarly, in *Ransom for a Dead Man* (pilot B), the first clue is that Leslie Williams doesn't inquire after her husband during the ransom call; nothing at that point suggests it isn't a kidnapping. It might be argued that the fact that the supposed kidnappers later take the money and leave the bag suggests something is amiss, but Columbo is already on her trail before then because of the behavioral clue, so we don't need an FCS at this point. In "Short Fuse" (#6), the single clue is Roger Stanford's nervous reaction to the tape. In "A Bird in the Hand" (#59), Harold McCain plants a bomb under his uncle's car (but unfortunately he blows up the gardener after the uncle is killed in a hit-and-run and the police need the Rolls moved out of the way). He says it must have been an expert from the outside, but Columbo thinks an insider would have known where the security cameras were. But his real first clues are FCMs—there are scrape marks on the driveway from Harold's cowboy boots as he lay under the car to plant the bomb, and the configuration of the bottom of a Rolls requires a left-handed individual, which Harold is. And in "Strange Bedfellows" (#63), another mob killing is intended, but even before Graham McVeigh completes the plan by killing Bruno Romano, Columbo suspects him because of the cigarette ashes in the victim's car. This is an odd clue, because it depends on McVeigh not having been in his brother's car at all that day, when there would be nothing incriminating about it if he had been in the car.

The fact that the movies and most of the first season episodes lack the full pattern of two first clues could merely be coincidence, or it could mean that it wasn't part of Levinson and Link's original structure for the program. The idea may have been that since the focus was not on whodunit but how the detective builds a case against the murderer, the identity of the killer need not require a leap of faith to grasp. Both movies have an identical premise: one spouse kills the other in order to inherit from and be rid of him/her. If they weren't robberies or kidnappings, it doesn't take a genius to figure out who killed them and no FCM is needed, although in each case, what we get is only an FCM and no FCS. In the first season, three of the episodes keep the murderer "in the family" (four if you count Ken Franklin, Jim Ferris's writing partner) so no FCM is needed. In later seasons, the list of murderers would expand to include blackmailers, business rivals and others whose association with the victim is often distant or apparently nonexistent. Indeed, in three later episodes, the murderers would claim that they didn't even know the victims: "Identity Crisis" (#32); "The Conspirators" (#43); and "Agenda for Murder" (#50). As the connection between the victim and the murderer became less obvious, it may have been a natural evolution of the program to introduce clues whose function was to point in the direction of the murderer.

Table 2: First Clues that the Setup is False (FCS) and as to Who the Murderer Is (FCM)

Episode	FCS	FCM
Death Lends a Hand (#2)	There is a distinctive cut on the victim's face.	Mr. Brimmer wears a ring that matches the victim's cut.
Dead Weight (#3)	Helen Stewart sees the shooting.	She sees Martin Hollister pull the trigger.
Blueprint for Murder (#7)	Goldie suspects foul play when Beau leaves town without telling her.	Beau's radio is set to classical, the favorite music of Elliott Markham.
Etude in Black (#8)	Victims "eyes" suggest she didn't kill herself, or lack of man in her photos, or that she allowed pet cockatoo to die of gas, or that her suicide note is typed and was placed back in typewriter	Alex Benedict comes to the victim's house and picks up a flower he claims to have just dropped on the floor, but maybe he lost it earlier.
The Greenhouse Jungle (#9)	Skid marks suggest a massive car has run the victim's Jaguar off the road.	Jarvis Goodland goes straight to his greenhouse after making the ransom money drop.
The Most Crucial Game (#10)	There is non-chlorinated water on the pool deck.	Paul Hanlon turns the radio off at the word "murder."
Dagger of the Mind (#11)	A rare book is left open face-down.	Water on the victim's car means he was in London, perhaps visiting the actors.
A Stitch in Crime (#13)	The people who know the victim do not believe that she hid drugs in her home.	Dr. Mayfield calmly resets his desk clock while hearing the news of the murder.
The Most Dangerous Match (#14)	The wrong toothbrush in the victim's bag means he didn't pack it himself.	Emmet Clayton shows Columbo a note the victim allegedly left to him.
Double Shock (#15)	The wet towel when the victim is found on an exercise bicycle suggests he was killed and then placed there.	Columbo spots a flat footprint outside and begins searching for flat-footed people like twins Dexter and Norman Paris.

Episode	FCS	FCM
Lovely But Lethal (#16)	The imprint of the jar removed from the victim's flour tin indicates that this was no ordinary robbery.	The victim has Viveca Scott's face on his dartboard.
Any Old Port in a Storm (#17)	The victim's car was left with its convertible roof open on a rainy day.	The victim didn't eat since Sunday, placing him last at his brother Adrian's winery.
Double Exposure (#19)	The victim gets up and leaves a screening room in the middle of a film.	Bart Kepple turned on a tape recorder despite the presence of a body in the hall.
Mind Over Mayhem (#21)	The victim's pipe is in the driveway, meaning he was killed there, not inside.	Marshall Cahill smokes cigars, as did the killer, who left a burned-out match.
Swan Song (#22)	The pilot's belt was unbuckled.	The victim's brother is accusing Tommy Brown of foul play.
A Friend in Deed (#23)	The victim's nightgown was under her pillow, meaning someone dressed her in another one.	The victim's husband knows about the gown under the pillow, but the husband's friend, who happens to be Columbo's boss, insists that he follow the robbery trail.
An Exercise in Fatality (#24)	Brown scuffmarks on the floor mean the victim was being chased through the spa.	The coffee burn on Milo Janus's arm puts him in the victim's office where there is a coffee stain on the rug.
By Dawn's Early Light (#26)	The sound of the cannon exploding was heard as far away as Westlake.	Col. Rumford hesitates in identifying the cleaning rag.
Troubled Waters (#27)	The victim must have died instantly and did not have time to write an "L" on her mirror.	A feather is found outside Hayden Danziger's hospital room, but hospitals don't use feather pillows.
Playback (#28)	There is no dirt inside the window where the thief supposedly climbed in.	Harold Van Wyck wrote where he would be on the back of a magazine for the first time.

Episode	FCS	FCM
A Deadly State of Mind (#29)	Nadia Donner is having difficulty keeping the facts straight on the robbery scenario that Marcus Collier has created.	The Lieutenant finds a flint on the floor on the night Collier doesn't use his cigarette lighter.
A Case of Immunity (#31)	The ashes indicate that the safe was blown before the fire was set.	A security chief failed to draw his gun suggesting someone he trusted killed him, like First Secretary Hassan Salah.
Identity Crisis (#32)	The victim's coat was removed, not necessary for a mugging.	Nelson Brenner is in a photo with the victim at the amusement park.
A Matter of Honor (#33)	It's odd that Hector Rangel would take it upon himself to destroy a valuable bull without permission.	Luis Montoya ordered the car that he could drive to be washed before Hector supposedly told him that he wanted to remain and work on the books.
Now You See Him (#34)	The position of the body indicates that the murderer opened the door.	Only an expert lockpick like The Great Santini could have opened the door.
Last Salute to the Commodore (#35)	The coroner establishes that the victim did not drown in a fall off his boat.	Charles Clay asked the gate guard to check the time, but Clay has an expensive watch.
Old Fashioned Murder (#37)	The supposed robber is in fancy dress as though he were going on a tropical vacation.	Ruth Lytton is the only member of the family calm enough to have shot both her brother and the guard/robber.
The Bye-Bye Sky High IQ Murder Case (#38)	The shots entered the body at the same angle even though the sound of it hitting the floor was heard between the shots.	The record playing right before the murder was preset to play a particular piece, and Oliver Brandt gave the club the player.
Murder Under Glass (#40)	Mario reports that his uncle was very angry just before he died of poisoning.	Paul Gerard, upon being told he had eaten dinner with a poisoned man, came right over.
The Conspirators (#43)	The moved whiskey bottle suggests more than the killing of a gun dealer was going on.	Joe Devlin's name is in the victim's book.

Episode	FCS	FCM
Murder, Smoke and Shadows (#45)	The victim's smashed-in face means he was not struck by lightning.	The book found near the body has Alex Brady's private phone number in it.
Sex and the Married Detective (#46)	The lack of keys makes Columbo wonder how the victim opened Dr. Allenby's clinic.	The woman in black was also seen at the concert where Allenby was that night.
Grand Deceptions (#47)	The leaves found under the victim's collar mean the body was moved.	Col. Brailie is far too arrogant to clean up mud in the victim's cabin, so he must think he left it there the night before.
Agenda for Murder(#50)	The dried blood under the gun means it was in the victim's hand for a long time.	The victim's phone indicates that the last call dialed was made to Oscar Finch.
Rest in Peace, Mrs. Columbo (#51)	The victim bet on sports and won, so he wouldn't have gone to an ATM for cash.	The last person the victim saw was Vivian Dimitri.
Murder in Malibu (#53)	Columbo quickly concludes that it wasn't a robbery.	The private eye hired by the victim's sister gives him lots of reasons to suspect Wayne Jennings.
Columbo Goes to College (#54)	The casing found outside the parking garage means something about the victim being shot in the garage is off.	The victim was supposed to have met Mr. Rowe, father of a student, for dinner.
Columbo and the Murder of a Rock Star (#56)	There is a break in the gardener's herringbone rake pattern.	The stars on the wine bottle corks indicate that one of the bottles came not from the victim's refrigerator, but from the one in Hugh Creighton's office.
It's All in the Game (#60)	The water in the refrigerator means someone turned off a circuit breaker.	The heat was turned on and Lauren Staton has a circulation problem.

Episode	FCS	FCM
Butterfly in Shades of Grey (#61)	The murderer had to have a key to get in.	Fielding Chase, whose daughter has a key that she thinks was missing on the day of the murder, was talking to the man on the phone at the time.
A Trace of Murder (#64)	The cut of the cigar end does not match the cutter used by Clifford Calvert.	Calvert's wife Cathleen knows forensic guy Patrick Kinsley.
Ashes to Ashes (#65)	The victim didn't feed her dog.	The last place the victim was known to have been was at Eric Prince's funeral home.
Murder With Too Many Notes (#66)	The victim did not scream when falling four floors, meaning he was already dead or unconscious.	The victim never wore dress shoes, so someone else dressed him and the most likely suspect is his mentor, Findlay Crawford.
Columbo Likes the Nightlife (#67)	The victim used mouthwash and clipped his toenails before committing suicide.	The date calendar on the victim's desk has a missing page, and a pencil rub of the next day reveals Justin Price's name.

Intermediate Clues and Some Delayed and Slippery Ones

If the "final clue" is what catches the criminal and the "first clue(s)" is/are what puts Columbo on the trail of the murderer, then the rest of the clues in the episode are "intermediate" clues. They don't seal anyone's fate, but they are important. At their best, these clues progress from one to another as they tighten the net. One of the best examples of this clue progression is in "Swan Song" (#22), the enjoyable episode in which singer Tommy Brown leaps out of a plane to kill his wife Edna and her associate, who will not allow him to keep any money he makes, but force him to donate it to the crusade. First, Edna's brother suspects foul play and Columbo's inspection of the plane crash site leads to his discovery that the navigation kit is empty.

Tommy explains but Columbo goes to Bakersfield to verify his story and learns that there was also a thermos on board (and it was not among the wreckage). When Columbo goes to ask Tommy about it, he finds him with a young singer (thereby suggesting a motive) and Tommy mentions that he was in the Air Force. An Air Force colonel reveals that Tommy was a parachute rigger and Columbo discovers that forty-five square yards of cloth are missing from the crusade's seamstress shop. This leads the Lieutenant to order autopsies of the victims, which in turn reveal that they had barbiturates in their systems, which is contrary to their religion. Columbo and the NTSB investigator confirm that forty-five square yards of cloth is sufficient to make a parachute that would fit in the empty navigation kit, but would have caused Tommy's descent to be faster than normal, which would explain how he broke his leg. With all of this evidence in hand, Columbo tricks Tommy into going back to find the parachute and the singer is caught.

Another episode with lots of great intermediate clues is "Negative Reaction" (#25). First, Columbo notes that it's odd that Alvin Deschler, the supposed kidnapper, would kill the victim before getting the ransom money and that Paul Galesko would shoot Deschler before learning the whereabouts of his wife. Next, Columbo notes that there are powder burns on Galesko's leg, but Thomas Dolan (the wino) recalls a gap between the shots. The motel manager says Deschler claimed someone stole his camera, but a criminal wouldn't draw attention to himself like that. Galesko wrote a little note when Deschler called, and on it he wrote "$20,000 in small bills" (something easy to remember), but not the location of a phone booth where he was supposed to go. The room where Deschler stayed has a newspaper in it that Deschler supposedly used to create the ransom note, but the maid says there was no newspaper when she cleaned up and what's more, you can't make the ransom note without creating lots of little bits of paper and there were none in the room. Columbo finds Galesko's book of photos from San Quentin and it contains many pictures of Deschler. There's a discarded photo in the fireplace of the room where the victim was shot, and Galesko claims Deschler tossed it because it was a bad picture, but only a photo expert would come to that conclusion. Finally, Columbo is bothered by the fact that witnesses report seeing Deschler ride around in cabs until the day of the murder, an expensive thing to do. He did rent a car just hours before the victim was kidnapped, but why did he wait so long? Columbo guesses that it was because Deschler, who was fresh out of prison, didn't have a driver's license and indeed he passed the test that morning, but that's not a very likely scenario for a kidnapper.

But intermediate clues do not work well when they are unnaturally delayed until later in the episode. Sometimes this is done so that Columbo and the murderer can maintain a rapport, as in "Murder: A Self Portrait" (#48). The clues lose their impact when they're all held until the end. Moreover, at that point, Columbo has the final clue in his pocket, so these clues are irrelevant. "Fade in to Murder" (#36), "Murder: A Self Portrait" (#48) and "Murder With Too Many Notes" (#66) feature final scenes that reveal clues that Columbo could have explained earlier. However, they do not involve the final clue and the reason appears to be (particularly in "Self Portrait") to preserve the friendly relations between detective and killer until the last possible moment.

Another example of a clue delayed occurs in "The Greenhouse Jungle" (#9), in which Columbo learns early on about the possibility of a bullet in the dirt in Jarvis's greenhouse, yet even after he has reason to believe Tony was shot with the same gun, it isn't until after Wilson takes over and searches for the gun planted at Cathy's house that Columbo uses the metal detector to find the incriminating bullet (this may provide them with a way of explaining the delay).

In "Try and Catch Me" (#39), in his very first examination of the murder scene, Columbo has spotted the paint under Edmund's fingernails, yet it isn't until the last scene that he follows the clue of the scratch marks left by Edmund on the metal boxes to the missing piece of paper hidden in the light bulb socket. The final clue is very powerful and clever in this episode, but it is diminished slightly because Columbo takes so long in following up on his early observation.

The newer episodes often have Columbo delay revealing his clues, sometimes so that he can form a relationship with the murderer (as in "Self Portrait," as just noted), although sometimes not. In "Columbo Goes to the Guillotine" (#44), he notices the screwdriver right away, but doesn't mention it to Eliot Blake until well into the episode. In "Sex and the Married Detective" (#46), Columbo notes that the victim did not have his keys, but he claims not to know what to make of this instead of stating the obvious—the lady in black opened the door to the clinic so she must be someone associated with it. Also the amount of ash in the ashtray is a clue delayed to the last scene when Columbo must have noticed it much earlier. In "Murder With Too Many Notes" (#66), Columbo delays nearly all the clues until the end; he almost tells Findlay Crawford the clue about the victim's dress shoes, but then changes the subject before hitting the main point, which is that they're the wrong size. Again, the problem is that these neat little observations lose their impact when they are delayed until the end, when the Lieutenant already has the solution to the case.

Another variation of the delayed clue is when Columbo starts to pick up a clue, but then drops it, because it would prove too much too soon. I call these "slippery clues." In "The Most Dangerous Match" (#14), Columbo's investigation encounters a "slippery clue" when he questions the match played between Emmet Clayton and Tomlin Dudek in the French restaurant. Clayton wants to make it look as if he beat Dudek and the old man was so distraught that he tried to run away, unfortunately tripping and winding up in the trash compactor in the hotel basement. Of course, it was actually Clayton who lost the game and if Columbo discovers this fact, the chessmaster's little game is up. So the plot unfolds this way: Columbo finds the proprietor of the restaurant, who remembers that Dudek made the "first move" by setting down the salt shaker on the checkered tablecloth, but when Columbo shows Clayton Dudek's chess book in which he has recorded that white won the game, Clayton insists that he played white and the Lieutenant drops the matter. Presumably, the writers drop this slippery clue because they want the investigation to take other turns.

Here are a few other examples of these slippery, intermediate level clues that seem to slip out of Columbo's grasp, because they would prove too much, too soon:

"Murder By the Book" (#1) may be unique in being the only episode to have Columbo investigate and then drop a clue that could wrap up the case in favor of what is perceived to be a more subtle clue. Ken Franklin takes Jim Ferris to his cabin in San Diego and suggests that Ferris call his wife Joanna in L.A. to say he's working late at the office (so Ferris won't feel so guilty about running off). As Ferris tells Joanna this lie, Franklin shoots him. Joanna immediately calls the police to say she heard a shot. Franklin will claim that the telephone call from his cabin to Joanna was the one he made to her fifteen or twenty minutes before (he actually made that call from a general store while Ferris waited in the car). But the significance of the timing of the two calls cannot be ignored: the one from Franklin's cabin in San Diego was followed *immediately* by Joanna's call to the police in L.A. In other words, Ferris must have been at Franklin's cabin when he was shot and Franklin was the murderer.

In "Now You See Him" (#34), we get a very unusual version of the slippery clue—an entire person disappears (and I don't mean the killer)! The idea of the episode is that The Great Santini's past is so shrouded in mystery that Columbo will not be able to uncover the fact that he was a Nazi, yet for some bizarre reason the writers give Santini a daughter. Of all the episodes in which a murderer might have relatives, this was not the place to include one (even if she doesn't know daddy's big secret, she could certainly help Columbo trace his prior movements in Europe). So, about half way through the episode, Della Santini simply disappears without explanation (yes, she is supposed to have run off with singer Danny Green, but Green is part of the last scene, so if Columbo could find him, he could definitely find Della). Now, there's a slippery clue.

Finally, here's an example from "Murder Under Glass" (#40) that isn't quite a slippery clue or a clue delayed. After Chef Albert explains how the bottle opener works, Columbo takes the cartridge in for testing (when he should take the whole opener), but as we learn, the poison was in the point of the opener, so no poison is found in the cartridge. This isn't exactly a clue delayed, because Columbo catches Paul Gerard not so much on physical evidence (which relates to his attempt to kill the Lieutenant, not the original crime) as on Gerard's ability to repeat the murder, which only the murderer would know how to do. And it isn't a slippery clue because, although it might prove too much if poison were discovered in the whole opener, that's not why he fails to examine the whole thing. The reason is that the writers want Gerard to switch the openers back and have Columbo subtly uncover the method Gerard used. The Lieutenant seems a lot cleverer this way in the end, but I still don't approve of him not following proper procedure earlier on to achieve this result. In addition, the episode should not hide the scene in which Gerard returns to the restaurant to exchange the openers a second time, because enough is kept hidden already (the exact method in which the murder is carried out) and because that's not playing fair.

Chapter 17:
Columbo Final Clues

Introduction to Columbo Final Clues

Columbo final clues fall into seven categories. The majority are of one of the following five kinds: evidence placing the murderer at the scene, tricks, confessions, alibi busters, and scenario busters. I invented this last term to describe those episodes that do not attack the murderer's explanation of where he/she was at the time of the crime (those are alibi busters), but which explode away the carefully constructed false scenario and leave the murderer exposed. For example, that's what it means in "Lady in Waiting" (#5) to show that the sequence of events doesn't fit the way Beth Chadwick describes (the shots in fact occurred before the alarm went off, so her brother didn't waken her from a deep sleep by breaking into her bedroom) and she must have shot him deliberately. See the essay "Busting Alibis, Busting Scenarios" for more on this kind of ending.

In addition, there are two special seldom-used endings. First, the "Kill Columbo Ending," in which the point is to finesse the murderer into recreating the details of the murder using Columbo as the victim. Second, the "Metaclue" ending in which Columbo demonstrates that the murder has been for naught. The murderer has sabotaged himself. See the essays that follow for more on these two special kinds of endings.

By far the most common ending is the one in which Columbo uncovers evidence that places the murderer at the scene of the crime. I find these endings to be the most satisfying in general, for several reasons. First, because they do not require the criminal to confess or slip up, I don't have to ask whether I believe they would actually make these errors. Second, assuming that the clue is a clever one (and it usually is), the ending is satisfying because Columbo wins the battle by finding something that the haughty criminal never imagined. This is especially true when the murderer thinks the Lieutenant is dull-witted and could not beat him or her. Not so surprisingly, my choices for the series' best episodes are those that employ this kind of ending: "By Dawn's Early Light" (#26) (Colonel Rumford's spotting of the cider fermenting places him next to the cannon on the morning that it blew up); "Columbo Cries Wolf" (#49) (Sean Brantley is caught with the body of Dian Hunter); "Try and Catch Me" (#39) (the deathbed testimony of Edmund's note is very powerful evidence, as the Lieutenant says); "Now You See Him" (#34) (the one-strike carbon ribbon not only provides the motive for why Santini killed Jesse Jerome, but the fact that, the night he was killed, Jerome was typing a letter and it has disappeared places the magician in the man's office); "Playback" (#28) (the presence on the video tape of the invitation Harold Van Wyck would later hand to the art gallery proves that he was there when his mother-in-law was killed; Columbo notes he had to step over the body to pick it up).

A particularly nice twist is when the murderer is caught because he sees something at the scene of the crime and, forgetting that he was not supposed to be there at that time, acts on this information and is incriminated. That's why it's so satisfying when Colonel Rumford's investigation into the fermenting cider proves to be his undoing. And that's why I like the trick in "A Deadly State of Mind" (#29). Marcus Collier thinks he can avoid capture by proving that his accuser is a blind man, not realizing that the only way he would know that a blind man was near the scene of the crime is that he almost ran over the man while speeding from the scene.

Of course, some "presence at the scene" final clues don't quite measure up. In "Dead Weight" (#3), finding the murder weapon hiding in plain sight at the Hollister exhibit is very conclusive (because it matches up to the bullet in the victim), but it wasn't a very clever plan for Hollister to leave it there. In addition, the whole device doesn't make sense because if Hollister decided years ago to pretend the gun was stolen, why did he and if he just made this up then the Marine Military Institute would be surprised. The flower that places Alex Benedict at the scene of the crime in "Etude in Black" (#8) leaves a lot to be desired because having it fall off there makes him look very sloppy. And in "Sex and the Married Detective" (#46), Joan Allenby is caught when a salesperson identifies the clothes she bought in Chicago to turn into "Lisa" the courtesan, but again, it's not particularly clever on her part to allow for this possibility.

The essays that follow will discuss the other kinds of endings in greater detail. Here is the complete list of episode endings (excluding the two McBain episodes, "No Time to Die" (#58) and "Undercover" (#62).

Episodes by kind of final clue:
I. Evidence of Presence at the Scene (24):
"Dead Weight" (#3) (the gun); "Etude in Black" (#8) (boutonniere); "The Greenhouse Jungle" (#9) (matching bullet); "A Stitch in Crime" (#13) (dissolving suture); "The Most Dangerous Match" (#14) (murderer had to be deaf); "Lovely But Lethal" (#16) (poison ivy); "Swan Song" (#22) (parachute); "An Exercise in Fatality" (#24) (changed victim's clothes); "By Dawn's Early Light" (#26) (cider); "Playback" (#28) (invitation); "Now You See Him" (#34) (message on carbon ribbon); "Fade in to Murder" (#36) (fingerprints on bullets); "Try and Catch Me" (#39) (message in safe); "The Conspirators" (#43) (scratch mark on bottle); "Sex and the Married Detective" (#46) (clothes); "Murder: A Self Portrait" (#48) (rag used on victim); "Columbo Cries Wolf" (#49) (the body); "Agenda for Murder" (#50) (piece of cheese); "Murder in Malibu" (#53) (victim's clothes); "Caution: Murder Can Be Hazardous to Your Health" (#55) (scratch mark on car); "Columbo and the Murder of a Rock Star" (#56) (berries in window well);

"Death Hits the Jackpot" (#57) (monkey's print on medallion); "A Bird in the Hand" (#59) (hair in Harold's hat); "Columbo Likes the Nightlife" (#67) (the body)

II. Tricks (18)
A. Piece of Evidence (8):
Ransom for a Dead Man (pilot B); "Blueprint for Murder" (#7); "Candidate for Crime" (#18); "Double Exposure" (#19); "A Friend in Deed" (#23); "Negative Reaction" (#25); "Troubled Waters" (#27); "Columbo Goes to College" (#54)

B. Incriminating Act (8):
"Death Lends a Hand" (#2); "Short Fuse" (#6); "Requiem for a Falling Star" (#12); "A Deadly State of Mind" (#29); "The Bye-Bye Sky High IQ Murder Case" (#38); "Make Me a Perfect Murder" (#41); "Murder, Smoke and Shadows" (#45); "A Trace of Murder" (#64)
C. Verbal Slip (2):
Prescription: Murder (pilot A); "Last Salute to the Commodore" (#35)

III. Confessions (8):
"Dagger of the Mind" (#11); "Mind Over Mayhem" (#21); "A Case of Immunity" (#31); "Old Fashioned Murder" (#37); "Rest in Peace, Mrs. Columbo" (#51); "Uneasy Lies the Crown" (#52); "It's All in the Game" (#60); "Strange Bedfellows" (#63)

IV. Scenario Busters (7):
"Murder By the Book" (#1); "Suitable for Framing" (#4); "Lady in Waiting" (#5); "Double Shock" (#15); "Publish or Perish" (#20); "Ashes to Ashes" (#65); "Murder With Too Many Notes" (#66)

V. Alibi Busters (5):

"The Most Crucial Game" (#10); "Forgotten Lady" (#30); "Identity Crisis" (#32); "Grand Deceptions" (#47); "Butterfly in Shades of Grey" (#61)

VI. Kill Columbo (3):

"Murder Under Glass" (#40); "How to Dial a Murder" (#42); "Columbo Goes to the Guillotine" (#44)

VIII. Metaclue (2):

"Any Old Port in a Storm" (#17); "A Matter of Honor" (#33)

The Three Cs of Columbo Trick Endings

Following evidence of the murderer's presence at the scene, the second most common type of ending is one in which Columbo catches the murderer by a trick. Tricks can be subdivided as follows: 1) those in which the murderer reveals a crucial piece of evidence; 2) those in which the murderer makes an incriminating act; and 3) those in which the murderer says something incriminating. I believe that these trick endings should be judged on the following criteria: conclusiveness, cleverness and credibility. Let's see how these factors are played out in the trick ending episodes.

Obviously, the final clue has to be conclusive. In other words, it has to be a piece of evidence or information that is so incriminating that it functions as the equivalent of hearing the killer confess or the jury say "we find the defendant guilty." For the most part, the show delivers conclusive final clues.

Pieces of evidence are particularly conclusive: the murderers can't argue their way out of it when they are caught with a tangible piece of evidence that incriminates them, like the missing body ("Blueprint for Murder" (#7)), the murder weapon ("Double Exposure" (#19)); "Columbo Goes to College" (#54)), the marked ransom money (*Ransom for a Dead Man* (pilot B)), their fingerprints on a pair of gloves (not the ones used in the murder, but a second pair used to try to frame someone else, in "Troubled Waters" (#27)), or some other piece of evidence that only they would possess or know about, such as the jewels in "A Friend in Deed" (#23), or the camera in "Negative Reaction" (#25). Nevertheless, the ending to "College," which looks a lot like the ending to "A Friend in Deed," does not work quite as well because "Friend in Deed" had the intermediary of the Bel Air Burglar black-mailing the murderers, leading to Commissioner Halperin trying to plant the "stolen" jewels at "his" apartment, only to learn that Columbo altered the file. In "College," the Lieutenant himself has to awkwardly reveal the information about the car to the frat boys and they put the murder weapon in what turns out to be Mrs. Columbo's car.

The second element by which a trick ending can be measured is its cleverness, which describes the trick itself (what Columbo does), as opposed to the issue of whether it is believable that the murderer would fall for this trick (that's the third element, credibility). In the episode "Candidate for Crime" (#18), there is no question that when Columbo pulls a bullet out of the wall (where Nelson Hayward fired it) and it matches the one in Harry Stone's body, that is a very conclusive clue. We also can't say that the trick was lacking in cleverness. Since cleverness really measures what Columbo does, it is difficult to apply that criterion here because Hayward pulls the trick on himself with no input from Columbo. And, to the extent that the issue is the cleverness of what Hayward sets up, I guess it is fairly clever. Naturally, all of these criteria are subjective, but I concede that this plan is an ingenious way to try to convince the police that Hayward is the target and not the murderer.

This brings me to the third factor, credibility, and here's where "Candidate" suffers. Ordinarily, credibility asks whether we can reasonably believe that the murderer would fall for the trick that Columbo has set in motion. But here the question is whether Hayward should attempt this stunt at all and I do not find it convincing that he would. In the first place, I wasn't convinced that Columbo put Hayward in a position where he would take this drastic step. Plus, he takes a significant risk of being caught (as he is) and conversely it is pure luck that Columbo can catch him by sacking out on the couch and waiting for Hayward to do it all himself.

Tricking the murderer into an incriminating action generally produces a conclusive ending, although "Requiem for a Falling Star" (#12) has a very inconclusive trick for a final clue—Nora Chandler doesn't even dig up her husband's body, but merely runs toward the fountain under which she buried it when Columbo shows her a Shriner's ring and implies that it belonged to her husband. This is probably because there's no plausible way to unearth the body: Columbo doesn't have enough for a warrant and Chandler (assuming she didn't notice that the ground was untouched) is unlikely to do all that dirty work. Thus, the episode cheats by having Chandler confess (to two murders, no less) without a good reason.

But the bigger issues with incriminating acts are their cleverness—that is, the measure of how creative Columbo's trick has been—and their credibility—whether we can believe that the murderer should fall into this trap. For example, our reaction to the ending of "Short Fuse" (#6) depends not only on whether we find the situation Columbo has put Roger Stanford in clever (trapped on the tram with an activated cigar box bomb), but also on whether, under the circumstances, we believe that Stanford would fall for it and attempt to get rid of the bomb. I do believe he would and I find that to be a powerful ending to this episode. The same questions can be asked of "The Bye-Bye Sky High IQ Murder Case" (#38). Is it clever of Columbo to finesse Oliver Brandt into supplying the missing piece of information about how the Rube Goldberg-type technique created the sound of the body falling (by setting a marker on the turntable so that the toner arm hit it and it fell on an unabridged dictionary between the squib "shots") and is it believable that Brandt would do it? Again, I think the answer to both questions is yes, although I know of others who disagree. I should also note that this ending can be seen as the germ of the Kill Columbo Ending later explored in the following seasons, but without the nagging question of why the murderer would take such a risk. (See the essay "The Kill Columbo Ending" for more on this topic.)

In "Death Lends a Hand" (#2), Columbo tricks Brimmer into attempting to dispose of a contact lens in his car trunk. Brimmer is made to believe that, as the victim's body was being transported, the contact fell out of her eye into the trunk. The Lieutenant admits to the victim's husband that both contacts are actually on the body, but says that he's arresting Brimmer based on his incriminating act. My problem with this ending is twofold. First, since it's obvious that Columbo planted the contact lens in the trunk, he ought to admit it. The fact that he doesn't raises the issue of whether the Lieutenant will admit to using unscrupulous methods to catch a murderer (see the essay "The Morality of Columbo II" for more on this topic). Second, and more important, since he's been dropping heavy-handed comments that he suspects Brimmer is the killer, if he put the contact lens in the trunk, Brimmer could legitimately argue that he was only trying to dispose of the false evidence the police had planted in an attempt to frame him for a crime he didn't commit. The trick is clever, and it's credible that Brimmer falls for it, but in the end it's not conclusive.

In "Make Me a Perfect Murder" (#41), Kay Freestone stashes the gun above the diffuser panel in an elevator. When she later thinks that the gun has become visible, she removes it and disposes of it. But this is not the real gun, because Columbo has already found it and replaced it with the one she tosses away. So she's caught based on her incriminating act, not a piece of evidence. It is conclusive (if she wasn't the murderer, she would just tell Columbo about the gun in the elevator), it is a clever idea and it is credible that she would fall for it. My problem is that hiding the gun in the way she did is not a good idea in the first place. It creates a "closed box" issue—there is no other solution than finding the gun that she put there, however cleverly Columbo goes about it.

"Murder, Smoke and Shadows" (#45) has a two-part ending that is very unsatisfying. Columbo almost connects Alex Brady to the victim's whereabouts by finding a ticket stub from the day of the murder in a yearbook in his game room. But Brady could have picked up the ticket stub himself and, even if Columbo places the victim in the game room, he fails to place Brady there at the same time. Indeed, Brady scoffs at this evidence and Columbo moves in for the kill by referring to Brady's conversation with his secretary in which he tried to bribe her to keep quiet about his having disposed of the phone log sheet for the day the victim called him. It's not just Brady's word against the secretary's because the entire conversation was overheard, in bits and pieces, by the busboy and waitress (both police officers) and the cocktail waitress (Brady's former lover, Ruth Jernigan). Setting aside the problems with the way this idea is executed (having people hear parts of a conversation makes it difficult to reconstruct, and you shouldn't use someone the murderer would recognize no matter how good it might feel for her), as an idea this is rather unimaginative. Any episode could end with a murderer trying to bribe a witness. It's not particularly clever, and since Brady is himself a master manipulator, I have a hard time buying that he'd fall for it. And as explained in "Get 'Em for the First Murder," the episode does not need to rely on these insubstantial clues when Columbo has in his possession a piece of film that incontrovertibly implicates Brady in another death, that of Lenny's sister Jenny years ago. Strangely, he shows the film, but only to serve as the motive for Lenny's murder.

On the other hand, "A Deadly State of Mind" (#29) has a fascinating trick ending. Marcus Collier is tricked into disputing the evidence against him—a man saying he saw him speed away from the murder scene—by claiming the witness is blind. Collier says this because, in fact, he nearly hit a blind man as he was speeding out of the driveway, and he thinks Columbo is trying to frame him with false evidence. But Collier hasn't seen through the layers of the Lieutenant's plan. Columbo has the brother of the blind man, who looks a lot like him, point the finger at Collier and of course he can see. As Columbo concludes, the eyewitness who puts Collier at the scene of the crime is none other than Collier himself. This is a brilliant trick which causes Collier to make an incriminating action (trying to discredit a witness's testimony on the grounds that he's blind), but only because it is so carefully constructed.

"A Trace of Murder" (#64) is disappointing because, although tricking the co-conspirators into pointing the finger at each other produces conclusive results, this technique is not very clever (it could be used anywhere). Also, at least with respect to Patrick Kinsley, a police forensic scientist who ought to know something about murder investigations, I think it's surprising that he falls for this old ploy so easily.

Tricking murderers into making a verbal slip is the least satisfying of the three kinds of trick. I have always said that what Columbo gets Dr. Flemming to admit at the end of *Prescription: Murder* (pilot A) is nearly impossible: I didn't kill my wife but if I did, it wasn't to be with my lover, but for the money and once the lover served her purpose I would have gotten rid of her too. Naturally, once Joan Hudson hears this, she turns on him so the clue is conclusive, but I don't believe that she would agree to fake her own death to test him in this way and I don't see how Flemming, brilliant psychiatrist that he is, would fall for this little charade. And "Last Salute to the Commodore" (#35), a bad episode in every measurable way, relies on a silly trick in which the murderer, upon having a ticking watch held next to his ear, says that it isn't the Commodore's watch because he broke it to frame his cousin for the murder. But even Swanny (who's none too bright) could and should say "who cares?" or "so what?" just like the other suspects gathered in the living room.

Confession Endings

There are various ways to describe the format of *Columbo*, but one of the most basic would be something like this: a brilliant villain plans and executes a murder convinced that the police will never figure it out. Enter a shabby cop, who keeps noticing little details that bother him, which he points out to the villain in a series of clever one-on-one dialogue scenes. The villain is alternately amused and frustrated by the cop, because he seems to be getting closer, but doesn't have enough to make an arrest. Then, in a powerful final scene, Columbo pulls out a piece of evidence that the criminal overlooked or could not have foreseen, or tricks the villain into producing a piece of evidence or making an incriminating act or slip of the tongue. Final curtain.

Sound familiar? That's a good description of most *Columbo* episodes, it's true, but how then do we account for a group of eight episodes in which the show ends with the villain's confession. A confession? From a villain who has kept the Lieutenant at bay for ninety minutes to two hours? Why? In other words, a confession ending is somewhat at odds with the basic *Columbo* structure and, for the most part, it really doesn't work as well as the ending in which Columbo pulls out a clue that nails the villain or the ending in which the villain is cleverly tricked into incriminating him or herself. These episodes are not among the show's best. Nevertheless, a confession ending can work if handled properly, and I want to briefly explore how it has been handled on *Columbo*, both successfully and otherwise.

First, let's list the confession ending episodes. It's true that Adrian Carsini agrees to confess, but it would be a disservice to say that "Any Old Port in a Storm" (#17) employs a confession ending. Nor do I consider it a confession ending if a sympathetic villain has been caught by a piece of evidence and then says "okay, I'll confess," as in "Swan Song" (#22). I count the ending as a confession only if the confession itself forms the basis for Columbo's arrest. After "Dagger of the Mind" (#11) and "Mind Over Mayhem" (#21), the next confession appears in "A Case of Immunity" (#31), followed by "Old Fashioned Murder" (#37). From the newer crop of episodes, we have four confession endings: "Rest in Peace, Mrs. Columbo" (#51); "Uneasy Lies the Crown" (#52); "It's All in the Game" (#60) and "Strange Bedfellows" (#63). And for the sake of completeness, I must mention "Forgotten Lady" (#30), in which we actually hear a confession (on the basis of which Columbo makes an arrest), but: 1) it's not from the actual murderer; and 2) Columbo has presented a typical (if rather weak) alibi buster final clue in the form of the time lapse, that is, why it took Grace Wheeler fifteen minutes to splice a broken section of film when the process can be completed in less than five. It is my contention that the episode deliberately utilizes a final clue designed to make Ned Diamond confess; it would be far less satisfactory if it had been used to nail Grace. In any event, it's not my focus here.

There are two criteria by which we can measure the success of a confession ending. To address the basic question of why a villain who has eluded capture would confess, the episode must provide a convincing answer or no one is going to buy it. There must be a very good reason why this person is confessing, and the situation in which the confession takes place should make sense to the viewers; if it doesn't, the ending fails. Thus far, the show has utilized three reasons: fear of greater harm from another person, compulsion arising from psychological illness, and desire to save another person (plus three episodes where villains confess for no apparent reason). Second, we must be convinced that the villain won't recant the confession. There are two ways to do this: the villain can provide a detail of the crime that only the murderer would know, or the situation must be so constructed that recanting is just not an option (this is often the case in the save someone else and fear of greater harm situations).

I think "Mind Over Mayhem" (#21) does a decent job. Marshall Cahill confesses because the case against his son Neil looks serious, because he doesn't know if Columbo will proceed with it (using a combination of real and fake clues) and because he killed to save Neil in the first place. Cahill isn't about to recant and let Columbo go after Neil again, so the ending is fairly solid. But Columbo's methods raise other issues (see "The Morality of Columbo II"). The other "save someone else" episode is "It's All in the Game" (#60). This episode troubles me for various reasons (see the two "Morality of Columbo" essays) but, as examined from the ending (when we know everything), Lauren Staton's confession is a lot like Marshall Cahill's. She confesses to save her daughter and she's not about to recant. That's the deal she makes with Columbo—he can have her, but not her daughter. Whatever I might think about Columbo's behavior in this episode (and I have a lot of issues about him letting off an accomplice, flirting with a suspect and lying to everyone), the confession ending works here as it does in "Mind Over Mayhem" (#21) and maybe a little better, since Staton's motive is more sympathetic than Cahill's.

The ending to "A Case of Immunity" (#31) works if we accept that the self-satisfied character of Hassan Salah would admit his crime in a scene in which he believes that: 1) he has diplomatic immunity protecting him from prosecution; 2) the Lieutenant has been taken off the case and is powerless to do anything; and 3) he gets a kick out of "congratulating" Columbo for his cleverness while still walking away scot-free. I think it is a very believable scene, as is Salah's actual confession and waiver of his diplomatic immunity to prevent prosecution in his own country. And Salah is certainly not going to recant or the King will take him home and remove his head (fear of greater harm). Less satisfying is the newer episode, "Strange Bedfellows" (#63). Well, since Graham McVeigh honestly believes that the mob was about to kill him and that the police were powerless to stop it, he probably would confess to save himself (who wouldn't?). And by having him reveal the location of an important piece of evidence, the episode ensures that he's not going to get out of it. But it isn't particularly clever to have the mob threaten to kill the man (as compared to the clever handling of the diplomatic immunity situation with Salah), not to mention the moral implications of Columbo getting into bed with these folks. So "Strange Bedfellows" (#63) works on a technical level, but it still leaves me feeling very unsatisfied. (See "The Morality of Columbo II" for more on this topic.)

The conclusion to "Rest in Peace, Mrs. Columbo" (#51) works, more or less, if we buy the premise of the deranged criminal who believes that she has killed Mrs. Columbo and that the Lieutenant himself is about to die from ingesting poison. As her psychiatrist explains, under such circumstances she would be compelled to admit the crime to get the satisfaction of it, regardless of any possible consequences to herself (and to her it looks as if there will be none). She also divulges an incriminating detail (that she made the ATM withdrawal) so she cannot recant. My problem is that I find this premise very poor for a *Columbo*. Note what I said above: the villains are supposed to be intelligent and clever, not crazy. Following her disturbed plan to its conclusion takes very little effort on Columbo's part, unlike plotting a trick designed to make a clever villain confess.

That leaves the three episodes where the villain confesses for no good reason. In "Dagger of the Mind" (#11), Columbo plants a bead in the victim's umbrella to trick murderers Nicholas Frame and Lillian Stanhope into thinking he has evidence that they were at the scene of the crime. Nicky starts babbling incoherently and Lilly finally turns to Chief Superintendent Durk and tells him that it was an accident. I should note here that I used to classify this ending as a trick, one designed either to induce the pair into incriminating themselves by their actions or to make them utter a verbal slip. I have changed my mind and reclassified it as a confession ending for two reasons. First, it was becoming impossible for me to draw any distinction between it and the ending to "Uneasy Lies the Crown" (#52), which is analyzed next. Almost all confession endings employ some kind of trickery, but the point is to induce the murderers to confess, not to produce incriminating evidence, engage in incriminating actions or make a verbal slip. Second, I concluded that, to the extent we can ask what Columbo was trying to accomplish here, the answer must be that he expected the murderers simply to give up when they saw that bead hit the floor. He could not have expected Nicky to lose his grip on reality, nor could he have anticipated that Lilly would turn to Chief Superintendent Durk for help when that happened. But there is no real reason why they should confess when they see the bead, nor should Nicky start quoting Shakespeare. The one scene that lays any ground for this is when Nicky, who is reluctantly preparing to kill Tanner, the first victim's butler who is blackmailing them, starts goofing around. But his wife just thinks he's acting and how do we know otherwise? More importantly, Columbo is not present, so he does not know that Nicky is teetering on the edge of sanity (if in fact he is). Thus, his plan (for them to toss in their hats upon seeing the false evidence) is a long shot and it's pure luck that it works, for any reason. On top of all that, the trick requires that Sir

Roger's umbrella hang on the wax figure's arm in a semi-closed position (without the strap being fastened) and it looks very unnatural. How did Columbo know the umbrella would be displayed in this fashion? Finally, nothing would prevent the pair from recanting later.

"Uneasy Lies the Crown" (#52), which has a lot of interesting clues and a complicated plot, has the same confession ending in response to a trick. It is one of the series' biggest letdowns. Why does Wesley Corman confess? Columbo hasn't proved a thing—Wesley falls for the trick with the laundry bluing because, we're told, he knows nothing about chemistry. But he's been a nasty villain until now, so why throw in the towel? And nothing stops him from recanting. It would have been far better if Columbo's trick made Wesley do something incriminating, or at least admit some detail of the crime that only he would have known. Or, as discussed in "The Kill Columbo Ending," this might have been one of those rare times when the Lieutenant should finesse the murderer into demonstrating the same technique (putting digitalis in a crown) that he used on the victim.

Finally, "Old Fashioned Murder" (#37) does not work, but that's par for the course for this confusing episode. Ruth Lytton kills her brother to save the family museum so that she can leave it to her niece, then frames the niece for the murder, and then confesses when Columbo agrees to withdraw his theory that Ruth killed the niece's father years ago?! This mess is inexplicable at any level, and Ruth's confession is far from convincing. I cannot imagine why she wouldn't recant tomorrow, given her knack for changing course, and the belt buckle clue (which is very insubstantial) won't stop her.

In conclusion, confession endings on *Columbo* work best if the situation is credible and recanting not possible, although they are not the most satisfying of endings. The episodes with these endings run the gamut from good ("A Case of Immunity" (#31)) to bad ("Old Fashioned Murder" (#37)).

Busting Alibis, Busting Scenarios

In an alibi buster ending, the murderer has created a scenario in which his or her entire strategy is to create an ironclad alibi. Thus, when Columbo cracks a hole in this alibi, the murderer is supposed to be left revealed. An alibi buster ending actually provides two inferences in one clue, because it demonstrates that the criminal knew at the time of the murder that he or she would have to fabricate this supposedly airtight alibi.

However, I usually find the alibi buster to be a less than satisfying ending. Not only does it not directly incriminate the murderer, but sometimes I can easily come up with arguments as to why it doesn't even carry much weight in its own right.

The first alibi buster appears in the second season episode "The Most Crucial Game" (#10). Paul Hanlon, manager of a football team, has killed the team owner, Eric Wagner, during a game for reasons that the episode never makes clear. The way he sets up the situation, he calls Wagner from the owner's box as a game is beginning. Wagner, who is at home dozing after a night of carousing, is told to get in the swimming pool because the men have to leave for a trip later. Then Hanlon, disguised as an ice cream vendor, leaves the stadium and drives to a location near the Wagner house. He calls a second time and uses a radio to make it sound as if he's still in the box. He is aware that the conversation is being recorded and he will use the tape to prove that he could not have killed Wagner several minutes later because he was miles away at the stadium. But Columbo busts this alibi by demonstrating that Hanlon wasn't in the box. At the time he called, a clock in the box chimed when it hit a half-hour mark, but the tape contains no chime.

This is a very weak ending. All Hanlon has to say is that the clock was running slow at that point, and he adjusted it during the week so that, when Columbo tests his theory one week later, it chimes at the proper time. Moreover, since the Lieutenant never investigates Hanlon's motive and has no other evidence against the man, the alibi buster feels very incomplete.

The second alibi buster is a special case, "Forgotten Lady" (#30). On the surface, it is also a weak ending. Columbo demonstrates to Ned Diamond that Grace Wheeler shot her husband because the film she was supposedly watching at the time broke and she didn't fix it for fifteen minutes because she wasn't really there. Of course there are plenty of other possibilities, the most obvious one being that Grace had fallen asleep and didn't awaken for eleven or so minutes. However, in this unusual episode, the point appears to be to get Ned to "confess" to a crime he didn't commit, because the Lieutenant is reluctant to arrest Grace, who doesn't even remember having killed her husband (see "The Morality of Columbo I" for more on this ending). Thus, the alibi buster doesn't have to bear as much weight, and so it fares better than the typical such ending in this one-time case.

The next two alibi busters are disappointing, however. In "Identity Crisis" (#32), Columbo proves that Nelson Brenner's audio tape of a speech was not made on the night when the killing occurred, but the next morning. Otherwise, the tape would not have contained the information that the Chinese were pulling out of the Olympics, news that had just been reported at 6:20 a.m. But because he's a spy, Brenner could claim any reason he wanted, particularly national security, for faking an alibi or anything else he does, so this is very inconclusive. Brenner has already told Columbo that he doesn't need an alibi, so there's no reason for him to accept defeat when the Lieutenant pokes holes in the one he provides. A more conclusive ending would have resulted if Columbo had demonstrated that Brenner was Steinmetz, so that the CIA would have dealt with him even if he couldn't be arrested for the murder, although the police artist's drawing showing that Brenner could have been dressed as Steinmetz is not definitive either.

A different problem plagues "Grand Deceptions" (#47), in which Columbo tries to prove that Colonel Brailie was not busy setting up Civil War miniatures for General Padget at the time of the murder because the box he received at that hour actually contained the books (he had set up the miniatures earlier in the day). In this case, the switched boxes idea simply doesn't work, because there would have to be either a paper trail or a human one. That is, if Brailie had the labels switched at the factory (assuming the same company manufactured both the miniatures and the books), someone would have made the switch and could be called as a witness. Alternatively, if both boxes were delivered to Brailie elsewhere, there would be a record of this transaction and this doesn't really explain why the miniatures don't arrive until nightfall. And if the General didn't keep the empty boxes, then the clue is impossible to prove because the two box sizes are too close for Columbo to rely on someone's memory as to which one came first. The idea might have worked better had the writers used the same size box with different weights (noted on the postmarks) for miniatures and books.

A variation on the alibi buster ending is what I call the "scenario buster." In these episodes, Columbo doesn't demonstrate that the criminal's alibi is full of holes. Rather, he punctures the scenario that the murderer has created and presumably, the only alternative is a scenario in which the villain stands incriminated. The first example occurs in the very first episode, "Murder By the Book" (#1). Ken Franklin takes his partner Jim Ferris to his cabin in San Diego. Because Ferris is worried about getting home late, Franklin asks him to call his wife Joanna and tell her he's working late at the office, as he often does. As he does so, Franklin shoots him. Joanna hears this and calls the police, who arrive to find Ferris's office ransacked. The body is not there, however—it arrives later when Franklin, who has driven back from San Diego, deposits it on his own front yard, setting up the scenario that Ferris was killed by mobsters about whom he was writing an exposé and the body was dumped at Franklin's to warn him not to continue Ferris's work.

Columbo claims to bust this scenario by scouring Ferris's notes and discovering that the whole plot was an idea the writers had for a mystery. I think that this is an interesting observation, but not a very conclusive piece of evidence. Mystery writers have lots of ideas, but the similarity of one to a murder doesn't mean it actually happened that way. What is more disappointing is that the episode already contains the seeds of a far better ending in the sequence of telephone calls. This clue is actually raised, but then dropped, so it qualifies as a "slippery clue" (see "Intermediate Clues").

The next scenario buster is the episode "Suitable for Framing" (#4). Dale Kingston kills his uncle to inherit his art collection, but the inheritance actually goes to Kingston's Aunt Edna (the uncle's ex-wife). So Kingston has to incriminate her, which he intends to do by placing some of the "stolen" paintings in her house and then getting the police to search it. Before Kingston has a chance to complete his plan, Columbo manages to touch the paintings while they are in Kingston's possession. When they are found in Aunt Edna's house, the Lieutenant shows that they have his prints on them. Note that Columbo's fingerprints don't place Kingston at the scene of the crime, but they do poke holes in the scenario he has created. My problem with this ending is not the idea but the execution of it. The manner in which the Lieutenant gets his prints on the paintings is very difficult to set up and (I think) hard to believe: he goes to Kingston's place to look around, falls asleep and is there to stick his hand into Kingston's briefcase when he comes home with the paintings.

The very next episode, "Lady in Waiting" (#5), also contains a scenario buster. Beth Chadwick shoots her brother Bryce and wants it to look like an accident—he lost his key and came in through her bedroom window, setting off the alarm. Unfortunately for her, Bryce has a spare key, so when she shoots him anyway, the shots ring out before she activates the alarm. Her fiancé, Peter Hamilton, who is just arriving at the house at that moment to have it out with Bryce, hears this sequence and that is what convicts her. Although conclusive, this is a weak ending to a weak episode. Beth does not come off looking very intelligent, because all of Columbo's clues result from her mistake.

In "Double Shock" (#15), Columbo builds a case that either Dexter Paris or his identical twin brother Norman killed their uncle, but he can't prove which one. The solution, he discovers, is that it took two people to commit the crime (demonstrated by the facts that it takes two people to lift a body out of the bathtub and that the short period of time the power was out means a second person was waiting in the basement to change the fuse) and they collaborated on it (see "Variations on a Theme by Jackson Gillis"). The final clue is a list from the telephone company, demonstrating that these two brothers, who have pretended to hate each other, actually spoke many times recently, presumably to plan this heinous deed. But that's resting far too much weight on the telephone calls, which is very uninspired.

The third season episode "Publish or Perish" (#20) is Peter Fischer's first attempt at writing for the series and he packs a lot into its ninety minutes. In the complicated plot, Riley Greenleaf hires Eddie Kane to shoot Allen Mallory and leave several clues. What Kane doesn't know is that it will look as if Greenleaf was being framed, and Kane is going to be the one doing it. Greenleaf completes the plan by blowing Kane up with one of the man's own homemade bombs. The scenario is that Kane killed Mallory and framed Greenleaf for it because the men stole his book idea. But Columbo busts this scenario by showing that the outline in Kane's filing cabinet (placed there by Greenleaf) impossibly contains the ending to the book that Mallory's agent just came up with. I admire Fisher's attempt here, but I think the better course would have been to have Columbo prove that Greenleaf killed Kane (see "Get 'Em for the First Murder"). This ending is difficult to explain and doesn't have a dramatic punch.

"Ashes to Ashes" (#65) and "Murder With Too Many Notes" (#66) are very similar and both employ a scenario buster ending. In "Ashes," mortician Eric Prince kills Verity Chandler and cremates her body while he is supposed to be cremating cowboy film star Chuck Huston. This requires him to cremate Huston the next day, together with some schlimazel named Mel Lerby. Columbo finds Huston's stainless steel shrapnel piece in Lerby's ashes and the scenario is busted. Or is it? All Prince has to say is that he didn't clean out the oven sufficiently after cremating Huston and his shrapnel piece was left and got mixed in with Lerby's ashes. I like the idea here, but they should have carried it one step further. If Columbo found a piece of Chandler herself (her pager, for example, which we're told was on the body), then he would really have Prince caught. Rather than merely busting the scenario, Columbo could have connected Prince to the crime itself.

In "Murder With Too Many Notes" (#66), movie music conductor Findlay Crawford tries to make it look like his protégé Gabriel McEnery fell off the roof where the younger man liked to conduct in time with Crawford. Columbo demonstrates that an elevator ascended and tossed the man off the roof. He points out that McEnery's baton fell down the shaft when it opened. Why didn't McEnery hear the elevator approaching? Because he was unconscious—Columbo demonstrates that McEnery was given seco-barbital (it dissipated in his system, but he cut his hand and that spot retained the drug). And Columbo points out that McEnery didn't put on his own shoes, because he didn't wear dress shoes and the ones on his feet are the wrong size. Columbo doesn't really have a final clue here, he just sums up the clues he's gathered and arrests Crawford, but the idea is that he busts the killer's scenario.

Finally, an interesting variation can be seen in "Butterfly in Shades of Grey" (#61). Fielding Chase creates a scenario in which it appears that Jerry Winters was shot in the back by a jealous lover as he happened to be talking to Chase on the phone. In fact, Chase is in Winters's den, on the extension. After he "hears the shots," Chase gets in his car and calls 911 on his cell phone. Columbo demonstrates that Chase could not have been at or near his home, because his cell phone cannot get a signal in the remote mountains where he lives. In one sense, this is an alibi buster: it proves Chase was not where he claims to have been right after the murder. But it also attacks the scenario, because the only way Chase could have called 911 moments after hearing the shots is if he had fired them himself. This is the program's most effective alibi/scenario buster ending.

Ironically, this situation is the reverse of the one presented in "Murder By the Book" (#1), in which the murderer tricks the victim into saying that he is "at the office" when he isn't and then shoots him. Even more ironically, "Butterfly" uses a telephone clue to catch Chase, which is what I propose as a better ending for "Murder By the Book" (#1). See "Intermediate Clues."

The Kill Columbo Ending

During the seventh season of the show in 1977-78, a new concept was introduced: the Kill Columbo Ending. First, a little definition is in order: the Kill Columbo Ending is not what happens any time a villain considers, or even tries to do away with the Good Lieutenant, nor is the point of the ending to arrest the villain for the attempted murder of Columbo. The Kill Columbo Ending cannot be used indiscriminately in any episode. Its use depends on the murder method containing some element of the unknown: either it looks like an accident or is in some sense committed by "remote control." The important characteristic is that there must be information about the murder known only to the murderer. If the victim was gunned down, having the murderer pull a gun on Columbo doesn't provide information that is known only to the murderer. Rather, the ending works like this: the murder investigation is missing a piece known to the killer. The villain is getting very irritated with the detective. Because the murder contains some element that cannot be proved, he decides to kill Columbo in the same way the original victim was killed. Finally, the opportunity presents itself. Of course this is no coincidence, because it is Columbo orchestrating these events, finessing the villain into this act and then using it to prove he knew how the original crime was committed.

Note that none of the following episodes use this ending: "Lady in Waiting" (#5) (when Beth Chadwick pulls a gun on Columbo, but he arrests her based on Peter Hamilton's remembered sequence of events); "Rest in Peace, Mrs. Columbo" (#51) (when Vivian Dimitri thinks she's poisoning the Lieutenant, but the purpose is to get her to confess); and "Butterfly in Shades of Grey" (#61) (when Fielding Chase begins to pull a shotgun out of his car trunk, but Columbo—who doesn't even see it—arrests him based on the fact that he could not have gotten a cell phone signal from the area near his house, so he must have called 911 from the murder scene). It is extremely dramatic, which is why its use has only occurred during episodes produced during the Richard Alan Simmons era, when emphasis was placed on the dramatic. It has only been used three times: "Murder Under Glass" (#40), "How to Dial a Murder" (#42), and "Columbo Goes to the Guillotine" (#44). Note that the seeds of this idea can be seen in "The Bye-Bye Sky High IQ Murder Case" (#38), in which the scenario contains an element of the unknown (how the sound of the body falling was made to occur between the sounds of the shots), and Columbo tricks the villain into revealing it during a recreation, at no peril to himself.

The problem with this ending, however, is that it raises at least two questions: 1) What will the murderer do next—leave town (which he could and should do before trying to do away with Columbo) or stay (hoping against hope that it will all go away now)? 2) Why did such a brilliant murderer resort to such a stupid move? One can debate whether Paul Galesko in "Negative Reaction" (#25) should know better than to identify the camera or whether Marcus Collier in "A Deadly State of Mind" (#29) should simply say "he's lying" instead of "he's blind," but both of these moves are a far cry from actually plotting out and attempting to kill the detective. The incriminating acts are arguably believable (perhaps under the strain, the murderers slipped, looking for a way out), but these preplanned murders are not. If the murderer plans to kill Columbo and then hop on the first plane out of the country, we must ask how he knows there aren't police hiding in the next room. Moreover, if escape was his intention, why not leave before the final meeting with Columbo, hoping to make a getaway before he's caught? The second possibility is even less credible—kill Columbo and resume life as usual in L.A. Even assuming that Columbo hasn't communicated his theory about the case to other police officers (and the murderer has no way of knowing that, although viewers who have seen even a few episodes know that Columbo works alone), there is usually enough information around for it to be impossible to claim that Columbo's death was an accident.

In "Murder Under Glass" (#40), the ending "fits" at least in a dramatic sense. Nevertheless, the ending does not answer the questions of why Gerard would make such a move and what he intends to do afterward. Neither of the two possible scenarios under which Gerard might try to kill the detective works in this case. First, his thought might be to kill Columbo and then hop on the first plane out of the country. But how does he know there aren't police surrounding the restaurant? If that was his intention, why not leave in the morning before his meeting with Columbo, hoping to make a getaway before he is arrested? Can he really believe that he could kill Columbo and resume life as usual in L.A.? Gerard has no way of knowing whether other police officers know what Columbo does. It is already officially known that Gerard was eating dinner with Rossi shortly before the man's death, that the poison was fugu and that Columbo would be meeting with the killer that day in order to have him under arrest by dinner time. Could Gerard really believe that he could get away with such a thing twice, that the police scrutiny would not be doubled, not merely for a second murder, but for that of a policeman? Can it be that this man, who so brilliantly orchestrated the cleverest how-to plot of the series, is so dumb that he is caught trying to bump off the investigator? I don't think so, and ultimately it is this major problem that causes me to relegate this episode to the very good category, and low in that category as well (see Appendix I).

Similarly, in "Columbo Goes to the Guillotine" (#44), the detective has passed along his suspicions that Max Dyson was murdered with the guillotine, so if he winds up beheaded as well, the LAPD is not about to sit still for it. Of course, the "Guillotine" episode has a lot more problems than these two questions, because the trick simply doesn't "work" there. Just because Eliot Blake knows how to operate a guillotine doesn't prove he used one to kill Max Dyson. Also, Blake doesn't alter how the object works, in the way that Gerard puts fugu in wine or in the way that Eric Mason trains his Dobermans to kill on hearing a specific word in "How to Dial a Murder" (#42). "Guillotine" is a less-than-satisfying episode on many levels, and its use of the Kill Columbo Ending is yet another one of them.

Surprisingly, "How to Dial a Murder" (#42) actually answers the two questions very nicely: Mason can return to life as usual (if that's what he plans on doing, although after murdering all the people close to him and driving out Joanne Nichols, one wonders what the point is) or escape because he has the best explanation anyone could ever ask for. He was resigned to the fact that the dogs would have to be destroyed, and it was this crazy Lieutenant who kept them alive and, in pushing them around, caused them to attack him. And the reason why he would attempt such a risky move as killing the detective is twofold: his method is so obscure that no one will be able to prove he did it, and Columbo has put all the clues pointing toward him right out on the billiard table. That's why I propose that Mason orders the dogs to kill not because Columbo taunts and insults him (a ridiculous notion considering that his profession is to teach people to take control of their lives and not let words control them), but because he sees the opportunity to do away with Columbo and all the physical clues. Could there be cops in the next room? Maybe, but unlikely (he probably would have passed them on his way in).

Thus, there are very few instances when this ending could be employed (and it has problems for the reasons cited above). Ironically, I think it might have been employed and worked better than the "Confession Ending" used in "Uneasy Lies the Crown" (#52) (where Wesley Corman confesses for no reason). Columbo could hound Corman until he prepares another crown filled with digitalis and prepares to put it in Columbo's mouth, only to be intercepted by Dr. Johnson and handed to the lab boys for analysis. It would have been a lot more satisfying than Corman's sorry confession because he bought the idea that digitalis would stain the victim's crown blue.

The Metaclue Ending

As much as everyone (including me) loves the episode "Any Old Port in a Storm" (#17), we must admit that the fascinating conclusion does not actually prove that Adrian Carsini killed his half-brother Ric by tying him up and leaving him in the wine cellar where he suffocated. It's true that Columbo's comment about the very hot day while Adrian was away induces the wine maker to check his stock of expensive wines in the cellar, but all that demonstrates is that Adrian knew that the air conditioning was off and that only now does he understand the effect the lack of air conditioning had on his collection. He could try to claim that he turned off the air conditioning to save money because it wasn't really necessary at this time of year, but that would be very inconsistent with his character, a man who just spent $5,000 on a bottle of wine (not so coincidentally, the same amount he sent to Ric knowing he'd get it back). The AC is on the day Columbo and Adrian go inside, and it still isn't the height of the summer, so that explanation just won't wash. But Adrian does have a very good option: he can simply claim that the AC malfunctioned while he was away and that he got it fixed but thought nothing of it until Columbo told him about the day it reached 109 degrees outside. That comports with all the facts and has nothing to do with Ric's death. But this is what I call a "metaclue" ending, and proving what happened is not the point.

In this variation on a theme, Columbo does not prove that the murderer killed the victim—not by trick, not by evidence that the murderer was at the scene, not by any means. Rather, he demonstrates that whatever the murderer was trying to accomplish has been for naught, that whatever item the murderer held dear and killed to protect has been harmed despite his best efforts. In so doing, Columbo creates a situation in which the murderer might as well give up and confess, because the whole point of the murder has been undermined and the murderer has nowhere else to go.

The only other example of the metaclue on *Columbo* is in the fifth season episode "A Matter of Honor" (#33), in which Columbo reveals the very thing Luis Montoya killed to keep secret—his cowardice when confronted by the bull. Columbo hasn't proved that Montoya killed Hector Rangel, but he reveals the motive, and that's even more damaging to the matador who was famous for his courage. When that happens, it knocks all the fight out of Montoya and he turns himself in. I object to the injection of a "traditional" *Columbo* final clue following the scene in the bullring. Columbo tells Comandante Sanchez about the lack of water marks on the cape, supposedly further eroding Montoya's claim that Rangel fought the bull later in the day. With the high winds at that hour Rangel would have had to use water to prevent the cape from flying around and attracting the bull's attention. This observation, although true, doesn't qualify as a *Columbo* final clue because it isn't very conclusive and, more importantly, because it is totally unrelated to the scene with Montoya and the bull. Columbo tells Sanchez that the lack of water marks convinced him that Montoya was lying about the timing of Rangel in the bullring, but he was already convinced that Montoya was the killer and this observation has no connection with the setup that reveals what Montoya worked so hard to keep quiet. Montoya isn't arrested because the water mark clue proves he did it; he hands his cape and sword to Columbo for having brought to light the only reason he killed his unfortunate friend in the first place. The writers should have stuck to their guns and gone with the metaclue ending, although I admit it is not as satisfying as the ending in "Any Old Port."

As these examples demonstrate, you can't use the metaclue randomly. Indeed, it should be used very sparingly or it loses its ability to satisfy the audience. First, it can only be used in a situation in which the murderer has killed to protect a secret about himself or to save some aspect of his life that he holds dear. It is completely inappropriate when the motive is money ("Double Shock" (#15)), or advancement ("A Stitch in Crime" (#13)), or the cover-up of past wrongdoing ("An Exercise in Fatality" (#24)). Second, although the revelation can be brought to light by Columbo, the actual undermining of the murderer's motive works best if the Lieutenant was not the cause of it. Perhaps this is why the ending to "Any Old Port" is more satisfying than that of "A Matter of Honor"—the poetic justice that it was Adrian himself who, in killing his brother, ruined his own wines. And, of course, it must be done cleverly or we won't appreciate it. If Columbo dropped off the blueprint with the board members in "By Dawn's Early Light" (#26) and thereby induced them to vote for the coed junior college that Rumford killed to prevent, I don't think we would be happy when Rumford confessed because his plan had not worked.

An example of where this scenario doesn't apply and/or work is the newer episode "Uneasy Lies the Crown" (#52). Columbo tells murderer Wesley Corman that his use of digitalis on the tooth of the victim has been stained blue, and "demonstrates" this proposition with a kid's chemistry set. When he goes to remove the actual tooth, Wesley simply gives up. This is not a metaclue ending for several reasons: 1) Wesley hasn't killed to protect a secret or keep some aspect of his life that means everything to him, just his gambling habit; 2) Columbo doesn't reveal that Wesley's plan was for naught, he merely tricks him into thinking that a piece of evidence points to him as the murderer (and it actually doesn't, as Columbo is making this up); and 3) if Wesley simply stood his ground, he'd be able to walk away, even though he wouldn't have a rich father-in-law anymore (any how long did he think he could shame the family that hated him into keeping him around anyway?).

While I'm not in favor of overuse of the metaclue, in the right circumstances (as in "Any Old Port"), it can make for a powerful conclusion.

ABC *Mystery Movie* Stars Gideon Oliver (Louis Gossett) Columbo (Peter Falk) and B.L. Stryker (Burt Reynolds)

Agenda for Murder with Oscar Finch (Patrick McGoohan)

Any Old Port in a Storm with Karen Fielding (Julie Harris)
and Adrian Carsini (Donald Pleasance)

Columbo Cries Wolf
with Sean Brantley
(Ian Buchanan)

Caution Murder Can be Hazardous to Your Health
with Wade Anders (George Hamilton)

Columbo Goes to the Guillotine

Columbo and the Murder of a Rock Star
with Hugh Creighton (Dabney Coleman)

Columbo gets Dog some water

Columbo meets Shera Danese

Columbo is winded after a run in
An Exercise in Fatality

Columbo teaches a class in *Columbo Goes to College*

Columbo's portrait from *Murder A Self Portrait*

Death Hits the Jackpot with Leon Lamarr (Rip Torn)

Double Shock with Dexter Paris (Martin Landau)

It's All in the Game with Lauren Staton (Faye Dunaway)

Leslien Williams (Lee Grant) gets a message in *Ransom for a Dead Man*

Make Me a Perfect Murder with Kay Freestone (Trish Van Devere)

Murder in Malibu with Wayne Jennings (Andrew Stevens)

Patrick McGoohan, guest murderer on 4 episodes

Peter Falk 1989

Peter Falk autograph

Playback with Harold Van Wyck (Oscar Werner)

Rest in Peace Mrs. Columbo with Vivian Dimitri (Helen Shaver)

Robert Culp as Jordan Rowe, father of a murderer in *Columbo Goes to College*

Sex and the Married Detective with Joan Allenby (Lindsay Crouse)

The Great Santini
(Jack Cassidy) in
Now You See Him

Thomas Mitchell who played Columbo in the *Prescription Murder* play

Uneasy Lies the Crown with Wesley Corman (James Read)

Chapter 18:
Variations and Non-Columbos

Variations on a Theme by Jackson Gillis

When an episode of *Columbo* opens with a credit that it was written by veteran mystery writer Jackson Gillis (formerly a writer on *Perry Mason*), it's anyone's guess what we're about to see. Sometimes (indeed, in six out of the eleven episodes which Gillis has at least partial screen credit for having written), the episode is completely traditional: the audience witnesses the murder first, and the Lieutenant follows the clues to a one-on-one dialogue with the killer, whom he eventually catches by trick or evidence. For the record, these episodes run the gamut from some of the series' best to some of its worst. They are: "Suitable for Framing" (#4), "Short Fuse" (#6), "Dagger of the Mind" (#11), "The Most Dangerous Match" (#14), "Lovely But Lethal" (#16)·and "Troubled Waters" (#27). But that's only half the picture. The other half of the time Gillis, a veteran mystery writer, experiments with the *Columbo* format, not as seriously as the changes wrought by trying to adapt Ed McBain novels into *Columbo* episodes (see "No Time for Columbo, No Place for McBain"), but in significant ways nonetheless. Here is a brief look at some of his variations on a theme.

Gillis's first experiment arrives in the second season episode "Requiem for a Falling Star" (#12). In that episode, Gillis allows the audience and Columbo to think that the murder of Jean Davis was a tragic mistake; what murderer Nora Chandler really intended to do was blow up nosy journalist

Jerry Parks, who may have some new dirt on her, not her own long-suffering secretary. Thus, Nora faints when she hears what really happened and appears to try again to kill Parks, but once again she misses. Columbo, however, tells her Parks is at death's door and that he "has" something on her— namely her late husband's Shriner's ring, which Columbo intimates was dug up from the fountain in her back yard where her husband is buried. Now we learn that Jean was the intended victim in the first place, because she knew of Nora's previous murder and might spill the beans to Parks if they wed. Unfortunately, this twist raises more questions than it answers. Why kill Jean if she hasn't revealed this secret before now? Why not kill Parks and be done with it? Also, Nora seems to assume that, by making Jean's death look like the attempted murder of Parks for which Nora appears to have a motive that she later proves doesn't exist, the police will keep looking for Parks's enemies (excluding her) and she'll never be suspected again. This hope is unrealistic. The plot puts her far too much in the spotlight, no matter who the intended victim is.

His second experiment comes in the second season finale "Double Shock" (#15). In this episode, Columbo cannot figure out whether Dexter Paris or his twin brother Norman killed their uncle, Clifford, but it turns out that they both collaborated in the crime. The idea of using identical twins (or even people who look alike), either one of which could have committed a murder, is not new. With twins, there is no piece of evidence that would accuse one but not the other, since their fingerprints are also identical. About the only way of establishing anything definitely is to determine where the innocent party was at the time of the murder, something this episode never goes into. Instead it pulls a switch by saying they both did it. Now, two people may well commit one murder, but being twins has nothing to do with it. Suppose they looked nothing alike; then everything would work the same, with one tiny and insignificant exception. Mrs. Peck, the imperious housekeeper, looks out the window and thinks she sees Dexter leaving, but it's actually Norman dressed as Dexter while his brother remains hidden in the house to deactivate the alarm. This could easily be done with two people who weren't twins, by simply dressing the second man in the same clothes as the first and having him walk away from the house, never turning his face to Mrs. Peck. In other words, after Columbo and the audience waste a lot of time trying to piece together which one of them did it, we're supposed to be caught off guard by the notion that both did, when the only purpose to be gained by having identical twins do it is a ten-second glimpse by Mrs. Peck. Columbo's Final Clue here, that the brothers who pretended to hate each other actually spoke frequently by phone to plan the murder, is also a real letdown (see "Busting Alibis, Busting Scenarios").

After "Double Shock" (#15), the next twist offered by Gillis appears in the fifth season finale "Last Salute to the Commodore" (#35). I put "Commodore" and "Double Shock" in a dead heat for worst episode (non-McBain adaptation), and "Commodore" wins (loses) the race by a nose. In addition to compromising the Columbo character (see "The Developing Character"), the episode attempts to function as a "traditional" mystery, with the killer hidden from the audience as well as Columbo. However, writer Gillis and director Patrick McGoohan don't play fair; important clues are deliberately withheld from us by being drowned in loud noise (when Columbo is in the shipyard) or obscured as a drunken character weaves into the camera while the important line is being spoken by someone else off screen (what Swanny says at the yacht club). Finally, when the mystery is revealed, it's a dull cliché (the secondary heir did it, and then framed the primary heir) which is brought to light by a sloppy verbal slip unworthy of any good mystery, not to mention the usually excellent *Columbo*. What if the killer said "who cares" to the watch noise just like everybody else in the scene?

In "Murder in Malibu" (#53), Gillis really gets us going. Oh, we witness a traditional *Columbo* murder all right, it's just that what we see is the second time Wayne Jennings has shot the victim, Theresa Goren. So when he's caught and then released because the coroner says she was killed earlier by a different gun, we're supposed to be lost because we (and Columbo) have to start from square one again. But is that true? Besides Jennings, the only other possible

215

suspect is Theresa's sister, Jess McCurdy, but she never really becomes a viable suspect (nor does Jennings make much effort to incriminate her), so, unless Columbo is willing to accept the bizarre coincidence of a burglar (and he's already found discrepancies with the burglary scenario) robbing and killing Theresa just before Jennings happened to arrive to shoot her, Jennings is the most likely suspect for first shooter, too. It's a twist without an effect.

Finally, Gillis has the variation in "A Bird in the Hand" (#59), in which we follow as Columbo investigates Harold McCain, who plots the murder of his uncle, Big Fred, by means of a car bomb and winds up blowing up the poor gardener by mistake when Big Fred is killed in a hit and run. However, we learn at the very end of the episode that Big Fred's wife Dolores was the driver of the vehicle that bumped off her husband in the first place. Dolores also later also kills Harold, when he puts the pieces together. This episode really contains an insider's view, as Columbo seems tickled by the idea that he can catch Dolores for the second murder (the "bird in the hand" of the title) rather than the first. But what makes that interesting or clever? It's only unusual if you have bought into the strange presumption of the show that Columbo always gets his murderer for the first crime, even if the second one is more clever (the remote-controlled suicide in "A Deadly State of Mind" (#29)) or bears a better link to the killer (the poison used to murder Shirley Blaine in "Lovely But Lethal" (#16)). See "Get 'Em for the First Murder" for more on this unwritten rule of the show.

In summary, then, it seems to me as if Jackson Gillis creates better *Columbo*s when he is not spinning a variation on a theme.

Get 'Em for the First Murder, No Matter What

Sometimes even the best-laid schemes of clever murderers on *Columbo* require another dastardly deed to keep the police away (or at least so they think). Sometimes the murderer must get rid of an accomplice who has served his/her purpose. This group of victims includes Tracy O'Connor in "Suitable for Framing" (#4), Eddie Kane in "Publish or Perish" (#20), Nadia

Donner in "A Deadly State of Mind" (#29), and Rahmin Habib in "A Case of Immunity" (#31). But more often the problem is some pesky individual (besides Columbo, of course) who has stumbled upon the crime and is in the way, like Sharon Martin in "A Stitch in Crime" (#13), Charles Clay in "Last Salute to the Commodore" (#35), or Harold McCain in "A Bird in the Hand" (#59). Then there are those who want to blackmail the murderer in return for keeping silent: Lilly La Sanka in "Murder By the Book" (#1), Tanner in "Dagger of the Mind" (#11), Shirley Blaine in "Lovely But Lethal" (#16), Roger White in "Double Exposure" (#19), and Linwood Coben in "Columbo Likes the Nightlife" (#67). There is yet another category—those poor souls (schlimazels, in Yiddish) whom the murderers get rid of (even if they posed no threat) to frame them for the crime or otherwise throw Columbo off the track: Harry Alexander in "A Stitch in Crime" (#13), Lisa Chambers in "Double Shock" (#15), Alvin Deschler in "Negative Reaction" (#25), Milton Schaeffer, the unlucky security guard in "Old Fashioned Murder" (#37) (to complete the setup that the murderer's brother interrupted a robbery), Bruno Romano, the mobster in "Strange Bedfellows" (#63) (to frame him for killing Teddy McVeigh), and Howard Seltzer, the schnook killed in "A Trace of Murder" (#64) to frame Clifford Calvert. This in itself is not surprising (see "Accomplices, Blackmailers and Schlimazels" for more on these second killings). What is odd is the unwritten rule on *Columbo* that the Lieutenant will pursue and ultimately catch the criminal for the first crime committed, even if the second one is more interesting, more sinister, or more blameworthy. The Lieutenant checks into these situations, but never as fully as the first murders.

"Lovely But Lethal" (#16) is a particularly apt example of this oddity. The first murder is an unfortunate heat-of-the-moment crime; in fact, Viveca Scott really didn't want to kill Karl Lessing because he had the formula that would save her company. Many clues come about (or should) as a result of the fact that the murder is unplanned (indeed, it's unlikely she would have selected a microscope as a murder weapon had she planned ahead, and thus neither she nor Columbo would have contracted poison ivy). And in all fairness, Lessing's behavior to her is rather despicable, so it seems a shame to lock her up for life as punishment. On the other hand, Shirley Blaine hints to Viveca that she knows who killed Lessing and wants an executive promotion to keep silent. She gets instead a poisoned cigarette that causes her to drive off the road to her death. Not only is this crime more dastardly and deliberate, it is also more clever and therefore more worthy of Columbo's talents. Wouldn't it be more satisfying for the Lieutenant to arrest Viveca for this crime rather than the accidental murder of Lessing?

This is also true of "Dagger of the Mind" (#11), in which Sir Roger Haversham is accidentally killed by a cold cream jar thrown at him in the middle of a fight with Nicholas Frame and Lillian Stanhope, but in which Tanner (Sir Roger's butler who tries to blackmail the murdering couple into serving them) is found deliberately hanged and framed for Sir Roger's murder. Granted, the couple does cover up Sir Roger's murder to make it look like an accident, but that's still not quite the same as doing off with Tanner in a premeditated plan. In "A Deadly State of Mind" (#29), Marcus Collier's murder of Karl Donner would almost seem to qualify as justifiable self-defense, as Donner is assaulting both his own wife Nadia and Dr. Collier at the time, as opposed to Collier's murder of Nadia Donner, which he accomplishes by means of a clever remote-controlled activation of a post-hypnotic suggestion in making her think she is going swimming. As satisfying as it is to watch Columbo catch Collier (and the blind man trick is very clever), it would be even more satisfying if the Lieutenant could prove how the man killed Nadia. And in "Columbo Likes the Nightlife" (#67), Tony Galper is killed accidentally when his ex-wife Vanessa Farrow pushes him and his head hits a glass coffee table, á la "Death Lends a Hand" (#2). Vanessa and her lover, Justin Price, hide the body, it's true, but then their actions become a lot more dastardly when they kill Linwood Coben, the tabloid reporter who has pictures of them standing over Tony's body and wants at least $250,000 to keep quiet about it. Columbo spends most of his time gathering evidence about the Coben murder, but he catches the duo by demonstrating that Tony's body is hidden beneath the fish tank in the floor of Justin's club.

Granted, in some cases, the first murder is cleverer and it seems perfectly appropriate for Columbo to catch the villains for those, rather than the after-the-fact cover-up murders. "Murder By the Book" (#1), "Suitable for Framing" (#4), "Double Shock" (#15), "Double Exposure" (#19), and "A Case of Immunity" (#31) all fall into this situation. In "A Stitch in Crime" (#13), the first (attempted) murder of Dr. Heideman is the cleverest, but Columbo has to work backwards from the actual murders of Sharon Martin and Harry Alexander to realize that Dr. Mayfield has put dissolving suture in Dr. Heideman. I understand the necessity for this mode of investigation, but it is something of a letdown that Columbo only arrests Mayfield for attempted murder. Columbo has some clues linking Mayfield to Sharon Martin's murder (there is barely any investigation into Harry Alexander's death), but he is nowhere near proving that the nurse was killed because of what she knew about the suture and that Mayfield was the killer.

"Publish or Perish" (#20) presents a special case. It is certainly true that the murder of Allen Mallory, for which Riley Greenleaf frames himself in order to later clear himself by means of an ironclad alibi and evidence suggesting that someone is trying to frame him for the crime, is very clever and complicated. By contrast, the murder of Eddie Kane (which is really all part of the same plan, as Eddie is to be the fall guy who will be blamed for the Mallory murder and the frame-up of Greenleaf) is not quite as challenging. Nevertheless, I would have suggested in this instance that Columbo pursue Greenleaf for the second murder because he stands a greater chance of being able to prove it. Indeed, I think writer Peter Fischer gave the Lieutenant too difficult a task in trying to prove not that Greenleaf fired the bullet that killed Mallory (Eddie Kane did that) or that he killed Eddie Kane, but that he hired Kane to kill Mallory in return for publishing his book on how to make bombs. The final clue in the episode (proof that Greenleaf knew the ending to Mallory's latest book and that Kane could not have typed this newly created ending nine months ago in an outline as Greenleaf has planted evidence to indicate) goes some way toward this difficult goal, but I'm not sure that it goes far enough.

Finally, the ultimate proof of how ingrained this "catch them for the first crime" idea is came to light when Jackson Gillis created one of his "Variations on a Theme" (see the preceding essay) by having Columbo catch someone for a second murder as though this were some bolt from the blue; he even names the episode "A Bird in the Hand" (#59). Now, I was content to see Dolores McCain arrested for Harold's murder, rather than the murder of her husband, Big Fred. Indeed, as the episode is constructed, the second murder is far more clever than the first, a hit-and-run that is not explored because Harold's attempt to kill Big Fred with a bomb (which unfortunately comes to light when the gardener goes to move the man's car) distracts Columbo (and the audience) from the fact that Big Fred is already dead and that Harold is not the murderer. My point here is simply that Gillis does what could have been done long before and that there is absolutely nothing odd about it.

On a related note, sometimes the murderer kills to silence a witness who could reveal a past murder, but Columbo never catches the criminals for these cold cases. In fact, he usually announces that he suspects the murderers of committing these crimes but throws up his hands at trying to prove them. He tells Eric Mason in How to Dial a Murder (#42) that he can't arrest him for killing his wife Lorraine six months ago (why not?). He indicates to Max Barsini in Murder: A Self Portrait (#48) that he can't use his late wife's dreams to prove he killed his art dealer, Harry Chudnow, years ago and buried him in the basement of Vito's Bar (but if they dig up Vito's basement and find old Harry's remains, won't Barsini be the prime suspect?). And he merely explains to Nora Chandler in Requiem for a Falling Star (#12) that he believes her husband's body is buried underneath the fountain in her yard and Nora confesses, not just to killing him but also her assistant, Jean Davis, who knew what happened and might blab it to her lover, Jerry Parks. But they never even bother digging up the body and instead Chandler awkwardly confesses to two murders.

And in the oddest twist on this theme, in Murder, Smoke and Shadows (#45), Columbo actually shows murderer Alex Brady a film clip that implicates him in the death of Jenny Fisher (she falls off a motorcycle while performing a stunt for him and he runs away), but only for the purpose of establishing Brady's motive for killing Jenny's brother Lenny when he arrives with the film and threatens to ruin the director with it. Neither Columbo nor the writers seem to realize what they have in hand, and instead the Lieutenant tries to tie Brady to Lenny's murder, first by means of placing Lenny in Brady's playroom with a ticket he bought for the studio tour (but Brady dismisses this clue and Columbo drops the idea) and then with an awkward scene in which Brady's secretary tells him she knows something and he bribes her to keep it quiet (overheard in bits and pieces by police officers posing as wait staff). Why not arrest Brady for his complicity in Jenny's death? It may not be first degree murder, but he would still go to prison for it.

In summary, the unwritten rule that Columbo should "get 'em for the first murder, no matter what" occasionally leads to some very strange results. It would have been better for the writers to leave open the possibility that Columbo could arrest the villain for the second (or past) murder, particularly if that crime was more clever or dastardly.

No Time for Columbo, No Place for McBain

After watching a show for two hours, what is it that leads viewers to say they've seen an episode of *Columbo*? Is it Peter Falk in a raincoat doing anything? Assuming that the answer to that question is no, then the program ought to be some kind of mystery (Falk giving an interview or painting in his studio just doesn't cut it). In my book (and this is my book), I have to take it another step and say that what makes the show *Columbo* are the aspects I describe in these essays. I'm willing to be flexible—not all aspects have to appear in an episode, but changing it into a police procedural is such a fundamental reworking that I think I (and lots of fans with whom I have spoken) can raise a legitimate objection to it. The writers can hide the murderer from us, obscure who the intended victim is or even have Columbo chase multiple villains for various murders, but these "episodes" went too far.

What do I mean by police procedural? Well, the following definition is from the Mystery Lover's Calendar published by the New York Public Library:

> In the most liberal sense a police procedural features a real police officer or detective as opposed to an amateur or private detective. In a stricter sense the police procedural is the type of book that has been perfected by Ed McBain and Joseph Wambaugh. In these mysteries the hero is a police officer who utilizes scientific techniques; personality is often downplayed, with the star of these books being modern forensics. In the police procedural there are no outlandish explanations of events—instead, fingerprints and blood samples are taken, witnesses questioned, and confessions obtained.

Now, I like a good police procedural, particularly one with a quirky cop as the main character (*Kojak* is an example). But this definition explains why *Columbo* is not a police procedural and why "No Time to Die" (#58) and "Undercover" (#62) do not qualify as episodes of *Columbo*.

Obviously, when talking about *Columbo*, the "stricter" definition of police procedural applies because, although the mysteries feature a "real" police detective rather than an amateur one, the tone or feel of the show is that of a private detective. As Mark Dawidziak puts it in his book, "Columbo belongs in the British drawing-room school of Doyle/Christie/Sayers . . . Columbo matched wits with suave, intellectual, sophisticated murderers." *The Columbo Phile* (p. 5). Thus, what makes the show unique is the delicate balance of character and clues, the point-counterpoint dialogue, and the brilliant idea of a common man for a hero that the villains often underestimate at their peril.

The McBain episodes also feature a level of violence unheard of on regular *Columbo* installments. In addition to the scene of the abductor getting blown away at the end of "No Time to Die" (#58), there are numerous uncomfortable moments of watching the psycho torture the victim, both psychologically and occasionally physically. In "Undercover" (#62), the camera provides close-up shots of the two men who murder each other at the beginning as well as the later murders of Mo Weinberg and Geraldine Ferguson. Columbo carries a gun and gets into an altercation with Weinberg. And worst of all, the Lieutenant himself is pistol-whipped when he opens the door of his hotel room and is surprised by a hooded figure.

Another point of contrast is the issue of time. In both McBain adaptations, the question of time is important. Dates or times appear on the screen to tell the audience how much time has passed. Particularly in "No Time to Die" (#58), the clock is ticking and the police have to find the victim in time, or else. By contrast, in a typical "regular" episode of the show, time is not a factor. The victim is already dead and Columbo's methodical investigation often takes a while. In fact, although there are some instances when it is clear exactly how much time has passed, they represent the exception rather than the rule: in "Troubled Waters" (#27), the Lieutenant takes a three-day cruise to Mexico and hands Hayden Danziger over to the authorities just before the ship docks at Mazatlan. And in "Columbo Goes to College" (#54), the Lieutenant is serving as a guest lecturer in a criminology class when the professor is killed. Exactly one week later, he recreates the scenario and solves the case. But most of the time, it's difficult to say how many days have passed, and it doesn't matter.

While *Columbo* focuses on a specific quirky character, shows the murder first and then has the murderer and detective engage in a nonviolent battle of wits and clues until the ending, McBain novels do none of these things. Police procedurals by definition do not focus exclusively on any one individual, but instead follow a group of officers as they investigate the case (McBain is perhaps best known for his 87th Precinct short stories and novels), probably coming closer to real life, but not necessarily making better fiction or a better show (McBain's stories were brought to television in a show called *87th Precinct* that lasted only one season, 1961-62). Putting Columbo into a McBain story makes for the worst of all possible combinations.

In "No Time to Die" (#58), there was no murder. Instead, Columbo's nephew, himself a cop, has gotten married, and he finds his bride has disappeared from the hotel room while he was showering. She was abducted by a crazed psychopath (the kind that flourish on television) and held captive in a room awaiting "marriage" to this fruitcake. While she tries to escape, the world's fastest-moving and talking Columbo, the nephew and assorted others gallop through mountains of material in search of clues, such as looking at every photo of the wedding and ticking off known guests, hoping that the psycho was there at the time. There is nothing clever, interesting or worth watching about this movie and it is frustrating for the manner in which the character and the show that we know so well are tossed aside so casually. Occasionally, the scene focuses on the psycho caressing the bride and talking to her in his demented fashion; Columbo will never get to address him, however.

In the end, the police kick in the door just as the psycho is about to consummate his "marriage" to the nephew's wife. The nephew, who is leading the charge (that's standard police procedure, isn't it?), blows the guy away with a fusillade of bullets, while a befuddled Columbo stands in the doorway, holding his gun. Does anything seem odd about this picture? Perhaps it's that, in the fifty-seven episodes and two movies that came before, the *murderers* (yes, that's right, murderers, not kidnappers or would-be rapists) were arrested and not killed. Or perhaps it's that the good Lieutenant is well known for not carrying a gun.

Not every tradition of the show was discarded, but all of the important ones were. The Lieutenant's first name is not revealed (although this requires having the nephew not call him anything), Mrs. Columbo does not appear at her own nephew's wedding (she is supposedly looking after her mother, who fell and broke her hip, in Chicago) and Columbo still drives the jalopy, although it works perfectly throughout the episode (it couldn't very well die on him in the middle of this intense investigation). He wears his usual raincoat, but it's covering the tuxedo from the wedding, which he never gets to change out of because of time pressures.

An interesting debate took place after the airing of this movie. Some people thought what was wrong was that the format had been changed, but others countered that the real objection to the movie was that Columbo's character was different. In fact, both schools of thought are correct. In essence, format and character are inextricably linked to one another, and neither can be altered without the other suffering as a consequence. In real life, the police may chase thieves down the street, engage in shootouts with drug dealers and (at least occasionally) face off against psychotic killers, but Columbo does not belong in these situations, just like Hercule Poirot, Father Brown and Miss Marple do not. These fictional "drawing room type" detectives, who solve mysteries by their brain power and not by the fist, cannot be placed in the scenario represented by "No Time to Die" (#58) without altering the nature of their character, and that is what happens here. Columbo *can't* be his usual "one more thing, sir" polite, apparently slow-witted self in this situation. The prognosis is far too grim, and time is running short. Besides, since he's talking to witnesses and police rather than the villain, what would be the point?

Similarly, "Undercover" (#62) follows the police as they put together puzzle pieces to find missing money. Columbo is the name of the guy who dons the costumes and does most of the legwork, but it's not the character of the series. Eventually, the movie tries to include a murder mystery when two witnesses are killed (and the Lieutenant is assaulted) and there's even an attempt at a *Columbo*-type of final clue (the murderer's fingerprint is on a coin in a parking meter near the scene of a murder when he is supposedly elsewhere). But the clue is presented to his girlfriend rather than to him, probably because it really only has to be enough to get her to tell what she knows, believing him to be caught already. The focus is on the methodical steps taken to solve the crime, not on the characters. Columbo again speaks in fast clips, and he seems pretty much like all of the other cops, except that he drives an odd car and wears the same suit all the time.

Could there be an episode that used McBain material without abandoning the format and therefore the character? It is difficult to say. It would take major rewriting of the McBain story to create the inverted format (show the murder first) and cat-and-mouse dialogue that the hallmarks of the show, and at some point it would probably be easier to simply start from scratch. And stop to think for a moment—Columbo does not usually work well with others (see the essay "Colleagues and Sidekicks" for more on this topic), primarily because his observations are outside the mainstream and his logic often comes at the answer by a most circuitous route. Isn't it enjoyable to see that even his superiors sometimes wonder what planet he's on, as when Captain Sampson asks why he considers Alvin Deschler's driving habits so important in "Negative Reaction" (#25)? Doesn't he gather important clues by wandering around the crime scene in "Candidate for Crime" (#18) instead of standing mute at the Commissioner's side as he's instructed to do? Why spoil all that by putting him in a precinct full of other cops, all doing their little part so that the resolution is a group effort?

Chapter 19:
Murderer's Options

Motive, Method and Appearance

A. Motive

There are only a few motives that have appeared on *Columbo* over the years. The majority of episodes (27) feature a villain out for money or power and the next group (20) have the murderer acting to silence someone who would reveal something unsavory that the murderer wants kept quiet (a scam bilking people, an affair, and so on; I put past murder under its own special category). The next group, what I have called "hold onto something dear" often (but not always) appear in an episode in which there is a sympathetic relationship between Columbo and the murderer (see essay on this topic). Obviously, if the individual is threatened with losing something that means so much to him or her, the audience and Columbo can have a lot more sympathy than if it's just someone out for money or to get ahead. But on the other hand, a lot depends on how the scenario is played out. Harold Van Wyck in "Playback" (#28) is threatened with the loss of the company that is his whole existence, but he hardly makes for a sympathetic character.

The "revenge" category is an interesting mixture of sympathetic murderer episodes ("Try and Catch Me" (#39), "Sex and the Married Detective" (#46), "It's All in the Game" (#60)) and those in which the murderer is anything but sympathetic ("How to Dial a Murder" (#42), "The Conspirators" (#43), "Columbo

Goes to the Guillotine" (#44), "Rest in Peace, Mrs. Columbo" (#51)). I suppose the difference results from whether or not we would "understand" the revenge under the circumstances. Dr. Joan Allenby striking back at her lover David Kincaid for having an affair and treating her with such disdain (in "Sex and the Married Detective" (#46)) comes off as sympathetic, while Dr. Eric Mason siccing his hounds on Charles Hunter (in "How to Dial a Murder" (#42)) for having slept with his wife (whom he also killed) just seems sick. As I recently read, the difference between revenge and justice is that revenge feels right only to those directly involved, but justice feels right even to outsiders.

Table 3: Motives

Money, Power	Fraud, Affair or Scam will be revealed	Hold onto something dear	Revenge	Past murder cover-up
Prescription: Murder (A)	Dead Weight (#3)	Any Old Port in a Storm (#17)	Try and Catch Me (#39)	Requiem for a Falling Star (#12)
Ransom for a Dead Man (B)	Blueprint for Murder (#7)	Candidate for Crime (#18)	How to Dial a Murder (#42)	Murder, Smoke and Shadows (#45)
Murder By the Book (#1) (James Ferris)	Etude in Black (#8)	By Dawn's Early Light (#26)	The Conspirators (#43)	Murder: A Self Portrait (#48)
Suitable for Framing (#4) (Rudy Mathews)	Double Exposure (#19) (Victor Norris)	Playback (#28)	Columbo Goes to the Guillotine (#44)	
Lady in Waiting (#5)	Mind Over Mayhem (#21)	Forgotten Lady (#30)	Sex and the Married Detective (#46)	
Short Fuse (#6)	An Exercise in Fatality (#24)	Old Fashioned Murder (#37) (Edward Lytton)	Rest in Peace, Mrs. Columbo (#51)	

Here is a complete list of motives featured in various episodes. I have not included "Undercover" (#62) (obviously, the motive there is money) or "No Time to Die" (#58), which does not contain a murder. However, I have included the second murders that appear in seventeen of the show's episodes, in the final two columns. The motive behind such second murders falls under one of two categories. In many cases, the motive is to get rid of an accomplice, witness or blackmailer. In the other instances, the motive is to complete the frame-up that the murderer intended from the beginning. Finally, I do count the attempted murder of Dr. Heideman in "A Stitch in Crime" (#13), for which Barry Mayfield's motive is to get ahead.

Accident/Self-Defense	Cowardice will be revealed	Get rid of accomplice, witness, or blackmailer	Complete the frame-up (2nd murder)
Death Lends a Hand (#2)	A Matter of Honor (#33) (hidden motive)	Murder By the Book (#1) (Lilly La Sanka)	A Stitch in Crime (#13) (Harry Alexander)
Dagger of the Mind (#11) (Sir Roger Haversham)		Suitable for Framing (#4) (Tracy O'Connor)	Double Shock (#15) (Lisa Chambers)
Lovely But Lethal (#16) (Karl Lessing)		Dagger of the Mind (#11) (Tanner)	Publish or Perish (#20) (Eddie Kane)
A Friend in Deed (#23) (Janice Caldwell)		A Stitch in Crime (#13) (Sharon Martin)	Negative Reaction (#25) (Alvin Deschler)
A Deadly State of Mind (#29) (Karl Donner)		Lovely But Lethal (#16) (Shirley Blaine)	Old Fashioned Murder (#37) (Milton Schaeffer)
A Bird in the Hand (#59) (Fernando)		Double Exposure (#19) (Roger White)	Strange Bedfellows (#63) (Bruno Romano)

Money, Power	Fraud, Affair or Scam will be revealed	Hold onto some- thing dear	Revenge	Past murder cover-up
The Greenhouse Jungle (#9)	Troubled Waters (#27)	Columbo Cries Wolf (#49)	It's All in the Game (#60)	
The Most Crucial Game (#10)	Identity Crisis (#32)	Butterfly in Shades of Grey (#61)		
A Stitch in Crime (#13) (Dr. Heideman)	The Bye-Bye Sky High IQ Murder Case (#38)			
The Most Dangerous Match (#14)	Murder Under Glass (#40)			
Double Shock (#15) (Clifford Paris)	Grand Deceptions (#47)			
Publish or Perish (#20) (Allen Mallory)	Agenda for Murder (#50)			
Swan Song (#22)	Columbo Goes to College (#54)			
A Friend in Deed (#23) (Margaret Halperin)	Caution: Murder Can Be Hazardous to Your Health (#55)			
Negative Reaction (#25) (Frances Galesko)	Columbo and the Murder of a Rock Star (#56)			
A Case of Immunity (#31) (Youseff Alafa)	Ashes to Ashes (#65)			
Last Salute to the Commodore (#35) (Otis Swanson)	Murder With Too Many Notes (#66)			
Make Me a Perfect Murder (#41)				

Accident/Self-Defense	Cowardice will be revealed	Get rid of accomplice, witness, or blackmailer	Complete the frame-up (2nd murder)
Columbo Likes the Nightlife (#67) (Tony Galper)		A Deadly State of Mind (#29) (Nadia Donner)	
		A Case of Immunity (#31) (Rahmin Habib)	
		Now You See Him (#34)	
		Last Salute to the Commodore (#35) (Charles Clay)	
		Fade in to Murder (#36)	
		A Bird in the Hand (#59) (Harold McCain)	
		Columbo Likes the Nightlife (#67) (Linwood Coben)	

Money, Power	Fraud, Affair or Scam will be revealed	Hold onto something dear	Revenge	Past murder cover-up
Uneasy Lies the Crown (#52)				
Murder in Malibu (#53)				
Death Hits the Jackpot (#57)				
A Bird in the Hand (#59) (Big Fred McCain)				
Strange Bedfellows (#63) (Teddy McVeigh)				
A Trace of Murder (#64)				
24	17	8	7	3

B. Method

There are only so many ways to do away with someone, and *Columbo* murderers have not been a particularly creative bunch in this regard. The vast majority of murders on the show (thirty-four, counting second victims and those that may have occurred in the past, but not those in "Undercover" (#62)) are accomplished by means of the old standard, a gun. Following that come the old hit-them-over-the-head method (13), tied exactly by "impact" murders (13), by which I mean running someone over with a car, sending someone over a cliff in a car or off a roof or high balcony without a net (and the plane crash episode, "Swan Song" (#22)). The methods I've combined under the heading "gassing, poisoning, drugging" have been used a total of seven times. Strangling and bombing are each used on six occasions. Drowning is the method of choice in six instances. That leaves a few out-of-the-ordinary murders: two each by electrocution, suffocation and mauling by animal and the one-time-only murders by beheading and knifing, and the attempt to murder by inserting dissolving suture into a heart valve.

Accident/Self-Defense	Cowardice will be revealed	Get rid of accomplice, witness, or blackmailer	Complete the frame-up (2nd murder)
7	1	13	6

If more than one method is employed, I count as the method only the one that actually succeeds. In "The Most Dangerous Match" (#14), Tomlin Dudek is killed when Emmet Clayton switches his drugs around; the first attempt at pushing him into the trash compactor failed. And in "Columbo Likes the Nightlife" (#67), Justin Price tries to strangle Linwood Coben to make it look like he hanged himself by jumping out the window with a rope tied to the radiator. Unfortunately, Linwood is a big guy and his weight pulls the radiator out of the wall, so the cause of death was probably the impact of the big man hitting the ground four stories down, then being hit by the radiator. "Murder With Too Many Notes" (#66) is tricky—it's not until late in the episode that it's made clear that the victim is unconscious (but not dead) when the opening elevator sends him to the street, so it's death by impact, not drugging. In an episode with more than one murder, there are multiple entries.

Table 4: Methods

#	Title	Shot	Blow to head	Impact	Bomb	Gas Poison Drugs
A	*Prescription: Murder*					
B	*Ransom for a Dead Man*	Paul Williams				
1	Murder by the Book	James Ferris				
2	Death Lends a Hand		Lenore Kennicut			
3	Dead Weight	Roger Dutton				
4	Suitable for Framing	Rudy Mathews		Tracy O'Connor		
5	Lady in Waiting	Bryce Chadwick				
6	Short Fuse				David Buckner, Quincy	
7	Blueprint for Murder	Beau Williamson				
8	Etude in Black					Jenifer Welles
9	The Greenhouse Jungle	Tony Goodland				
10	The Most Crucial Game					
11	Dagger of the Mind		Sir Roger Haversham			
12	Requiem for a Falling Star		Al Cumberland (past)		Jean Davis	

Strangled	Drowned	Electrocuted	Mauled by animal	Suffocated	Other Method
Carol Flemming					
	Lilly La Sanka				
	Eric Wagner				
Tanner					

#	Title	Shot	Blow to head	Impact	Bomb	Gas Poison Drugs
13	A Stitch in Crime		Sharon Martin			Harry Alexander
14	The Most Dangerous Match					Tomlin Dudek
15	Double Shock			Lisa Chambers		
16	Lovely But Lethal		Karl Lessing	Shirley Blaine		
17	Any Old Port in a Storm					
18	Candidate for Crime	Harry Stone				
19	Double Exposure	Victor Norris, Roger White				
20	Publish or Perish	Allen Mallory			Eddie Kane	
21	Mind Over Mayhem			Howard Nicholson		
22	Swan Song			Edna Brown, Maryann Cobb		
23	A Friend in Deed					
24	An Exercise in Fatality					
25	Negative Reaction	Frances Galesko, Alvin Deschler				
26	By Dawn's Early Light				William Haynes	

Strangled	Drowned	Electrocuted	Mauled by animal	Suffocated	Other Method
					Dr. Heideman dissolving suture, attempted
		Clifford Paris			
				Ric Carsini	
Janice Caldwell	Margaret Halperin				
Gene Stafford					

#	Title	Shot	Blow to head	Impact	Bomb	Gas Poison Drugs
27	Troubled Waters	Rosanna Welles				
28	Playback	Margaret Midas				
29	A Deadly State of Mind		Karl Donner	Nadia Donner		
30	Forgotten Lady	Henry Willis				
31	A Case of Immunity		Youseff Alafa	Rahmin Habib		
32	Identity Crisis		"Geronimo"			
33	A Matter of Honor					
34	Now You See Him	Jesse Jerome				
35	Last Salute to the Commodore		Otis Swanson, Charles Clay			
36	Fade in to Murder	Claire Daley				
37	Old Fashioned Murder	Edward Lytton, Milton Schaeffer				Peter Brandt (past)
38	The Bye-Bye Sky High IQ Murder Case	Bertie Hastings				
39	Try and Catch Me					
40	Murder Under Glass					Vittorio Rossi
41	Make Me a Perfect Murder	Mark McAndrews				

Strangled	Drowned	Electrocuted	Mauled by animal	Suffocated	Other Method
			Hector Rangel		
	Phyllis Galvin (past)			Edmund Galvin	

#	Title	Shot	Blow to head	Impact	Bomb	Gas Poison Drugs
42	How to Dial a Murder			Lorraine Mason (past)		
43	The Conspirators	Vincent Pauley				
44	Columbo Goes to the Guillotine					
45	Murder, Smoke and Shadows			Jenny Fisher (past)		
46	Sex and the Married Detective	David Kincaid				
47	Grand Deceptions					
48	Murder: A Self Portrait		Harry Chudnow (past)			
49	Columbo Cries Wolf					
50	Agenda for Murder	Frank Staplin				
51	Rest in Peace, Mrs. Columbo	Charlie Chambers				
52	Uneasy Lies the Crown					Adam Evans
53	Murder in Malibu	Theresa Goren				
54	Columbo Goes to College	D.E. Rusk				

Strangled	Drowned	Electrocuted	Mauled by animal	Suffocated	Other Method
			Charles Hunter		
					Max Dyson, Beheaded
		Len Fisher			
					Lester Keegan, Knifed
	Louise Barsini				
Dian Hunter					

#	Title	Shot	Blow to head	Impact	Bomb	Gas Poison Drugs
55	Caution: Murder Can Be Hazardous to Your Health					Budd Clark
56	Columbo and the Murder of a Rock Star					
57	Death Hits the Jackpot					
59	A Bird in the Hand	Harold McCain		Big Fred McCain	Fernando	
60	It's All in the Game	Nick Franco				
61	Butterfly in Shades of Grey	Jerry Winters				
63	Strange Bedfellows	Teddy McVeigh, Bruno Romano				
64	A Trace of Murder	Howard Seltzer				
65	Ashes to Ashes		Verity Chandler			
66	Murder With Too Many Notes			Gabriel McEnery		
67	Columbo Likes the Nightlife		Tony Galper	Linwood Coben		
	Totals	34	13	13	6	7

Strangled	Drowned	Electrocuted	Mauled by animal	Suffocated	Other Method
Marcy Edwards					
	Freddy Brower				
6	6	2	2	2	2

C. Appearance

One other way to categorize *Columbo* episodes is by what the murder is made to look like, its appearance. The most common tack taken by the murderer (thirty-five instances) is to make the murder look like natural causes or an accident, probably to avoid any police investigation at all (fat chance of that). Following that come the twenty-three cases where the killer makes the murder look like it happened during a robbery, kidnapping or other crime, but does not attempt to frame any specific individual. Next come the

Table 5: Appearances of the Murders

#	Title	Accident or natural causes	Robbery or other crime
A	*Prescription: Murder*		Carol Flemming
B	*Ransom for a Dead Man*		Paul Williams
1	Murder by the Book	Lilly La Sanka	James Ferris
2	Death Lends a Hand		Lenore Kennicut
3	Dead Weight		
4	Suitable for Framing	Tracy O'Connor	Rudy Mathews
5	Lady in Waiting	Bryce Chadwick	
6	Short Fuse	David Buckner, Quincy	
7	Blueprint for Murder		
8	Etude in Black		
9	The Greenhouse Jungle		Tony Goodland
10	The Most Crucial Game	Eric Wagner	
11	Dagger of the Mind	Sir Roger Haversham	
12	Requiem for a Falling Star		Jean Davis

twenty scenarios in which the murderer does attempt to frame someone in the episode for the crime. On eight occasions, the murderers hide the body to avoid any investigation. On six occasions, the murderers attempt to make the crimes look like suicide. Finally, on two occasions, they make the murder look like self-defense.

Past murders are included in this list, as is the attempted murder of Dr. Heideman in "A Stitch in Crime" (#13). However, the murders of "Undercover" (#62) are not included.

Frame-up of a specific person	Hide the body	Suicide	Self-defense
	Roger Dutton		
	Beau Williamson		
		Jenifer Welles	
		Tanner	
	Al Cumberland (past)		

#	Title	Accident or natural causes	Robbery or other crime
13	A Stitch in Crime	Dr. Heideman (attempted), Harry Alexander	
14	The Most Dangerous Match	Tomlin Dudek	
15	Double Shock	Clifford Paris	
16	Lovely But Lethal	Shirley Blaine	Karl Lessing
17	Any Old Port in a Storm	Ric Carsini	
18	Candidate for Crime		Harry Stone
19	Double Exposure		
20	Publish or Perish	Eddie Kane	
21	Mind Over Mayhem		Howard Nicholson
22	Swan Song	Edna Brown, Maryann Cobb	
23	A Friend in Deed		
24	An Exercise in Fatality	Gene Stafford	
25	Negative Reaction		
26	By Dawn's Early Light	William Haynes	
27	Troubled Waters		
28	Playback		Margaret Midas
29	A Deadly State of Mind		Karl Donner
30	Forgotten Lady		
31	A Case of Immunity	Rahmin Habib	
32	Identity Crisis		"Geronimo"
33	A Matter of Honor	Hector Rangel	
34	Now You See Him		Jesse Jerome

Frame-up of a specific person	Hide the body	Suicide	Self-defense
Sharon Martin			
Lisa Chambers			
Victor Norris, Roger White			
Allen Mallory			
Janice Caldwell, Margaret Halperin			
Frances Galesko			Alvin Deschler
Rosanna Welles			
		Nadia Donner	
		Henry Willis	
Youseff Alafa			

#	Title	Accident or natural causes	Robbery or other crime
35	Last Salute to the Commodore	Otis Swanson	Charles Clay
36	Fade in to Murder		Claire Daley*
37	Old Fashioned Murder	Peter Brandt (past)	
38	The Bye-Bye Sky High IQ Murder Case		Bertie Hastings
39	Try and Catch Me	Edmund Galvin, Phyllis Galvin (past)	
40	Murder Under Glass	Vittorio Rossi	
41	Make Me a Perfect Murder		Mark McAndrews
42	How to Dial a Murder	Charlie Hunter, Lorraine Mason (past)	
43	The Conspirators		Vincent Pauley
44	Columbo Goes to the Guillotine	Max Dyson	
45	Murder, Smoke and Shadows	Jenny Fisher (past)	
46	Sex and the Married Detective		
47	Grand Deceptions	Lester Keegan	
48	Murder: A Self Portrait	Louise Barsini	
49	Columbo Cries Wolf		
50	Agenda for Murder		
51	Rest in Peace, Mrs. Columbo		
52	Uneasy Lies the Crown		
53	Murder in Malibu		Theresa Goren

Frame-up of a specific person	Hide the body	Suicide	Self-defense
Edward Lytton, Milton Schaeffer			
	Len Fisher		
David Kincaid			
	Harry Chudnow (past)		
	Dian Hunter		
		Frank Staplin	
Charlie Chambers			
Adam Evans			

#	Title	Accident or natural causes	Robbery or other crime
54	Columbo Goes to College		
55	Caution: Murder Can Be Hazardous to Your Health	Budd Clark	
56	Columbo and the Murder of a Rock Star		
57	Death Hits the Jackpot	Freddy Brower	
59	A Bird in the Hand	Big Fred McCain	Fernando, Harold McCain
60	It's All in the Game		Nick Franco
61	Butterfly in Shades of Grey		
63	Strange Bedfellows		
64	A Trace of Murder		
65	Ashes to Ashes		
66	Murder With Too Many Notes	Gabriel McEnery	
67	Columbo Likes the Nightlife		
	Totals	35	22

*In "Fade in to Murder," it is not clear whether Ward Fowler is trying to make Claire Daley's death look like a robbery or whether he's trying to frame her husband Sid for the crime.

Frame-up of a specific person	Hide the body	Suicide	Self-defense
D.E. Rusk			
Marcy Edwards			
Jerry Winters			
Teddy McVeigh			Bruno Romano
Howard Seltzer			
	Verity Chandler		
	Tony Galper	Linwood Coben	
20	8	6	2

Accomplices, Blackmailers and Schlimazels

The original victim is not the only one in a number of *Columbo* episodes. Sometimes, the murderer uses an accomplice, who is then a liability that must be removed. On other occasions, some individual stumbles upon the murder and decides to blackmail the murderer—they usually wind up as victim number two. And finally there are those poor souls who are killed as part of a larger plan or by accident.

In *Prescription: Murder* (pilot A), Ray Flemming's plan begins to unravel in large part because of his reliance on his patient and lover, Joan Hudson, as an accomplice. She nearly crumbles under Columbo's surprisingly (at least in retrospect) tough interrogation (see "The Developing Character") and later she agrees to fake her own death in order to hear whether Flemming loves her and what he plans for the future. What is perhaps most ironic about this turn of events is that it demonstrates precisely what Flemming preached to Columbo but did not himself practice—creating the perfect murder requires a murderer who calculates every possibility and takes account of every contingency. His plan included a weak accomplice who betrayed him and, even if his intention was to get rid of her, he was unable to prevent Columbo from getting to her before he could carry out his plan. Succeeding *Columbo* murderers have also used accomplices, but on almost every occasion they have carried it off with greater success than Flemming.

In "Suitable for Framing" (#4), Dale Kingston gets impressionable art student Tracy O'Connor to stay with the body of his dead uncle and keep it warm until a security guard arrives so as to provide Kingston with an alibi for the delayed "time of death." Although Columbo has his suspicions about Tracy, he is unable to find her before Kingston knocks her unconscious and sends her over a cliff in her car. Ultimately, Kingston is caught on the basis of Columbo's fingerprints being on the paintings Kingston planted at his Aunt Edna's house.

In "Publish or Perish" (#20), Riley Greenleaf hires Eddie Kane to kill Allen Mallory and plant evidence suggesting that Greenleaf himself did it. This is part of his plan, because he will provide himself with an alibi (he was involved in a parking lot fender bender with a couple outside a bar at the time). In addition, Kane is going to become the second victim, and then Greenleaf can plant evidence indicating that the whole thing was his doing. He sets one of the man's own homemade bombs to explode (Kane is a bizarre character) and lets the police find the connections he wants in the rubble. Columbo catches Greenleaf by demonstrating that the scenario he has concocted (namely that Kane killed Mallory and framed Greenleaf for the deed to retaliate against both men for stealing his book) simply isn't possible. The conclusion to the book was thought up by Mallory's agent recently and couldn't be in Kane's synopsis.

In "A Friend in Deed" (#23), Mark Halperin uses the opportunity of helping his friend Hugh Caldwell conceal the accidental killing of Caldwell's wife to manipulate Caldwell into helping him kill his own wife, Margaret. Caldwell remains a weak character throughout the episode and provides an easier target than Halperin when Columbo has the real Bel Air Burglar threaten to expose the two men. But ultimately Halperin is caught when he plants the jewelry taken from Caldwell's wife in what he believes to be the burglar's apartment, but which turns out to be a set-up staged by Columbo, who actually rented the apartment.

In "A Deadly State of Mind" (#29), we have a scenario very similar to *Prescription: Murder*: a murdering psychiatrist uses a patient and lover as a weak accomplice who has the potential for bringing about his downfall. After the death of Karl Donner, Marcus Collier constructs a robbery scenario and depends upon his weak but trusting patient Nadia to assist by claiming that her husband was killed by two men in stocking masks. Columbo soon notices significant flaws in Nadia's story, but he also finds independent evidence implicating Collier. Collier takes advantage of his position by suggesting that Nadia undergo a lie detector test to satisfy Columbo's suspicions, all the while intending to use the occasion to do away with his vulnerable accomplice. Using hypnosis supposedly designed to prepare Nadia for the test, Collier instead gives her a post-hypnotic suggestion that will lead to her diving off a balcony in the belief that she is going swimming. Unlike Flemming, Collier brilliantly eliminates the potential weak link, and even though Columbo has many "little things" that bother him (the phone left off the hook after Collier's triggering call, the clothes she removed and folded in neat piles as if going swimming), he cannot prove that Collier killed Nadia. The detective is left trying to prove that Collier was at the Donner house that day, which he manages to do by presenting Collier with a witness who "saw" him at the scene of the crime. In reality the man at the scene (but not the one Columbo brings out) was blind, and Collier seals his own fate by letting on that he knew this fact. See "Get 'Em for the First Murder" for more.

In "A Case of Immunity" (#31), Hassan Salah has idealistic young Rahmin Habib pose as the driver who gets away after the security guard is killed both to steer the police in another direction and to obscure the time of death. But long before Columbo can get to Salah through Habib, Salah has killed off his accomplice by knocking him unconscious and sending him over a cliff in his car. There are several clues which lead Columbo to believe that Salah has murdered Habib, but he catches Salah by cajoling him into confessing in the unseen presence of his country's king.

"Columbo Cries Wolf" (#49) could easily be renamed "Accomplice to Murder" (I suggest as much in "Creative Columbo Titles"). Sean Brantley needs Tina, one of the models at The Chateau, to pretend to be his partner, Dian Hunter, after he murders Dian and wants to make it look like she drove away from the complex that night. Whether or not Tina knows what Brantley has done is not clear. She never reveals where she was during the first "fake" murder and after the real act has been committed, Columbo has just one chance to catch Brantley, which he brilliantly does with the beepers. Dian herself could be called an accomplice to her own murder, because her participation in the first scheme unknowingly set the stage for what happened next. And even Columbo could be called an accomplice, because his very thorough investigation into the fake scenario allows for the real one and almost prevents him from catching the murderer.

In "Columbo and the Murder of a Rock Star" (#56), Hugh Creighton asks his associate Trish Fairbanks to go on a "research project" which involves speeding down a street in Pasadena in his car with a mask of his face so as to establish an alibi while he murders his lover, Marcy. Not surprisingly, Trish figures out what really happened and creates her own insurance policy in the form of an envelope to be sent to the police in the event of her "accidental" death. She uses this knowledge to blackmail Creighton into giving her a partnership in his law practice and his social life, with the promise of marriage in six months. Although Creighton at first appears uncomfortable with this arrangement, later in the episode he seems to have accepted it. Columbo never confronts Trish, but it is unlikely that she would betray either herself or Creighton. Ultimately, the detective catches Creighton by placing him at the scene of the murder when he demonstrates that Trish's car (which Creighton used) has berries in its window washer well that fall only on a street near where the crime was committed (it's unclear whether he also plans on arresting Trish).

In "Death Hits the Jackpot" (#57), Leon Lamarr murders his nephew Freddy in order to keep Freddy's lottery winnings and he uses Freddy's almost-divorced wife (and his lover) Nancy as an accomplice to stay with the body and call him an hour later when he has the alibi of being at a costume party. The use of an accomplice in this episode makes very little sense, since Nancy keeps inquiring about her share of the money, and Lamarr would eventually have to decide to pay her or kill her, too. By the end of the episode, he has done neither. Additionally, she creates the problem of a liability that is never adequately dealt with. Although Nancy says nothing to implicate Lamarr, her explanations of her own behavior are very shaky and suspicious. In the end, after Columbo catches Lamarr by placing him at the scene of the crime (a chimpanzee that was present grabbed the shiny medallion on Lamarr's Halloween costume and left its fingerprint on it), then the Lieutenant has Nancy brought in and congratulates her on inheriting her husband's lottery money. This so infuriates Lamarr that he reveals her assistance in the murder. Ironically the primary murderer is used to catch the accomplice!

In "It's All in the Game" (#60), the use of an accomplice not only makes sense, but is required (both women have been hurt by this man and are preventing further injury by killing him first). But they make a serious mistake in not having Lisa leave immediately. Or they could have chosen to have Lisa stay but come out of hiding (they seem to forget that Lisa's presence is only incriminating if she is connected to Nick Franco, not to her own mother). Columbo uses the accomplice against the murderer here, but in a very unusual way. His decision to let Lisa go in order to obtain a confession from Lauren is bizarre and not easily understood. Obviously, he considers the motive for killing Franco to be sympathetic, but he arrests Lauren nonetheless. The same should apply to Lisa. This suggests that the real reason Columbo lets Lisa go is not out of sympathy for her, but because of his feelings for Lauren. See the two "Morality of Columbo" essays for more on this episode.

In "Columbo Likes the Nightlife" (#67), Vanessa Farrow accidentally kills her ex-husband Tony when she pushes him away and his head strikes a glass coffee table. She calls her lover, Justin Price, who needs Tony's money to open his dance club, and Justin takes over as prime mover, much like Mark Halperin in "A Friend in Deed" (#23). He comes up with the idea of making it look like Tony is still alive for two more days (until the money he needs is transferred to his account), he hides the body and then, when the couple is approached with incriminating photographs of them standing over Tony's body, Justin viciously kills tabloid photographer Linwood Coben and makes it look like a suicide. Columbo separately investigates Justin and Vanessa and they react differently. Justin has answers to the Lieutenant's probing questions, but Vanessa just becomes nervous and asks him to leave. Then she calls Justin, who is obviously frustrated by her inability to cope with the situation. For a time, it looks like the Lieutenant will get Vanessa to break or that Justin will decide that Vanessa is too much of a liability to keep around. But in the end, Columbo catches both of them by demonstrating that Tony's body is in the floor beneath the fish tank in Justin's newly-opened club.

Sometimes the accomplices are not arrested or killed. Despite the title of "The Conspirators" (#43) and the fact that the killer's friends are informed of the murder of arms dealer Vincent Pauley and agree to keep silent about it, Joe Devlin is never in any danger of being betrayed by the O'Connells (matriarch Kate and her son George) or even young Kerry Malone. Columbo gathers clues implicating Devlin in both the planned gun running and the murder and ultimately catches him for the latter on account of the poet's use of a diamond to scratch a line on every bottle of Irish whiskey he drinks, including the one left at the scene of the murder as an ironic joke. Columbo does get something out of the O'Connells, though—he recognizes their house flag on the tugboat and realizes that it must be where Devlin has hidden the guns he is shipping to Ireland.

Oscar Finch creates the scenario of having been in his office with a client when he was actually off killing Frank Staplin in "Agenda for Murder" (#50), but when Columbo starts to get too close, Finch enlists the aid of his friend Paul Mackey to claim that he was the client at the office that night. Columbo has evidence to disprove Mackey's story (principally the single dry spot in Finch's parking lot) but he places Finch at the scene of the crime by proving that a piece of cheese left on Staplin's desk has the same bite mark pattern as a piece of gum from Finch's office. It's not clear from the ending whether Mackey will be arrested as an accessory after the fact, or even if Finch's arrest will hurt his run for vice-president (although the latter certainly seems likely).

Here are some examples of accomplices who are not true accomplices. Paul Gerard uses Eve Plummer to withdraw the payoff money he receives from the restaurateurs in "Murder Under Glass" (#40), but Eve is unaware of the true nature of the scam, much less that Gerard has done away with Vittorio Rossi when Rossi refused to continue paying and threatened to expose him. Columbo uses Eve to find out where Gerard purchased the blowfish from which he extracted the poison to kill Rossi, but he catches Gerard only when the food critic tries to dispatch the good Lieutenant by the same means (see "The Kill Columbo Ending").

In "Uneasy Lies the Crown" (#52), Wesley Corman enlists the aid of his brother-in-law David Sherwin to make the death of Adam Evans look like an accident. But David is not a true accomplice since he believes Evans died when he accidentally ingested some of Wesley's wife Lydia's digitalis, when in fact Wesley engineered Evans's death by putting a time-release dose of digitalis in a filling in the actor's mouth earlier that day. David disappears from the story after he admits his role in moving the body to Columbo. In the end, Columbo "demonstrates" that the digitalis would stain Evans's teeth blue and Wesley confesses (even though the evidence is fake—Columbo used laundry bluing to create the desired effect).

In summary, the use of an accomplice, although helpful in certain respects, also contains potential problems. These problems appear to be resolved best if the accomplice is removed from the scene before Columbo has a chance to start asking questions, as in "Suitable for Framing" (#4), "A Deadly State of Mind" (#29) and "A Case of Immunity" (#31), or if the murderer is convinced that the accomplice will keep quiet because he or she has as much to lose as the primary murderer, as in "A Friend in Deed" (#23) and "Columbo and the Murder of a Rock Star" (#56). Accomplices who do not fall into either of these categories can be used to turn on the murderer (*Prescription: Murder*) and can be tricked into revealing their cohorts ("Death Hits the Jackpot" (#57)—although in that case it was the other way around).

Then there are those episodes that do not involve an accomplice initially, but in which someone becomes an accessory after the fact by stumbling upon the murder and trying to blackmail the killer. "Murder By the Book" (#1), "Dagger of the Mind" (#11), "Lovely But Lethal" (#16) and "Double Exposure" (#19) all contain the same structure: an individual comes upon evidence of the murder and tries to parlay that knowledge into a reward from the murderer. But Lilly La Sanka, Tanner, Shirley Blaine and Roger White all meet the same fate when the murderers remove them from the scene and make their murders look like a suicide, an accident or another framed murder. Columbo always has his suspicions about these second deaths and even some evidence pointing to the killers, but he catches the villains by finding evidence that they were at the scene or by use of clever tricks (see "Get 'Em for the First Murder").

Sharon Martin, the first victim in "A Stitch in Crime" (#13), is actually killed because she suspects that Barry Mayfield put dissolving suture into Dr. Heideman, who is supposed to die a few days later "of natural causes." And Charles Clay, who at first looks like the murderer in "Last Salute to the Commodore" (#35), becomes the second victim because he merely moved the body when he thought his wife killed the Commodore, but later concluded that her cousin Swanny was the true killer.

Of course, there is the complicated episode "A Bird in the Hand" (#59). Harold McCain, who Columbo is investigating for having planned the murder of his uncle, Big Fred (which doesn't come to pass as planned because Big Fred is hit by a truck), discovers that Big Fred's actual killer was his wife, Dolores. When Harold tries to blackmail Dolores, he winds up a victim himself. As discussed in greater detail in the essays "Variations on a Theme by Jackson Gillis" and "Get 'Em for the First Murder, No Matter What," Columbo arrests Dolores for Harold's murder, noting that he doesn't have to prove that she killed Big Fred.

Finally, there are those schlimazels (Yiddish for bad-luck sad sacks) who are killed as part of a bigger plan. They include: Harry Alexander in "A Stitch in Crime" (#13) (killed to complete the scenario that Sharon Martin was killed by someone to whom she sold drugs); Lisa Chambers in "Double Shock" (#15) (killed by the Paris brothers to implicate attorney Michael Hathaway in her murder as well as the original one, that of their Uncle Clifford, also so that she cannot collect under Clifford's will), Alvin Deschler in "Negative Reaction" (#25) (killed by Paul Galesko to complete the scenario that Deschler kidnapped and killed Galesko's wife Frances); Milton Schaeffer in "Old Fashioned Murder" (#37) (killed by Ruth Lytton to make it appear that her brother Edward, the main victim, caught him robbing the family museum); Adam Evans in "Uneasy Lies the Crown" (#52) (killed by Wesley Corman to implicate his wife Lydia, so that he can curry favor with her father by getting her committed rather than arrested); Bruno Romano in "Strange Bedfellows" (#63) (killed by Graham McVeigh "in self-defense" to complete the scenario that Romano killed Graham's brother Teddy); and Howard Seltzer in "A Trace of Murder" (#64) (killed by Patrick Kinsley and Cathleen Calvert solely to frame her husband Clifford for the crime so that he will be arrested and she can remain with Kinsley). Then there is the sad case of Fernando in "A Bird in the Hand" (#59), who is killed by accident when he starts a car wired by go off by Harold McCain. The intended victim is Harold's uncle, Big Fred, but he was already killed, at first we are led to believe by a drunk driver, but then we learn that it was a premeditated act by Fred's wife Dolores. These people must be cursed.

Chapter 20:
Columbo's Relationship with the Murderer

The Sympathetic Murderer Relationship

The sympathetic murderer relationship between Columbo and the murderer was introduced in the third season episode "Any Old Port in a Storm" (#17). Episodes that feature this relationship contain at least three points of commonality that identify them as examples of this type of relationship, as opposed to the usual antagonistic relationship between Columbo and the murderer, or the occasional example (see the following essay) of the "all-in-the-game" paradigm in which the murderer appears to be enjoying Columbo's company, but is in fact faking it. First, the murderer has a sympathetic motive for his or her acts (hence the name for this paradigm). Thus, if the victim threatens to take away something that means everything to the murderer (a winery, a military academy, a last opportunity to dance, etc.), both the audience and Columbo will have some sympathy for this individual, although we do not condone the murder. This simply isn't possible if the motive is to inherit money ("Suitable for Framing" (#4), "Double Shock" (#15)) or to cover up a scandal ("Mind Over Mayhem" (#21)) or to hide an affair ("Candidate for Crime" (#18)), or to achieve other nefarious purposes. On a related point, there is no way that this individual could ever commit a second murder because the extreme circumstances precipitating the first one just will not recur and the audience would no longer be sympathetic if the murderer goes around knocking off witnesses, etc. (e.g., Abigail Mitchell of "Try and Catch Me" (#39) isn't about to close the safe door on Columbo).

Second, there is often a scene, unnecessary to the plot, in which the Lieutenant and the murderer share a quiet moment together enjoying an activity that is meaningful to the murderer, and it is both touching and significant. When he tries Adrian Carsini's wines, or enjoys Tommy Brown's music or Grace Wheeler's dancing, or shares a cigar while discussing retirement with Colonel Rumford, we can see that the Lieutenant has made a connection that transcends the murder investigation. Finally, in the last scene there is either a moment of regret evident in Columbo's manner or he makes a gesture to soften the blow. Easy example: his offering of the bottle of dessert wine to Carsini. It wasn't necessary, but it was very poignant and the perfect ending to the episode.

Now, one might suppose that the show would employ this paradigm whenever a female murderer was featured, but this has not been the case. Fascinatingly, the first three examples were male villains, although they have all been females more recently (but not every female murderer on the show is a sympathetic character). Of course, the first time this paradigm was used was in the episode many people consider the best of the best, "Any Old Port in a Storm" (#17). In this episode the motive of stopping his brother Ric from selling the winery that is Carsini's whole life is entirely sympathetic, Columbo slowly bonds with Carsini as he learns about wines and uncovers the key to solving the case (witness the scene in which he delights Carsini by demonstrating that he has learned the rudiments of wine appreciation, as well as his display of knowledge at the dinner), and the ending contains a wonderful sympathetic gesture as the Lieutenant allows Carsini to sip a dessert wine as he drives him downtown.

"Swan Song" (#22) is the second example. Tommy Brown may not be the most moral guy in the world (taking sixteen-year-old Maryann to hotels is rather disgusting), but Edna takes his "punishment" too far, and his desire to escape from her clutches makes him a sympathetic character. Clearly, he becomes fast friends with Columbo (even calling him "little buddy") and the Lieutenant really means it when he says he enjoyed Tommy's concert. Columbo makes a nice gesture at the end when he turns on the radio and remarks that anyone who can sing like that can't be all bad.

Next on the list of sympathetic murderers is Colonel Rumford of "By Dawn's Early Light" (#26). He may be a tough commander to the cadets, but his motive (to keep the academy that means so much to him) is sympathetic, and he does indeed connect with the Lieutenant in the famous scene in the office where they share a cigar and Rumford asks Columbo if he has a first name (see "You Can Call Him Lieutenant"). At the end, Columbo allows the proud man a last moment with his cadets to tell them that there will be discipline for the cider brewing, although he won't be around to administer it. The camera freezes on that poignant scene.

The next episode is "Forgotten Lady" (#30) and I doubt this call will surprise anyone. Grace Wheeler's motive (to dance again despite her skinflint husband, so she thinks) is very sympathetic and ultimately tragic. Columbo really does love old musicals and he gets a thrill out of spending time with Wheeler. She clearly likes him, and the ending is the greatest gesture of sympathy the Lieutenant can make—he doesn't arrest her. See "The Morality of Columbo I" for more on this episode.

Then comes a tough call, "Old Fashioned Murder" (#37). This episode has problems—lots of them—but I think what they're going for here is a Type II episode. Ruth Lytton kills her brother to stop him from selling the family museum that is the only place where she has ever felt comfortable (like Carsini in his winery). She and Columbo share a love of beautiful old objects and museums, and he offers two gestures to her at the end: he withdraws his theory that she killed Peter Brandt years ago in return for her confession to the crime at hand, and he offers her his arm (like the gentlemen callers that her sister has succeeded in wooing while Ruth spent her life running the museum) on their way out. Of course, it is difficult to maintain sympathy for Ruth as she frames her niece Janie for the crime, not to mention the fact that she also kills an innocent man in the first place (Milton Schaeffer may be a shady character, but he isn't involved in closing down her museum) and makes wisecracks as she does so. A mess, to be sure, but the underlying idea is a sympathetic murderer relationship.

In "Try and Catch Me" (#39), the motive of killing Edmund, who murdered her niece Phyllis and got away with it, is incredibly sympathetic. Abigail Mitchell really takes a liking to Columbo (telling him he's a nice young man and kind and so on) and they bond in the scene on the pier when he tells her how he likes to bring Dog out to see the ocean. And the Lieutenant clearly regrets having to arrest her at the end. Whether or not he should arrest her and whether his justification for doing so should be that he takes his job seriously are matters for discussion in another essay (see "The Morality of Columbo I"), but this is a terrific sympathetic murderer relationship episode.

From the newer episodes, "Sex and the Married Detective" (#46) is another sympathetic murderer situation. Dr. Joan Allenby's life has been shattered by her lover's betrayal, so her motive is sympathetic. She and Columbo like each other, and he is very compassionate with her in the ending when he tells her he understands what has driven her to this act. Finally, I put "It's All in the Game" (#60) in this category. I realize that I am about to use the phrase "all-in-the-game" to describe the next type of Columbo/murderer relationship and this one does at times appear to be the sort of situation where the murderer and Columbo are only pretending to enjoy each other's company, but ultimately I think it more naturally falls here. The twist, of course, is that we don't know what the motive is until the very end, so that we assume Lauren Staton is a typical non-sympathetic murderer. Then, in watching her interact with Columbo, it is not clear whether they really like each other or whether she is pretending and he is playing along in order to catch her. In other words, while watching it for the first time, I thought it was an "all-in-the-game" episode . . . until the ending. Now we learn that her motive—to save her daughter and herself from the batterer Nick Franco—is highly sympathetic. Now Columbo makes the grand gesture of allowing daughter Lisa to leave in return for Staton's confession. In light of all of this, I think the bond between Columbo and Staton is genuine.

What about the very end, when the Lieutenant tells Barney that it was just a trick to catch Staton? Well, writer Peter Falk never quite made up his mind as to what he wanted to do. Having Columbo actually fall for Staton would be fascinating, but at the same time insulting to the notion that the Lieutenant has always been faithful to his wife. So he goes the other way at the end and pretends as if it's all been a game. There is no clear answer to this, but it seems that Columbo likes Staton enough to be sympathetic to her situation, particularly when he finds out what it is, even if he isn't as attracted to her as he appears to be.

On the other hand, "Lady in Waiting" (#5) does not present a sympathetic murderer situation. As noted above, she pulls a gun on Columbo at the end, and that's just not something a sympathetic murder would do. In addition, Beth Chadwick's motive is key. At the beginning, it appears to be to escape from her brother Bryce's overpowering control, or perhaps to be free to marry Peter Hamilton. Of course, she could accomplish either goal without killing Bryce, and Hamilton says he would have quit the company to be with her. But ultimately I don't think that these were her motives, or if they were, she has abandoned them for less sympathetic ones by the end. She doesn't merely live her own life after Bryce is gone, she takes his place and begins to run the company her own way. This motive, had it been revealed at the beginning, would not make her a very sympathetic character. In fact, this scenario should sound familiar, because it is exactly what was used in the next episode, "Short Fuse" (#6). Roger Stanford may look sympathetic at the beginning when he stops his evil uncle from throwing him out of his late father's company, but later when Roger takes over the company and starts implicating an innocent man for the murder, neither the audience nor Columbo could find him very likeable. And Beth reveals herself to be such a domineering person (it must run in the family) that Peter Hamilton has all but called off the engagement before Columbo makes his arrest. What about her interaction with Columbo? Well, they never seem to connect in any way, and in the scene at the company offices, she orders him never to bother her again (not exactly a bonding situation). Finally, when she pulls the gun on him at the end, Columbo does not say that he understands her situation, only that she's "too classy" to do that and what would be the point with police outside? He is polite, but I don't think he genuinely feels sorry for her. Under the circumstances, why should he?

The All-in-the-Game Relationship

As hinted at in "The Sympathetic Murderer Relationship," there are actually three types of relationships between Columbo and the murderers on the show. Most of the time, we get what might be called the usual antagonistic relationship. The murderers don't particularly like Columbo, and although they may be amused at first by this odd little man, they quickly become increasingly frustrated by his incessant questioning, and ultimately they are at least flabbergasted, if not infuriated, when caught by this guy. Then there is the sympathetic murderer situation, first dramatized in the excellent episode "Any Old Port in a Storm" (#17).

And that's that . . . or is it? I have come to the conclusion that there is a third type of episode. The name for this paradigm should be obvious: "All-in-the-Game." In this version of the Columbo/murderer relationship, Columbo and the murderer seem to be consciously taking note of the fact that they are engaging in a game of wits and games are referred to throughout as a kind of motif. They may appear to be having fun together, but we can see that the murderer is faking it and we know Columbo realizes that, deep down, this person isn't nice. This is the defining characteristic of the paradigm and it carries over to the final scene. Columbo doesn't make a kind gesture, nor does he regret having to make the arrest. And the murderer isn't angry; instead he (there have been no fully-realized episodes of this type with female murderers) is still caught up in the game he has lost. He compliments Columbo on solving the case, as if he was just an observer looking in from the outside and was not about to be taken downtown. Not so surprisingly, it is in this type of episode that the murderer often casually asks when Columbo first suspected him and the Lieutenant obliges by revealing the first clue (or one of them).

Inklings of the game idea can be seen in the first pilot (*Prescription: Murder*) in the scene in Dr. Flemming's office in which he and Columbo discuss the "hypothetical murderer." In addition, some of the scenes in *Ransom for a Dead Man* (pilot B) also suggest the idea, as when Leslie Williams tells Columbo that his little trick of reproducing how she used a machine to play a tape of her husband's voice for the ransom call didn't work and when she makes him sick by flipping her airplane upside down. She even compliments him at the end, saying he's "very smart" and he returns the compliment. But the characters don't play games with each other and they don't really pretend to like one another.

The first full-fledged instance of an "all-in-the-game" episode does not occur until the third season in "Double Exposure" (#19). Columbo and Bart Kepple do not like each other by any stretch of the imagination. But they do engage in the battle I've described, both in Kepple's office in that terrific scene discussing the second print of the film and on the golf course when Columbo interferes, at least temporarily, with Kepple's game (Kepple even says "I'll play" when the Lieutenant asks him to go along to check out the murder of Roger White). At the end, Kepple seems genuinely tickled by the fact that Columbo caught him using his own technique of subliminal cuts. He has a big grin on his face when Columbo comments that, if there were a reward for Kepple's capture, the Lieutenant would support his claim to it. Writer Stephen J. Cannell, who admired what might be described as "taking off the gloves" scenes in which Columbo drops his polite manner, carries the idea one step further here and creates this new type of Columbo/murderer relationship.

"All-in-the-game" does not appear again until the fifth season, in

"Identity Crisis" (#32). Again, the references to the game motif are present (indeed, they are very heavy-handed); the murderer has a number of games in his house, and they connect one of them, mah-jongg, to the Chinese at the end of the episode. Nelson Brenner doesn't miss a beat after hearing the final clue (a rather disappointing alibi buster—see "Busting Alibis, Busting Scenarios") before asking whether it was the coat that kept bothering Columbo, and the Lieutenant replies yes; a mugger would not have touched the coat but it was removed because the victim was wearing a shoulder holster.

Next comes "Fade in to Murder" (#36). Despite Ward Fowler's comment at the end about the murderer having the sympathetic part, the fact is that he doesn't. However, Fowler (or at least his alter ego, Lieutentant Lucerne) engages in very bizarre behavior because Lucerne keeps pointing to evidence that implicates Fowler. The actor and the Lieutenant form a gaming relationship, even to the point where the last scene (where Columbo has the final clue in his pocket) begins with Fowler and Columbo playing around with his video camera and VCR.

This paradigm is a favorite of episodes produced under Richard Alan Simmons, because three of the five episodes in the seventh season fall into this type: "Murder Under Glass" (#40), "How to Dial a Murder" (#42) and "The Conspirators" (#43). In "Murder Under Glass" (#40), the final scene is the amazing one in which Columbo cooks a meal while explaining how Paul Gerard murdered Vittorio Rossi with a wine opener tinged with fugu poison, while Gerard attempts to repeat the process with the detective. But Columbo is one step ahead of him, and the glass full of poison is the evidence he needs to catch the wily Gerard. When Gerard asks Columbo when he first suspected him, the Lieutenant explains that Gerard's prompt arrival at the scene of the crime (rather than going to a hospital) after being told he had eaten dinner with a man who had been poisoned was "the damnedest act of good citizenship I've ever seen."

In "How to Dial a Murder" (#42), the game theme runs throughout from

Eric Mason's comment that Columbo has won "the game" when he presents the telephone clue, to the word game they play, to the extraordinary ending in which Columbo reveals clues by shooting billiard balls into the pockets on Mason's pool table! Mason says "remarkable" after he recovers from his shock that Columbo has learned the kill word and reprogrammed the dogs. Then he compliments Columbo on having taken control and comments that he could swear that the Lieutenant had taken one of his courses. "No sir," responds Columbo, "it's just that I enjoy the pleasure of the game." It's true that Nicol Williamson sometimes plays the scenes as Mason in a very imposing way, using his stature to intimidate, and he doesn't ask when Columbo first suspected him (this question is not a necessity; it just fits nicely into this paradigm). But on the whole it is an "all-in-the-game" episode.

Finally, "The Conspirators" (#43) uses the game theme repeatedly, from the first scene in which Columbo meets poet Joe Devlin and they play pinball, to their dart games in the pub and the limerick-telling contest. In the end, Devlin raises his glass to salute the cop who beat him and tells him it wasn't luck.

In addition, I would include in this group the first episode from the Simmons era, "The Bye-Bye Sky High IQ Murder Case" (#38) from the end of the sixth season in 1977. Now, I'm not about to say that this episode fits neatly anywhere, but it is best described as an "all-in-the-game" episode. Oliver Brandt is not a sympathetic character—he kills his partner Bertie because he has discovered that Brandt is stealing from his clients. Brandt and Columbo invoke the gaming theme, using the brainy organization to which Brandt belongs as a jumping off point, and including the scene in which Columbo has to solve the bags-of-gold minimum information problem. And when caught, Brandt gets into that Type III area, the inquiry about the first clue ("It was the cuing that bothered you? Remarkable!") The reason this episode doesn't fit very well is that Brandt is such a weak villain that he can't play the game properly and he comes off as a sweaty, nervous, ineffectual opponent. It's true that the men have a sort of bonding scene in which

Brandt talks about the difficulties of being born "smart" and Columbo relates how he decided to work twice as hard in order to keep up the smart guys on the force. My take on this scene is that it is an example of Columbo's basically good nature, as he explains in "Try and Catch Me" (#39)—he tries to find good qualities in everyone, even murderers. Thus, he appreciates the challenges Brandt has faced, but he still intends to arrest him for the crime he committed. See "The Developing Character" for more on that scene.

The other on-the-fence episode is one of the newer ones produced by Simmons, "Grand Deceptions" (#47). In that episode, there is a kind of game theme introduced through the I-Ching sticks and Frank Brailie asks at the end when Columbo first suspected him. But I have concluded that this is not a real "all-in-the-game" episode because Brailie doesn't play along. He finds Columbo annoying and seems frustrated in the final scene. Columbo is the one who leaves the I-Ching stick indicating a trap is afoot and Brailie does not compliment the Lieutenant on catching him. Instead, he shrugs in resignation.

Of the new episodes, the first one that fits into this type is "Murder: A Self Portrait" (#48) (which is Simmons's last episode as executive producer). Again, it doesn't fit well, but here the awkwardness is caused by those dream scenes that seem to bother some people (although I liked at least the first two). Or more specifically, because Max Barsini is painting Columbo's portrait, the writers could not allow the Lieutenant to present his usual probing clues, so they use the suggestive but ephemeral dream memories instead and have Columbo hold all of the real clues until the end (see "Intermediate Clues"). Thus, a sort of false camaraderie is engendered, but even so, the men taunt each other, and Barsini does seem to be rather objective at the end when he asks what would have happened if he'd used a clean rag to knock out Louise, and the Lieutenant's answer takes us back to the First Clue, the one contact in/one out observation.

"Ashes to Ashes" (#65) looks like an all-in-the-game episode, but it really isn't. Part of the question is how much of the relationship between Eric Prince and Columbo is colored by the personal friendship between Patrick

McGoohan and Peter Falk (see "Peter Falk as Columbo"). There really is no game theme invoked although the men do taunt one another. It's a very odd moment at the end when Eric Prince announces that he's going to the police car, apparently giving up when all Columbo has done (or tried to do) is bust the scenario that Prince cremated Chuck Huston one day and Mel Lerby the next (in fact, the first cremation was victim Verity Chandler and the second consisted of Houston and Lerby together, so Huston's piece of shrapnel winds up in Lerby's ashes). Prince does not ask when Columbo first suspected him, although he does step outside the situation to compliment Columbo at the end.

"Murder With Too Many Notes" (#66) also looks a little like a Type III episode. Although Findlay Crawford asks Columbo at the end if he knows of a symphony he can conduct in prison, his attitude toward the Lieutenant throughout is not that of gamesmanship. In point of fact, it's not a clear attitude. Sometimes he seems bemused by Columbo, but at other moments he is frustrated by him. Nevertheless, this does not really qualify as a Type III episode: there is no game theme, Crawford does not ask when Columbo first suspected him and he does not compliment the Lieutenant at the end.

Some people have suggested that there are episodes when Columbo really dislikes the murderer, such as Barry Mayfield of "A Stitch in Crime" (#13), Milo Janus of "An Exercise in Fatality" (#24) and Paul Gerard of "Murder Under Glass" (#40). I have thought about this idea, but I can't quite buy into it. For one thing, two of the episodes involve instances when "Columbo Gets Angry" and, as explained in the essay with that title, I think he's really angry, but not because the murderer is a particularly heinous individual. Rather, it's because he has tried or actually gotten away with murder *again*, right under the Lieutenant's nose (similarly, he is angry with Marcus Collier in "A Deadly State of Mind" (#29) because Collier succeeds in committing a second murder on Columbo's watch and he's angry with Anita Borden because she's concealing evidence that could help convict Collier). But the larger issue is that we never know what Columbo is really thinking, so there's no reason to believe he hates anybody.

Moreover, I just don't see why Columbo would despise Paul Gerard. I know, he says he doesn't like very much about him, but he is responding to Gerard, who said it first. I have never been happy about that line, as it is the first time he says something like this. It doesn't add anything to the episode, and it doesn't answer the question of why Columbo would despise Gerard. Yes, he's a snob but so is Adrian Carsini. Yes, he has killed a person people admire (Vittorio), but the same is true of many other murderers (Leslie Williams, Ken Franklin, Beth Chadwick, Alex Benedict, Emmet Clayton, Riley Greenleaf, Mark Halperin and Luis Montoya come to mind). Yes, he tries to kill Columbo, but that is the Lieutenant's plan and he doesn't seem particularly upset by it, nor is he upset in "How to Dial a Murder" (#42) or "Columbo Goes to the Guillotine" (#44) (the other episodes that employ the "Kill Columbo Ending"; see essay by that title). He doesn't even mind all that much in "Rest in Peace, Mrs. Columbo" (#51) when Vivian Dimitri tries to do away with his wife, at least not when he anticipates this move and uses it as a way to catch her (in fact, Columbo's comments to Dimitri at the end support my theory that he's basically a good guy; he's a lot more understanding of this woman who plotted to kill his wife than I imagine most men would be). And Gerard doesn't measure up to the really heinous qualities of Mayfield or Janus—he isn't killing any witnesses or besmirching any characters. So I prefer to think of this episode as the quintessential "all-in-the-game" scenario: Gerard doesn't really like Columbo, but he plays a deadly game with him while faking a smile the entire time. As for how Columbo feels about Gerard, I would suggest the following: although the Columbo character develops over the years, I think the description that fits him best is the one he provides in the speech in "Try and Catch Me" (#39)—he doesn't dislike murderers, only the acts they do. And, true to that speech, he finds something to admire in Gerard—his knowledge of food. So his comment that he hasn't found much else to like about the man strikes me as out of character for this quintessentially polite guy. In any event, it doesn't mean that he despises Gerard.

In some of the newer episodes, Columbo announces that he doesn't like the murderers or otherwise insults them. He tells Alex Brady in "Murder, Smoke and Shadows" (#45) that it will be a pleasure to arrest him. He asks Frank Brailie in "Grand Deceptions" (#47) if he would agree that they don't like each other, and he tells Brailie he's too arrogant to have cleaned up the mud on the floor unless he was worried that he left it there during the commission of the murder. And he announces to Eric Prince in "Ashes to Ashes" (#65) that he's been catching guys like him for twenty-five years (an odd assessment of time, see "Hello, Continuity Department?") and that Prince stole a diamond necklace off a corpse years ago because telling him makes Columbo "feel good." These comments are unnecessary. In my opinion, they do not fit the Columbo character. To the extent that they suggest that Columbo really despises these guys, I don't understand why.

Of course, there is no "right" answer here; these are merely various ways of looking at the show. But I particularly like my system because it allows me to explain moments in the series that do not seem to fit. For example, in "Etude in Black" (#8) when Alex Benedict calls Columbo a "genius" in the last scene, it feels out of character for the relationship in that episode. The problem is that Benedict's comments are Type III in an episode that has been Type I all along. Indeed, the scene is even inconsistent internally, as Benedict tells his wife that he loves her and tells Columbo that this is embarrassing and then calls him a genius. It just doesn't belong there. I apply the same observation to a gesture Justin Price makes in "Columbo Likes the Nightlife" (#67). He should not send Columbo a colorful shirt because he doesn't even pretend to enjoy the Lieutenant's company. It's an "all-in-the-game" moment in an episode where it doesn't belong.

Columbo Gets Angry

Among the many fascinating aspects of *Columbo*, one that generates more attention than most is the question of those few times when the Lieutenant loses his cool. Is it for real? Is he faking it as a new approach to unnerve the murderer? Perhaps the reason this question is so intriguing is that it touches on the deeper unknowable issue of what is actually on Columbo's mind. Often, he is described as "faking" or deliberately acting to get under the murderer's skin when he fumbles for that piece of paper or gets lost on a tangent about his wife. (It was fascinating back in 1996 to hear people ask the same questions about Frances McDormand's Oscar-winning performance as the pregnant police chief in the movie *Fargo* and more than a few critics noted the character's Columbo-like qualities.) Thus, when he "drops the façade" and gets angry with the murderer, we want to know why.

Some people have suggested that Columbo's explosions are part of his act because they come late in the episodes, after his usual methods have not produced results. Thus, they say that the Lieutenant uses badgering to get Joan Hudson to confess or at least implicate Ray Flemming in *Prescription: Murder* (pilot A), that he explodes at Barry Mayfield to induce him to incriminate himself by removing the dissolving suture he used to sew the valve into Dr. Heideman in "A Stitch in Crime" (#13), and that he gets angry at Milo Janus to trick him into slipping up in "An Exercise in Fatality" (#24).

I admire this analysis and I agree with it, at least in part. The faking-it concept works well for *Prescription: Murder*, even though I do not believe it is credible that Joan Hudson would turn on Flemming so quickly without even talking to him, and I do not accept that Flemming would fall for it. But we must remember that the Columbo of the first movie is not the same individual who appears in seasons two and four. In the first movie, he was essentially a polite civil servant, who would not hesitate to badger a witness if it became necessary. But as the series progressed, he became a more likeable person all around, and the outbursts seemed even more out of character. See "The Developing Character" for a further discussion of this issue.

The problem with the faking-it explanation is that it is quite unnecessary in "A Stitch in Crime" (#13) and inapplicable to "An Exercise in Fatality" (#24). In the former episode, Columbo is letting Mayfield know that if Heideman dies, an autopsy will be performed on the body and Mayfield will be caught. The Lieutenant does not have to shout to get that point across; he could say it very casually, because the words themselves would tell Mayfield he is in trouble. As for "An Exercise in Fatality" (#24), Janus has already told the Lieutenant to direct all further inquiries to his lawyer. He simply is not the type of individual who will be cowed into making an incriminating move if Columbo gets angry with him.

Here is my suggestion for what is going on in those two scenes. Columbo really is angry, and for a very specific reason. The Lieutenant's job is to catch murderers, and that means by definition that when he arrives on the scene someone is already dead. There is nothing he can do about this except catch the perpetrator, which he proceeds to do. But suppose that, while he is at work and before he can catch the murderer, that same individual strikes again right under the Lieutenant's nose. Now there is something to be angry about, and that is precisely what happens in both of these episodes. In "A Stitch in Crime" (#13), Sharon Martin and (I believe) Harry Alexander are dead, but Columbo has it in his power to prevent Dr. Heideman from dying and he is not about to let it happen on his watch. And in "An Exercise in Fatality" (#24), Ruth Stafford, the widow of the victim who turns to drink in her grief, tries to confront Milo Janus, but when he is unmoved by her accusations and makes threats of his own, she nearly dies of an overdose of alcohol and sleeping pills. Janus even has the guts to feign concern over her well-being. You had better believe Columbo is angry about her overdose.

I would also include in this list Nadia Donner of "A Deadly State of Mind" (#29). Granted, she is an accomplice to Marcus Collier's killing of her husband, but she is so completely under Collier's control that it is difficult to blame her directly. So I say Columbo is really angry at Collier. That would explain why the Lieutenant is short with him throughout the episode, but particularly after Nadia's murder, and why he loses his cool with Anita Borden when she is reluctant to tell him about the drugs she knows Collier is using and Columbo believes he used to trick Nadia into diving off the balcony. This murderer actually struck again on Columbo's watch, and he's not taking it lightly.

My comment about Ruth Stafford and Dr. Heideman being innocent (and Nadia Donner being completely under Collier's control) is an important caveat. Obviously, there are many other episodes with second murders, but the difference is that in those cases, the second victim at least partially has him/herself to blame. This person either has stumbled onto the murder or was an accomplice to it and is trying to blackmail the murderer when he or she meets an untimely end: Lilly La Sanka in "Murder By the Book" (#1), Tracy O'Connor in "Suitable for Framing" (#4), Tanner in "Dagger of the Mind" (#11), Shirley Blaine in "Lovely But Lethal" (#16), Roger White in "Double Exposure" (#19), Eddie Kane in "Publish or Perish" (#20), Rahmin Habib in "A Case of Immunity" (#31). (See "Accomplices, Blackmailers and Schlimazels" for more on this topic.) Thus, we can understand why the Lieutenant is not overly upset about this falling out among criminals. And in addition, he was completely unaware of the existence of or the connections to these people, so there was nothing he could have done to prevent their deaths. He never meets some of them at all, and others he talks to, but does not know that they possess knowledge that will result in their deaths.

There are exceptions, of course (how could there not be, in a show written by so many different people over the years?). Thus, Lisa Chambers is a second innocent victim in "Double Shock" (#15), but the Lieutenant does not explode at the Paris brothers. Of course, dealing with Mrs. Peck probably has him walking on eggshells, and attacking the Paris brothers would not help the situation. And the murder of Tomlin Dudek is essentially a second murder in "The Most Dangerous Match" (#14) because the method (mixing up Dudek's medications) is completely divorced from Emmet Clayton's first attempt (pushing Dudek into the trash compactor), yet the Lieutenant does not explode when he is unable to prevent the completion of this murder (he does yell at Clayton at the end, but that's just to prove the point that Clayton could not hear the trash compactor when his hearing aid was not working). But in general, my thesis works fairly well. That is why I conclude not that Columbo dislikes Mayfield and Janus, but that he is momentarily angry with them for trying to kill again while he is on the case (see "The All-in-the-Game Relationship" for more on Columbo-murderer relationships).

Chapter 21:
More About the Character

The Developing Character

Who is Columbo? One of the most fascinating aspects of the show is that the main character is not set in stone. Indeed, he's something of a moving target: one episode, he's a nice guy who hates to see someone with decent qualities commit heinous deeds and get put away for it; the next, he seems almost happy to slap the cuffs on the culprit. In part, these differences can be attributed to the passage of time and different writers being involved, but the character's development is not fully linear. I want to explore it a bit further here. In addition, I want to discuss how the newer episodes have explored Columbo's characteristics, or how they have failed to do so.

Not surprisingly, the Columbo of *Prescription: Murder* (pilot A) bears only a slight resemblance to the character of the show, particularly in the later years. For one thing, Peter Falk plays the role very seriously and he speaks in a soft monotone, rather than his distinctive New York accent. His gestures are small. He also mostly carries his raincoat, and hardly puts it on. He seems for the most part like a worn-out career officer who views his job as putting criminals away. When psychiatrist Ray Flemming describes Columbo's behavior as a textbook example of compensation (he uses the fact that he doesn't look threatening to lull suspects into a false sense of security), the Lieutenant's response is "you got me pegged, Doc." He even uses heavy-handed interrogation on Joan Hudson, badgering her and accusing her of portraying the victim's wife on the plane where they fake an argument and she leaves (which is what they staged). The Columbo of later years would not have acted in this manner. See "Columbo Gets Angry" for further discussion of this topic.

Many changes in the character are evident as early as the second TV movie, *Ransom for a Dead Man* (pilot B). Columbo is introduced in the movie as he searches for his lost pen on Leslie Williams's front porch, in a much lighter approach. Falk uses his regular voice. Note how gently he treats the annoying step-daughter, Margaret. His kindness pays off as Margaret learns to trust him and ultimately helps him catch Leslie Williams, who actually believes that Margaret will go away if she is given a share of the phony ransom money. Finally, his love of chili and pool, friendship with Bert (of Barney's Beanery) and fear of flying are all introduced in this movie.

During the first season, more characteristics were added: the car (a dilapidated 1959 Peugeot that Falk found—with its engine missing—in the studio lot) is introduced in "Murder By the Book" (#1), he gets seasick in "Dead Weight" (#3) and he demonstrates a fear of heights in "Short Fuse" (#6). "Death Lends a Hand" (#2) establishes that he does not carry a gun and that he was a bit of a prankster as a kid (he learned to disable a car by putting a potato in the exhaust pipe). Also in "Dead Weight" (#3), he talks about his niece who married a cop and the context suggests that he may be making it up. And in "Suitable for Framing" (#4), Columbo reveals that he's rather shy about the subject of sex when he has difficulty questioning artist Sam Franklin while the man is painting a nude model.

In the second season, Dog is introduced in "Etude in Black" (#8). (See "Bert, Barney and Dog" for the history of Columbo's canine pal.) In "A Stitch in Crime" (#13), he demonstrates a fear of needles and the sight of blood. This is also the first time he eats a hard-boiled egg at the crime scene, although he also comments that he missed breakfast that morning, so this may not be his usual routine. He does do it again in the first episode of the third season, "Lovely But Lethal" (#16). In fact, his search for salt to put on his egg leads to an important clue (the empty flour tin with the octagonal print left in the bottom by the hidden jar of vanishing cream the victim stole from Viveca Scott). Thereafter, it would become his morning routine, although it is not employed all that often.

Columbo's Italian heritage is clearly suggested by his name and is commented on in "Dead Weight" (#3) (Hollister observes that it's odd that a man with the name Columbo is so uncomfortable on a boat), but it is not really explored until "Any Old Port in a Storm" (#17) in the third season. In that excellent episode (which also contains lots of other "firsts"), he tells Joan Stacey, Ric Carsini's fiancée, that he will help her search for Ric because "he's Italian and we Italians have to stick together." He admits to being Italian on both sides. Then he bonds with the murderer, winemaker Adrian Carsini, by allowing Adrian to teach him all about fine wines; his prior knowledge was limited to helping his grandfather stomp the grapes in the basement. He gains the man's respect by acquiring a lot of information (ironically, as it turns out, when he uses his newfound knowledge to catch Carsini by demonstrating that his act of turning off the air conditioning to suffocate his brother also ruined his priceless collection of rare wines by causing them to overheat).

From the very beginning, Columbo is always holding and smoking cheap cigars that he buys at the supermarket. He does attempt to quit in "Blueprint for Murder" (#7) and again in "Last Salute to the Commodore" (#35), but he never quite succeeds. Interestingly, cigar smoking is a trait he shares with all four murderers played by Patrick McGoohan: in "By Dawn's Early Light" (#26), the Lieutenant and Colonel Rumford share a cigar of quality in the Colonel's office; in "Identity Crisis" (#32), Columbo and Nelson Brenner enjoy a cigar in Brenner's opulent home; in "Agenda for Murder" (#50), Oscar Finch must smoke because he uses a lit cigar to suggest he had a late-night meeting in his office; and in "Ashes to Ashes" (#65), Eric Prince lights up. Columbo's knowledge of smoking comes in handy on several occasions. In "Mind Over Mayhem" (#21), he sees a match burnt from top to bottom and knows a cigar smoker was at the scene of the crime, so when Marshall Cahill pulls a cigar out of his pocket, the Lieutenant immediately suspects him. In "Caution: Murder Can Be Hazardous to Your Health" (#55), the Lieutenant notices differences in how cigarettes at the scene of the crime were extinguished (some crushed, some twisted) and the lack of staining on the filter means the victim didn't actually smoke the one found burning in his hand (the murderer had to remove the real fatal cigarette, as it was loaded with nicotine sulfate). And in "A Trace of Murder" (#64), the Lieutenant notices that the cigar left at the scene of the crime was not cut the same way that Clifford Calvert cuts his cigars, which leads Columbo to think that Calvert is being framed for the crime.

Many of the characteristics introduced in the first, second and third seasons were developed further as the show continued. He demonstrates his skill at the pool table in "The Greenhouse Jungle" (#9), when he "can't miss a shot" as he annoys Jarvis Goodland by pointing out inconsistencies in the kidnapping scenario. And he astonishes Eric Mason by shooting balls into various pockets of his pool table and pulling out clues in the conclusion of "How to Dial a Murder" (#42). As for chili, he humorously orders it at a fancy restaurant in "Publish or Perish" (#20), making the snooty waiter turn up his nose until Jeffrey Neal asks him to accommodate his friend. The car often serves as comic relief, as when the mechanic in "Etude in Black" (#8) refuses to work on it or when he drives it to the abandoned junkyard where Alvin Deschler has been murdered in "Negative Reaction" (#25) and a beat cop tells him the place has been closed for months. It stalls out on him completely in "A Friend in Deed" (#23) and is involved in fender-benders in "A Matter of Honor" (#33) (stranding poor Columbo in Mexico, which leads to his involvement in a case there), "Old Fashioned Murder" (#37) and "Make Me a Perfect Murder" (#41). In "The Conspirators" (#43), the car gets a flat tire.

He expands on the Italian aspect of his character in "Identity Crisis" (#32), in the scene in which he bonds with Salvatore DeFonte (Vito Scotti, see "The Supporting Cast" for details). They speak a little Italian together and DeFonte is happy to give "a fellow paisano" a copy of the speech that Nelson Brenner wrote for him. In "Murder Under Glass" (#40), Columbo actually interrogates a witness in Italian. Moreover, he uses the language throughout the episode to talk to Mario, the victim's nephew, whose information about his uncle's last moments is helpful in getting Columbo on the right track. Finally, his Italian heritage is used in "Death Hits the Jackpot" (#57). A little old Italian lady is annoyed by his presence at the funeral until he explains who he is in Italian. Oddly, the writer felt the need to have his dialogue subtitled, when it was not done in "Murder Under Glass" (#40). It was also a nice touch to have him pretend not to understand Italian when approached by the Mafia don in "Strange Bedfellows" (#63), although this small gesture does not quite address the whole uncomfortable collaboration (see "The Morality of Columbo II: How Far Will He Go?").

The fact that he doesn't carry a gun and doesn't like them is raised again in "Troubled Waters" (#27), when he asks murderer Hayden Danziger to fire the gun into the mattress so that he can do a crude ballistics check. However, he does fire the gun into the sandbox in "Playback" (#28) to demonstrate that the noise would have caused a door in the murderer's gadget-filled house to open, although he tells Harold Van Wyck that he hates guns. (This is the only time he fires a gun on the show.) But the idea gets carried too far in "Forgotten Lady" (#30) when he is hounded by police bureaucrats for failing to take his regular firing range test (see "Does Columbo Exist?" for more on this issue). The gun presents yet another problem with "No Time to Die" (#58)—the police procedural requires the main character to carry a gun, although he doesn't use it. And in the second Ed McBain adaptation, "Undercover" (#62), Columbo carries a gun and seems prepared to use it if necessary. He actually winds up getting pistol-whipped, in a most uncomfortable and un-Columbo-like scene (see "No Time for Columbo, No Place for McBain"). But the Lieutenant's non-gun-carrying habit is nicely used in "Butterfly in Shades of Grey" (#61), first when Fielding Chase notices at his office that Columbo is unarmed and then at the end when he starts to remove a shotgun from his trunk and remarks that Columbo is foolish to allow himself to be alone and unarmed with him (Columbo acknowledges that he is unarmed, but then leans on the horn of the disabled car and, as the police arrive, remarks that he is certainly not alone).

Here's a seemingly simple question with no clear answer: does Columbo drink when he's "on duty"? Setting aside the episodes where he must imbibe to form a relationship with the murderer (e.g., "Any Old Port in a Storm" (#17) when he allows Adrian Carsini to teach him about fine wines, and "The Conspirators" (#43), when he joins Joe Devlin for beer and Irish whiskey at various bars around L.A. so the men can tell each other limericks and play darts), the fact is that in some episodes he accepts a drink and in others he says he's "on duty" or asks for a soft drink. Even the two pilot movies can't agree on this one—in *Prescription: Murder* (pilot A), he and Ray Flemming have bourbon together, but in *Ransom for a Dead Man* (pilot B) he tells Leslie Williams he'll have a root beer and she comments how that makes her feel decadent. In other examples, he has another bourbon with Ken Franklin in "Murder By the Book" (#1), accepts a drink from Lizzi Fielding in "Etude in Black" (#8) and has a glass of wine with Nelson Brenner in "Identity Crisis" (#32) and with Eric Mason in "How to Dial a Murder" (#42). But on the other hand, he turns down an offer of a drink in "Candidate for Crime" (#18), tells Paul Galesko that he's "on duty" in "Negative Reaction" (#25), requests a cream soda in "A Deadly State of Mind" (#29), has a cup of tea with Abigail Mitchell in "Try and Catch Me" (#39), and tells Vincenzo Fortelli, the Mafia don in "Strange Bedfellows" (#63) and Eric Prince in "Ashes to Ashes" (#65) that he's on duty. Personally, I like the idea that he's a "cream soda kind of guy" (as he tells Fortelli at the end of the episode, when he's off duty) or at least that he wants to keep his head clear, as he says when he turns down a cognac offered by Commissioner Halperin in "A Friend in Deed" (#23).

Richard Alan Simmons became the executive producer of the show beginning with "The Bye-Bye Sky High IQ Murder Case" (#38) at the end of the sixth season. He changed the Columbo character by making him more formidable: he arrived at the scene in a cloud of smoke, surprising the murderer. Simmons continued to craft dramatic entrances for Columbo. In "Try and Catch Me" (#39), he emerges from a safe where the murderer thinks the victim's body is; in "Murder Under Glass" (#40), he is first seen eating at a restaurant where the victim died of food poisoning; in "Make Me a Perfect Murder" (#41), the murderer finds him lying in the position she left the victim in; in "How to Dial a Murder" (#42), the murderer finds Columbo playing with his two Dobermans after they've just mauled a man to death; and in "The Conspirators" (#43), the murderer finds Columbo playing pinball in his parlor although he's certain there's no connection between him and the victim.

In addition, in these episodes, Columbo's gestures become broader, as when he tells Oliver Brandt at the end of "The Bye-Bye Sky High IQ Murder Case" (#38) that he could never leave the force and he flails his arms around as he says so. In "Make Me a Perfect Murder" (#41), Columbo (whose questionable driving was previously a mild source of humor) gets into a major car wreck when his rear-view mirror falls off and then he spends most of the episode in a silly neck brace. And in "The Conspirators" (#43), he actually goes bar-hopping with the murderer, which is essential to the plot (it's how he learns about the murderer's habit of marking the bottle with his distinctive diamond ring), but is unnatural and seems to be carrying the "All-in-the-Game Relationship" just a wee bit too far.

In the Simmons's era, Columbo makes two speeches, each of which represents an interesting insight into his character, or at least the character he had become. The first, in "The Bye-Bye Sky High IQ Murder Case" (#38), is the one in which he explains how he decided to work twice as hard as all those "smart guys" on the force. He tells Oliver Brandt that he really enjoys his job. Of course, he may be lying and may actually be very quick-witted, but I think there's a ring of truth in what he says. It certainly fits in with his little character traits of losing pencils, fumbling for bits of paper in his pocket and so on. Personally, I rather like the idea that Columbo is the everyman who works twice as hard to catch the criminal, rather than the notion that he is a quick thinker but just hides it with the façade of a bumbler.

The second speech, in "Try and Catch Me" (#39), is in my opinion even more important. After murderer Abigail Mitchell humorously brings him up to speak before a ladies' luncheon, he lights a cigar and says the following:

> About my work being dark and frightening, I'll tell you the truth, I'm not sure about that either. I like my job; oh, I like it a lot. And I'm not depressed by it. And I don't think the world is full of criminals and full of murderers, because it isn't. It's full of nice people, just like you. And if it wasn't for my job I wouldn't be getting to meet you like this. And I'll tell you something else: even with some of the murderers I meet, I even like them too. Sometimes . . . like them . . . and even respect them. Not for what they did—certainly not for that. But for that part of them which is intelligent, or funny, or just nice. Because there's niceness in everyone, a little bit anyhow. You can take a cop's word for it.

Now admittedly, the speech is ambiguous. It could refer only to "Sympathetic Murderers," but then that wouldn't necessarily cover the ones who are intelligent and funny, like Bart Kepple in "Double Exposure" (#18) or Joe Devlin in "The Conspirators" (#43), and he does say there is niceness in everyone. I think that Columbo is saying that, at this point, he believes deep down that murderers (just like all people) have good and bad impulses, that they may have many fine qualities, but unfortunately they act on these bad impulses. He doesn't judge them or despise them, but it's his job to bring them to justice for what they've done. This sounds like something that might be said by Father Brown, the gentle sleuth created by G.K. Chesterton, but not an L.A. police officer. Then again, Columbo is not a typical cop and the mysteries are drawing-room type and not police procedurals (which is why the McBain adaptations were such a bad idea; see "No Time for Columbo, No Place for McBain" for more).

The newer episodes (for which Simmons returned as executive producer, ten years later) continued the course of making the character broader and eventually it crossed the line into self-parody. In "Columbo Goes to the Guillotine" (#44), the last scene goes way over the top. Columbo has occasionally taken some solace in putting away a particularly heinous murderer, but most of the time he simply does his job. Sticking a fake gun in Eliot Blake's face from which a flag saying "Bang" erupts changes the tone of the episode from one of seriousness (the capture of the murderer) to one of silliness. Here is a possibility that might have worked: if Columbo had pulled out a real but unloaded gun and pointed it at Blake, then pulled the trigger. As Blake stood there in shock, Columbo would say, "Now you know how Mr. Dyson felt as the blade came down on him. And you didn't even need to read his mind." If done in complete seriousness it might have been very effective, but what was done here was disappointing.

The silliness continues in the next episode, "Murder, Smoke and Shadows" (#45). First, rather than merely telling Alex Brady that his attempted bribery of his secretary was overheard, Columbo "proves" it to him by bringing out the waiter and busboy, who are both police officers, as well as the cocktail waitress, played by his former lover, an actress (a dangerous stunt, since he could have recognized her). Then Columbo takes a bow and appears to be dressed in a ringmaster's outfit. In addition to raising the old "Does Columbo Exist?" problem, this scene is disappointing because it serves no function except to draw attention to its own bizarre nature. The next episode, "Sex and the Married Detective" (#46), contains a contrived and pointless scene in which Columbo plays the tuba for a group of children.

"Grand Deceptions" (#47) manages to convey only the gestures, not the spirit of the Columbo character. In addition to the scene in which Columbo overdoes it when he discovers the flashlight (see "Peter Falk as Columbo"), there are the scenes in which he tells Frank Brailie that it will be a lot of paperwork now that it's a murder and in which he amazes General Padget with Civil War knowledge based on his nephew's taking part in reenactments (does the nephew stage these scenes for his uncle?). Naturally, the last scene is also problematic, what with Columbo fumbling around for a Miranda card and then stumbling through the words every kid can recite by heart. Meanwhile, the visual is of the Civil War battlefield scene, and the camera comes to rest on a miniature of . . . Columbo? It's silly and insulting to the character. (See "Does Columbo Exist?" for more on the existential issues raised by this scene.) Beyond this, Columbo makes unnecessary insults to the murderer at the end ("we don't like each other, would you agree with that?" and "you're too arrogant to clean up mud"). "Murder Under Glass" (#40) had such an exchange of unpleasantries, but it was begun by the murderer, not Columbo. As discussed in "The All-in-the-Game Relationship," this situation is not the kind where Columbo and the murderer are faking being friends. Brailie is not very likeable, but he gets his comeuppance.

In "Rest in Peace, Mrs. Columbo" (#51), writer Peter Fischer recalls some aspects of the character that were long neglected. He reminds us of Columbo's love of chili and has him comment on how he likes old-fashioned things, includes a scene at the police station, and uses an assistant who isn't an incompetent fool. In "Murder in Malibu" (#53), frequent contributor Jackson Gillis remembers the Lieutenant's habit of eating hard-boiled eggs, which had not been seen in a long time. Another hard-boiled egg-eating scene occurs in "A Trace of Murder" (#64), as Columbo waits to meet with the victim's lawyer to tell her the sad news.

In "Caution: Murder Can Be Hazardous to Your Health" (#55), Columbo takes way too long to put some obvious pieces together to conclude that the car of murderer Wade Anders has a scratch on it left by the victim's dog, who is missing a claw. First, he meets the dog, then he notices that she has scratched his car, then he and the murderer have a collision and only then does he notice the scratches on Anders's car. He doesn't put all the pieces together until he picks Dog up from a grooming and is told the animal has had a pedicure. This episode also contains a comment that seems out of character. When Columbo watches the dancers at the Television Awards rehearsal, he remarks "great legs," which does not jibe with his usual charming awkwardness around the subject of sex. Witness his sole comment about all the young beauties at The Chateau in "Columbo Cries Wolf" (#49): "They sure have their health." Similarly, he turns red when Joan Allenby asks him how things are at home (i.e., in the bedroom) in "Sex and the Married Detective" (#46).

In "Columbo and the Murder of a Rock Star" (#56), it was a good choice not to have Columbo order his usual chili. Instead, he uses the opportunity to order a feast that surprises Hugh Creighton, who can certainly afford it. In "It's All in the Game" (#60), writer Peter Falk remembers Columbo's hard-boiled-egg-and-juice routine at the murder scene, and the pajama top was a nice touch. In "Forgotten Lady" (#30), he is awakened from a sound sleep to go to the murder scene and he comments that it's lucky he didn't show up in his pajamas.

In "Death Hits the Jackpot" (#57), there are too many scenes of supposed comic relief, involving Columbo searching for a 25th anniversary gift for his wife, interacting with the victim's neighbors and showing up in places so that his presence will be humorous. A little of this last element goes a long way, but here we have the following: he arrives to tell Leon Lamarr (the murderer) about his nephew Freddy's death and finds that he's at a Halloween party where his raincoat is mistaken for a costume by an "eccentric millionaire"; he drives his car to an upscale dealership where the snooty salesman says "no trade-ins"; he interrupts a silent bid auction when his habit of waving to people from across the room puts him in an unintentional bidding war with Lamarr; and he appears at Freddy's funeral where his presence inexplicably annoys the old Italian lady, until Columbo surprises her by speaking Italian.

In "Butterfly in Shades of Grey" (#61), the car appears, as does "This Old Man" and the cigar, which is used for good effect in Fielding Chase's office. In "Undercover" (#62), there are bad attempts at humor when Geraldine Ferguson (Shera Danese) refers to Mo Weinberg (played by Burt Young) by saying he looks like the guy from *Rocky* (he *is* that guy). There is also another bad attempt at humor in the movie, objectionable for a much more serious reason. When Columbo meets Lucia, she asks his name and he responds "Columbo." She tells him it's an honor to meet a member of "that family." See "Does Columbo Exist?" for more on this scene. In addition, the Columbo character is compromised in this movie by having him placed in such dangerous situations. It was shocking to see him disarming Mo Weinberg and of course even more shocking to see him beaten up. The writers mention his habit of not wearing a gun only to discard it and of course the disguises turn him into someone other than the mild-mannered fellow he has been for the past twenty years. There is an occasional attempt to lighten the mood, as when Detective Brown brings Columbo some colorful baggy pants to get him out of the hospital, but it wasn't very funny, nor did it relieve the tension of seeing the beloved Lieutenant pistol-whipped.

In "Strange Bedfellows" (#63), Columbo's upset stomach from the clams, although a humorous idea in theory, gets a little bit too gross. In "A Trace of Murder" (#64), there are several moments of parody. For one thing, Columbo announces that a cat who is missing from the victim's apartment "could be the only witness to this terrible crime." He also goes around tossing fruit to people. And he tells Patrick Kinsley that "three eyes are better than one," implying that he (like Peter Falk) has a glass eye. Previously, there was no reason to believe this was true. Also, the language used in this episode was unfortunate. No, it isn't Columbo who says "that son of a bitch" (the co-conspirators do, when each thinks the other has turned state's evidence against him or her), but still, the program never saw the need to employ this language before, and it adds nothing here. (Back in "Agenda for Murder" (#50), Columbo refuses to repeat the word "Jesus" when Oscar Finch tells him the victim says it; again, Columbo as a mild-mannered fellow is a nice touch, but making him foul-mouthed just turns him into every other TV cop.)

In "Ashes to Ashes" (#65), Columbo mentions in passing that his wife won't talk about their final departure, but this topic was handled much better in a brief scene in "Swan Song" (#22) with Vito Scotti as Mr. Grindell.

"Murder With Too Many Notes" (#66) has the cigar and, of course, the car is put to use in the somewhat overly long scene of driving Findlay Crawford home. But someone forgot Columbo's fear of heights. While Sergeant Degarmo keeps a healthy distance from the edge of the roof, the Lieutenant keeps walking up and looking down four stories to the street, and it isn't even necessary to catch the murderer. Also, Columbo comes off as a fool when he seems not to know anything about music and can scarcely recognize such popular tunes as the themes from *Jaws* and *Psycho*. What's very odd is that, although the murdering conductor is involved in this skewering of the character, it is joined in fully by the members of the orchestra, who have no reason to dislike the Lieutenant.

In fact, it was unnecessary and somewhat offensive to have the orchestra make fun of Columbo for not knowing some obvious movie tunes and for being ignorant of classical music. It's one thing for Findlay Crawford to try to make Columbo look foolish—indeed, that fits in with the show's theme that murderers underestimate him—but why does the script have a musician call out that he's surprised the Lieutenant has even heard of Tchaikovsky? In fact, past episodes reveal that he does appreciate and know a thing or two about classical music: he has arrested one maestro before in "Etude in Black" (#8), he is captivated by classical pieces while pursuing Elliot Markham in "Blueprint for Murder" (#7) and he states that *Madame Butterfly* is his wife's favorite opera in "Identity Crisis" (#32). Finally, he spends a lot of time listening to Tchaikovsky in "The Bye-Bye Sky High IQ Murder Case" (#38), in which a piece of the composer's *Romeo and Juliet* is crucial to the plot. Naturally, Columbo does not take offense at these insults, but this scene continues the process of the character becoming a caricature of himself, and that is a shame.

Finally, in "Columbo Likes the Nightlife" (#67), Columbo drives his car around a bit and smokes a cigar briefly at the beginning, but the roughness of the episode seems out of place (the violence of the second murder and Columbo sticking his hand into a toilet). It was interesting to note that, although the Mafia makes another appearance on the show, in this instance Columbo politely declines all offers of help and solves the case on his own. This is a far cry from his behavior in "Strange Bedfellows" (#63), when he collaborated with mob boss Vincenzo Fortelli to convince murderer Graham McVeigh to confess. (See "The Morality of Columbo II" for more on this topic.)

Peter Falk as Columbo

Every once in a while in the arts, there is a perfect marriage of actor and character. It isn't so much that another actor could not play the role as it is that the particular choice becomes so indentified with the role that we could not imagine what anyone else would do with it. And when that character is on a television show, the repetition allows the actor to put something of him/herself into the character. A few examples would include: Leonard Nimoy as Mr. Spock on *Star Trek*, Carroll O'Connor as Archie Bunker on *All in the Family*, Raymond Burr as Perry Mason, and obviously, Peter Falk as Columbo.

As the history indicates, Falk was not the first person to play the role, either on television (Bert Freed was the character in "Enough Rope") or on the stage (see "Prescription: Mitchell" for more details). And he wasn't the first choice to play the part. Lee J. Cobb and Bing Crosby were first offered the role, but both turned it down. But once the first pilot aired in 1968 and ever since, there has been only one Columbo and there is no doubt that Falk has made the character the one we know and love, and love to discuss. (I'd be curious to know how Norm Boucher and others handled the part in *Columbo Takes the Rap*—did they try to emulate Falk or go their own way?)

Now, the Columbo of *Prescription: Murder* (pilot A) bears only a slight resemblance to the character of the show, particularly in the later years. For one thing, Falk merely carries his raincoat and rarely puts it on. More significantly, he plays the role very seriously and he speaks in a soft monotone, rather than his distinctive New York accent. These elements would change in *Ransom for a Dead Man* (pilot B). Also, the character becomes less of just a polite civil servant and more of the guy we recognize: more gentle-natured (consider his treatment of the murderer's step-daughter Margaret), more fumbling for that pen (indeed, that's how he is introduced, searching for his lost pen on Leslie Williams' front porch) and quirkier (his love of chili and fear of heights are introduced in this movie). See "The Developing Character" for more.

It has been reported that Falk was more than a little disorganized. He brought the character his stature (or lack thereof) and squinting of his glass eye. As time went on, he exaggerated these features, so that in later episodes he seems to be hunched over and his eye is more noticeably half-closed. There are great lines in "Swan Song" (#22) when he tells the NTSB investigator that he "doesn't even like being this tall" and in "Fade in to Murder" (#36) when he responds to the deli owner's comment that the murderer was short, that is, about his (Columbo's) height by saying "average height." These habits were accentuated when Richard Alan Simmons took over as executive producer with "The Bye-Bye Sky High IQ Murder Case" (#38) and continued throughout his tenure, ending with "Murder: A Self Portrait" (#48). (Again, see "The Developing Character" for more.)

Falk made Columbo more likeable, more eccentric, more entertaining to watch. He kept finding new angles on the character, enriching and deepening his performance. There is no question that, had the show been made with someone else, it would not have been as good or as memorable.

Falk gave the character his greatest moments . . . and some not so good ones. I personally believe that Columbo works best as an understated character, a quiet little guy who has more going on than he allows others to realize. Less is more and here are some examples to prove it.

In "Now You See Him" (#34), Columbo has learned from a magic store owner that the devices that Santini might have used to throw his voice from one room to another aren't so much magic as they are the tools of "a gaffe in a head act." That is, the guy who sits on stage and amazingly knows what the person in the twentieth row has whispered to his assistant. He knows because the assistant is wired with a microphone behind her ear and he has a receiver in his. Shortly thereafter, Columbo is talking to Michael Lally, a retired trapeze artist who knew Santini years ago in Europe. Lally reports that when he first met Santini (then using a different name), he was "the gaffe in a head act." Now here's an "aha" moment if there ever was one. But Columbo, who is in the foreground when Lally says this, seems not to even notice (he's too fascinated by the guy's cheap apartment). Naturally, he does hear the information and the significance of it is not lost on him or the audience. But what a brilliant stroke it was to have him not make a big deal of it.

On the other hand, we have the scene in "Grand Deceptions" (#47) in which Columbo's men discover the flashlight the victim was carrying when he died. As he will later explain to murderer Frank Brailie, the flashlight is found in a spot where it could not have fallen naturally, so someone must have put it there. But that's no reason for his behavior at the time, which is to hold the flashlight over his head and yell out "this object that I hold in my hand is a flashlight, right?" To which his men respond, "yes, Lieutenant." What's the point of this business? It makes Columbo seem silly, rather than observant.

I also think it works better when other characters' reactions to his eccentricities are played out subtly. For example, in "A Case of Immunity" (#33), Hassan Salah is right behind Columbo to steady the priceless objects the Lieutenant keeps bumping. He finally asks politely if they might move the discussion to another room and Columbo says sure. Similarly, Raymond the butler in "Forgotten Lady" (#30) (memorably played by Maurice Evans) silently follows Columbo around with an ashtray and hands it to him before the Lieutenant can make a mess.

These moments are nicely done. By contrast, in "Double Shock" (#15), Mrs. Peck, the fussy housekeeper, scolds Columbo on three occasions over his slovenly behavior and he skitters away in fear. It is not only unrealistic (the police don't need to walk on eggshells in anyone's house and any other cop would tell her where she could file her complaints), but it is also not funny. And it detracts from Columbo's investigation.

In "Make Me a Perfect Murder" (#41), the misogyny in the episode (see

"Recurring Problems") wouldn't be so hard to swallow if Columbo didn't join in it by insulting Kay Freestone. Columbo insists that "no one kills someone for just a job" (which is what happened); it must be that she was jilted by Mark McAndrews, too. Also there's the farce with the car crash and neck brace—if he's that bad a driver, let's stop laughing and get him off the road.

In "The Conspirators" (#43), Columbo's act of boozing it up with Joe Devlin is inappropriate to the seriousness of the poet's deeds, and it also leads to too many gift clues, like the recurring whiskey bottles everywhere they go, ultimately leading to the "Final Clue" of the marked whiskey bottle that catches the poet. At the conclusion of "Columbo Goes to the Guillotine" (#44), Columbo sticks a fake gun in the murderer's face and a flag saying "Bang" comes out of it. In the newer episodes, it is sad to see the character becoming a parody of himself; see "The Developing Character" for more details.

Falk occasionally allows his friendships with other actors (or directors) to alter his performance. The most glaring example of this occurs in "Last Salute to the Commodore" (#35), when Falk starts goofing around, no doubt because his buddy Patrick McGoohan (who is behind the camera) encourages it. He laughs when noise in the shipyard prevents him from hearing an important clue (what the Commodore bought—stencils and marine paint—which eventually lead to the discovery that he was about to rename his boat "Lisa S." and marry the young yoga lover). Then he seems to be performing the circus act of seeing how many clowns he can fit in his car and he assigns a young assistant to drive while he stands up and yells instructions. Later, he uses the actual murderer to play the part of the victim just to prove to the victim's grief-stricken daughter that a guard who thought he saw her father that night really didn't, and he interrupts the conclusion to comment to one of the suspects that Sergeant Kramer has been with him for a while, but "Mac" Albinsky is a new guy. As I've always said about this episode, it's too much "comic relief" and not enough substance to be relieved from.

Falk and McGoohan also enjoy themselves a bit too much in McGoohan's last appearance, as mortician Eric Prince in "Ashes to Ashes" (#65). They yell at each other across a room instead of approaching each other, Prince asks too many questions about the cousin who helped Columbo figure out what "SB" means (an inside joke meaning that McGoohan is having fun with Columbo's habit of conveniently having a relative for every occasion, something Prince wouldn't know) and at the end, he announces that he's going to the police car because . . . well, why is he exactly? Columbo doesn't tell him to do so, and the final clue of ashes being mixed together doesn't go far enough, so there's no reason for Prince to turn himself in.

The other criticism that can be fairly leveled at Falk is his decision, as executive producer, to attempt to "adapt" two Ed McBain police procedural novels into episodes of Columbo (see "No Time for Columbo, No Place for McBain"). Not only do the two not go together, but to make this marriage, Falk actually has to abandon many elements of the show he fought so hard to keep in over the years. Lack of violence, fighting and shooting? "No Time to Die" (#58) features a young woman being tortured and almost raped and killed by a crazed psychopath, who is ultimately blown away at the end in a hail of bullets. "Undercover" (#62) contains a close-up shot of two men who murdered each other, has two other murders, shows Columbo disarming a criminal and then getting beaten up. Great clues? There are none to be found in either show.

The Morality of Columbo I: To Arrest or Not to Arrest

Although the role of the fictional detective is to bring the criminal to justice, there are many occasions when these detectives have chosen not to do so. They are often private detectives, who are not bound to the follow the rules like the police, but in any event they decide that a higher morality has been satisfied or that no good would come of prosecuting this particular individual. Lieutenant Columbo has encountered three such situations, and he has treated them differently. Let us examine these instances and see if his decisions are consistent, or at least explainable.

The first instance occurs in the fifth season episode "Forgotten Lady" (#30), with guest star Janet Leigh as Grace Wheeler, a former dancer trying to make a comeback despite the objections of her ailing aged husband, Dr. Henry Willis. When Henry refuses to give Grace the money to finance her new show, she drugs and shoots him in his bed, making it look like a suicide. Columbo proceeds with his usual course of narrowing in on Grace, but something unusual is going on. Grace keeps forgetting Columbo's name and then the details of the suicide. Eventually, the Lieutenant finds a coded medical file in Henry's records and discovers that Grace has an inoperable aneurysm of the brain, which is slowly eating away at her memory and her life; she has only a few months left to live. Columbo reveals this information not to Grace but to Ned Diamond, Grace's former dancing partner and life-long love. He has invited Diamond to a showing of a movie at Grace's house to demonstrate the significance of the unexplained additional time the movie took to run that night. Because Grace was upstairs shooting her husband, she was unavailable for several minutes to repair the movie, which had broken while she was away. By this time Grace has actually forgotten that she killed Henry so Ned, acting out of his love for Grace, "confesses" to the crime and asks the Lieutenant to take him in. "It won't take long to break your story," says Columbo. "It might take a couple of months," suggests Ned, and the Lieutenant nods in agreement—"yes, yes it might."

The idea of Columbo opting not to arrest Grace is very compassionate, but he apparently needs help in arriving at this course of action and that creates a difficulty with this episode and its moral compass. He tells Ned that he has "a problem with this case" referring to the fact that Grace doesn't even remember the murder anymore. But of course that isn't his "problem" at all; it falls to the district attorney to decide which cases to prosecute. In this instance either the D.A. would recognize, or a judge (on motion of the defense attorney) would rule that Grace Wheeler was incompetent to stand trial because of her failing memory and medical condition. Grace would never have to face a jury on a murder charge, assuming that she lived long enough to stand trial, which is unlikely given the situation. Columbo doesn't need to feel that he is the bad guy when he arrests Grace—it is the job of the police to arrest offenders on the basis of the evidence, not to decide which ones should stand trial.

Perhaps the Lieutenant means to say something else. From a humanitarian point of view, he doesn't want to condemn Grace, whose crime was the result of a tragic misunderstanding, to spend her few remaining days in police custody awaiting a competency hearing. Indeed, given her memory loss, there is a good chance that even revealing to her that she committed this crime would come as a tremendous shock and who can say what the effect of that would be? In this unfortunate situation, Ned Diamond sees a way out—he confesses to the crime and lets Grace and Columbo off the hook. Now she'll be able to live out her last days peacefully and Ned will be released when there is no evidence to support his confession.

But wait a minute. Unquestionably, Ned Diamond comes out of this looking like a hero. But does Columbo? Supposing we all agree that not arresting Grace is the "right" answer—why doesn't the Lieutenant think of it himself? He appears to want to straddle the fence without making a decision. On the one hand, he invites Ned to the movie, reveals the truth to him and accepts Ned's offer to confess. But he appears genuinely surprised by Ned's confession and he was on the verge of actually arresting Grace (Ned interrupts him to confess to Grace).

And, to really shake things up, consider this: why does Columbo have to arrest anybody? Wouldn't the most humane thing to do under the circumstances be to "recognize" that Henry shot himself and leave it alone? What does Columbo accomplish by arresting Ned, who didn't do it—does he satisfy some bizarre notion that somebody should pay? Is he making sure that his record of catching criminals doesn't suffer (of course, it will in two months when Ned is released)? Or to put it another way, who would be injured by calling it a suicide? Grace isn't going to be shooting anyone else, so the only possible answer is "society" but how is society made whole by the arrest of Ned Diamond?

There are plenty of precedents for Columbo to follow in this case, most notably the famous ending to Agatha Christie's *Murder on the Orient Express*, in which Hercule Poirot provides two "possible" solutions to the crime and then allows the director of the railroad company to "choose" the more humane solution. Likewise, Columbo could offer the explanation of how Grace killed Henry as one possible scenario, the other being his suicide. Then, acting out of compassion, he would say to Ned, "I guess we'll never know what really happened, so I think I'll report this as suicide after all." "Thank you, Lieutenant," the dancer would say.

What difference does it make how Columbo avoids arresting Grace? There is one all-important difference—this way Ned gets to remain with Grace during her final days, instead of languishing in a cell for a crime he didn't commit. As compassionate as it is of Ned to go to jail on Grace's behalf, he should realize that he will be unable to comfort her during what time she has left and that is a shame. To the extent that Columbo reaches the "right" answer (don't arrest Grace), he lacks the conviction to do it by himself and he should go further and arrest no one.

In the second instance, "Try and Catch Me" (#39), Columbo reaches the opposite conclusion. Abigail Mitchell, a famous mystery writer, locks her niece's husband Edmund Galvin in her airtight safe and he suffocates. Columbo lines up the evidence against Abigail, including the final clue, a note left by Edmund accusing Abigail of the crime, which constitutes a powerful piece of "death-bed testimony" that carries much weight in the courtroom.

Abigail asks to be let go, and not merely because she is an old woman who will hurt no one else. During his investigation, Columbo has also uncovered the motive for the crime: Edmund had killed his wife, Abigail's beloved niece Phyllis, and made the murder look like a boating accident. Abigail could not live with the fact that Edmund had gotten away with this awful crime and so she took action. Doesn't her motive, easily the most sympathetic of any murderer on the series, warrant some compassion on the Lieutenant's part?

No, he answers, he is "a professional" who finishes the job he has been assigned, just as she would do. Abigail laments that if only he had investigated Phyllis's death originally, none of this would have been necessary. And that is that.

Once again, however, I want to argue that the Lieutenant has come to the "right" solution for the wrong reason. Although a case could be made that he should let her go, a stronger argument exists for why he should not. Being a "professional" has nothing to do with it and it is a rather cold and heartless thing to say to her under the circumstances. Ironically, the episode already contains the proper reasoning for why Columbo must arrest Abigail Mitchell.

In the middle of the episode, Columbo finds Abigail at a luncheon where she is addressing a women's club about ancient duels and poisonings. She spots Columbo and invites him to speak to the group about his depressing profession, humorously suggesting the name of some complicated technological technique that she knows he will not recognize. Instead, Columbo gives a speech that summarizes an unspoken attitude that he has come to hold as the series progressed (he did not at the beginning): he isn't depressed by his job and he doesn't hate murderers, just the murders they commit. He believes that the world is full of good people and he even admires the murderers for other qualities they possess (see "The Developing Character" for this speech in full).

In the last scene, therefore, Columbo should ask Abigail if she remembers this speech. Yes, she would answer— the Lieutenant admires murderers for their other qualities and since in her case the motive for the murder is so sympathetic, this is all the more reason why he should look the other way. "No, ma'am," he would explain, "you don't understand." In that speech he was referring to Edmund who, however despicable his crime of murdering Phyllis, still may have had redeeming qualities that make it unthinkable to the detective that he should be killed by an avenging relative. It is true that the criminal justice system didn't succeed in catching Edmund, but it would fail again if it failed to arrest Edmund's murderer. Now, this isn't to say that

Abigail should necessarily spend the rest of her life in prison. In this case, the proper forum to hear the mitigating circumstances is in the courtroom and Columbo will be there to offer what he has learned about why she committed this crime. Perhaps Abigail will receive a very short sentence, perhaps even none at all, but that decision is to be made elsewhere and by other people, not the police.

In the third trial of the Lieutenant's morality, "It's All in the Game" (#60), he faces a pair of women who have killed a man he learns was a "scumbucket," but he doesn't know why. At the request of his primary suspect, Lauren Staton, he lets her accomplice, Lisa Fiore, go even before he learns the whole sympathetic story. It turns out that the victim, one Nick Franco, had met Lisa, who is Lauren's daughter, in Rome and romanced her. Through her, he learned she had a wealthy mother in L.A. and he secretly flew over to woo her as well. When Lisa put the pieces together, she confronted him. But rather than back down, he told her he would marry her mother for her money and when Lisa threatened to tell all, he sliced her neck with a razor and threatened her to keep silent. She didn't and the two women killed him first.

Columbo's decision to let Lisa go sounds sympathetic, but in fact he could apply the same reasoning to Lauren herself to let her go. What's really going on in writer Peter Falk's "almost love story" is that the Lieutenant has fallen for Lauren and would do anything (short of letting her go) to solve the case. When she requests that he let Lisa go, he acquiesces, as a favor to Lauren and in order to obtain her confession. As my review of the episode notes, I have a lot of problems with this decision. The episode also raises questions as to the Lieutenant's methods, which are discussed in the next essay, "The Morality of Columbo II: How Far Will He Go?"

The Morality of Columbo II:
How Far Will He Go?

In "Columbo Goes to College" (#54), the Lieutenant is asked whether he would ever make up evidence to catch a criminal. He responds that, once he gets the scent, "there's very little that I wouldn't do in order to solve the case." In that instance, his methods were not questionable. But in two 1970s episodes two of the newer installments, his methods do raise issues about just how far he will go to arrest the murderer.

The first example of questionable methods occurs in the first season episode "Death Lends a Hand" (#2). In that case, private investigator Mr. Brimmer strikes Lenore Kennicut when she refuses to accede to his blackmail and threatens to expose him. She falls backwards and hits her head, with fatal results. Brimmer moves the body and makes it look like a mugging. He is caught trying to dispose of a contact lens in his car trunk. Columbo has led him to believe that the contact lens fell out of the body while it was being transported. But Columbo comments to Lenore's husband that her lenses are still in her eyes. This comment suggests that the Lieutenant planted the evidence, but he doesn't admit it. He contends that Brimmer has incriminated himself regardless of how the lens wound up in the trunk. The problem is that Columbo has been rather heavy-handed in his suggestion that he thinks Brimmer is the culprit. He made a point of telling Brimmer that a private investigator was the murderer and he knows Brimmer did some PI work for Lenore's husband in the past; he observed that Brimmer was ambidextrous and Lenore was struck by a left-handed person; he noted Brimmer's explosive temper and commented that Lenore was struck in anger; he remarked that "if only the murderer were here" he'd know to look for the missing contact lens; and he came to Brimmer's place and complimented him on his deep pile rug.

In other words, Columbo has provided Brimmer with the opportunity of claiming that the Lieutenant was trying to frame him for the murder and that he only went to his car (which mysteriously failed earlier that day) to remove the planted false evidence, the contact lens. The more steps Columbo takes to provide Brimmer with fake evidence to see how he reacts, the more Brimmer's reactions become indistinguishable from those of an innocent person who is being framed. (See "The Three Cs" for more on this topic.) For a more conclusive and satisfying ending, Columbo should trick Brimmer into doing something that only the murderer would know about, not something that he could put together from the situation the Lieutenant has created. But the question raised by this episode is whether planting false evidence against a suspect is ever acceptable.

The second instance is the third season episode "Mind Over Mayhem" (#21). In that episode, Marshall Cahill runs Howard Nicholson over because Nicholson is about to reveal that Cahill's son Neil did not do the research for which he will receive an award. Rather, Neil stole the work from Carl Finch, a now-deceased scientist. In essence, Neil committed this fraud to please his tyrannical father, a fact that he admits to his therapist, Nicholson's much-younger wife Margaret. It's also obvious that Neil is attracted to Margaret, but that she loves her husband. When Columbo tries to question Margaret about Finch (Cahill has removed the file from Nicholson's filing cabinet), she invokes therapist-patient privilege. But she does encourage Neil to confess his fraud, and he complies. In the end, Columbo comes to arrest . . . Neil. Not only does the Lieutenant have the motive of the cover-up of the plagiarism, but he claims to have a second, simpler motive: Neil was having an affair with Margaret and he killed her husband. He claims that the tire of the car Neil was driving that night has tobacco impacted in it, tobacco from Nicholson's pipe. He even brings out a hotel manager who states that he saw Neil and Margaret check in together.

This is not true. Columbo knows that Cahill committed the murder: a burned-out match left at the scene of the crime indicates that the murderer smokes cigars, as he does; one of the institute cars has a dent in the front where he hit Nicholson; and he has no alibi because he could have programmed the robot to type the war-game scenario into the computer that night. Columbo also knows the motive. And he knows something else—Cahill thinks he's a dimwitted bureaucrat who would do anything to close the case. So, putting all of this together, he decides to frame Neil for the crime (the tobacco in the tire evidence is fake and the hotel manager is lying), hoping that Cahill will confess to save the son he killed to protect in the first place. The plan works and the Lieutenant gets the right result, but at what cost? Again, he seems to think nothing of planting false evidence, whether against the murderer or even against an innocent party to induce the murderer to confess.

Interestingly, these are the only episodes from the 1970s in which Columbo goes to such lengths to arrest a murderer. "Death Lends a Hand" (#2) is the first episode ever written, and "Mind Over Mayhem" (#21) is from the third season, at which point the character of Columbo was in transition from his original state as a polite but dogged civil servant who takes on the guise of a slow-witted bumbler in order to lull the murderer into a false sense of security. See "The Developing Character" for more. By the time the seventh season episode "Try and Catch Me" (#39) aired, the Lieutenant gives a speech in which he indicates that he is a decent man who looks for good qualities in all people, even as his job requires him to arrest those who have committed murder. Thus, it seemed unlikely at that point (to me anyway) that he would again resort to the tactics he employed in "Death Lends a Hand" (#2) and "Mind Over Mayhem" (#21).

But things change. In "It's All in the Game" (#60), Columbo enters into a bizarre flirting relationship with murderer Lauren Staton and he lies about it, if not to his wife and his friend Barney, then to himself.

Peter Falk has said that he had the idea of an "almost love affair" for the Lieutenant some time ago and finally put it together in this episode. However, I find the relationship between the Lieutenant and Staton disturbing and I don't think Falk ever seems to decide exactly what is going on. On the one hand, during the scenes when they are together, there is no question that Columbo is flattered by Staton's attention and that he really likes her, and she likes him. He admits as much in a scene with Barney, and Falk even allows

Barney to make some rather insightful comments about the whole situation. But in other scenes, particularly the one at the end, Columbo tosses off the whole business as a show he put on to play along with Staton and ultimately catch her for the crime. Was he attracted to her? Of course not; why he's taking the wife bowling tonight. The real Lieutenant Columbo would never cheat on his wife or even allow himself to fall for another woman, right?

I'd like to examine the whole issue from the perspective of lies and truth-telling, because I think this analysis points to the central contradiction Falk has created here. We are well aware of course that Columbo lies to the suspects; there's nothing unusual or even unethical about that (but see comment below). But here the Lieutenant's lying knows no bounds. If his behavior during the scenes with Staton and the scene in which he keeps telling Barney "this is a tough case" are to be believed, then he is lying to Barney at the end. Also, while he does give Barney the tie to give to his nephew Vince, Columbo does not make a point of getting rid of the doggie bed that he was so tickled to receive from Staton. Yes, he makes a cute quip about Barney being a "damn fool" for believing what a cop told him, but Barney is his friend, not a suspect in a case. He has no reason to lie to Barney and it's insulting of him to do so (he could have simply avoided the topic altogether). In addition, although it is never stated, the implication is that he is not telling Mrs. Columbo about Lauren Staton and their mutual flirtation; this much is suggested by a scene in Barney's bathroom in which he removes the tie before he goes home. In other words, he is now lying to his wife as well.

More significantly (and not even subject to dispute), he lies to his fellow police officers when he tells them that the interrogation of Lisa is going nowhere and he lets her go. This is not even a very good lie, because the cops know that Franco called Lisa twelve times; that's how Columbo got to her in the first place. Apparently, the Lieutenant has no scruples or morals whatsoever. He treats the other police officers and his friends just like suspects, lying to them whenever it is convenient to do so. Ultimately, I think a good case can be made that the Lieutenant is really lying to himself. He is attracted to Staton and he lets Lisa go because Staton asks him to do this. But he can't admit this, so he tells Barney that it was all an act.

Given all this lying, one might legitimately ask why Columbo follows through on his promise to let Lisa go. After all, he only needs to let Staton think that's what he's doing and then bring Lisa back in to be arrested. Now, the Columbo I've gotten to know over the years would never do such a thing, but then again he'd never do a lot of what he does in this episode either. In other words, if Columbo thinks nothing of lying, why be true to his word with a murderer, of all people? (It's interesting to note that he considers it very significant to tell Staton that he'd never lie about playing poker, the way Franco did.) One might make the argument that, whatever lies he tells suspects, fellow cops or even his wife, the fact is that when the Lieutenant makes a promise, he is a man of his word. The problems with this argument are that: 1) it draws an arbitrary line; 2) he doesn't actually promise Staton that he will let Lisa go; and 3) he has so undermined his ethics in this episode that it is cold comfort to know that he keeps his promises. At least in "Mind Over Mayhem" (#21), he gets the right result when the proper murderer is arrested. He says, and I'm willing to take his word for this, that he set Neil up because it was his only way of catching Cahill and he never would have pursued the phony case. Here he doesn't catch the accomplice, but only the main murderer and his methods don't play fair with anyone. Neither the ends nor the means fit the character we've come to know.

Finally, there is the 1995 episode "Strange Bedfellows" (#63). In that case, Graham McVeigh murders his brother Teddy and pins it on Bruno Romano, a restaurateur with mob connections, whom McVeigh then kills in "self-defense." Columbo's investigation is proceeding along its usual course when suddenly he is forcibly transported to the mansion of Vincenzo Fortelli, a local "retired" mob figure. Fortelli demands that the Lieutenant arrest McVeigh or else he will have to take matters into his own hands. As events unfold, it looks like Fortelli is living up to his promise, as he traps McVeigh in his restaurant and tells Columbo to leave or else he will be killed too. McVeigh confesses to Columbo and even provides a detail of the crime that only the murderer would know, so he cannot repudiate his confession. But then it turns out that this was all a scam. Columbo and Fortelli collaborated to make McVeigh think he had no choice but to confess. The title gives it all away: Columbo and Fortelli make strange bedfellows, but they succeed in their mission.

But it's troublesome, as even Columbo seems to recognize. The episode has Fortelli contact him, he is wary about talking to the mob don, and in the end, when Fortelli suggests they share a drink, Columbo passes, saying "I'm a cream soda kind of guy and you're not." Well, the Lieutenant can draw all the distinctions he likes, but the tough question is what separates the police from the mob if they join forces like this? Interestingly, in the last episode of the series, "Columbo Likes the Nightlife" (#67), a mobster's son disappears and "the family" sends a messenger to see how Columbo is doing. The Lieutenant is polite to the man, but he does not collaborate. At the end, when he catches the murderers without any help, he returns the business card offered by the messenger, clearly indicating he wants nothing to do with the Mafia.

A less severe but still troublesome issue is the Lieutenant's occasional practice of stealing clues. In "The Bye-Bye Sky High IQ Murder Case" (#38), Columbo comes to understand how the murder was committed when he switches umbrellas with Oliver Brandt, and he finds powder burns and bits of paper in Brandt's umbrella left behind by exploding squibs. As the Lieutenant admits, he can't get evidence that way. The good news is that he does not arrest Brandt based on that illegally obtained piece of evidence. Rather, Brandt incriminates himself when Columbo recreates the scene of the crime and Brandt supplies the missing detail of how he made the club members think they heard the sound of the body falling in between the shots in the library.

Columbo also steals a toothbrush from Colonel Brailie's apartment in "Grand Deceptions" (#47), which he uses to get Jenny Padget to admit her affair with Brailie. This is not quite as objectionable, because it's used against Jenny rather than the murderer (and Columbo then drops the matter).

But his act of stealing the cleaning rag in "Murder: A Self Portrait"

(#48) cannot be so easily excused. The rag becomes a very important clue. Indeed, it's the episode's "Final Clue" (see essay with this title for more on this topic). It places Max Barsini at the beach with his ex-wife who drowned, because the rag has paint cleaner on it (which knocked her out), and because she has "Barsini red" paint on her face from the rag. Thus, the Lieutenant has finally arrested a murderer using a piece of evidence that he took without a warrant and without permission. Needless to say, this kind of evidence would not hold up in court. But it's also dissatisfying to see the character sink to these levels.

Finally, I want to make one more point about Columbo's lying. Naturally, he should not be expected to tell murderers what he's thinking; they lie to him for the sole purpose of covering up their heinous deeds, so they don't have a right to know how his case is progressing. But sometimes the Lieutenant seems to lie about matters that don't reveal anything to the murderer. For example, in "Ashes to Ashes" (#65), he lies at length to Eric Prince about how he learned what "SB" means. Prince seems fascinated to learn about the relative who provided the Lieutenant with this information and how Columbo repaid him. Columbo dutifully answers all of Prince's questions, but he's lying. He found out that "SB" stands for Sunset Boulevard by talking to a guy at a taxi station. Does it make a difference? Why lie about where he came across the information?

Does Columbo Exist?

Now, this may seem like an odd title for an essay in a book about Columbo. Of course Columbo exists! What is this all about?

The issue here has to do with an idea that surfaces from time to time on the show: the suggestion that, even in the fictional world he inhabits, Columbo is somehow "not real." Occasionally, the writers take the "rule" laid down by creators Richard Levinson and William Link a little too far. On the one hand, they created a character who is "real" enough to be believable. He has a wife, a dog and a large extended family, lives a simple life, comes from an Italian background, and likes to work hard at his job (they didn't create all of these aspects, but they set the stage for them to be added by others). Of course, he isn't "real" in the sense of being an everyday police officer—no one could afford to spend the time on a single case that he does (it might be beneficial to the force if someone did, though), police officers rarely have the time or patience to be polite to suspects (especially ones they consider guilty) and a cop who can't bear to carry or fire a gun would probably not rise to the rank of lieutenant. But these things have to be accepted for the purpose of making the drama more interesting to watch, just like Dirty Harry's rejection of authority and Jessica Fletcher's ability to walk into any crime situation and assume the role of advisor to the police (just what they would want).

The problem of surrealism arises out of Levinson and Link's secondary set of caveats about the character: never show Columbo in his office, never show him talking to superiors, don't reveal his first name. In the years after the first season (when they served as executive producers of the show), all of these rules (except the first name one) were broken, at no cost to the character. In "Any Old Port in a Storm" (#17), considered by many people to be the finest episode (I rank it 9.7 on a scale of 10; see Appendix I for details), Columbo is shown in his office. And in "Negative Reaction" (#25), Captain Sampson asks him why he's still investigating the Galesko case, and he provides a terrific explanation about how little things really do bother him (it's not just a show for the suspects). Rather than diminish the character, I think this scene improves upon it.

At times, though, it seems that the writers really don't want Columbo to be a real policeman, even a fictional real one. They seem to like the idea that Columbo only exists where there's a murder, as if afterwards another cop turns to ask him a question and finds only cigar ash. "Who was that man in the raincoat?" Some of this works very well—not showing his wife makes her more three-dimensional than showing her would. But much of it serves only to create unnecessary friction between competing concepts.

The first example of this issue occurs in "Forgotten Lady" (#30), when Columbo is confronted about not completing his pistol range requirements.

It would be best never to mention this subject, instead of having a police officer say to him "I've never seen you around before," which makes no sense. First of all, he is shown in his office in "Any Old Port in a Storm" (#17). He wanders around police headquarters and works out of Lieutenant Duffy's office in "A Friend in Deed" (#23). He tells Lewis Lacey that he's usually in his office in the mornings in "An Exercise in Fatality" (#24). He works with Sergeant Hoffman in a police central room and he arrests the murderer in the property room in "Negative Reaction" (#25). And he constantly greets and is recognized by lots of other police officers in every single episode. So the idea that he doesn't exist in the same world as all the rest of the L.A.P.D. officers on the show runs counter to practically every episode to precede this one. Now, is there a requirement in Columbo's world that police officers carry guns and practice firing twice a year or not? If not, then he's fine. If there is, then he must have fulfilled this requirement because he is conscientious, even if he's no fan of guns.

Then, having set up this situation, the episode builds the tension until there is no way out of it. Certainly, the solution Columbo finds (he has someone else go to the firing range for him) will not work. The authorities would be observing at this point to make sure he goes through with it. Author William Harrington picked up on this issue in his books, which refer to Columbo's trying to get out of his firing range requirements. This is even odder, considering that Harrington's novels are more in the nature of police procedurals than adventures of the Columbo character, and in a police procedural world the police have and comply with firing range requirements.

Two eighth season episodes contain scenes that raise the notion of whether Columbo is "real." In "Murder, Smoke and Shadows" (#45), he appears in a ringmaster's uniform at the end, although it seems as though this only occurs in murderer Alex Brady's mind. It's a very odd moment no matter how you slice it. But in "Grand Deceptions" (#47), he becomes a figurine on the Civil War battlefield, and there is no suggestion that this is a mirage imagined by murderer Frank Brailie. This might work as the last scene of the very last episode, as a sort of "farewell," but not at the end of a season when they knew he was coming back.

On the other hand, since Columbo does inhabit a fictional world, I think it was a mistake to have Lucia, the little old Italian lady in "Undercover" (#62), tell him that she was pleased to meet a member of "that family," clearly referring to the infamous Columbo group of Mafiosi in New York. That unfortunate fact does not have to enter this fictional program, for the same reason that no one needs to ask whether he's named after a brand of yogurt or the capital of Sri Lanka. (William Link has explicitly stated that he and Richard Levinson had never heard of the New York syndicate by that name.) Interestingly, in the Ed McBain novel *Jigsaw*, which was the inspiration for this episode, 87th Precinct character Steve Carella approaches Lucia as himself, without a costume, and she answers his questions.

Finally, I have to add a comment about a related topic that surfaces from time to time: does Mrs. Columbo exist? Now, it is certainly true that the Lieutenant mentions a plethora of relations who seem to arise coincidentally to contribute to the plot at hand: a brother-in-law who is a lawyer to whom Columbo shows Beau Williamson's will in "Blueprint for Murder" (#7), a cousin named Ralph who's so perfect that he's a bore, just like Leslie Williams's husband in *Ransom for a Dead Man* (pilot B), a nephew who's majoring in dermatology at UCLA just when he needs someone to examine his poison ivy in "Lovely But Lethal" (#16), and so on. I'm perfectly willing to accept the idea that he's making up these folks or at least employing them to appear less intimidating than if he said he approached a lawyer or scientist at the police department or D.A.'s office. The show leaves these matters delightfully ambiguous. (However, it is clear that he has a number of relatives when his wife calls him in "Any Old Port in a Storm" (#17) and lists a bunch of them who are coming for dinner, and in "Columbo and the Murder of a Rock Star" (#56), he asks a young guy at the beginning where he bought his boom box, because he wants to get one for his nephew, and at the end of the show he has bought the boom box at Dhoti's Discount just as the guy suggested.)

But that's a far cry from claiming that his wife doesn't exist. To accept that idea, you have to believe that Columbo doesn't exist, which is silly for the reasons explained above. Or we would have to accept that he actually lives by himself. Now, does it make sense that this everyday fellow would be a complete loner, unconnected from society? Or is it more likely that, like most men who lived in that era, he married and had a life at home?

Well, whatever you make of those questions, the fact is that, according to events on the show, Mrs. Columbo *does* exist. The Lieutenant speaks to her *four* times on the phone: in "Any Old Port in a Storm" (#17) (he calls to ask her what the weather was one day last week and she tells him to call the weather bureau); in "An Exercise in Fatality" (#24) (she calls him to ask him what to make for dinner and he looks in the victim's garbage can, sees the empty Chinese food containers and suggests he bring home Chinese); in "Troubled Waters" (#27) (the Columbos can't find each other at first on the ship and connect by phone); and in "Rest in Peace, Mrs. Columbo" (#51) (after presenting the audience with the possibility that she is dead, the show rewards us with a phone conversation at the end in which we learn that she's had the flu and is concerned that she missed her soap opera). What is fascinating about these scenes is that the murderers aren't present for any of them, so they aren't being faked for anyone's benefit. In fact, the Lieutenant is usually the only person in the room. And as noted, in "An Exercise in Fatality" (#24), Mrs. Columbo calls him so if someone insists she doesn't exist, that example is particularly hard to explain (his secret assistant calls him? why?).

In addition to all of this, she clearly is on the cruise with him in "Troubled Waters" (#27). The episode opens with Columbo running to catch her as she's already boarded the ship. As just noted, they talk on the telephone. When the purser comes knocking at his door late at night, Columbo hilariously asks whether the problem is his wife (she does get carried away enjoying herself, you know). At the end of the show, Columbo has gotten separated from her again, and the purser points her out (the camera remains focused on Columbo, so the audience never sees her, but she's there). And in "Identity Crisis" (#32),

CIA agent Nelson Brenner has the Columbo house bugged. When Columbo says that *Madame Butterfly* is his wife's favorite opera, Brenner responds "I know." Clearly, he heard the Columbos talking about it.

People who think Mrs. Columbo doesn't exist have confused the Lieutenant's habit of referring to unseen relatives with the show's concept that Mrs. Columbo will not be seen in person. The unseen relatives are a part of the characterization and they may or may not exist. Mrs. Columbo does exist, but is not shown to the audience as a literary device.

So while the idea of keeping some elements of the Columbo character (his wife, his first name, true details about his family) hidden from the audience has a lot of appeal, the show sometimes goes overboard in suggesting that he doesn't really exist, even in the fictional world he inhabits. I think that these instances take the concept too far and create awkward, bizarre moments in an otherwise brilliant show.

You Can Call Him Lieutenant

Over the years, probably no topic has raised as much interest as Columbo's first name. It's a whole category on the Ultimate Columbo website, and European fans in particular seem fascinated by this question. The simple answer is this: the program has never given him a first name, nor did William Harrington in his novels. Some years ago, the game Trivial Pursuit gave a false answer to the question (it said "Phillip") and a rumor was spread that it came from the playbill to the theatrical production (although the character's first name wasn't used in the play either). The playbill did not list a first name for Columbo. In fact, the Trivial Pursuit false answer has an interesting story behind it. A man named Worth, who wrote a number of trivia books, had the idea of planting a false piece of information so that he could prove that others were trying to steal his material. When Trivial Pursuit came out, he sued, pointing to the Columbo first name Q&A as his little trap. He lost the case, but the rumor that Columbo has a first name that only a few people know about has persisted.

More recently, technology has created another twist that didn't exist before. You can pause the frame when Columbo shows his badge to Major General Hollister in "Dead Weight" (#3) and to the Mexican police in "A Matter of Honor" (#33) and guess what? It says "Frank Columbo." Well, now, that certainly answers the question, right?

Not so fast. William Link, the surviving co-creator of the show, was asked this very question on an interview in 2009 or thereabouts. His answer was that a prop guy, acting without permission and without anyone noticing, made the badge and included a first name on it. No one ever realized this or gave permission for his name to be Frank. Indeed, they would not have put his name on a badge and never said it.

Personally, I found all this discussion rather silly. When you stop to think about it, the murderer and witnesses should call him "Lieutenant," as should the police officers working under him, and the rare superior calls him "Columbo." As he says in "By Dawn's Early Light" (#26), he has a first name, but only his wife uses it. I have considered the idea that perhaps he has a very distinctive Italian name (say "Eduardo" or "Armando"), but I certainly wouldn't push the point.

It's notable that, despite all the ethical lines the Lieutenant crosses in "It's All in the Game" (#60) (see the two essays "The Morality of Columbo"), he refuses to give Lauren Staton his first name and instead she has to awkwardly call the man she's almost dating "Lieutenant." Similarly, his lack of a first name creates a weird situation in the episode "No Time to Die" (#58), because his nephew is a major character and he ought to call him "Uncle [First Name]." Instead, he does not call him anything. This is one more reason why making that episode was a mistake (see "No Time for Columbo, No Place for McBain" for more on this topic).

The character without a first name has a long history on television. The idea was often employed in Westerns, which featured a "mysterious stranger" who would help others. For example: Shane, Tate, The Virginian and Paladin (from *Have Gun, Will Travel*). Two other mystery movie characters had no first names the audience knew about: Quincy and McCoy. It does make the character a bit more mysterious. But had the creators given Columbo a first name, I wouldn't have minded.

Another issue that seems to fascinate people is the origin of the name "Columbo." Over the years, people have asked Levinson and Link this question and the pair have confessed that they don't really recall how they came up with it. Perhaps it was a restaurant in Philadelphia called Palumbo's. Or perhaps it came from Columbus. In the foreword to his 2010 book *The Columbo Collection,* Link suggests a new theory for how he and Levinson came up with the name Columbo: they loved to watch the fights and Rocky Marciano's fight trainer was named Allie Colombo. Finally, when I spoke with him in preparing this book for publication, Link had another thought: in 1959, he and Levinson were staying at the big apartment in New York City when a movie from one of their favorite writer/directors, Billy Wilder, opened and they went to see it. You may have heard of it: *Some Like It Hot,* and the villain's name is . . . Spats Colombo.

Again, I'm not sure what all the fuss is about. Do people ask how McCloud and McMillan, Jim Rockford and Thomas Magnum, Frank Cannon and Barnaby Jones got their names? In any event, it will have to go down as a mystery unsolved.

Chapter 22:
Other Actors and Characters

Prescription: Mitchell by Mark Dawidziak

About halfway through director Frank Capra's last Hollywood film, *A Pocketful of Miracles* (1961), two delightful actors collide for a brief hallway scene. Look for the moment. Freeze it. There they are: crafty screen veteran and an equally crafty newcomer with one common role in their future—slovenly homicide detective Lieutenant Columbo. Thomas Mitchell was 68. Peter Falk was 33.

At the same time that *A Pocketful of Miracles* was being sneak previewed to summer audiences in preparation for a December release, NBC aired "Enough Rope," a one-hour installment of *The Chevy Mystery Show.* A live drama by Richard Levinson and William Link, the episode was based on the writing team's 1950s short story "May I Come In" (also known as "Dear Corpus Delecti"). Character actor Bert Freed played Lieutenant Columbo. The distinction of being the first actor to portray Columbo means little to Freed. He doesn't even remember the production.

Levinson and Link were not pleased with the direction and low production values of "Enough Rope." Capra, saddled with a difficult star (Glenn Ford), was not pleased with *A Pocketful of Miracles.* The entire production was agony . . . except for Peter Falk.

"Peter Falk was my joy, my anchor to reality," Capra wrote in his charming and candid 1971 autobiography, *The Name Above the Title.* "Introducing that remarkable talent to the techniques of comedy made me forget pains, tired blood, and maniacal hankerings to murder Glenn Ford. Thank you, Peter Falk."

Mitchell was another of Capra's joys. A member of the director's stock company, Mitchell had played fugitive swindler Barnard in Capra's *Lost Horizon* (1937), Washington reporter Diz Moore in *Mr. Smith Goes to Washington* (1939) and forgetful Uncle Billy in *It's a Wonderful Life* (1946). "Tommy Mitchell was heaven's answer to our prayer," Capra said of the busy supporting actor's casting in *Mr. Smith Goes to Washington*. "In fact, he was soon to become heaven's answer to many a director's prayer—including John Ford's."

Almost immediately after "Enough Rope" aired, Levinson and Link began working on a stage version. They would need a big-name actor to play Lieutenant Columbo. The answer to their prayer was Thomas Mitchell.

The producer who agreed to stage Levinson and Link's play—now titled *Prescription: Murder*—assembled an impressive cast. Joseph Cotten (drunken Leland in *Citizen Kane*) would play Ray Flemming, the psychiatrist who comes up with the seemingly perfect way to murder his wife. Agnes Moorehead, another graduate of Orson Welles's Mercury Players, would play Flemming's wife. And Mitchell was their choice to play Lieutenant Columbo, a cigar-smoking bulldog of a New York City police detective.

"We met for our first rehearsal at the American Legion Hall on Hollywood Boulevard," Bill Link recalls. "It was a difficult cast to work with. We were young writers with no reputation, and nobody was nice to us. Joseph Cotten was very difficult. Agnes Moorehead was very forbidding, almost like Mrs. Danvers in *Rebecca*. And the first thing Thomas Mitchell said to us was, 'In my theater, writers sit in the last row.' That scared Dick and me to death. You can imagine the impact of that on young writers hoping that their play is on its way to Broadway."

Other problems emerged. Mitchell, who was not in good health, did not want to learn new lines. He decreed that the script would not change. This was particularly chilling news to Levinson and Link because they wanted to use a national tour to strengthen their play. They knew the third act was weak. The murder and the alibi were so good that the resolution wasn't strong enough.

"Mitchell was very crusty," Link says. "He had infrequent good days. One of those days was when we rehearsed at his home. I was just starting to collect art, and he had a wonderful collection. He showed it to me with great pride, so that was a nice day."

Prescription: Murder had its world premiere at the Curran Theatre in San Francisco. It was the start of a lucrative 25-week tour through the United States and Canada. When the producer suggested Broadway, Levinson and Link demanded changes for the third act. Why mess with a play making money? The producer backed Mitchell's original demand: no changes. Levinson and Link replied by threatening to slap an injunction on the play. So *Prescription: Murder* was denied a New York opening.

"We were relieved," Link says. "We didn't want our first Broadway show to be a play we knew was structurally flawed."

Yet the 1962 tour of *Prescription: Murder* was of great value. Mitchell proved the great appeal of Lieutenant Columbo. Flemming was supposed to be the central character. Cotten was supposed to be the star. But in San Francisco, Fargo and Detroit, the applause would go crazy for Mitchell, then drop off when Cotten took his bows. The cop was the real star, and it took that tour to make Levinson and Link realize it. Dressed in a heavy overcoat and dropping cigar ashes everywhere, Mitchell was turning on the Irish charm and winning over audiences in city after city.

"He played it far straighter than Peter's Columbo," Link explains. "He was more the standard Irish homicide investigator. But there was a sense of humor. You did see that twinkle. There was a bit of the leprechaun to his portrayal."

Who was this pre-Falk Columbo? Thomas Mitchell was born in Elizabeth, New Jersey, on July 11, 1892. Despite his crack to Levinson and Link about writers, he actually had a deep respect for the process. He started out as a reporter with the *Elizabeth Daily Journal*. And Mitchell penned several plays.

His play *Little Accident,* written in collaboration with Floyd Dell, was made into a 1944 film for Gary Cooper, *Casanova Brown.* Until 1935, Mitchell was an active writer, director, producer, actor and play doctor for the Broadway theater. One columnist described him as "a quiet genius of theater."

He arrived in Hollywood with *Craig's Wife* (1936); however he concentrated almost exclusively on acting. Two roles established him as one of the most sought-after character actors in Tinsletown: Henry Barnard in *Lost Horizon* and Dr. Kersaint in director John Ford's *The Hurricane* (1937).

Mitchell's peak year, though, was Hollywood's peak year: 1939. He worked with five great directors in five of the greatest films in Hollywood's greatest year—as Diz in Capra's *Mr. Smith Goes to Washington,* as Scarlet O'Hara's father in Victor Fleming's *Gone With the Wind,* as the drunken doctor in Ford's *Stagecoach,* as Cary Grant's pilot buddy in Howard Hawks's *Only Angels Have Wings,* and supporting Charles Laughton's Quasimodo in William Dieterle's *The Hunchback of Notre Dame.* Any one of those roles might have earned him the Academy Award for best supporting actor. He won for *Stagecoach.*

Other memorable film roles include Dr. Gibbs in *Our Town* and Jonas Henderson in *High Noon* (1952). Mitchell also is one of the few actors to have won an Oscar, an Emmy (best actor of 1952) and a Tony (for the 1935 musical *Hazel Flagg*).

Columbo was the last stage or film role of Mitchell's career. He collapsed while *Prescription: Murder* was in Levinson and Link's hometown, Philadelphia. Rushed to the hospital, Mitchell was diagnosed as having cancer. His understudy, Howard Wieram, finished out the run. A few months later, in mid-December, Thomas Mitchell died at the age of seventy. It was the second cancer death in two days among the stars of Hollywood. The other was Mitchell's *Hunchback of Notre Dame* co-star, Charles Laughton.

Multiple Murderers

On *Columbo*, several people appear in multiple episodes as guest murderers. When they found someone good, they just kept bringing him back.

Jack Cassidy appeared in three episodes, beginning with the first one, "Murder By the Book" (#1). Each time, he plays the same sort of villain (arrogant but willing to "play along" with Columbo, at least for a while). In the first episode, he is Ken Franklin, the lesser half of a writing duo who decides to murder his partner, Jim Ferris, before Ferris can leave him, as he's announced, and go on to write on his own. Columbo lets Franklin know that his second, cover-up murder (knocking out Lilly La Sanka, who was blackmailing him, and dumping her body in the lake) was sloppy, but the original idea (having Ferris claim to be in office when he shoots him) was clever, so it must have been Ferris's. Ironically, Franklin says it was his idea, the only good one he ever had. Cassidy appears clean-shaven in this episode.

Cassidy appears next in the third season episode "Publish or Perish" (#20) playing Riley Greenleaf, an unscrupulous publisher who kills novelist Allen Mallory before he can defect to a rival, and then kills Eddie Kane, the psychopath who he had commit the first murder. Greenleaf is grumpy when Columbo interrupts him watching a porno movie, and even seems annoyed when the Lieutenant calls him in to arrest him as he has "guests waiting."

Finally, Cassidy makes his last and best appearance in the fifth season episode "Now You See Him" (#34), playing a magician known as The Great Santini. When the club owner keeps taking his profits, holding over Santini the knowledge that he is an ex-Nazi, Santini shoots the man during his famous water tank illusion. He sports grey hair and a mustache and has more confidence than Franklin or Greenleaf. Each of Cassidy's villains is a powerful performance.

This is not exactly true with respect to Robert Culp, who also appeared as a guest murderer in three episodes. First, he was Mr. Brimmer, the private detective who lashes out when a client's wife threatens to reveal his blackmail in "Death Lends a Hand" (#2). But his character is rather wooden and the only distinguishing trait is his temper, which flairs once for Columbo's benefit. He wears thick glasses, which are used to show how he disposes of the body as the images are projected on them.

In the second season, he appears as Paul Hanlon in "The Most Crucial Game" (#9). Hanlon manages sports teams for owner Eric Wagner, but he murders Wagner for reasons that are never made clear. Hanlon is a lot like Brimmer, except that he sports a handlebar mustache and shouts at Columbo.

Culp does create a good character in Dr. Bart Kepple in the third season episode "Double Exposure" (#19). Kepple is a motivational researcher, who uses subliminal cuts of a cold drink to lure his victim to a water fountain, where he shoots him. Kepple has two great scenes with Columbo, one in his office in which he cannily challenges the Lieutenant to find the print with the cuts in it, and another on a golf course where he deflects the clues Columbo throws at him and says he won't let Columbo interfere with his golf game. Finally, Culp appears for a fourth time, but not as a murderer. In "Columbo Goes to College" (#54), he plays Jordan Rowe, university counsel and father of one of the pair of murdering frat boys, Justin Rowe. The elder Rowe is a tough father and he's also tough on Columbo, who he thinks is on the wrong track. But it was odd that he wasn't present at the end to respond when his son suggests the father will get him out of this predicament.

Patrick McGoohan holds the record for the most appearances and each one is a completely different character. First, he appears as Colonel Lyle Rumford in "By Dawn's Early Light" (#26), which gets my vote for best episode. He deservedly won an Emmy for his complex portrayal of the strict military man who sees his world disappearing. He speaks with a clipped Southern accent and has his hair blond and cut short, as appropriate for the role.

McGoohan next appears as Nelson Brenner, "consultant" by day and CIA operative by night, in "Identity Crisis" (#32). He wears his hair (or a piece) long and red and speaks in a very affected manner, no doubt riffing on his spy roles in Danger Man and The Prisoner. It was his least memorable performance.

But then McGoohan appears as Oscar Finch, the lawyer and right-hand man to a vice presidential candidate in "Agenda for Murder" (#50). His hair is graying and he has a mustache and thick glasses. He has the habit of nibbling all the time as he rushes about at a manic pace, and this leads to his undoing. He also has a sense of humor, as he laughs at jokes Columbo tells. He again won an Emmy for this performance.

Finally, McGoohan is Eric Prince, funeral home director in "Ashes to Ashes" (#65). This time, he has a full beard and a slower pace, but it's still an excellent performance.

William Shatner appears twice, years apart in totally different roles. First, he is miscast as the overpaid actor playing the part of a dandy TV detective in "Fade in to Murder" (#36). The character has some serious identity issues, as he frequently becomes his TV persona, Lieutenant Lucerne, and accuses himself of the crime, although he does also attempt to frame the victim's husband. Still, the scenes of Shatner munching on celery in his dressing room and prancing around the set as Lucerne are silly.

Years later, he appears as Fielding Chase, a right-wing radio host out to destroy his enemies (one of them literally) in "Butterfly in Shades of Grey" (#61). He does a great riff on Rush Limbaugh and has several scenes where he does a slow burn waiting for Columbo to get to the point.

George Hamilton follows a similar pattern, although his first appearance is better than the second one. First, in "A Deadly State of Mind" (#29) he is Marcus Collier, a psychiatrist sleeping with his patient and using drugs on her to deepen her hypnotic state and help him write a book. He is suave and charming and Columbo gets angry with him when he manages to kill his lover before she tells the police too much.

Years later, he is Wade Anders, host of *Crime Alert* in "Caution: Murder Can Be Hazardous to Your Health" (#55). Unfortunately, he keeps using his on-air voice, a deep monotone, in scenes when he's not on camera and it makes for a rather uninspired character.

Finally, I must mention Robert Vaughn, who many people would put in this category. But the fact is that he only appears once as a murderer, in

"Troubled Waters" (#27), the episode at sea. When he guest stars again in "Last Salute to the Commodore" (#35) as Charles Clay, he appears to have murdered his father-in-law, then dumped the body at sea and made it look like an accident. But we learn later that he only discovered the body and, thinking his drunken wife Joanna had killed her own father, tried to clean up the mess for her. Even this wasn't true, however. It turned out that the Commodore was killed by his nephew, "Swanny" Swanson (Fred Draper) and he later killed Clay, too. So Vaughn makes only one appearance as a murderer; in the other instance, he is a victim!

The Thirty-One Hats of Michael Lally

Back in 1996, I was watching two episodes of *Columbo* in a row when I stumbled onto something odd. I suddenly experienced a sense of déjà vu. In the second episode, a short older man with white hair appeared on the scene, spoke perhaps a line in his distinctive somewhat raspy voice and then disappeared. Wait a minute, I thought, I've seen this man before. So I went back to the other episode and, sure enough, there he was again. By now intrigued with this idea, I proceeded over a several week period to watch each and every episode from the 1970s, staring at the screen like Columbo checking for discrepancies in the video tapes in "Playback" (#28) or listening over and over again to the audio tapes in "The Most Crucial Game" (#10) for a sound that didn't belong. And like the good Lieutenant, I am pleased to report that I hit pay dirt—this guy was everywhere!

I could not tell who he was at first. I thought he was never billed in the credits, even on the one occasion when he has a substantial role—"Now You See Him" (#34), where he played the meaty role of "Michael Lally," the retired high wire artist who recognizes Santini from his days in Europe and who talks to Columbo at length in his simple apartment (watch him there first to get to know him so you can spot him in his other briefer appearances). I checked with Mark Dawidziak and William Link, and neither of them knew.

But then I received a communication from Peter Falk himself, and I learned that the gentleman was a gofer on the show, an "old union guy from Chicago." He was cast in various brief roles because he was very natural at playing a variety of characters. John Cassavetes came to like him very much, and Mr. Falk remembered attending the man's funeral with Cassavetes years later.

And his name? It was Michael Lally. That's right, the show uses his real name in his biggest role, that of the retired trapeze artist who knows a little about Santini's background in "Now You See Him" (#34). The scene, in which Columbo goes to talk to Lally, but winds up inquiring about the cost of his bare-bones apartment, is a highlight of the show. Thus, his name seems to be provided twice in the credits (but not in "Now You See Him" (#34)). The name Michael Lally is listed for the role of TV cameraman in "Swan Song" (#22), although this credit actually refers to his son, Michael Edward Lally. I am indebted to the Ultimate Columbo Website for this bit of information; the site notes that the son also appears as the property room officer who gives Columbo Alvin Deschler's personal effects and who appears in the final scene of "Negative Reaction" (#25). Michael Lally the father plays different roles in "Swan Song" (#22) and "Negative Reaction" (#25), as explained below. And he is positively identified as the "second bartender" in "A Friend in Deed" (#23).

The pattern is as follows: Mr. Lally's appearance is always very brief and he gets only one line of dialogue (and sometimes none). Thus, he can often be found among the assorted cops at the scene of the crime (on at least three occasions, he is the police photographer), or else he appears very briefly in a scene during the episode as a bartender (four times by my count), security guard (three times), cab driver, bank clerk, auto mechanic and so on. Thus far, I have been unable to spot him in only twelve out of the show's forty-three episodes from the 1970s: "Death Lends a Hand" (#2), "Dead Weight" (#3), "Suitable for Framing" (#4), "The Greenhouse Jungle" (#9), "The Most Crucial Game" (#10), "Dagger of the Mind" (#11), "The Most Dangerous Match" (#14), "A Matter of Honor" (#33), "Fade in to Murder"

(#36), "Try and Catch Me" (#39), "How to Dial a Murder" (#42), and "The Conspirators" (#43). Now, I'm not really surprised that he didn't go along on the foreign excursions, although he is in "Troubled Waters" (#27).

I should point out that the early appearances are particularly brief and hard to catch. In "Murder By the Book" (#1), he appears to be one of the cops checking out James Ferris' body after Ken Franklin puts it in his own front yard. Later in the episode, he could also be the waiter who brings the strawberries to Lilly La Sanka when she dines with Ken Franklin in that same episode, but since the man never shows his face, we'll never be sure.

His next walk-on is in "Lady in Waiting" (#5), and it is a quick one at that. Beth Chadwick has finished at the beauty parlor and she steps to the outer office to pay her bill and schedule her next appointment, Columbo tagging along. As she pays the bill, freeze the frame: Lally is in the background, picking up a pedestal from another desk and carrying it off screen. That's it.

You also have to look quickly for him in "Short Fuse" (#6). Columbo, Everett Logan and Roger Stanford are racing to board the tram that will serve as the location for the episode's climax. Watch carefully as Lally is the tram loader—he ushers the previous carload of people off and shuts the door as the threesome board. Finally, in "Blueprint for Murder" (#7), he again makes a fleeting and anonymous appearance—he is the second person standing in line behind Columbo as the Lieutenant prepares to inquire how much it will cost to dig up the pile in Elliot Markham's building where the body may be hidden.

In "Etude in Black" (#8), Lally has a name, but still no lines. He is Frank, an assistant in Mike's garage who brings Mike a socket wrench and nods sympathetically at the beginning of the episode when Mike, upon hearing Alex Benedict blow the horn, comments, "It must be his nibs again." Lally finally gets his first line in "Requiem for a Falling Star" (#12). When Columbo rushes into the studio at the end of the episode to tell Nora Chandler the "news" about Jerry Parks, a security guard (Lally) runs after him saying he can't go in there. Columbo flashes his badge and is allowed to pass. In "A Stitch in Crime" (#13), Lally has his first of many bit roles as one of the cops at the scene of the crime. In this case, he is the one who brings a weary Columbo some orange juice and informs the Lieutenant that they're still working on finding coffee. And, winding up the second season in "Double Shock" (#15), Lally is a bank clerk who asks Norman Paris to sign for $554,000 in cash in the scene where Columbo talks to Norman at the bank where he works.

Lally has many jobs in the third season (three times he's a bartender, once a cop, once a security guard, and assorted others), and the character actor is there in every one of the eight episodes. But sometimes you really have to look for him. You will need the pause button to catch him in "Lovely But Lethal" (#16), the season opener. He is again a cop at the murder scene, but he has no lines and he is seen only in passing as the camera moves across a group of policemen to discover Columbo walking up the path and checking Karl Lessing's mailbox before going inside.

Lally has a much more substantial appearance in the terrific episode "Any Old Port in a Storm" (#17). He's the bartender at the bar where Columbo watches the news report about Ric Carsini's death and realizes that he needs to find out if it rained last Tuesday when Ric supposedly parked his car and went scuba diving. Columbo asks Lally if he remembers if it rained last Tuesday and the bartender responds, "Mister, I can't remember what happened this morning." He then makes change for a quarter so that the Lieutenant can call the weather bureau (remember back when phone calls cost a dime?).

In "Candidate for Crime" (#18), Lally is a member of Nelson Hayward's crew. He appears in the scene in the house just before Hayward goes outside to tape his campaign ad. His appearance in "Double Exposure" (#19) is also fleeting; he is the security guard who says "Good evening, Mr. Norris" and allows the victim's car to pass into Kepple's institute. But that's nothing compared to his almost invisibility in "Publish or Perish" (#20)—he is behind a character on one of three split screens! Watch very carefully as Riley Greenleaf starts making trouble in the bar and throws the drink at the bartender. No, Lally isn't the bartender who gets wet; he's another bartender standing behind that poor fellow.

Lally gets back into the swing of things in "Mind Over Mayhem" (#21), playing a lab technician who reports the computer simulations to the military personnel playing the war games. "China air attack 1300," he tells them at first, then "submissile attack China." In "Swan Song" (#22), he is a worker for the crusade, responsible for counting the money they make at each concert. He tells Edna Brown after the Bakersfield concert that they have taken in $30,000, of which $15,000 goes to the tabernacle escrow fund.

Finally, it's back to the bartending job in "A Friend in Deed" (#23). No, he's not the bartender at the ritzy club where Hugh Caldwell pretends to call his wife; his job is at the dive that Artie Jessup (the Bel Air Burglar) uses as his office. He's there throughout, but his only line is when he tells Artie (who is talking to the Lieutenant) that his wife called to tell him to come home, he's taking her shopping.

In the show's fourth season, Lally displays a wide variety of professions, all the way from cops and police photographers to bums on the street, and he's present in every one of the season's six episodes. Sometimes you really have to look for him, and on one occasion he is heard but not seen!

In "An Exercise in Fatality" (#24), he gets in shape as "Charlie," who is working out on a stationary bicycle as Janus first enters the Chatsworth spa to confront Gene Stafford. Janus knows him, as he responds to Charlie's greeting. But he has hit the skids by "Negative Reaction" (#25)—he is the old man on the street (Columbo addresses him as "Pop") who directs the Lieutenant to the mission to locate Thomas Dolan, but the implication is that Pop is down on his luck as well. (I think the Ultimate Columbo website has an error. It claims Lally's voice can also be heard in a conversation at the cabin where Frances Galesko's body is found, but the identifiable voice is that of Fred Draper, playing the fingerprint man, see "The Supporting Cast.")

He has rejoined the force in "By Dawn's Early Light" (#26). He is one of the cops on the scene at the academy; in fact, he is the one who tells Sergeant

Kramer that he found the victim's car keys. Later, after Columbo has wandered back toward the cars, Lally asks Kramer how long they have to stay and the Lieutenant tells them they can go.

Lally takes a temporary leave from the force to sail away in "Troubled Waters" (#27), but he gets a job on the ship as a bartender (one of his favorite sidelines). He is seen twice in the episode, which is something of a rarity. First, he brings a drink to the table where band members are sitting just as Lloyd Harrington makes his move by going over to be dumped by Rosanna Welles. Then, much later in the episode, he brings scotch and waters for Hayden Danziger and Columbo in the crucial scene in which the Lieutenant finesses Danziger into planting the powder-burned glove to seal the case against Harrington.

Lally gets to relax a bit in "Playback" (#28). He is one of three men (the one on the left) sitting at the bar watching the football game. This will give Columbo the inspiration to check the tape of the murder and find the proof he needs to nail Harold Van Wyck.

Now we come to Lally's most interesting appearance of the entire show, when he is heard but not seen in "A Deadly State of Mind" (#29). How is this possible? Well, the feat is the result of the way the scene is shot. Columbo is sitting on the couch at the Donners' beach house, exploring some doubts he has about Nadia Donner's story, when a car with the "lab boys" pulls up. The camera continues to focus on the Lieutenant as we hear the three men enter the room and talk amongst themselves. Of course, I can't prove it, but I'd be willing to bet that "Lou the photographer" is none other than Michael Lally. By the time I watched this episode carefully looking for Lally, his raspy voice had become unmistakable to me, and Lou (whose line is something about the job never being easy) is Lally's most subtle appearance.

Now for the fifth season. In "Forgotten Lady" (#30), he is a guest at the home of Grace Wheeler and in fact he is the person to ask for a dance from the new show, which Grace and Ned perform. In "A Case of Immunity" (#31), Lally returns to the role of police photographer when he tells

Columbo that he is blocking the shot and that the tire iron that was the murder weapon was found in the driveway. In "Identity Crisis" (#32), he is the cabdriver who identifies the photograph of "Mr. Henderson" for Sergeant Kramer as being the man he took to Long Beach Amusement Park. Lally did not take the trip to Mexico, or at least I can't spot him in "A Matter of Honor" (#33), but he more than makes up for this with his signature piece, playing "Michael Lally," the retired trapeze artist in "Now You See Him" (#34) who knows that Santini used to travel around Europe with a "British" name and a German accent. Finally, he returns to his steady police photographer job for "Last Salute to the Commodore" (#35). He has no lines, but he can be observed taking pictures of Charles Clay's body.

Finally, we come to Mr. Lally's appearances in the show's sixth and seventh seasons. Unfortunately, there were only eight episodes in these last two seasons of the 1970s and Lally only appears in some of them. He does not appear (or at least I have been unable to find him) in "Fade in to Murder" (#36), "Try and Catch Me" (#39), "How to Dial a Murder" (#42) and "The Conspirators" (#43).

But, he does drop in to "Old Fashioned Murder" (#37), as the cop at the murder scene who whistles at Milton Schaeffer's wild shirt that the man bought because he expected to take a tropical trip after the robbery (there's a bit of an inconsistency about the name—in the scene Columbo calls him "Carter," but later he tells Ruth Lytton that "Sergeant Shaw" whistled at the shirt). And he is a member of the Sigma Club in "The Bye-Bye Sky High IQ Murder Case" (#38), where he is visible in the background when Oliver Brandt enters at the beginning and a short time later, when he is observed playing chess with another member.

In the show's seventh season, he plays Paul Gerard's unnamed assistant, who holds the bag while the restaurant critic goes food shopping in an open-air market while discussing his alternative theories of the murder with Columbo in "Murder Under Glass" (#40). And finally, he is the security guard in "Make Me a Perfect Murder" (#41) who nearly ruins Kay

Freestone's plan by stopping to flip through a (dirty?) magazine as she is running back to the projection room.

Mr. Lally passed away on February 15, 1985, before new episodes were produced in 1988. But I want to acknowledge Mr. Lally's contribution to the show. His realistic characterizations of ordinary people made the whole atmosphere more realistic and believable and we are in his debt. My thanks to Mr. Falk and hats off to Mike Lally for his terrific character roles.

The Supporting Cast

Obviously, the main interaction in any *Columbo* episode is between the detective and the guest murderer. But in addition, there is a small group of actors who have appeared several times in supporting roles. The following individuals have appeared four or more times in a notable supporting role.

John Finnegan is a character actor who has appeared on the show thirteen times, more than any other supporting actor except for Michael Lally's thirty-one brief appearances (see "The Thirty-One Hats of Michael Lally"). His plain speaking and New York accent always make his characters very believable. Some of his characters are "Colleagues and Sidekicks" to Columbo (the cop in "Lovely But Lethal" (#16), Lieutenant Duffy in "A Friend in Deed" (#23)) and they are discussed in the essay by that title. He also plays the role of Barney of Barney's Beanery in three episodes, and they are discussed in "Bert, Barney and Dog." Here are his eight other appearances. He first can be seen as Carl, the construction crew chief in "Blueprint for Murder" (#7). Carl explains to Columbo the process of digging a hole and putting in a pile (building foundation). The Lieutenant clearly suspects that architect Elliott Markham has buried a body in this way and Markham is happy to keep Columbo going in that line of reasoning.

He is another workman in "The Most Dangerous Match" (#14); in fact, he's the one who explains to Columbo that Dog would not have been seriously hurt if he had fallen into the trash compactor because the machine automatically shuts itself off (see "Bert, Barney and Dog"). This is significant because Columbo realizes that chess master Emmet Clayton must have pushed his victim into the compactor while his hearing aid was broken, or he would have heard the machine shut off and would have turned it back on.

In "Last Salute to the Commodore" (#35), Finnegan plays the guard who provides Charles Clay with the time when Clay wants to establish an alibi for himself. In "Fade in to Murder" (#36), he is the assistant director who escorts Columbo outside after the Lieutenant's noisy entrance ruins a take by *Lieutenant Lucerne* star Ward Fowler.

In "Columbo Cries Wolf" (#49), Finnegan plays the police chief who is impressed with Columbo's clue that the woman in the airport tape was not Dian Hunter because she put cream in her coffee. But when the Lieutenant fails to find Dian's body, the chief loses faith in him. Then Dian disappears a second time and the chief announces that Columbo is not to go near The Chateau, but luckily he is already on his way there.

Finnegan has a small but important role in "Uneasy Lies the Crown" (#52) as a waiter with a cold (he's not Barney, although the Beanery is mentioned in the episode). He is not impressed by the colorful capsules he was given to take, but Dr. Sherwin's discussion of how they work (time-release gel) gives Columbo the notion of how Wesley Corman committed the time-delay murder.

Then Finnegan is back as the chief, now named Quentin Corbett, in the episode "Columbo and the Murder of a Rock Star" (#56). Corbett tells Columbo to cooperate with Hugh Creighton by giving the man the file on his murdered lover, Marcy Edwards. And the chief has a menu recommendation for the Lieutenant, who is meeting Creighton at a fancy restaurant for dinner.

Finally, after his three appearances as Barney in "It's All in the Game" (#60), "Strange Bedfellows" (#63) and "A Trace of Murder" (#64) (see "Bert, Barney and Dog" for details), Finnegan plays Sean Jarvis in "Columbo Likes the Nightlife" (#67). Jarvis is the man who calls Linwood Coben to demand the rest of the money Coben promised. When Columbo inquires what the money was for, he learns that Jarvis's property overlooks Vanessa Farrow's house. It was while hanging out in a tree on Jarvis's yard that Coben observed and photographed Farrow and her boyfriend Justin Price disposing of the body of Farrow's ex-husband, Tony Galper.

Bruce Kirby made nine appearances on the show. However, seven of them are as a sergeant, at first named George Kramer and then named Brindle; these appearances are discussed further in "Colleagues and Sidekicks." His other two appearances are as the lab attendant in "Lovely But Lethal" (#16) whose job is to destroy the octagonal-shaped jars that once had miracle wrinkle removing cream in them, and as a TV repairman in "Make Me a Perfect Murder" (#41), who wishes Columbo would just buy a new set.

Shera Danese, also known as Mrs. Peter Falk, made six appearances on the show. She climbed the ladder from bit player to accomplice to victim to actual murderer. She first can be seen as Molly in "Fade in to Murder" (#36). Molly is Sid Daley's secretary and it turns out he was really with her, and not a friend playing chess, the night his wife Claire was murdered.

Danese next appears as Eve Plummer, Paul Gerard's assistant in "Murder Under Glass" (#40). Plummer is an accomplice, but only to the fraud Gerard is pulling by having restaurateurs pay him money so he will write good reviews of their establishments (she plays the role of the owner of the bank account, Mrs. Irene Demilo). She has no idea that Gerard poisoned Vittorio Rossi when he refused to pay up anymore. She is helpful in telling Columbo where Gerard buys his fish, specifically the blowfish he used to make the poison.

Danese has a major role as Vanessa Barsini in "Murder: A Self Portrait" (#48). Vanessa is Barsini's second wife, who manages his business affairs. However, she has no idea that he once murdered his art dealer and that he has just murdered his first wife Louise so that she will not spill the beans about this past crime. Vanessa and Julie (Barsini's current model) fight and later bond as they realize that they have been caring too much about his needs and not at all about their own.

In "Columbo and the Murder of a Rock Star" (#56), Danese moves all the way to being an accomplice after the fact. Hugh Creighton murders his mistress and asks his assistant Trish Fairbanks (Danese) to try an "experiment" for him while he's doing it. Since the experiment consists of speeding down a street with a mask of Creighton on her face so that he can be caught on camera by an automatic ticketing machine, it doesn't take long for her to figure out that she's become his alibi. She parlays this knowledge into an instant partnership with his law firm and a personal relationship with him to secure her position. Danese also performs the vocals for the rock star in this episode, which makes for a nice moment in the closing credits when Columbo is driving down the road and starts singing along to the victim's song "Closer, Closer." See "This Old Man" for more detail.

In "Undercover" (#62), Danese is Geraldine Ferguson, owner of an art gallery and possessor of one of the pieces of the puzzle that reveal the location of some hidden robbery money. Columbo has several discussions with her, trying to get her to admit what she knows. Unfortunately, the murderer (Irving Krutch) also figures out that she has a piece of the puzzle and he kills her for it.

Finally, Danese becomes a full-fledged murderer in "A Trace of Murder" (#64), although she has her partner Patrick Kinsley actually pull the trigger. Cathleen Calvert is having an affair with Patrick and they want to get her rich but embarrassing husband Clifford out of the way. They decide that the best solution is to frame him for the murder of Howard Seltzer, a meek businessman with whom Clifford has a business dispute. Patrick shoots Seltzer, leaves a cigar end from one of Clifford's stogies at the scene, and collects fibers from the scene and gives them to Cathleen, who wipes them on Clifford's suit. The frame is very good, but Columbo eventually is onto both of them. He tricks them into incriminating each other.

Vito Scotti always brought humor and distinctiveness to his six characters. He first appears in the fantastic third season episode "Any Old Port in a Storm" (#17) as the maitre d' who, along with the wine steward, are apologetic when they learn that the rumpled guest they've seated near the kitchen is the dining companion of fussy winemaker Adrian Carsini. They're even more taken aback when Carsini explodes that the rare dessert wine Columbo has ordered was ruined by exposure to heat.

Scotti next plays the role of Mr. Chadwick in "Candidate for Crime" (#18). Columbo goes to see the exclusive tailor to find out if Nelson Hayward ordered his new jacket before his campaign manager was shot dead while wearing it. But before revealing the purpose of his visit, the Lieutenant inquires about getting a new jacket himself for his wife's bowling league banquet. Prissy Mr. Chadwick is not interested and is not capable of rushing the order, even for a friend of Nelson Hayward.

In "Swan Song" (#22), Scotti is Mr. Grindell, owner of a funeral home. When Columbo has to wait a few minutes for the victim's brother to emerge, Grindell uses the opportunity to ask if the Lieutenant has made any plans for his final departure. Columbo can barely discuss the subject himself and, he explains, if he brought it up with his wife, she'd think he was working on something dangerous.

Scotti is very memorable in "Negative Reaction" (#25) as Thomas Dolan, a wino who is sleeping in the junkyard where Paul Galesko shoots Alvin Deschler. Dolan tells the police that there is a gap between the two shots when Galesko's story has them happen simultaneously. But once he sobers up, Dolan can't recall the details, although he is extremely gracious to Columbo, who comes to find him at a mission.

In "Identity Crisis" (#32), Scotti is Salvatore DeFonte, an Italian businessman for whom Nelson Brenner, in his cover job as a consultant, has written a speech. DeFonte has a wonderful scene with Columbo, clearly enjoying the chance to speak to a fellow paisano (in Italian, no less) and offering him some grapes for the road.

Finally, Scotti was given an appropriate role as "Vito," owner of Vito's Bar, in "Murder: A Self Portrait" (#48). Vito gave artist Max Barsini and his wife Louise a place to live back in the hard early days and is grateful that Barsini has come to paint a picture of his bar now. But the project is merely

Barsini's alibi. He painted the picture before, and he goes out to murder Louise while he's supposedly doing it now. Vito has some good scenes with Barsini and Columbo, including one in which he imitates Harry Chudnow, Barsini's first art dealer.

Fred Draper appeared on the show six times, sometimes in very minor roles and sometimes in somewhat more prominent ones. Unfortunately, his characters were usually not very convincing. He first appears unbilled as the cab driver in "Lady in Waiting" (#5). After Beth Chadwick murders her brother Bryce, her mother arrives by cab from her home in Palm Desert. Mistaking Columbo for a workman, she orders him to pay the cab driver and get her bags. Draper enjoys watching the Lieutenant haul her heavy bags to the house and when Columbo gives him a tiny tip, he comments, "you're a sport."

In "Lovely But Lethal" (#16), Draper has a large part as Dr. Murchison, who supposedly stumbles upon a successful wrinkle cream formula but then, after his sneaky assistant Karl Lessing steals it, thinks he made a mistake and retires to the bottle. His boss, cosmetics queen Viveca Scott, tries to get him to recreate it by sobering him up and forcing him to exercise at her fat farm, but it doesn't look like he can reproduce the results. Draper overplays the role, giving speeches about Scott being the "goddess of beauty" and does not convey a realistic scientist (even a bad one).

Draper's next role is unbilled—he plays the fingerprint man in "Negative Reaction" (#25) who comments that Alvin Deschler's prints are all over the cabin where the victim is found. He does a good job a few episodes later in the small but important role of David Morris in "A Deadly State of Mind" (#29). As murderer Marcus Collier speeds from the scene of the crime, he almost runs over a blind man. Columbo catches Collier with an ingenious trick. He has a man (Draper) walk in and identify Collier as the driver of the car. No way, claims Collier, this guy is blind. But he isn't. Draper is David Morris, but it was his brother Daniel, whom he resembles, who is blind and who Collier almost hit that day. By insisting that his accuser is blind, Collier incriminates himself.

Draper has his largest role in "Last Salute to the Commodore" (#35). He plays Swanny Swanson, nephew of the murdered Commodore and, it turns out in the end, the actual murderer. Although the plot makes it look like Charles Clay commits the deed, we learn that he merely discovers the body, thinks his wife had done it and disposes of the old man to save her. When Clay later realizes what had occurred, he must confront Swanny (the scene is not shown) because Clay is murdered himself. Draper plays Swanny as perpetually drunk and even when he is revealed at the end, he merely babbles incoherently. It's one of the series' worst moments in the worst episode (excluding the non-Columbo McBain adaptations).

Finally, Draper appears as a bit actor in "Fade in to Murder" (#36). In an ironic moment, this actor, who plays the part of a man named Joseph, appears at the end of an episode of the fictional *Lieutenant Lucerne* show and bungles his one line by saying "It'll be a kleasure to pill you, Lieutenant Lucerne." The director laughs it off, but star Ward Fowler says "get rid of him."

Val Avery is a large man with a face that suggests that his four characters have had their hard knocks, which is usually true. He first appears as Harry Barnes in "Dead Weight" (#3). Barnes has a good line or two as he rents a boat to Helen Stewart and her mother Mrs. Walters. It's a miracle the two of them bring the boat back in one piece. Barnes unknowingly becomes part of the plot when Major General Martin Hollister, who concludes that someone on a boat must have seen him commit a shooting, innocently asks Barnes who his "friend" was who waved to him earlier in the day. He supplies Stewart's name and address and Hollister goes off to meet and woo her into changing her story.

Avery next appears in "The Most Crucial Game" (#10) as Ralph Dobbs, a seedy private investigator who is caught by Columbo when he breaks into the house of Eric Wagner to remove bugs that were planted there. Dobbs reluctantly admits that he was hired by Wagner's lawyer, Walter Cannell, who was spying on team manager (and murderer) Paul Hanlon. In point of fact, Hanlon knew about the bugs and used them to set up his alibi (his phone call to Wagner in which he is supposed to be at the stadium, but is in reality a few blocks away at a phone booth). Dobbs becomes exasperated when Columbo won't return his listening equipment until he reveals how it was placed at Hanlon's house and he finally admits that he got his friend Eve Babcock to pretend to be a secretary and hide the bugs there.

Avery's next role (his most significant) is as Artie Jessup, the "Bel Air Burglar," in "A Friend in Deed" (#23). In this great portrayal, Jessup is a jewel thief who operates out of a seedy bar. When Hugh Caldwell kills his wife in a fight and then his friend Mark Halperin kills his wife for the inheritance, the men place the blame on the Bel Air Burglar, who's been hitting the neighborhood. But Jessup wouldn't hurt anyone and Columbo quickly picks up on this. He cleverly uses Jessup to trick Caldwell and Halperin into making a mistake. Avery has some notable scenes with Thelma, Jessup's nagging "wife" and one in which she calls while he's talking to Columbo to say "come home, you're taking her shopping." Lastly, he appears as Louie the bartender in "Identity Crisis" (#32). Louie notices that the victim, a man who turns out to be a spy code-named "Geronimo," was followed out of the bar by Lawrence Melville and that sets Columbo on Melville's trail and eventually to the real killer, Nelson Brenner.

Finally, Steven Gilborn makes four appearances on the newer shows as Dr. George Johnson, the medical examiner. He first appears in "Uneasy Lies the Crown" (#52), where he plays the significant role of explainer at the end. Columbo brings dentist Wesley Corman into the lab to show him how he murdered Adam Evans, who was having an affair with Corman's wife Lydia. He puts some digitalis into a crown in Evans's mouth and, a few hours later, the drug hit his system and killed him. To "prove it," Columbo demonstrates that digitalis on porcelain, when heated to body temperature, turns blue. Wesley confesses. But after he's taken away, Dr. Johnson announces that Columbo is bananas. Why, the only thing that is blue in the room is laundry bluing, like the kind Columbo has in splotches on his shirt. Is that so, asks the wily Lieutenant.

Gilborn appears again as Johnson in "Columbo Goes to College" (#54), "Caution: Murder Can Be Hazardous to Your Health" (#55) and "Columbo and the Murder of a Rock Star" (#56). In "Caution," he provides the important information that the victim died of nicotine sulfate poisoning.

Bert, Barney and Dog

Columbo talks a lot about his personal life, or at least he seems to (whether or not he's telling the truth about all of those relatives is another story). But we don't get to see him other than when he is on the job. (See "Does Columbo Exist?" for examples of when this idea gets carried too far.) So the little tidbits we do get to see of him when he is not talking to murderers or other witnesses are very important. This essay explores three of Columbo's friends, humans Bert and Barney and the Lieutenant's faithful companion, Dog.

Although Columbo keeps to himself, he does have a regular hangout while he's working: Barney's Beanery, where he orders his favorite meal, chili. Bert (played by Timothy Carey) appears twice, in the second pilot, *Ransom for a Dead Man* and the first season episode "Dead Weight" (#3). In the second instance, Bert actually helps Columbo when he talks about how he simply could not give up his war trophies. This convinces the Lieutenant that General Hollister still has access to his famous pearl-handled pistol. In fact, Hollister used the weapon to commit the murder and then put it in a display case along with the rest of the exhibit honoring him at the Marine Military Institute.

Barney is the closest thing the Lieutenant has to a regular friend on the show. When the series returned in 1989, the Lieutenant began eating at Barney's Beanery again. In "Rest in Peace, Mrs. Columbo" (#51), the Lieutenant has chili at a place that could be Barney's, although he refers to it as "the diner." The eatery is mentioned in "Uneasy Lies the Crown" (#52), when Wesley Corman tells Columbo that he'll meet the Lieutenant at Club Fifth Avenue rather than Barney's Beanery. John Finnegan appears later in the episode as a sneezing waiter, but he is not supposed to be Barney. Barney does not actually appear until "It's All in the Game" (#60), where he provides a crucial sounding board for the Lieutenant's bizarre flirting relationship with murderer Lauren Staton. Barney is given some very insightful lines and Columbo does not really treat him very well. The Lieutenant ignores Barney's questions about how far he would go to catch Lauren and at the end, Columbo claims that the whole flirtation was an act, designed to catch her. As explained in greater detail in the essays "The Morality of Columbo I" and "The Morality of Columbo II," the Lieutenant's last-minute about-face is not very convincing. Barney appears again in "Strange Bedfellows" (#63). Columbo is having some chili at Barney's when murderer Graham McVeigh comes to tell him that he's being threatened by mob boss Vincenzo Fortelli. And Barney appears in "A Trace of Murder" (#64). At the end of the episode, after murderers Patrick Kinsley and Cathleen Calvert have been caught, Columbo explains to Barney and his busboy, John, how it was while having coffee at the restaurant that the Lieutenant learned that the two knew each other. Patrick passed Cathleen the artificial sweetener and then opened the front car door for her on the way out, knowing she gets carsick in the back seat.

In these appearances, Barney is played by character actor John Finnegan. Finnegan has also played a number of other roles on the series over the years. See "Colleagues and Sidekicks" for a discussion of his roles as the sergeant in "Lovely But Lethal" (#16) and Lieutenant Duffy in "A Friend in Deed" (#22) and "The Supporting Cast" for his other appearances.

Dog, the sad but lovable basset hound, was introduced in "Etude in Black" (#8) to be Columbo's "sidekick" in response to network pressure. But the animal soon proved to be a valuable addition to the show. In his first appearance, he helped Columbo bond with Audrey, a neighbor of the victim, and this relationship was beneficial to Columbo in advancing his case against maestro Alex Benedict. He also helped Columbo bond with Elizabeth Van Wyck, wife of murderer Harold Van Wyck in "Playback" (#28). He even makes an impression on Abigail Mitchell in "Try and Catch Me" (#39), in the scene on the pier when Columbo explains how he likes to take Dog to see the ocean. In "Make Me a Perfect Murder" (#41), Dog and

Columbo watch the TV movie *The Professional* while they wait for a repairman to fix the set and the Lieutenant realizes that the murderer must have
changed the film just before the projectionist came back into the room, not
several minutes before as her scenario suggested. And Dog becomes part of
the plot in "It's All in the Game" (#60): after Lauren Staton sees Columbo
and his dog, she buys a doggie bed as part of their mutual flirtation.

On four occasions, Dog's presence has been integral to the plot. First, in
"The Most Dangerous Match" (#14), he provides Columbo with the means to
catch murderer Emmet Clayton when he almost falls into the trash compactor and a worker explains that the machine shuts off if anything falls in. Now
Columbo understands why the victim wasn't killed when Clayton pushed
him into the compactor—the machine shut off and Clayton, whose hearing
aid was not working, walked away without turning it back on. Second, in
"Mind Over Mayhem" (#21), Dog helps Columbo bond with "boy genius"
Steve Spelberg and Steve, working with his robot and Columbo, conclude
that Marshall Cahill could have programmed the robot to type the war-game
commands into the computer, leaving Cahill free to drive off and kill the victim. Third, in "Caution: Murder Can Be Hazardous to Your Health" (#55),
Dog again provides Columbo with the inspiration for the final clue when he
gets a pedicure and the Lieutenant concludes that the victim's dog, which
is missing a claw, scratched the murderer's car and placed him at the scene
of the crime. Finally, in "Ashes to Ashes" (#65), Dog provides the first clue
when he signals that another dog is present. The victim's puppy, a bulldog
named Louella, is crying because she has not been fed, and Columbo cannot
believe the scenario that the victim came home at night and did not feed the
dog. Something is amiss.

Of course, in many cases, Dog simply provides comic relief and texture
to the Columbo character. In "Forgotten Lady" (#30), Columbo feeds Dog
his favorite ice cream flavor, vanilla, and takes him for a walk in the park. This
makes for a counterpoint to the sad story of Grace Wheeler and her tragic
murder of her husband. In "Now You See Him" (#34), Columbo tells Dog to

look the other way if anyone tries to steal the stiff new raincoat his wife bought for him. In "Murder, Smoke and Shadows" (#45), Dog makes his first reappearance after the ten-year hiatus when he rides in the car with Columbo when the Lieutenant pulls up to talk to murderer Alex Brady. In "Grand Deceptions" (#47), Columbo asks Dog to keep watch when he leaves the car outside General Padget's house. And in "Murder: A Self Portrait" (#48), Dog tries to get in on the act when Max Barsini arranges to paint a portrait of Columbo, but Barsini tells the Lieutenant he doesn't paint dogs. It also seems as if Dog provides some insight into the motive for the murder when he bites Columbo and Dr. Hammer explains that the animal was jealous. But somewhat oddly, it turns out that Barsini murdered his ex-wife not out of jealousy but rather to prevent her from telling Hammer about how he killed his art dealer years ago.

In "How to Dial a Murder" (#42), Columbo presents Dog to Miss Cochrane and asks if the animal can be trained to protect his wife while the Lieutenant is working. Miss Cochrane suggests that Mrs. Columbo learn karate. Although this is a humorous scene, the writers missed an opportunity to really put Dog to use in this episode. When Eric Mason returns home after the murder, he finds Columbo playing with Laurel and Hardy, the two Dobermans that Mason trained to kill the victim. But Columbo is not the bravest of souls, so why would he approach the Dobermans with blood dripping from their mouths? Here is where Dog would come in handy. If he wandered over and started sniffing Laurel and Hardy, Columbo might notice that they didn't seem vicious.

Bert and Barney provide valuable sounding boards for Columbo in their appearances. And where would Columbo be without his loyal and lovable companion Dog?

Colleagues and Sidekicks

Columbo generally works alone. Of course, in almost every episode, there are other cops around and the first cop on the scene will report what he or she saw to the Lieutenant. But occasionally he has collaborated with a colleague of equal stature. Naturally, Columbo has to work with the local authorities when he is out of his jurisdiction. The first such instance is when he works with Chief Superintendent Durk of Scotland Yard in "Dagger of the Mind" (#11). Durk, played delightfully by Bernard Fox, is Columbo's tour guide of the Yard and London, but the men wind up putting their heads together to solve the case of the death of Sir Roger Haversham. Although Columbo takes the lead in working the case, Durk has to admit that the Lieutenant is usually right. The men become friends and, years later, Durk calls Columbo when a woman from Los Angeles fails to arrive in London as scheduled in "Columbo Cries Wolf" (#49). Although this scene is not shown to the audience, it is a nice touch to remember the Chief Superintendent in this fashion.

Columbo has an interesting relationship with Captain Gibbon (Patrick Macnee) on the ship in "Troubled Waters" (#27). On the one hand, the Captain, who has asked for the Lieutenant's help when the singer on board is found murdered in her cabin, is uncomfortable when Columbo starts questioning the guests and being conspicuous when the home office told the Captain to keep sailing but keep the matter quiet. He's even more put out when the evidence points toward band member Lloyd Harrington, but Columbo keeps investigating Hayden Danziger, who has framed Harrington for the crime. But the Captain eventually comes around when Columbo, with the help of ship's doctor Frank Pierce, convinces him that the scenario Danziger has staged just won't hold water. In the end, the Captain is on hand to ask Danziger why he would plant a powder-burned glove in a fire hose and to order Danziger to be handed over to the Mexican police when they reach Mazatlan.

Columbo works well with Comandante Emilio Sanchez (excellently portrayed by Pedro Armendariz, Jr.) in Mexico in "A Matter of Honor" (#33). Sanchez admires Columbo—he knows about how the Lieutenant solved the case aboard the cruise ship on its way to Mazatlan in "Troubled Waters" (#27) and he relishes the opportunity to spend a little time with the man when a fender bender strands Columbo in Mexico for a few days. Then, when Columbo spots some inconsistencies in the death of Hector

Rangel, Sanchez is only too happy to have Columbo take the lead in investigating Luis Montoya. There is a wonderful scene in an open-air café when Columbo slowly brings Sanchez around to see that the scenario that Rangel faced off alone against the bull to prevent his son from being injured or killed is false and that Montoya is the most likely suspect. Montoya is a powerful retired bullfighter who would make life miserable for Sanchez if he started asking too many questions. Sanchez remains very involved in the case and at the end he arrests Montoya when Columbo reveals the motive: the matador killed Rangel because Rangel had seen him demonstrate cowardice rather than bravery when he faced off against a bull.

Columbo also works with Roland Pangborn (played by John Dehner), an investigator for the National Transportation Safety Board, following the plane crash in "Swan Song" (#22). Pangborn is impressed by Columbo's ability to spot evidence like the fact that the pilot's seat belt was unbuckled. Although Pangborn is skeptical at first of Columbo's theory that Tommy Brown jumped out of the plane he was flying, he has to admit that Brown, who was a parachute rigger in the Air Force, could have made his own chute small enough to fit in the navigation kit.

Columbo works with a fellow lieutenant in "A Friend in Deed" (#23). Lieutenant Duffy of the robbery division (played by frequent character actor John Finnegan, see "Bert, Barney and Dog" and "The Supporting Cast" for his other appearances) would be happy to arrest Artie Jessup, the Bel Air Burglar, for the recent murders of two women, but Jessup has an alibi for both nights. More significantly, Duffy and Columbo concur that Jessup is a burglar, not a murderer. Columbo does not let Duffy know that he suspects that the murders were actually committed by their boss, Deputy Police Commissioner Mark Halperin. But in the end, Duffy is present when Columbo arrests Halperin, who has planted jewelry "stolen" from the first house in what he thought was the burglar's apartment. But the apartment was actually rented by Columbo and only Halperin saw the file with the false address.

Lieutenant Schultz, who appears in "Murder in Malibu" (#53), is also from the robbery division. But Schultz is played for comic relief by Floyd Levine. He takes everything as given. He sees no flaws in the robbery scenario, when Columbo immediately spots that the window need not have been broken. He has trouble reading a Miranda card that every kid can recite by heart. And he and Columbo are embarrassed at the end as they examine a female mannequin dressed in women's undergarments.

Lieutenant John Robertson (played by Frank McCrae) is a more serious character. Robertson, who appears in "A Bird in the Hand" (#59), is present not only at the beginning, when he investigates the hit-and-run accident that killed Big Fred McCain, but also much later in the episode, when they look into the murder of Harold McCain. Robertson is not present when Columbo arrests Dolores McCain (Tyne Daly) for the murder of Harold.

In addition to the collaborations, Columbo is often assisted by a sidekick, usually a sergeant who hangs around after the initial investigation of the crime scene and lends a hand. The first example of a sidekick is also one of the most memorable, Bob Dishy's portrayal of Sergeant Wilson in "The Greenhouse Jungle" (#9). Wilson provides comic relief as he meticulously handles the details of the investigation, but seems to miss the big picture. But he also helps solve the case, even if unintentionally. He is the one who introduces the idea of using a metal detector. Unfortunately, he uses it to look for the missing gun in Cathy Goodland's house, where it was planted for him to find by murderer Jarvis Goodland. But Columbo picks up on the idea and uses the metal detector in Jarvis's greenhouse. He discovers a bullet, fired over a year before at a burglar, that matches the bullet in the victim's body, and Jarvis is caught.

Wilson returns to play a similar role in "Now You See Him" (#34). He and Columbo talk through a lot of the evidence, which helps the Lieutenant conclude, for example, that the murderer must have picked the lock and opened the door. Wilson is also instrumental in catching the murderer, the magician known as The Great Santini. Wilson shows Columbo how newer typewriters work, with a ball instead of a carriage and with a single-strike, crisp carbon tape for a clear image. This tape can be unrolled from the spool and the message on it is the final blow that nabs the wily magician. (Of course, there is a bit of an inconsistency in that Wilson's first name is "Freddy" in "The Greenhouse Jungle" (#9) and "John J." in "Now You See Him" (#34); see "Hello, Continuity Department?")

The next recurring character is Sergeant George Kramer, introduced in "By Dawn's Early Light" (#26). Played by Bruce Kirby, Kramer is usually crusty and in a bad mood. He finds Columbo's meandering investigation frustrating and he just wants to get the whole thing over with. He appears again in "A Deadly State of Mind" (#29), "Identity Crisis" (#32), and "Last Salute to the Commodore" (#35). Sergeant Phil Brindle, who looks exactly like Kramer (he's also played by Bruce Kirby) first appears (unnamed) in "Columbo Cries Wolf" (#49), when he alerts the chief that Dian Hunter is missing a second time. The same unnamed sergeant assists Columbo in the next episode, "Agenda for Murder" (#50), although he resists trying the Lieutenant's proffer of cheese (Parmigiano reggiano) left at the scene of the crime. Sergeant Brindle is finally given a name in "Strange Bedfellows" (#63). In that episode, he and Columbo meet with murderer Graham McVeigh at Barney's Beanery and Brindle is the one who suggests the idea of putting a loose tail on McVeigh in case the mob comes after him. At the end, Brindle waits at McVeigh's horse farm for the call from Columbo and the message to search under the birdbath to find a crucial piece of evidence.

Then there is the strange case of Sergeant Burke. He has the most appearances of any Columbo sidekick (5), but he is played by three different actors! He first appears in "The Bye-Bye Sky High IQ Murder Case" (#38), where he is portrayed by Todd Martin. Burke prevents murderer Oliver Brandt from leaving the Sigma Society and sends him upstairs, where Columbo is waiting to catch him. In the very next episode, "Try and Catch Me" (#39), Sergeant Burke is played by Jerome Guardino, who previously appeared as the cop (named "Harris" in the credits) who agrees to take Columbo's firing range practice for him in "Forgotten Lady" (#30). Burke meets with

Abigail Mitchell before Columbo comes bursting out of the safe and he stays around to look for the victim's missing keys. Todd Martin comes back to play the part in "Murder Under Glass" (#40), but Guardino gets the role again in "Make Me a Perfect Murder" (#41), where Burke informs Columbo that he has found the missing gun. When the series returned in 1989, so did Sergeant Burke. Guardino played him a third time in "Murder, Smoke and Shadows" (#45). But in his final appearance, Sergeant Burke was played by Stewart J. Zully in "Sex and the Married Detective" (#46) (Zully would also play Detective Archie Sewell in "Murder, Smoke and Shadows" (#45) and "investigator number 3" in "It's All in the Game" (#60).). At the end of the episode, Burke tells murderer Joan Allenby to come to her therapy clinic because they have found the mysterious "Lisa" and Allenby arrives to be met by Columbo and the final clue (see the episode write-up and the essay "Final Clues" for more on this topic).

Two of the more recent episodes feature Sergeant Degarmo, played by Richard Riehle. He first appears in "Ashes to Ashes" (#65), where he has the victim's roll of film developed for Columbo and they find a picture of a house that is important to the case. He appears again in "Murder With Too Many Notes" (#66), where he and the Lieutenant have a friendly disagreement as to whether the victim was dead or merely unconscious when the ascending elevator tossed him off the roof. In the end, Columbo demonstrates that the victim was unconscious and Degarmo is there for the arrest of the murderer.

In other cases, a sidekick appears in only one episode. The first such instance is probably Sergeant Murray, played by Dabney Coleman, in "Double Shock" (#15) (he would return years later to play the murderer in "Columbo and the Murder of a Rock Star" (#56)). Murray, who is constantly chewing gum and is not afraid of housekeeper Mrs. Peck like Columbo, is around at the end to arrest the Paris twins when Columbo demonstrates that they collaborated in killing their uncle. In the next episode, "Lovely But Lethal" (#16), an unnamed sergeant (another role played by John Finnegan) comes to search Viveca Scott's office at the fat farm, just after she has thrown away the incriminating cosmetics jar. But Columbo catches her anyway, because she has poison ivy on her hand from having touched the victim's microscope, which had the stuff on it. In "Candidate for Crime" (#18), Sergeant Vernon (played by Robert Karnes) is head of the security detail protecting Nelson Hayward after Hayward and his campaign manager fake death threats to attract attention. Vernon rushes into the candidate's hotel room at the end after Hayward has set off a squib to simulate a gun shot, but Columbo knows that the shot was fired hours before.

One of the best sidekicks the Lieutenant has is Sergeant Hoffman, played by Michael Strong. In "Negative Reaction" (#25), Hoffman works with Columbo throughout the case and is involved in the ending, when Paul Galesko is tricked into identifying the camera he used in the commission of the crime.

In "Rest in Peace, Mrs. Columbo" (#51), Sergeant Brady (played by Tom Isbell) helps Columbo catch murderer Vivian Dimitri. Brady lends the Lieutenant his house, which doubles for Columbo's, and he tapes the scene as Dimitri confesses that she killed Mrs. Columbo (or at least she thinks she has) and Charlie Chambers. In "Columbo and the Murder of a Rock Star" (#56), Sergeant Hubach (played by Sondra Currie) tracks down the gardener and assists Columbo at the end. She puts on a flat mask of Columbo's face, to show how murderer Hugh Creighton used his assistant Trish Fairbanks to make it look as if Creighton was speeding through Pasadena when he was actually murdering his lover at the beach house.

In "Death Hits the Jackpot" (#57), Sergeant Jack Stroller is played mostly for laughs by Warren Berlinger. He holds the props for Columbo in the final confrontation with the murderer, Leon Lamarr. Then, after the case is over, he and Columbo have a conversation about the Lieutenant's 25th wedding anniversary. Columbo thinks he should get "the old car" a new coat of paint, and Stroller asks which car he means. Sergeant Riley is more serious in "It's All in the Game" (#60). As played by Doug Sheehan, Riley seems exasperated by Columbo, but he does help prove that the victim got a new telephone number ten days before his death and had the bills sent to a post office box so they would not be seen in his apartment. Finally, there is Officer Will (played by Will Nye) in "A Trace of Murder" (#64). Will finds the missing cat, which leads to the cigar end clue. And he drives Cathleen Calvert to meet Columbo and Patrick Kinsley at Barney's. This becomes important when Columbo watches Kinsley open the front door for Cathleen. Will confirms for the Lieutenant that Cathleen sat in the front seat on the ride over as well, and the men agree that she must get carsick if she rides in the back seat. This is crucial, because it means Kinsley knows her and they worked together to frame Cathleen's husband for the crime they committed. In the end, Officer Will escorts Cathleen to see the D.A. after Columbo has tricked her into believing that Kinsley, her co-conspirator, has plotted against her.

Chapter 23:
Titles, Music and More

Creative Columbo Titles

Back in the 1970s, many dramatic programs had episode titles. This particularly made sense for the elements of *The NBC Mystery Movie* which were, after all, ninety-minute or two-hour movies. Beginning in the 1980s, shows like *Hill Street Blues* featured multiple characters, multiple storylines and stories and characters that developed over many weeks, so the use of titles began to fade. Today most dramas do not employ episode titles.

Thankfully, *Columbo* returned as part of a mystery movie wheel and then appeared as an occasional TV movie, so the individual episodes continue to have titles. What's more, some of these titles reflect the cleverness and originality of the ones from the series' first run. But many do not. In *The Columbo Newsletter*, I commented on the episode titles and suggested alternatives when I found the title less than inspiring. Here I want to gather those remarks together and make a few observations about the use of titles on the show.

Many of the titles from the 1970s reveal a good deal of ingenuity. They often take a famous phrase, directly or slightly modified, and use it to refer to the profession of that episode's murderer. Examples from the first season include: "Murder By the Book" (#1)(usually meaning to do things in a prescribed way, here tying into the fact that the plot idea was jotted down by the mystery writers and then put into action by one of them); "Death Lends a Hand" (#2)

(Mr. Brimmer, the murderer, not only assists Columbo with the investigation, but also killed by means of striking the victim with his hand); "Suitable for Framing" (#4)(nicely tying in the notion that the killer works in the world of art and that he frames his aunt for the crime); "Lady in Waiting" (#5)(originally referring to a woman who attends a queen, etc., but here meaning that Beth Chadwick has been waiting for her brother's death to emerge as her own individual); "Blueprint for Murder" (#7)(capturing that the murderer is an architect—I would also have suggested "Architect of Destruction").

From the second season: "Etude in Black" (#8)(bringing in the musical reference); "The Most Crucial Game" (#10)(referring to sports and the game between Columbo and Paul Hanlon); "A Stitch in Crime" (#13)(nice tweak of the phrase "a stitch in time saves nine" incorporating the plot twist that a heart surgeon uses dissolving suture to kill his patient); "The Most Dangerous Match" (#14)(referring to chess matches and the match between Emmet Clayton and Columbo); "Double Shock" (#15)(we're surprised when the man we assume to be the murderer turns out to have an identical twin, and the victim has quite a shock when one of them drops a mixer in his bathtub).

From the third season: "Any Old Port in a Storm" (#17)(referring to wine and the sea, both of which play a part in the plot); "Candidate for Crime" (#18)(the murderer is running for office on an anti-crime platform); "Swan Song" (#22)(Tommy Brown, a singer, parachutes from the sky and this murder is indeed his last performance); "A Friend in Deed" (#23)("a friend in need is a friend indeed," but here two friends commit the same deed, murder).

From the fourth season: "An Exercise in Fatality" (#24)(great title, achieved by altering one letter in the phrase "an exercise in futility" and referring to the murderer who owns exercise clubs); "Negative Reaction" (#25)(referring to photography); "By Dawn's Early Light" (#26)(calling to mind "The Star-Spangled Banner" in this military-themed episode, as well as the point that the important event occurs early in the morning); "Troubled Waters" (#27)(troubled by murder aboard a ship); "Playback" (#28)(episode filled with technological gadgets); "A Deadly State of Mind" (#29) (psychiatrist with deadly intentions).

From the fifth season: "Identity Crisis" (#32)(Nelson Brenner has multiple identities, including that of double agent); "Now You See Him" (#34) (great reference to magician's mantra, "now you see him, now you don't," and specifically indicating that, at the end, the Great Santini is revealed to be an ex-Nazi murderer).

From the sixth season: "Fade in to Murder" (#36)(fade in being a phrase used in film production and the murderer is an actor).

From the seventh season: "Murder Under Glass" (#40)(referring both to food—as in "pheasant under glass"—and to the magnifying glass typically used by traditional detectives)

From the newer episodes: "Agenda for Murder" (#50)(not a bad reference to the plans of the scheming murderer Oscar Finch); "Rest in Peace, Mrs. Columbo" (#51)(I don't like this entry, but since the point is to fool Vivian Dimitri and the audience into thinking the Missus is dead, they might as well convey it in the title); "Uneasy Lies the Crown" (#52)(the crown in this case referring not to royalty but to a dentist's porcelain crown, filled with digitalis; I would also offer "A Bite Out of Crime," since it's rumored that the McGruff crime dog is based on Columbo); "No Time to Die" (#58) (I may despise this attempt to make an Ed McBain mystery into a *Columbo*, but the title works); "Undercover" (#62)(same comment as "No Time"); "A Trace of Murder" (#64)(nicely captures the idea that the murderers leave a subtle trail pointing toward the man they want to frame).

However, not every attempt yields such a great result. Here are the ones that did not quite make it: "Dead Weight" (#3) (sure, the victim is excess baggage for the murderer, but that's always true; my suggestion is "General Discharge," which refers to a military discharge when the individual does not qualify for the honorable variety, and of course here the discharge is from a gun); "The Greenhouse Jungle" (#9)(must be based on *The Asphalt Jungle*, but I think "A Green Thumb for Murder" might better capture the idea); "Dagger of the Mind" (#11)(a quote from *Macbeth*, the play the murderers are putting on, but it doesn't fit them; a better reference would be something like "Foul Play is Fair"); "Requiem for a Falling Star" (#12)(way too serious for this fluffy episode; I offer "Acting in Self-defense"); "Lovely But Lethal" (#16)(this describes Viveca Scott, but that's about all; I suggest "Formula for a Beautiful Cover-up," although admittedly her cover-up leaves a lot to be desired); "Double Exposure" (#19)(referring to photography, which is relevant, but a better option would be "Murder Most Subliminal"); "Publish or Perish" (#20) (the literal phrase doesn't fit, because the victim publishes and perishes; I suggest "Final Rejection"); "Forgotten Lady" (#30)(well, Grace Wheeler is not so much forgotten as she is forgetting; I offer "Musical Tragedy"); "A Case of Immunity" (#31)(sort of gives away the ending; I suggest "Diplomatic Corpse," altering by one letter the phrase diplomatic corps to refer to this murder at a legation); "A Matter of Honor" (#33)(so close, but the title should be "Point of Honor," which means the same thing and brings in the idea of a sword as well); "Try and Catch Me" (#39)(Ruth Gordon has a ball as Abigail Mitchell, but she also has a very serious motive; I suggest "Murder, She Wrote"); "How to Dial a Murder" (#42)(that's very pedestrian; they should have tried "Dogged Pursuit"); "The Conspirators" (#43)(the conspirators don't do much, and the title should refer to Joe Devlin's profession, like "Poetic Justice").

From the newer episodes: "Murder, Smoke and Shadows" (#45)(dull, I suggest "In the Direction of Murder," referring both to Alex Brady's line of work and the fact that he already committed a crime of omission when he left someone to bleed to death, so now he's graduated to outright murder); "Murder in Malibu" (#53)(yes, there's a murder in Malibu, so what? I offer "Hapless Romantic"); "Death Hits the Jackpot" (#57)(doesn't tell us much; I suggest "Dead Giveaway"); "A Bird in the Hand" (#59)(refers only to the ending; the title should make some reference to gambling, such as "Cashing in the Chips" or "Loaded Dice"); "It's All in the Game" (#60)(like "Try and Catch Me" (#39), too frivolous a title for what's really at stake; I suggest "All's Fair in Love and Murder," which is certainly the case here); "Strange

Bedfellows" (#63)(that gives away the ending; I offer "Mob Scene"); "Ashes to Ashes" (#65)(not bad, but the episode itself suggests two better ideas—Verity Chandler's intended title for her TV segment, "Grisly Undertakings," and Columbo's closing comment to Eric Prince, "It's Your Funeral").

Then there are the ones that don't make any sense: "Short Fuse" (#6) (Roger Stanford doesn't have a quick temper; I suggest "A Serious Case of Exploding Cigars," which refers both to the murder method and the case Columbo has to solve); "Mind Over Mayhem" (#21)(what does this mean? I suggest "Research and Destroy"); "Last Salute to the Commodore" (#35) (unless Swanny braining the old man with a belaying pin counts as a "salute," the title doesn't work; I suggest "Who Killed the Commodore?" since the whole point of the episode is to make the audience guess for a change); "Old Fashioned Murder" (#37)(Ruth Lytton may be old fashioned, but her murders are not; try "Museum Piece," which refers to old items that belong in a museum as well as this "piece" of *Columbo* set in a museum); "The Bye-Bye Sky High IQ Murder Case" (#38)(okay, the cutesy title refers to Oliver Brandt's immaturity, like the silly song "Baby Oh So Blue," but it's too much; I suggest something like "Accounting for Murder"); "Make Me a Perfect Murder" (#41) (what—they forgot the "babe" part! The obvious title is "Murder on Cue").

From the newer episodes: "Grand Deceptions" (#47)(huh? I offer "Model of a Civil War," referring to the general's collection and the battle between Columbo and Colonel Brailie); "Murder: A Self Portrait" (#48)(references to the artist murderer should not be difficult, such as "Brush With Death" or "Still Life on a Beach"); "Caution: Murder Can Be Hazardous to Your Health" (#55)(not just silly, but inappropriate, since that old Surgeon General's warning on cigarette packs had long since been replaced; I don't know why they changed it from the originally planned titled, "Smoke Screen"); "Butterfly in Shades of Grey" (#61)(I have yet to hear anyone explain this oddity; I suggest "Murder on the Line"); "Murder With Too Many Notes" (#66)(meaning what? I suggest "Facing the Music").

The newer episodes also introduced the unfortunate idea of including

Columbo in the title. I think this is a mistake, both because it's unnecessary (his name is already the title of the show) and because it requires no creativity. "Columbo Goes to Military School" would be accurate for "By Dawn's Early Light," but not advisable.

Here are my alternatives: "Columbo Goes to the Guillotine" (#44)(I suggest "Reunion in a Magic Show," since this is the second episode to feature a magician murderer, plus it was our reunion with this program after a ten-year hiatus); "Sex and the Married Detective" (#46)("Dangerous Liaisons" seems like the obvious choice); "Columbo Cries Wolf" (#49)(I offer "Accomplice to Murder," which has the beauty of referring to Tina, Dian and even Columbo, who unwittingly plays into Sean Brantley's hand by investigating Dian's disappearance so thoroughly); "Columbo Goes to College" (#54)(I offer "Extracurricular Execution"); "Columbo and the Murder of a Rock Star" (#56) (this title refers to everyone but the murderer; I suggest "Devil's Advocate"); "Columbo Likes the Nightlife" (#67)(not even accurate—I offer "Club Dead").

"This Old Man": Columbo's Theme Song

As documented elsewhere (in *The Columbo Phile* at p. 156, for example), Peter Falk introduced the ditty "This Old Man" in the episode "Any Old Port in a Storm" (#17), in yet another of that amazing episode's list of innovations. Specifically, he starts singing the song while dialing the telephone at the winery and then does it again in "Candidate for Crime" (#18) while waiting to talk to Nelson Hayward at his campaign headquarters (oddly, Hayward, who has not heard him, begins humming it himself in a later scene). It quickly became part of the character. The little children's song fit perfectly, particularly as Falk made the character more likeable and more of a good guy (see "The Developing Character").

The song was used very effectively in "Murder Under Glass" (#40) as the background for the banquet Columbo attends. It was also the closing music in "Last Salute to the Commodore" (#35).

In the newer episodes, "This Old Man" first reappears when it is incorporated somewhat into the basset hound music at the beginning of "Murder: A Self Portrait" (#48), which was a nice touch in the scene with Dog. Columbo hums it shortly before arresting the murdering frat boys in "Columbo Goes to College" (#54). The song does not appear again until "Death Hits the Jackpot" (#57), and it is a poor version of the ditty that is used. And it should not have been used at the beginning of the episode, while future victim Freddy Brower is driving around in his van. Since the show has no official theme song, the music at the beginning has always related in some way to the murder, not the Lieutenant.

Then, and very oddly, it is heard over the closing credits of "No Time to Die" (#58), the attempt to fit an Ed McBain police procedural into a *Columbo* that abandons just about everything else about the character (see "No Time for Columbo, No Place for McBain"). It's also a bizarre choice after the climactic ending, with the would-be rapist being blown away and the tension filling the room to hear this children's song. "Strange Bedfellows" (#63) has a decent version of the ditty at the end, but "Ashes to Ashes" (#65) has a lackluster version of the song heard occasionally in the background.

Of course, "Murder With Too Many Notes" (#66) uses the song quite a bit, particularly at the end, where Columbo asks Rebecca to play it. But it was a bizarre choice to have Columbo say that it's his wife's favorite tune, rather than his own. That doesn't fit in with the years of him humming it or its incorporation into the show's music on many occasions. Also, the notion that he needs help in learning how to play the notes is belied by "Try and Catch Me" (#39), where he actually does so; he also plays *Chopsticks* in "Etude in Black" (#8). See "Hello, Continuity Department?"

Some other episodes have great individual music. At first, the music on the show was rather forgettable, although "Murder By the Book" (#1) has an interesting sound with a typewriter being put through a synthesizer. One of the better pieces of music occurs in "The Greenhouse Jungle" (#9), a catchy tune that would be used again in "Double Shock" (#15) and as one of many snippets that make up the music in "Requiem for a Falling Star" (#12).

"Dagger of the Mind" (#11) has a rousing tune that fits perfectly with Big Ben and the sights of London. "Swan Song" (#22) has Johnny Cash singing *I Saw the Light* throughout and it fits the episode perfectly. I love the little jingle about Milo Janus played as the credits roll in "An Exercise in Fatality" (#24). "By Dawn's Early Light" (#26) has appropriate military music, including the counting off that is played as the scene freezes on Colonel Rumford caught at the end. "Troubled Waters" (#27) has a fun ship-board theme as Columbo sails away to Mexico.

"Forgotten Lady" (#30) has old movie musicals playing, including *Walking My Baby Back Home* which actually starred Janet Leigh. "A Case of Immunity" (#31) hits the right notes with its theme evoking the Mideast. "Now You See Him" (#34) has a terrific mysterious theme that plays over the opening credits, as well as Henry Mancini's *Charade* which is sung during the episode by Danny Green. "The Bye-Bye Sky High IQ Murder Case" (#38) has a silly little children's song ("Baby Oh So Blue") which plays as Oliver Brandt sets up his Rube Goldberg device and again over the end credits. At first, I didn't like it, but then I decided that it perfectly fit this villain, who is really a big baby looking for comfort from his wife. "Try and Catch Me" (#39) has a lovely little tune that suggests an old lady and plays each time Abigail Mitchell takes some action. Similarly, in "Sex and the Married Detective" (#46), Patrick Williams creates a sort of leitmotif that appears each time Joan Allenby puts on the Lisa outfit, and the effect is very striking. And "The Conspirators" (#43) has that great Irish theme as Columbo goes speeding over the bridge toward the end as well as Joe Devlin singing "Whiskey in the Jar," the perfect complement to this fun episode.

In "Grand Deceptions" (#47), the music creates a theme of the toy soldiers that recurs throughout, although the mood is a bit too festive given the brutal murder and Brailie's wooden attitude. In "Columbo Cries Wolf" (#49), the music, although somewhat modern for a *Columbo* episode, fits perfectly on this outing.

In "Agenda for Murder" (#50), naturally, "Happy Days Are Here Again" is an appropriate piece of music to recall politics, but it is overused in the episode, particularly at the end where it is inappropriate.

"Columbo and the Murder of a Rock Star" (#56) features good music for the episode, well sung by Shera Danese over the opening and closing credits. It is particularly nice at the end, where Columbo, in a little music video (unique for the show), rolls down the road singing along to "Closer, Closer" (a song by the victim, rock star Marcy Edwards) on the boom box he bought at Dhoti's Discount, as the kid had suggested at the beginning of the episode.

Of course, you can't go wrong with a good piece of classical music, as used in "Etude in Black" (#8), "Playback" (#28) (Chopin) and "Identity Crisis" (#32) (*Madame Butterfly*).

Hello, Continuity Department?

Despite the fact that new episodes of *Columbo* aired (on and off) for thirty-five years and that it was written, directed and produced by many, many different individuals, there is a surprising amount of continuity. As noted in "The Developing Character," all of the character traits were essentially set during the first three seasons and then explored further thereafter (his wife, car, coat, Italian heritage, dog, and his favorite ditty, "This Old Man"). Not much new is introduced after that and there are many times when an episode picks up on something that has happened before. For a specific example, when Sergeant Wilson, first introduced in the second season episode "The Greenhouse Jungle" (#9), returns three years later in "Now You See Him" (#34), his character is given the same role: the young cop who knows the technology but doesn't see the big picture, as Columbo does.

Still, there are some inconsistencies. Naturally, when you see "Now You See Him" (#34), you can't help noticing that the writers forgot Wilson's first name—it's Freddy in the first episode and John J. in the second. But that's nitpicking.

For the most part, inconsistencies in Columbo's character don't matter. If he tells one murderer that he has kids and another that he doesn't, I'm willing to accept that he's lying to one person and he shouldn't reveal the true information anyway. But every once in a while, a situation arises that cries out for a reference to something we've seen before, and it doesn't happen.

In the very first new episode, "Columbo Goes to the Guillotine" (#44), the Lieutenant is shown two trick guillotines: a finger version and the murder weapon. He is amazed. But wait. In "Now You See Him" (#34), the murderer was a magician and, during a trip to a magic shop to get some information, he was shown a trick wrist guillotine. He didn't learn how it worked (unless he bought the item), but he was certainly familiar with the concept.

In "Columbo Cries Wolf" (#49), there is an unusual and delightful connection to a prior episode. Since the victim disappeared on her way to meet an important person in London, the writers have Columbo say that he was contacted by his old friend, Chief Superintendent Durk of Scotland Yard. This character was introduced in "Dagger of the Mind" (#11) and it was a nice touch to remember him (even if the audience is not privy to this conversation).

In "Agenda for Murder" (#50), however, the writers once again fail to take the opportunity to refer to a previous episode, the prior campaign entry "Candidate for Crime" (#18). There are many points in the episode when his prior experience would have come in handy, and was worth mentioning.

In "Uneasy Lies the Crown" (#52), there is some inconsistency in the Lieutenant telling Wesley Corman he takes cream in his coffee, because for the last twenty-two years he has ordered it black. This is particularly odd after "Columbo Cries Wolf" (#49), a few episodes before, made a clue out of the fact that a character not known to take cream in her coffee does just that on the security tape from the airport (suggesting it isn't her). Although there are no references to previous episodes here, there is an interesting connection to the preceding episode ("Rest in Peace, Mrs. Columbo" (#51)) in that Columbo mentioned that he needed to find a new dentist since his had moved away. It's almost as if that comment was part of the inspiration for this episode.

"Columbo Goes to College" (#54) has some nice moments of Columbo interacting with the class, a new venue for him. However, I do not understand his reference to "the Devlin case," which does not exist. Why didn't the writers have him refer to a real past episode? (in fact, he actually does comment on "Agenda for Murder" (#50)).

In "Columbo and the Murder of a Rock Star" (#56), someone was asleep at the wheel when Columbo was given the line that this was the first time he has ever put down the top on his car. To name just a few examples, he had it down in "Lady in Waiting" (#5) when he and Peter Hamilton ate at the drive-in restaurant, in "Short Fuse" (#6) when he drove Roger Stanford and Everett Logan to the cable car, in "The Most Dangerous Match" (#14) when he drove Emmet Clayton back to the restaurant where he and Dudek had dined the previous evening, and in "Last Salute to the Commodore" (#35) when he allowed "Mac" to drive the car (the top had to be down in this last scene, because Columbo was standing up in the back seat of the car yelling out instructions). Incidentally, the original car was gone when the show was resurrected in 1989, but the producers managed to find a "back up" car that was used for the rest of the series.

"Death Hits the Jackpot" (#57) has a side story about Columbo searching for his wife's anniversary present, but is not seriously dealt with, as Columbo first inquires about the lingerie Nancy sells, then Leon Lamarr's jewelry, only to discover in each instance that they are above his price range (surprise, surprise). At the end of the show, with time to spare, Columbo and Sergeant Stroller leave the room and the Lieutenant comments that maybe he'll get "the old car" a new coat of paint (this is an anniversary present?). The flunky asks which one and Columbo says "I didn't hear that" (this is funny?). According to details provided in "Columbo Goes to College" (#54), aired one year before, his wife's car is a 1976 green Ford coupe, and he drives a 1960 Peugeot, so his must be "the old car"! In any event, what does he buy her? There was more resolution in "Columbo and the Murder of a Rock Star" (#56), when the Lieutenant in the closing credits is listening to a CD on a boom box bought for his nephew at the store recommended by the kid at the beginning of the show.

The other issue raised in "Death Hits the Jackpot" (#57) and other new episodes is how long Columbo has been married and has been on the force. The idea that the Columbos have only been married for twenty-five years, despite the fact that they were "childhood sweethearts" and the unspoken certainty that the Lieutenant is somewhere in his early sixties in 1991, strains credulity quite a bit. After all, that means they were married in 1966, just two years before *Prescription: Murder* (pilot A) aired and at that time Columbo was in his thirties. He said thirty years to Vivian Dimitri in "Rest in Peace, Mrs. Columbo" (#51) in 1990, a year a half before this episode aired. That number sounded more realistic, and it was given to a murderer who was planning on killing Mrs. Columbo!

In "No Time to Die" (#59), it is interesting to see which aspects of the Columbo character the writers tried to keep and which they abandoned here. Of course, Columbo's usual mannerisms have to go and the car works perfectly as it must under the circumstances (it probably would have been better to use a different one). Mrs. Columbo is not present and although the explanation is credible, it also seems convenient. Naturally, the other cops and witnesses refer to him as "Lieutenant" or "Columbo," but there is a problem with Andy and Melissa. At least to his nephew, he should be known as Uncle [First Name], so the movie has Andy not call Columbo anything. He wears the raincoat over the tuxedo, but it's not really clear why he does so. In the end, it's ironic that so many minor aspects of the character are maintained in a movie that abandons the show's format completely.

In "Strange Bedfellows" (#63), he says he's been trying to find a way to tell people their loved ones have been murdered for twenty years. This episode was filmed in 1994 and aired in 1995, so that means he's talking about 1974 at the earliest, which is the middle of the third season. As always, he is not required to tell murderers the truth about anything, but what's the point of lying about this detail?

In "Ashes to Ashes" (#65), the Lieutenant tells Eric Prince he's been at this for twenty-five years. Columbo must be living in some kind of time warp, because the character has been in existence on television since 1968, which is thirty years prior to this episode's airdate! Even using the first season as a starting point, that was in 1971, which was twenty-seven years before this episode. Of course, Columbo can tell Prince anything he likes, but again, what's the point of lying about this piece of information?

I liked the old days, when his comments on these questions made sense, like in "Negative Reaction" (#25) (1974), when he said he'd been on the force fifteen years, meaning he joined in 1959. Of course, he could be lying to the suspects, but sometimes (for instance, in "Death Hits the Jackpot" (#57)) his comments are made to fellow officers and I don't understand why he would lie about these details. It seems more likely that a little vanity is involved. Columbo and Falk ought to be about the same age, but the actor kept aging while the character did not.

"Ashes to Ashes" (#65) also has an interesting moment when Columbo tells Prince that he got the information that "SB" means Sunset Boulevard from his cousin and fills in lots of details about the man (he's on his father's side, he sees him once a month, he repaid him for the info by giving him three golf balls) when the fact is that he got the information from a guy at the cab company. Interesting, but odd really. It's another example of the Lieutenant lying to the murderer without any real reason to do so. (See the essay "The Morality of Columbo II" for more on this topic.)

Columbo's Accolades

Columbo at the Emmys

In the 1970s, *Columbo* amassed an impressive number of Emmy awards, including three for Peter Falk as best actor (1971-72, 1974-75, 1975-76). In addition, Levinson and Link won outstanding writing in a drama series for "Death Lends a Hand" (#2), Lloyd Ahern won best cinematography for "Blueprint for Murder" (#7), Harry Wolf won best cinematography for "Any Old Port in a Storm" (#17), Richard Glouner won best cinematography for "Playback" (#28), Edward Abroms won outstanding achievement in editing (1971-72), *Columbo* won outstanding limited series (1973-74) and Patrick McGoohan won outstanding single performance by a supporting actor in a comedy or drama series for his role in "By Dawn's Early Light" (#26).

The program continued to receive Emmy Awards when it returned in 1989. Here is a summary of the results by year, both nominations and winnings.

1989-90 Awards

Peter Falk was nominated for and won Best Actor in a Dramatic Series. Patrick McGoohan was nominated for and won Outstanding Single Performance by a Supporting Actor in a Dramatic Series for "Agenda for Murder" (#50).

1990-91 Awards

Peter Falk was nominated for Best Actor in a Dramatic Series. Dabney Coleman was nominated for Best Guest Actor in a Dramatic Series for "Columbo and the Murder of a Rock Star" (#56).

1993-94 Awards

Peter Falk was nominated for Best Actor in a Dramatic Series. Faye Dunaway was nominated for and won Best Guest Actress on a Drama Series for "It's All in the Game" (#60).

Other Awards and Recognition

In the 1990s, *TV Guide* began compiling lists of "the best" and *Columbo* and Peter Falk have been on many of them. The Lieutenant's first appearance was ranked as thirty-nine out of the 100 best moments on television, and Peter Falk was named number twenty-one out of fifty influential TV stars. In April 1993, *TV Guide* named *Columbo* the best cop show of the 1970s. In June 1997, the magazine provided a list of the 100 best episodes of all shows that ever aired (comedies and dramas, so this was really a subjective compilation). Number sixteen from the top was "Murder By the Book" (#1). In October 1999, *TV Guide* named the Fifty Greatest Characters Ever. Clocking in at number seven, between Emma Peel and Mr. Spock, was Lieutenant Columbo. In July 2000, TV Guide listed the greatest detectives of all time and Columbo came in second, losing out only to Jim Rockford of *The Rockford Files.*

In 1996, Peter Falk received a Chevalier of Arts and Letters, France's highest honor. Fans in Germany report that he received a Bambi (their version of an Emmy?) in 1993.

In 1989, Richard Levinson (posthumously) and William Link were awarded the Ellery Queen Award for Lifetime Achievement in the Art of Mystery from the Mystery Writers of America (MWA). In 2002, Link was made president of the MWA.

In 1995, in a much overdue moment of recognition, the TV Academy of Arts and Sciences inducted into its Hall of Fame the writing team of Richard Levinson and William Link. Peter Falk made the presentation and the award was graciously accepted by Mr. Link and Mr. Levinson's widow. The special aired on CBS, but not until April 18, 1996.

Falk on Columbo

In addition to having his biography aired on the A&E program *Biography* on February 28, 2000 (hosted in this instance by Jerry Orbach), Falk appeared on *Inside the Actor's Studio*, a production of the Bravo Channel, in 1999 and gave an extensive and wide-ranging interview with host James Lipton.

Chapter 24:
Columbo Everywhere

Columbo on the Air

Columbo fans were indeed lucky during the 1990s and forward. Previously (from 1979 to 1985), the only way to watch the show had been on *The CBS Late Movie*, where it was edited terribly. Entire scenes were cut to make the show fit the time slot, with disastrous results. But *Columbo* stopped rotating on CBS late night in 1985, and the *Late Movie* itself was canceled in 1989. Beginning in 1994, the cable station A&E (Arts and Entertainment) began showing all of the episodes from the 1970s. For a while, it was possible to catch a two-hour episode or two ninety-minute episodes on various days of the week. During the month of May 1996, A&E ran a special feature: four two-hour episodes with introductory remarks by Peter Falk himself. Dubbed "Columbo's Favorite Columbos," they were: "Any Old Port in a Storm" (#17); "Forgotten Lady" (#30); "Now You See Him" (#34); and "Identity Crisis" (#32). On February 28, 2000, A&E featured Peter Falk on its acclaimed show *Biography*.

In October 1995, a cable channel that changed names a number of times (first it was The Family Channel, then Fox Family, then ABC Family) began showing the newer episodes of *Columbo* on Sunday nights. This was a good resource for those who missed them the first time around, although the channel insisted on "cleaning up" the language in the shows, leading to humorous moments such as when Jess McCurdy (Brenda Vaccaro) says "damn" in "Murder in Malibu" (#53) but there is, instead, a lengthy pause.

In 2002, A&E purchased the rights to the newer episodes and it aired them, as well as the original forty-three, on a rotating basis, for several years. A&E did not edit the episodes for time or harsh language, so they could be enjoyed in their entirety. *Columbo* currently can be seen on a cable station that airs old TV shows called MeTV.

New Links

Columbo co-creator William Link has not been resting on his laurels since the cancellation of *The ABC Mystery Movie* in 1990. He has been the creative force behind several shows, including *Over My Dead Body* (1990-91), a sort of *Murder, She Wrote* with Edward Woodward as a mystery writer assisted by reporter played by Jessica Lundy, and *The Cosby Mysteries* (1994-95), with Bill Cosby as a retired forensic scientist (Link also appeared in this series as Cosby's music teacher).

On April 15, 1991, ABC aired a most unusual movie. Called *The Boys*, it was Link's homage to his late partner, Richard Levinson, but with more than a few twists. James Woods and John Lithgow starred as mystery writing partners Walter Farmer and Artie Marguiles. Artie is a life-long chain smoker, but as the movie opens it's Walter who gets the news that he is dying of lung cancer, very possibly the result of second-hand smoke he breathed in while working in the same room as Artie for many years. Walter resolves to use his remaining time to settle his accounts and make sure that those around him will be all right after he's gone. His hardest challenge is to make Artie quit smoking. In reality, Levinson the smoker died of a sudden heart attack in 1987, and the movie is not so much a cry against the evils of second-hand smoke as it is a story about two friends and how they deal with this unexpected turn of events.

As noted in the Epilogue, Link wrote a new Columbo play, *Columbo Takes the Rap*, which toured regional theaters in 2006 and 2007. And in 2010, he published a new book, *The Columbo Collection*, with twelve original stories featuring Columbo (see "Columbo in Print").

Columbo for Purchase

During the 1990s, Columbia House Video began producing episodes of the show from the 1970s for purchase. In 1996, the company produced a set of ten episodes: the two pilots (*Prescription: Murder* and *Ransom for a Dead Man*); "Murder By the Book" (#1); "Death Lends a Hand" (#2); "Etude in Black" (#8); "A Stitch in Crime" (#13); "Any Old Port in a Storm" (#17); "A Friend in Deed" (#23); "By Dawn's Early Light" (#26); and "Try and Catch Me" (#39). These high-quality videos are complete and unedited and they provide a great way to see the episodes in all their original glory.

Mark Dawidziak, author of *The Columbo Phile*, who helped Columbia House select the first set of ten videos and wrote the liner notes on the boxes, asked me to poll the *Columbo Newsletter* readership for a list of favorites for a second set, which was produced beginning in 1997. They were: "Suitable for Framing" (#4); "The Most Dangerous Match" (#14); "Double Exposure" (#19); "Negative Reaction" (#25); "Playback" (#28); "A Deadly State of Mind" (#29); "A Matter of Honor" (#33); "Last Salute to the Commodore" (#35); "Murder Under Glass" (#40); and "How to Dial a Murder" (#42). Following this came the third set of ten episodes: "Lady in Waiting" (#5); "Short Fuse" (#6); "Blueprint for Murder" (#7); "Dagger of the Mind" (#11); "Requiem for a Falling Star" (#12); "Double Shock" (#15); "Publish or Perish" (#20); "Mind Over Mayhem" (#21); "An Exercise in Fatality" (#24); and "Fade in to Murder" (#36). Thus far that is the total, thirty out of the original forty-five pilots and episodes. The best ones were not always those produced. Sometimes, the cost of "clearing the rights" to a particular episode (for example, the Henry Mancini music in "Now You See Him" (#34)) was too high.

Finally, in the new millennium, Universal began creating high-quality DVDs of the show by season. Oddly, although Peter Falk still had an office at Universal at the time, the studio made no effort to approach him to put extra material on the DVDs and now that opportunity is lost. On September 7, 2004, it released a 5-disc set of the first season, including the two pilots as a bonus. Further sets were produced approximately once a year, as follows.

On March 8, 2005, a 4-disc set of the second season was released (no bonus feature). On August 9, 2005, a 2-disc set of double-sided discs of the third season was released, with "Murder is a Parlor Game" (the Donald Pleasance episode of the disastrous show *Mrs. Columbo*) as a bonus.

On March 14, 2006, a 3-disc doubled-sided set of the fourth season was released, with "A Riddle for Puppets" (again *Mrs. Columbo*) as a bonus feature. On June 27, 2006, a 3-disc set of the fifth season was released, with "Caviar With Everything" (*Mrs. Columbo*) as a bonus feature. On November 21, 2006, a 3-disc set of the sixth and seventh seasons was released (no bonus feature). On April 27, 2007, a 3-disc set of the five episodes aired in 1989 (that is, the four from season eight plus "Murder: A Self Portrait" (#48)) was released, with a bonus feature called "Top 10 Sleuths." On February 1, 2009, a 3-disc set of the six episodes from 1990 (that is, the rest of the ninth season plus "Columbo Goes to College" (#54)) was released, with previews as the bonus feature. On February 8, 2011, a 3-disc set of six episodes from 1991-93 (that is, from "Caution: Murder Can Be Hazardous to Your Health" (#55) to "It's All in the Game" (#60)) was released, again with previews as a bonus feature. Finally, on January 10, 2012, the final 3-disc set of the seven movies from 1994 to 2003 (from "Butterfly in Shades of Grey" (#61) to "Columbo Likes the Nightlife" (#67)) was produced, with previews as a bonus feature.

Columbo in Print

Columbo was not confined to television or even the theater stage. Over the years, the character has appeared in several series of books. In addition, the show has been written about. Details about these writings follow

1970s Tie-in Books

In the 1970s, with the popularity of *Columbo* on television, a number of "tie-in" books were printed. Although they are now out of print and difficult to find, here is a listing of them.

1) *Columbo* (1972) by Alfred Lawrence, an original novel.

2) *The Dean's Death* (1975), also by Lawrence, another original novel.

3) *Any Old Port in a Storm* (1975) by Henry Clement, is a retelling of the third season episode of the same name (#17).

4) *By Dawn's Early Light* (1975), also by Clement, is an adaptation of the fourth season episode of the same name (#26).

5) *Murder By the Book* (1976), by Lee Hays, is an adaptation of the first episode (#1).

6) *A Deadly State of Mind* (1976), also by Hays, is an adaptation of the fourth season episode of the same name (#29).

7) *Columbo and the Samurai Sword* (1980) by Walter J. Black and Craig Schneck, is an original novel with some un-Columbo-like elements, including a high-speed chase, graphic details of the murder and a scene in which the killer advances on Columbo with a sword.

Stay Tuned/Murder on the Air

In 1980, Richard Levinson and William Link wrote a book called *Stay Tuned*, about their experiences in television. One chapter of the book deals with *Columbo*: the difficult time they had finding writers who could produce scripts with good clues and clever dialogue but without violence, sex, etc., their battles with network executives to keep the character as written and not to add violence, sex, etc., their battles to keep Peter Falk away from the scripts, and how they resisted Falk's request to direct an episode and then (when they had no choice) they gave him "Blueprint for Murder" (#7), set in a real building construction zone full of dust and loud machines, which made the task nearly impossible. Finally, they explain why they decided to leave as executive producers after the first year and why the expansion of the show to two hours was a mistake (see "The Bloating Problem").

In 1989, Ric Meyers wrote a book about TV mysteries called *Murder*

On the Air. The last chapter, entitled "The Fine Line," talks extensively about Levinson and Link, particularly their work on *Columbo* and *Murder, She Wrote.*

The Columbo Phile

In 1989, Mark Dawidziak wrote *The Columbo Phile: A Casebook* (Mysterious Press, New York). This book was the first time all of the 1970s episodes were discussed at length, the history of the show was explored and there were lots of interviews with Falk, Link, Levinson, and many of the guest stars, writers and directors. It is truly a delight to read and enjoy. Although the book is out of print, it can still be found in used copies and on eBay. Reading the book led to my correspondence with Mark, who suggested the idea of a Columbo newsletter. From 1992 to 2002, I edited this quarterly publication, occasionally including Mark's contributions, to further explore the 1970s episodes in depth and to briefly discuss the then-newly appearing 1980s and 1990s episodes.

Harrington Books

Beginning in 1993, mystery writer William Harrington (who also contributed to research for books written by Harold Robbins, Margaret Truman and Elliott Roosevelt) began writing original *Columbo* novels (that is, not adaptations of any aired episodes). Although he maintained some traditions (not giving the Lieutenant's first name, for example), his novels often contained graphic material and connections to real-life murders that the show never featured (e.g., JFK's assassination). In addition, although Harrington followed the program's format of showing the murder first and then bringing in Columbo, his novels read more like police procedurals with an eccentric main character. The Lieutenant seems like a slightly unusual member of the force who hangs out with other cops and reporters. He talks to many witnesses rather than engaging in a series of one-on-one dialogues with the murderer. He constantly accepts drinks offered to him, rather than politely refusing them because he's on duty. And Harrington has him say and think things that were mentioned on some or even one episode of the show (so we have no idea whether they were truly his thoughts or not) such as that he likes "anything from the sea" or that he's a bad shot. Sometimes, he even contradicts what he has said on the show; in *The Game Show Killer* he states that only his wife goes bowling, but in "It's All in the Game" (#60) (aired three years before this book was published), he tells Barney (not Burt—Harrington has not updated Columbo's favorite eatery) that he is taking his wife bowling).

In all, Harrington wrote six novels: *The Grassy Knoll* (1993); *The Helter Skelter Murders* (1994); *The Hoffa Connection* (1995); *The Game Show Killer* (1996); *The Glitter Murder* (1997); and *The Hoover Files* (1998). On November 8, 2000, Harrington was found dead in his Greenwich, Connecticut home, an apparent suicide at age sixty-eight.

Just One More Thing

Peter Falk titled his 2006 book of memories (he refused to call it an autobiography) *Just One More Thing*, after Columbo's favorite catch-phrase. Much of the book is devoted to Falk's musings about various topics, his retelling of stories from his travels around the world and various acting parts and his marriage to Shera Danese. But he does talk about *Columbo*: his love for the character, his devotion to finding good scripts and clever clues and his battles with the network to maintain quality.

The Columbo Collection

In 2010, Link wrote a new book, *The Columbo Collection* (Crippen & Landru Publishers, Norfolk, Virginia). It contains twelve brand-new *Columbo* stories, not adaptations of previously aired episodes. Many of the stories are very short and bare-bones; they contain just the murder, Columbo's initial observations and the final scene. Some of them are longer. Interestingly, the character returns to his original portrayal from Levinson and Link's TV telecast ("Enough Rope") and first play—he is the worn-down civil servant, badly in need of a shave, haircut and a nap, polite but not the nice guy as Falk would portray him in later years of the show. This is not surprising, as Link is on record as not entirely approving of Falk's broadening of the character, the humor and the gestures. See "The Developing Character" for more. In a foreword, Link provides the history of how *Columbo* came to be, and dispels some popular myths. Peter Falk did not actually like cigars (he was a cigarette smoker for many years until he gave it up).

Offspring

Columbo is unique, but that doesn't mean there haven't been attempts to copy its qualities. The following shows are unquestionably offspring of *Columbo*.

First of all, Levinson and Link, along with Peter S. Fischer, made their own follow-up show by the name of *Murder, She Wrote* (CBS 1984-96). The show starred Angela Lansbury as Jessica Fletcher, a mystery novelist and amateur detective in the small town of Cabot Cove, Maine. Jessica was always stumbling across murder mysteries and helping the local authorities, both in Cabot Cove and in other locations to which she traveled. Like *Columbo*, the show focused on clever clues and did not contain much violence or sex. And like *Columbo*, after it left its regular time slot, the character appeared in a series of TV movies.

Link also produced *Over My Dead Body* (CBS 1990-91), with Edward Woodward as crusty English mystery novelist Maxwell Beckett and Jessica Lundy as his assistant. And later he was behind *The Cosby Mysteries* (NBC 1994-95), with Bill Cosby as retired criminologist and forensics expert Guy Hanks. Link even appeared in several episodes as Hanks' music teacher.

Another descendent of *Columbo* was *Matlock* (NBC 1986-92, ABC 1993-95), with Andy Griffith as Benjamin L. Matlock, a gentlemanly lawyer in Atlanta who lulled his opponents into a false sense of security with his unassuming but canny manner. Matlock was like Perry Mason channeling Columbo. He always got his clients off, but no one saw it coming. He also spent a lot of time shining his old pair of shoes, something Columbo could identify with.

Then there was *Diagnosis Murder* (CBS 1993-2001), with Dick Van Dyke as Dr. Mark Sloan, chief of internal medicine at Community General

Hospital in L.A. by occupation and amateur sleuth by avocation. Sloan worked with the police to solve crimes, and his contact was none other than his son, Detective Steve Sloan (played by Van Dyke's son, Barry).

The strangest twist on *Columbo* was *Monk* (USA 2002-09), with Tony Shalhoub as Adrian Monk, former San Francisco detective on "administrative leave" following the death of his wife. Monk was like Columbo taken to the nth degree. Instead of eccentricities, he had phobias and a psychiatrist and he was accompanied in his crime-solving by a full-time nurse, Sharona Fleming (Bitty Schram).

Columbo on the Web

I highly recommend The Ultimate Columbo Website, http://www.columbo-site.freeuk.com. It contains lots of information about the series, including an interview with Michael Lally's son. It's the best resource for visual goofs, such as the two helicopters the show uses interchangeably during "A Friend in Deed" (#23) in the scene in which Commissioner Halperin flies over his own neighborhood and sees "the Bel Air Burglar" (actually his accomplice, Hugh Caldwell) dumping his wife's body into the swimming pool. It also has an FAQ section and fun trivia about the series and the character.

Naturally, there are lots of other websites that discuss *Columbo*, including William Link's own website, http://www.williamlink.tv, which contains lots of interviews that Link has given about the show that are a delight to listen to.

Finally, every *Columbo* fan should check out the Internet Movie Data Base, www.imdb.com, which contains full credits and information for practically every movie and TV show ever made, and certainly all of the *Columbo* episodes. Hyperlinks allow you to jump from actor to show and from show to actor. When you wonder, where else have I seen that actor? Check IMDB for the answer. IMDB also lists actors who went unbilled during the shows aired during the 1970s, but I have not included them in this book because I cannot independently verify them (except for Robert Shayne, who has no lines but does play the victim, Rudy Mathews, in Suitable for Framing (#4)—good catch, IMDB!)

Appendices

Appendix I.
Complete Ranking and
Commentary

When I first decided to rank the episodes, I did so without setting forth any criteria. To my surprise, I discovered that I came up with a list that was based upon articulable factors. Simply put, my rankings told me that the most important element of a *Columbo* episode is the plot. This is not all that amazing, when you stop to think that what makes a good mystery in general are good clues. Specifically, the most important piece of all is the final clue: it must prove enough to satisfy us that the murderer will not only be arrested but also convicted and it must not be something so obvious that Columbo or anyone else could have spotted it much earlier. Having tried this myself, I realize that this is no easy task. It is a simple matter to write verbal slips and tricks wherein the murderer says the wrong thing or does something he should not know how to do, but ultimately these endings are often disappointing. I have a great deal of respect for those final clues which are particularly clever, and that is why I feel justified in criticizing the writers when they settle for less than they should.

After the final clue, the most important piece is the first clue, the means by which Columbo comes to suspect the real murderer. Unlike the final clue, the first clue must not reveal too much or it makes the murderer look like a fool. On the other hand, it must be more than mere intuition on Columbo's part. In other words, the first clue must find the middle ground between too much and too little. As described elsewhere (see "First Clues"), in many of the episodes, there are actually two first clues: 1) Columbo's First Clue that the Scenario (the FCS) created by the murderer is false; and 2) Columbo's First Clue as to the Murderer (the FCM), the individual that we in the audience already know is the guilty party. Then come the rest of the intermediate clues that make up the episode—they too must increase suspicion but not catch the murderer too soon.

After the clues, I take more intangible elements into account: the character of the murderer, the delving into the murderer's profession, the opportunity to learn more about Columbo's past or his family, and so on. That is why certain episodes which would fall into a lower ranking on the basis of their clues alone rise to a higher position, for example, "Forgotten Lady" (#30), "The Most Dangerous Match" (#14) and "Try and Catch Me" (#39). Also, I consider the acting of both Peter Falk and the actor playing the murderer, then the contribution by the supporting players. Finally, I ask if the music, direction, title and other supporting aspects have any outstanding characteristics. It is far from a precise science, and I hardly expect others to agree with me at every turn, if at all.

What I have not taken into account are the opinions of others, neither those who produce the show nor the Academy of Television Arts and Sciences. Instead, I have relied solely upon my own reasoning and I have tried at every opportunity to express the reasons why I have made certain choices. Thus, for example, there is no conflict between my rankings of "By Dawn's Early Light" (#26) and "Death Lends a Hand" (#2). This is so because I call "By Dawn's Early Light" (#26) the best episode based on my criteria, not the Academy's Emmy to Patrick McGoohan for his excellent acting in the episode. I disagree with the Academy in its award to "Death Lends a Hand" (#2) as the best written dramatic episode of the year, but because my decisions are extrinsic to theirs, I see no gap and have no reason to "explain" the Academy's decision.

I do not rank the series' two pilot movies, because they were never intended to be thought of as anything more than one-shot deals. I enjoy watching them to see the origin of the character and *Prescription: Murder* is still very good in many respects and not even dated although it was produced in 1968.

At the beginning, I also did not anticipate that the categories themselves would come to take on unique characteristics, but since then I have discovered that I can describe common features of episodes that all fall into a single category. Here then are the seven categories and the rough descriptions of the kinds of episodes that belong in them.

Excellent

Episodes in this category are the best the series has to offer. They contain the finest clues, the best acting by Falk and the guest stars and the best exploration of the intangible elements that make *Columbo* far better than the average detective program. The episodes that make up this category are ones I enjoy every time I watch them; in fact, each time I see them I notice some nuance that I hadn't caught before.

Very Good

Episodes in this category are highly praiseworthy, and contain excellent clues and fine acting. They also seem to have the curious property of one-time experimentation ("the one episode that . . . "). For instance, "A Matter of Honor" (#33) is the "hidden motive" episode, "A Stitch in Crime" (#13) is the "slow apparently natural death" idea (giving Columbo time to figure it out), and so on. What they lack are the little flourishes that elevate episodes into the excellent category. For instance, the problems I have with "Murder Under Glass" (#40) (too many witnesses, the "Kill Columbo Ending") made me, after considerable deliberation, move the episode from the excellent category to the very good category.

Good

There are two kinds of episodes in this category. First there are the solid episodes with good clues and strong but not outstanding endings ("Swan Song" (#22) and "Troubled Waters" (#27) epitomize this description). Then there are those episodes which contain only mundane clues but are elevated on the basis of well-written intangibles, outstanding acting and other elements ("The Bye-Bye Sky High IQ Murder Case" (#38) and "Lovely But Lethal" (#16)). Some of the confessional final clue episodes fall into this category ("Mind Over Mayhem" (#21), "A Case of Immunity" (#31), "Uneasy Lies the Crown" (#52)), suggesting the difficulties raised by this sort of ending (see essay on this topic).

Fair

Episodes in the fair category are filled with mundane clues and are undistinguished by fine acting, fine direction or other intangibles. This is not to say that they don't occasionally contain good clues or that the clues presented don't work, but only that the writers can and have done better. These are fair by comparison with the ones above, of course.

Poor

In a way, this is the worst category. Episodes that fall in the "bad" group simply had no ambition or contained so many problems that they were disastrous, but here by contrast what I sense is failed potential. The writers put forward an idea, such as a rival detective as the killer always keeping one step ahead ("Death Lends a Hand" (#2)) or an acting couple spiraling downward on the tragic path of Macbeth and Lady Macbeth ("Dagger of the Mind" (#11)), but the tree never bears fruit, the result being so disappointing as to make the effort a shameful waste. Also, these episodes are characterized by overacting by the guest stars and occasionally even by Falk. Nothing so undermines the character of a humble detective as the ego of the actor playing him, and scenery chewing by the murderers is not only inappropriate, but distracting.

Bad

As stated above, these episodes either contain no ambition ("Lady in Waiting" (#5), "Grand Deceptions" (#47)), or they make so many mistakes that I can't give them much credit ("Requiem for a Falling Star" (#12)). The final clues are often of the cheapest kind, such as verbal slips ("Last Salute to the Commodore" (#35)). The acting is uniformly overdone and distracts from what is supposed to be a dramatic program, not a comedy. And they attempt to tamper with the format of the program for no other reason than to attract attention (see "Variations on a Theme by Jackson Gillis" for more on this topic). In "Etude in Black" (#8), the final clue (the dropped flower) hits us over the head like a brick long before Columbo even enters the scene. There is great disparity between those episodes at the top of this category and those at the bottom.

Not Columbo

As the title suggests, these are the Ed McBain story "adaptations" that Executive Producer Peter Falk tried on two occasions, in "No Time to Die" (#58) and "Undercover" (#62), that bear no resemblance to the show we know. Either there is no murder, or there are many but we don't care, we don't learn who the villain is until the end so there is no opportunity for Columbo to joust with the murderer, he doesn't have his charming qualities and indeed he could be any cop on the force (which is appropriate for a police procedural like McBain's 87th Precinct stories, but not a character driven piece like Columbo). See "No Time for Columbo, No Place for McBain" for more on this topic.

Here then is my complete listing

Excellent

10.0   "By Dawn's Early Light" (#26)

9.9   "Columbo Cries Wolf" (#49)

9.8   "Try and Catch Me" (#39)

9.7   "Any Old Port in a Storm" (#17)

9.6   "Now You See Him" (#34)

9.5   "Negative Reaction" (#25)

9.4   "A Deadly State of Mind" (#29)

9.3   "Playback" (#28)

9.2   "A Friend in Deed" (#23)

Very Good

8.9   "An Exercise in Fatality" (#24)

8.8   "Blueprint for Murder" (#7)

8.7   "A Stitch in Crime" (#13)

8.6   "The Most Dangerous Match" (#14)

8.5   "A Matter of Honor" (#33)

8.4   "Murder Under Glass" (#40)

8.3   "Forgotten Lady" (#30)

8.2   "How to Dial a Murder" (#42)

8.1   "Double Exposure" (#19)

Good

8.0   "Swan Song" (#22)

7.9   "Troubled Waters" (#27)

7.8   "Lovely But Lethal" (#16)

7.7   "Columbo Goes to College" (#54)

7.6   "The Bye-Bye Sky High IQ Murder Case" (#38)

7.5   "A Case of Immunity" (#31)

7.4   "Uneasy Lies the Crown" (#52)

7.3   "The Conspirators" (#43)

7.25 "Mind Over Mayhem" (#21)

7.2   "Publish or Perish" (#20)

7.15 "Agenda for Murder" (#50)

7.125 "Columbo Likes the Nightlife" (#67)

7.1   "Murder With Too Many Notes" (#66)

7.05 "Ashes to Ashes" (#65)

Fair

7.0   "Columbo and the Murder of a Rock Star" (#56)

6.9   "Caution: Murder Can Be Hazardous to Your Health" (#55)

6.8   "The Greenhouse Jungle" (#9)

6.7   "Short Fuse" (#6)

6.6   "Butterfly in Shades of Grey" (#61)

6.5   "Murder By the Book" (#1)

6.4   "Murder: A Self Portrait" (#48)

6.3   "A Trace of Murder" (#64)

6.2   "It's All in the Game" (#60)

Poor

6.0   "Murder in Malibu" (#53)

5.9   "Suitable for Framing" (#4)

5.8   "Fade in to Murder" (#36)

5.7   "Sex and the Married Detective" (#46)

5.6   "Murder, Smoke and Shadows" (#45)

5.5   "The Most Crucial Game" (#10)

5.4   "Candidate for Crime" (#18)

5.35   "Death Lends a Hand" (#2)

5.3   "Death Hits the Jackpot" (#57)

5.25   "A Bird in the Hand" (#59)

5.2   "Strange Bedfellows" (#63)

5.15   "Dagger of the Mind" (#11)

5.1   "Dead Weight" (#3)

Bad

5.0   "Etude in Black" (#8)

4.9   "Lady in Waiting" (#5)

4.8   "Old Fashioned Murder" (#37)

4.7   "Grand Deceptions" (#47)

4.6   "Requiem for a Falling Star" (#12)

4.5   "Rest in Peace, Mrs. Columbo" (#51)

4.4   "Make Me a Perfect Murder" (#41)

4.3   "Identity Crisis" (#32)

4.2   "Columbo Goes to the Guillotine" (#44)

4.1   "Double Shock" (#15)

4.0   "Last Salute to the Commodore" (#35)

Not Columbo

3.5   "Undercover" (#62)

3.0   "No Time to Die" (#58)

Season Averages, Best to Worst

1)   Fourth Season (1974-75): 9.17

2)   Third (1973-74): 7.83

3)   Seventh (1977-78): 7.62

4)   Tenth (1990-91): 7.20

5)   Fifth (1975-76): 7.03

6)   Ninth (1989-90): 6.89

7)   TV Movies (1994-2003): 6.55

8)   First (1971-72): 6.18

9)   Sixth (1976-77): 6.07

10)   Second (1972-73): 6.06

11)   Thirteenth (1993-94): 5.43

12)   Twelfth (1992): 5.25

13)   Eighth (1989): 5.05

14)   Eleventh (1991-92): 4.15

Appendix II.
Columbo by the Numbers

Writing

Episodes written by Jackson Gillis (11): "Suitable for Framing" (#4); "Short Fuse" (#6); "Dagger of the Mind" (#11); "Requiem for a Falling Star" (#12); "The Most Dangerous Match" (#14); "Double Shock" (#15) [story]; "Lovely But Lethal" (#16); "Troubled Waters" (#27)[story]; "Last Salute to the Commodore" (#35); "Murder in Malibu" (#53); "A Bird in the Hand" (#59). See "Variations on a Theme By Jackson Gillis" for a discussion of his tweaking of the format.

Individuals Who Wrote Seven Episodes

Steven Bochco: "Murder By the Book" (#1); "Lady in Waiting" (#5); "Blueprint for Murder" (#7); "Etude in Black" (#8); "Double Shock" (#15) [co-writer]; "Mind Over Mayhem" (#21) [co-writer]; "Uneasy Lies the Crown" (#52)

Peter S. Fischer: "Publish or Perish" (#20); "A Friend in Deed" (#23); "An Exercise in Fatality" (#24); "Negative Reaction" (#25); "A Deadly State of Mind" (#29); "Rest in Peace, Mrs. Columbo" (#51); "Butterfly in Shades of Grey" (#61)

Richard Levinson and William Link: *Prescription: Murder* (pilot A); *Ransom for a Dead Man* (pilot B) [story]; "Death Lends a Hand" (#2); "Etude in Black" (#8) [story]; "Dagger of the Mind" (#11) [story]; "The Most Dangerous Match" (#14) [story]; "Double Shock" (#15) [story]

Individuals Who Wrote Three Episodes

Jeffrey Bloom: "Agenda for Murder" (#50); "Columbo Goes to College" (#54); "Death Hits the Jackpot" (#57)

William Driskill: "Troubled Waters" (#27); "Forgotten Lady" (#30); "Identity Crisis" (#32)

Dean Hargrove: *Ransom for a Dead Man* (pilot B); "Candidate for Crime" (#18) [co-writer]; "Mind Over Mayhem" (#21) [co-writer]

William Read Woodfield: "Columbo Goes to the Guillotine" (#44); "Columbo Cries Wolf" (#49); "Columbo and the Murder of a Rock Star" (#56)

Individuals Who Wrote Two Episodes

Howard Berk: "By Dawn's Early Light" (#26); "The Conspirators" (#43)

John T. Dugan: "Dead Weight" (#3); "The Most Crucial Game" (#10)

Peter Feibleman: "Fade in to Murder" (#36) [co-writer]; "Old Fashioned Murder" (#37)

Roland Kibbee: "Candidate for Crime" (#18) [co-writer]; "Mind Over Mayhem" (#21) [co-writer]

Stanley Ralph Ross: "Any Old Port in a Storm" (#17); "Swan Song" (#22) [story]

Lou Shaw: "A Case of Immunity" (#31); "Fade in to Murder" (#36) [co-writer]

Lawrence Vail: "Old Fashioned Murder" (#37) [story]; "Strange Bedfellows" (#63)

Robert Van Scoyk: "Murder Under Glass" (#40); "No Time to Die" (#58)

Stories by Larry Cohen (4): "Any Old Port in a Storm" (#17); "Candidate for Crime" (#18); "An Exercise in Fatality" (#24); "A Matter of Honor" (#33) [co-writer]

Stories by Ted Leighton (2): "Lady in Waiting" (#5) [co-writer]; "Blueprint for Murder" (#7) [co-writer]

Directing

Episodes directed by Vincent McEveety (7): "Rest in Peace, Mrs. Columbo" (#51); "Death Hits the Jackpot" (#57); "A Bird in the Hand" (#59); "It's All in the Game" (#60); "Undercover" (#62); "Strange Bedfellows" (#63); "A Trace of Murder" (#64)

Episodes directed by James Frawley (6): "Try and Catch Me" (#39); "Make Me a Perfect Murder" (#41); "How to Dial a Murder" (#42); "Murder, Smoke and Shadows" (#45); "Sex and the Married Detective" (#46); "Murder: A Self Portrait" (#48)

Episodes directed by Patrick McGoohan (5): "Identity Crisis" (#32); "Last Salute to the Commodore" (#35); "Agenda for Murder" (#50); "Ashes to Ashes" (#65); "Murder With Too Many Notes" (#66)

Individuals Who Directed Four Episodes

Harvey Hart: "By Dawn's Early Light" (#26); "A Deadly State of Mind" (#29); "Forgotten Lady" (#30); "Now You See Him" (#34)

Bernard Kowalski: "Death Lends a Hand" (#2); "An Exercise in Fatality" (#24); "Playback" (#28); "Fade in to Murder" (#36)

Individuals Who Directed Three Episodes

Alan J. Levi: "Uneasy Lies the Crown" (#52); "Columbo and the Murder of a Rock Star" (#56); "No Time to Die" (#58)

Leo Penn: "Any Old Port in a Storm" (#17); "The Conspirators" (#43); "Columbo Goes to the Guillotine" (#44)

Richard Quine: "Dagger of the Mind" (#11); "Requiem for a Falling Star" (#12); "Double Exposure" (#19)

Individuals Who Directed Two Episodes

Edward Abroms: "Short Fuse" (#6); "The Most Dangerous Match" (#14)

Hy Averback: "Suitable for Framing" (#4); "A Stitch in Crime" (#13)

Robert Butler: "Double Shock" (#15); "Publish or Perish" (#20)

Nicholas Colasanto: "Etude in Black" (#8); "Swan Song" (#22)

Daryl Duke: "Columbo Cries Wolf" (#49); "Caution: Murder Can Be Hazardous to Your Health" (#55)

Ben Gazzara: "A Friend in Deed" (#23); "Troubled Waters" (#27)

Richard Irving: *Prescription: Murder* (pilot A); *Ransom for a Dead Man* (pilot B)

Alf Kjellin: "Mind Over Mayhem" (#21); "Negative Reaction" (#25)

Ted Post: "A Case of Immunity" (#31); "A Matter of Honor" (#33)

Boris Sagal: "The Greenhouse Jungle" (#9); "Candidate for Crime" (#18)

Sam Wanamaker: "The Bye-Bye Sky High IQ Murder Case" (#38); "Grand Deceptions" (#47)

Music

Music by Dick de Benedictis (23): "Etude in Black" (#8); "The Most Crucial Game" (#10); "Dagger of the Mind" (#11); "The Most Dangerous Match" (#14); "Double Shock" (#15); "Lovely But Lethal" (#16); "Any Old Port in a Storm" (#17); "Candidate for Crime" (#18); "Double Exposure" (#19); "Mind Over Mayhem" (#21); "Swan Song" (#22); "A Friend in

Deed" (#23); "An Exercise in Fatality" (#24); "Troubled Waters" (#27); "Old Fashioned Murder" (#37); "A Bird in the Hand" (#59); "It's All in the Game" (#60); "Butterfly in Shades of Grey" (#61); "Undercover" (#62); "Strange Bedfellows" (#63); "A Trace of Murder" (#64); "Ashes to Ashes" (#65); Murder With Too Many Notes (#67)

Music by Bernardo Seagall (10): "Negative Reaction" (#25); "By Dawn's Early Light" (#26); "Playback" (#28); "A Deadly State of Mind" (#29); "A Case of Immunity" (#31); "Identity Crisis" (#32); "A Matter of Honor" (#33); "Now You See Him" (#34); "Last Salute to the Commodore" (#35); "Fade in to Murder" (#36)

Music by Patrick Williams (9): "Try and Catch Me" (#39); "Make Me a Perfect Murder" (#41); "How to Dial a Murder" (#42); "The Conspirators" (#43); "Murder, Smoke and Shadows" (#45); "Sex and the Married Detective" (#46); "Murder: A Self Portrait" (#48); "Murder in Malibu" (#53); "No Time to Die" (#58)

Music by Billy Goldenberg (7): Ransom for a Dead Man (pilot B); "Murder By the Book" (#1); "Suitable for Framing" (#4); "Lady in Waiting" (#5); "A Stitch in Crime" (#13); "Publish or Perish" (#20); "A Friend in Deed" (#23)

Music by Gil Mellé (4): "Death Lends a Hand" (#2); "Dead Weight" (#3); "Short Fuse" (#6); "Blueprint for Murder" (#7)

Music by John Cacavas (3): "Columbo Goes to the Guillotine" (#44); "Grand Deceptions" (#47); "Caution: Murder Can Be Hazardous to Your Health" (#55)

Music by James di Pasquale (2): "Uneasy Lies the Crown" (#52); "Columbo Goes to College" (#54)

Music by Steve Dorff (2): "Columbo and the Murder of a Rock Star" (#56); "Death Hits the Jackpot" (#57)

Acting

Actors who have portrayed the murderer multiple times:

Patrick McGoohan (4): "By Dawn's Early Light" (#26); "Identity Crisis" (#32); "Agenda for Murder" (#50); "Ashes to Ashes" (#65) [see "Multiple Murderers"]

Robert Culp (3): "Death Lends a Hand" (#2); "The Most Crucial Game" (#10); "Double Exposure" (#19) [and he appeared in "Columbo Goes to College" (#54) as Jordan Rowe, father of one of the pair of murdering frat boys] [see "Multiple Murderers"]

Jack Cassidy (3): "Murder By the Book" (#1); "Publish or Perish" (#20); "Now You See Him" (#34) [see "Multiple Murderers"]

George Hamilton (2): "A Deadly State of Mind" (#29); "Caution: Murder Can Be Hazardous to Your Health" (#55) [see "Multiple Murderers"]

William Shatner (2): "Fade in to Murder" (#36); "Butterfly in Shades of Grey" (#61) [see "Multiple Murderers"]

Other actors who have appeared multiple times

Michael Lally (31): see "The Thirty-One Hats of Michael Lally" for details

Dog (15): see "Bert, Barney and Dog" for details

John Finnegan (13): see "Bert, Barney and Dog," "The Supporting Cast" and "Colleagues and Sidekicks" for details

Bruce Kirby (9): "Lovely But Lethal" (#16) (lab attendant); "By Dawn's Early Light" (#26) (Sgt. Kramer); "A Deadly State of Mind" (#29) (Sgt. Kramer); "Identity Crisis" (#32) (Sgt. Kramer); "Last Salute to the Commodore" (#35) (Sgt. Kramer); "Make Me a Perfect Murder" (#41) (TV repairman); "Columbo Cries Wolf" (#49) (sergeant); "Agenda for Murder" (#50) (sergeant); "Strange Bedfellows" (#63) (Sgt. Phil Brindle) [see "Colleagues and Sidekicks" and "The Supporting Cast" for details]

Six appearances

Shera Danese: "Fade in to Murder" (#36) (Molly); "Murder Under Glass" (#40) (Eve Plummer); "Murder: A Self Portrait" (#48) (Vanessa Barsini); "Columbo and the Murder of a Rock Star" (#56) (Trish Fairbanks) [accomplice]; "Undercover" (#62) (Geraldine Ferguson) [victim]; "A Trace of Murder" (#64) (Cathleen Calvert) [murderer] [see "The Supporting Cast" for details]

Fred Draper: "Lady in Waiting" (#5) (cab driver); "Lovely But Lethal" (#16) (Dr. Murcheson); "Negative Reaction" (#25) (fingerprint man); "A Deadly State of Mind" (#29) (David Morris); "Last Salute to the Commodore" (#35) (Swanny Swanson) [murderer]; "Fade in to Murder" (#36) ("Joseph") [see "The Supporting Cast" for details]

Vito Scotti: "Any Old Port in a Storm" (#17) (maitre d'); "Candidate for Crime" (#18) (Mr. Chadwick); Swan Song (#23) (Mr. Grindell); "Negative Reaction" (#25) (Thomas Dolan); "Identity Crisis" (#32) (Salvatore DeFonte); "Murder: A Self Portrait" (#48) (Vito) [see "The Supporting Cast" for details]

Five appearances

Ed McCready: "Rest in Peace, Mrs. Columbo" (#51) (plainclothesman); "Death Hits the Jackpot" (#57) (security guard); "A Bird in the Hand" (#59) (Ed); "It's All in the Game" (#60) (detective number 2) Strange Bedfellows (#63) (man in bar)

Four appearances

Val Avery: "Dead Weight" (#3) (Harry Barnes); "The Most Crucial Game" (#10) (Ralph Dobbs); "A Friend in Deed" (#23) (Artie Jessup) [framed]; "Identity Crisis" (#32) (Louie the bartender) [see "The Supporting Cast" for details]

Steven Gilborn: "Uneasy Lies the Crown" (#52); "Columbo Goes to College" (#54); "Caution: Murder Can Be Hazardous to Your Health"

(#55); "Columbo and the Murder of a Rock Star" (#56) (all as the medical examiner, Dr. Johnson) [see "The Supporting Cast" for details]

Jerome Guardino: "Forgotten Lady" (#30) (Harris); "Try and Catch Me" (#39) (Sgt. Burke); "Make Me a Perfect Murder" (#41) (Sgt. Burke); "Murder, Smoke and Shadows" (#45) (Sgt. Burke) (see "Colleagues and Sidekicks")

Gerry Okuneff: "Death Hits the Jackpot" (#57) (patrolman); "A Bird in the Hand" (#59) (dealer); "It's All in the Game" (#60) (plainclothes detective) Strange Bedfellows (#63) (Walter Sterling)

Three Appearances

Timothy Carey: *Ransom for a Dead Man* (pilot B) (Bert); "Dead Weight" (#3) (Bert); "Fade in to Murder" (#36) (Tony) [see "Bert, Barney and Dog" for more details]

Cliff Carnell: "Blueprint for Murder" (#7) (Officer Wilson); "The Most Crucial Game" (#10) (plainclothesman); "Identity Crisis" (#32) (Don)

Carolyn Carradine: "Grand Deceptions" (#47) (major's wife); "Columbo and the Murder of a Rock Star" (#56) (receptionist); "Butterfly in Shades of Grey" (#61) (first biker)

Manuel DePina: "The Most Dangerous Match" (#14) (second reporter); "Double Exposure" (#19) (first detective); "An Exercise in Fatality" (#24) (photographer)

Robert Donner: "Any Old Port in a Storm" (#17) (drunk); Caution: Murder Can Be Hazardous to Your Health (Arnie) (#55); "Undercover" (#62) (Zeke Rivers)

Alan Fudge: "Publish or Perish" (#20) (David Chase); "Columbo Goes to the Guillotine" (#44) (Mr. Harrow); "Columbo Goes to College" (#54) (Mr. Redman)

Harvey Gold: "Negative Reaction" (#25) (Harry Lewis); "Forgotten Lady" (#30) (deputy coroner Henderson); "A Case of Immunity" (#31) (coroner)

Victor Izay: "An Exercise in Fatality" (#24) (medical examiner); "Now You See Him" (#34) (Lassiter); "Fade in to Murder" (#36) (Conroy)

Morgan Jones: "Columbo Cries Wolf" (#49) (Wilson); "Uneasy Lies the Crown" (#52) (lab technician); "Columbo Goes to College" (#54) (crime lab man)

Jimmy Joyce: "Blueprint for Murder" (#7) (workman); "Last Salute to the Commodore" (#35) (handwriting expert); "Fade in to Murder" (#36) (workman)

Milt Kogan: "Make Me a Perfect Murder" (#41) (dubbing chief); "Columbo Goes to the Guillotine" (#44) (medical examiner); "Grand Deceptions" (#47) (medical examiner)

Charles Macaulay: *Ransom for a Dead Man* (pilot B) (Richard); "Etude in Black" (#8) (Durkee); "Mind Over Mayhem" (#21) (Farnsworth)

Vincent J. McEveety [son of director Vincent McEveety]: "A Bird in the Hand" (#59) (second policeman); "It's All in the Game" (#60) (policeman); "A Trace of Murder" (#64) (busboy)

John Petlock: "Murder in Malibu" (#53) (plainclothesman number 2); "A Bird in the Hand" (#59)(medical examiner); "It's All in the Game" (#60) (male guest)

Dennis Robertson: "Double Exposure" (#19) (Det. Marley); "Mind Over Mayhem" (#21) (first reporter); "An Exercise in Fatality" (#24) (Jerry)

Richard Stahl: "The Most Crucial Game" (#10) (Mr. Fremont); "Lovely But Lethal" (#16) (Burton); "Double Exposure" (#19) (ballistics man)

Bill Zuckert: "Negative Reaction" (#25) (Captain Sampson); "A Case of Immunity" (#31) (Captain August); "Murder in Malibu" (#53) (Mrs. Shannon's father)

Steward J. Zully: "Murder, Smoke and Shadows" (#45) (Det. Archie Sewell); "Sex and the Married Detective" (#46) (Sgt. Burke) (see "Colleagues and Sidekicks"); "It's All in the Game" (#60) (investigator number 3)

Two appearances

Robin Bach: "Rest in Peace, Mrs. Columbo" (#51) (waiter); "Columbo Goes to College" (#54) (maitre d')

Alice Backes: "Negative Reaction" (#25) (Mrs. Mayland); "A Trace of Murder" (#64) (Harriet Jenkins)

Frank Baxter: "Lady in Waiting" (#5) (Fred); "Fade in to Murder" (#36) (Walter Gray)

Ed Begley, Jr.: "How to Dial a Murder" (#42) (Officer Stein); "Undercover" (#62) (Irving Krutch) [murderer]

Alma Beltran: "Double Exposure" (#19) (housekeeper); "A Friend in Deed" (#23) (Mrs. Fernandez)

Sorrell Booke: "Swan Song" (#22) (J.J. Stringer); "The Bye-Bye Sky High IQ Murder Case" (#38) (Bertie Hastings) [victim]

Lew Brown: "Short Fuse" (#6) (Farrell); "Candidate for Crime" (#18) (second detective)

Joshua Bryant: "A Friend in Deed" (#23) (Dr. MacMurray); "Last Salute to the Commodore" (#35) (Wayne Taylor)

William Bryant: "Requiem for a Falling Star" (#12) (Sgt. Jeffries); "Mind Over Mayhem" (#21) (Fields)

Morris Buchanan: "A Deadly State of Mind" (#29) (lab man); "Old Fashioned Murder" (#37) (second detective)

Bart Burns: "Requiem for a Falling Star" (#12) (Sgt. Fields); "Playback" (#28) (Thompson)

Larry Burrell: "Candidate for Crime" (#18) (newsman); "Swan Song" (#22) (TV reporter)

David Byrd: "Murder: A Self Portrait" (#48) (Ralph); "No Time to Die" (#58) (Bill Bailey)

Don Calfa: "Rest in Peace, Mrs. Columbo" (#51) (Rudy); "Strange Bedfellows" (#63) (Rudy the bartender)

Dabney Coleman: "Double Shock" (#15) (Det. Murray) [see "Colleagues and Sidekicks"]; "Columbo and the Murder of a Rock Star" (#56) (Hugh Creighton) [murderer]

Regis J. Cordic: "Any Old Port in a Storm" (#17) (Lewis); "Candidate for Crime" (#18) (deputy commissioner)

Sondra Currie: "Murder in Malibu" (#53) (Mrs. Rocca); "Columbo and the Murder of a Rock Star" (#56) (Sgt. Hubach) (see "Colleagues and Sidekicks")

Tyne Daly: "A Bird in the Hand" (#59) (Dolores McCain) [murderer]; "Undercover" (#62) (Dorthea McNally)

John Dehner: "Swan Song" (#22) (Roland Pangborn) [colleague] [see "Colleagues and Sidekicks"]; "Last Salute to the Commodore" (#35) (Otis "the Commodore" Swanson) [victim]

Bob Dishy: "The Greenhouse Jungle" (#9); "Now You See Him" (#34) (both as Sgt. Wilson) [see "Colleagues and Sidekicks"]

Walker Edmiston: "Dagger of the Mind" (#11) (gardener); "Any Old Port in a Storm" (#17) (auctioneer)

Stephen Elliott: "A Deadly State of Mind" (#29) (Karl Donner) [victim]; "Grand Deceptions" (#47) (Gen. Jack Padget)

Jude Farese: "Candidate for Crime" (#18) (highway patrolman); "An Exercise in Fatality" (#24) (Al Murphy)

Bernard Fox: "Dagger of the Mind" (#11) (Chief Superintendent Durk) [see "Colleagues and Sidekicks"]; "Troubled Waters" (#27) (Purser Preston Watkins)

Michael Fox: "Etude in Black" (#8); "The Most Dangerous Match" (#14) (both as Dr. Benson, the veterinarian)

Anne Francis: "Short Fuse" (#6) (Betty Bishop); "A Stitch in Crime" (#13) (Sharon Martin) [victim]

Robert Gibbons: "Blueprint for Murder" (#7) (clerk); "Now You See Him" (#34) (Rogers)

Redmond Gleeson: "A Deadly state of Mind" (#29) (Arnold); "Now You See Him" (#34) (George Thomas)

James Gregory: "Short Fuse" (#6) (David Buckner) [victim]; "The Most Crucial Game" (#10) (Coach Larry Rizzo)

Molly Hagan: "Murder, Smoke and Shadows" (#45) (Ruth Jernigan); "Butterfly in Shades of Grey" (#61) (Victoria Chase)

Deidre Hall: "Mind Over Mayhem" (#21) (receptionist); "Columbo Cries Wolf" (#49) (Dian Hunter) [victim]

Mariette Hartley: "Publish or Perish" (#20) (Eileen McRae); "Try and Catch Me" (#39) (Veronica Bryce)

Lenny Hicks: "Columbo Goes to the Guillotine" (#44) (Eddie); "Murder: A Self Portrait" (#48) (morgue attendant)

Rosanna Huffman: "Suitable for Framing" (#4) (Tracy O'Connor) [victim]; "Rest in Peace, Mrs. Columbo" (#51) (Mrs. Thornwood) [note: Rosanna Huffman was the wife of Richard Levinson, co-creator of the show]

Wilfrid Hyde-White: "Dagger of the Mind" (#11) (Tanner) [victim]; "Last Salute to the Commodore" (#35) (Kittering)

Robert Karnes: "The Greenhouse Jungle" (#9) (Grover); "Candidate for Crime" (#18) (Sgt. Vernon)

Don Keefer: "Death Lends a Hand" (#2) (medical examiner); "The Most Crucial Game" (#10) (deputy coroner)

Jefferson Kibbee: "Mind Over Mayhem" (#21) (Jeff); "Swan Song" (#22) (Frank)

Bernie Kuby: "Murder By the Book" (#1) (Mike Tucker); "A Friend in Deed" (#23) (Nathan Flowers)

Michael Edward Lally (Michael Lally's son): "Swan Song" (#22) (cameraman); "Negative Reaction" (#25) (property room guy)

Ida Lupino: "Short Fuse" (#6) (Doris Buckner); "Swan Song" (#22) (Edna Brown) [victim]

Arlene Martel: "The Greenhouse Jungle" (#9) (Gloria West); "A Friend in Deed" (#23) (saleswoman) [note: it's true that the credits list her as "Tanya Baker" in "Double Exposure" (#19), but she does not appear in the episode!]

Todd Martin: "The Bye-Bye Sky High IQ Murder Case" (#38); "Murder Under Glass" (#40) (both as Sgt. Burke) [see "Colleagues and Sidekicks"]

John McCann: "Any Old Port in a Storm" (#17) (officer); "The Conspirators" (#43) (Brandon)

James McEachin: "Etude in Black" (#8) (Billy); "Make Me a Perfect Murder" (#41) (Walter Mearhead)

Lucille Meredith: "Candidate for Crime" (#18) (Lucy); "Swan Song" (#22) (head seamstress)

Ray Milland: "Death Lends a Hand" (#2) (Arthur Kennicut); "The Greenhouse Jungle" (#9) (Jarvis Goodland) [murderer]

Leslie Nielsen: "Lady in Waiting" (#5) (Peter Hamilton); "Identity Crisis" (#32) ("Geronimo"/A.J. Henderson) [victim]

Stuart Nisbet: "Short Fuse" (#6) (pinstripe); "The Most Dangerous Match" (#14) (Dr. Sullivan)

Jeanette Nolan: "Double Shock" (#15) (Mrs. Peck); "The Conspirators" (#43) (Kate O'Connell)

Tim O'Connor: "Double Shock" (#15) (Michael Hathaway) [framed]; "Old Fashioned Murder" (#37) (Edward Lytton) [victim]

Patrick O'Neal: "Blueprint for Murder" (#7) (Elliott Markham) [murderer]; "Make Me a Perfect Murder" (#41) (Frank Flanagan)

Michael Prince: "The Conspirators" (#43) (Michael Moore); "Death Hits the Jackpot" (#57) (Mr. Weatherford)

Barbara Rhoades: Lady in Waiting (#4) (hostess); "Identity Crisis" (#32) (Joyce)

Richard Riehle: "Ashes to Ashes" (#65); "Murder With Too Many Notes" (#66) (both as Sgt. Degarmo) [see "Colleagues and Sidekicks"]

Clete Roberts: "Dead Weight" (#3) (TV newsman); "Candidate for Crime" (#18) (TV anchorman)

Bill Edward Rogers: "Columbo Cries Wolf" (#49) (policeman); "Rest in Peace, Mrs. Columbo" (#51) (uniformed policeman number 2)

Penny Santon: "Death Hits the Jackpot" (#57) (old Italian lady); "Undercover" (#62) (Lucia)

George Skaff: "A Case of Immunity" (#31) (Kura); "Make Me a Perfect Murder" (#41) (the producer)

George Sperdakos: "Now You See Him" (#34) (Thackery); "The Bye-Bye Sky High IQ Murder Case" (#38) (Mr. Wagner)

Dean Stockwell: "The Most Crucial Game" (#10) (Eric Wagner) [victim]; "Troubled Waters" (#27) (Lloyd Harrington) [framed]

Daniel Trent: "Death Hits the Jackpot" (#57) (Det. Braverman); "It's All in the Game" (#60) (detective number 1)

Joyce Van Patten: "Negative Reaction" (#25) (Sister of Mercy); "Old Fashioned Murder" (#37) (Ruth Lytton) [murderer]

Jay Varela: "Candidate for Crime" (#18) (Sgt. Rojas); "A Case of Immunity" (#31) (Capt. Ortega)

Robert Vaughn: "Troubled Waters" (#27) (Hayden Danziger) [murderer]; "Last Salute to the Commodore" (#35) (Charles Clay) [victim]

Danny Wells: "A Deadly State of Mind" (#29) (Gary Keppler); "Forgotten Lady" (#30) (bookstore clerk)

William Windom: *Prescription: Murder* (pilot A) (Burt Gordon); "Short Fuse" (#6) (Everett Logan)

Darrell Zwerling: "Mind Over Mayhem" (#21) (motel manager); "An Exercise in Fatality" (#24) (Lewis Lacey)

Switching Gears

Peter Falk wrote "It's All in the Game" (#60) and directed "Blueprint for Murder" (#7)

As noted above, Patrick McGoohan appeared in four episodes: "By Dawn's Early Light" (#26), "Identity Crisis" (#32), "Agenda for Murder" (#50) and "Ashes to Ashes" (#65); he also directed five episodes: "Identity Crisis" (#32); "Last Salute to the Commodore" (#35); "Agenda for Murder" (#50); "Ashes to Ashes" (#65); and "Murder With Too Many Notes" (#66). And he co-wrote "Murder With Too Many Notes" (#66).

Robert Douglas, who appeared as Dr. Pierce in "Troubled Waters" (#27), directed "Old Fashioned Murder" (#37)

Peter Feibleman, who appeared as Milton Schaeffer in "Old Fashioned Murder" (#37), wrote both that episode and "Fade in to Murder" (#36) [co-writer]

Dennis Dugan, who appeared as Theodore "Mac" Albinsky in "Last Salute to the Commodore" (#35), directed "Butterfly in Shades of Grey" (#61)

Miscellaneous Information

Most Often Used Professions of Murderers

Actor/Actress (5): "Dagger of the Mind" (#11); "Requiem for a Falling Star" (#12); "Fade in to Murder" (#36); "Murder in Malibu" (#53); "Columbo Likes the Nightlife" (#67)

Author/poet (3): "Murder By the Book" (#1); "Try and Catch Me" (#39); "The Conspirators" (#43)

Lawyer (3): *Ransom for a Dead Man* (pilot B); "Agenda for Murder" (#50); "Columbo and the Murder of a Rock Star" (#56)

Military person (3): "Dead Weight" (#3); "By Dawn's Early Light" (#26); "Grand Deceptions" (#47)

Radio/TV Show Host (3): "Double Shock" (#15), "Caution: Murder Can Be Hazardous to Your Health" (#55), "Butterfly in Shades of Grey" (#61)

Conductor (2): "Etude in Black" (#8); "Murder With Too Many Notes" (#66)

Motivational scientist (2): "Double Exposure" (#19); "How to Dial a Murder" (#42)

Police personnel (2): "A Friend in Deed" (#23); "A Trace of Murder" (#64)

Psychiatrist (2): *Prescription: Murder* (pilot A); "A Deadly State of Mind" (#29)

Scientist (2): "Short Fuse" (#6); "Mind Over Mayhem" (#21)

Total number of murderers: 73 (excluding "Undercover" (#62))

Male murderers: 58

Female murderers: 15

Total number of victims: 87, that is, one per episode/movie (excluding "Undercover" (#62)), or 67, plus:

two victims in the crime as planned: "Short Fuse" (#6), "Swan Song" (#22),

"Negative Reaction" (#25), "Old Fashioned Murder" (#37) and "Strange Bedfellows" (#63) (5 more), plus:

Follow-up murders of blackmailers, accomplices and schlimazels (see "Accomplices, Blackmailers and Schlimazels"): "Murder By the Book" (#1) (Lilly La Sanka), Suitable for Framing (#5) (Tracy O'Connor), "Dagger of the Mind" (#11) (Tanner), "A Stitch in Crime" (#13) (Harry Alexander), "Double Shock" (#15) (Lisa Chambers), "Lovely But Lethal" (#16) (Shirley Blaine), "Double Exposure" (#19) (Roger White), "Publish or Perish" (#20) (Eddie Kane), "A Friend in Deed" (#23) (Margaret Halperin), "A Deadly State of Mind" (#29) (Nadia Donner), "A Case of Immunity" (#31) (Rahmin Habib), "Last Salute to the Commodore" (#35) (Charles Clay), A Bird in the Hand (Fernando, Harold McCain), "Columbo Likes the Nightlife" (#67) (Linwood Coben) (15 more)

Past murders: "Requiem for a Falling Star" (#12) (Al Cumberland), "Old Fashioned Murder" (#37) (Peter Brandt), "How to Dial a Murder" (#42) (Lorraine Mason), "Murder, Smoke and Shadows" (#45) (Jenny Fisher), "Murder: A Self Portrait" (#48) (Harry Chudnow); and "Try and Catch Me" (#39) (Phyllis Galvin, tricky because she's not a prior victim of the murderer, Abigail Mitchell, but of the man she kills, Edmund Galvin) (total=6)

Most victims per episode:

1) "A Bird in the Hand" (#59) (3)

2) "A Stitch in Crime" (#13) (2 plus 1 attempted)

3) "Old Fashioned Murder" (#37) (2 plus 1 in the past)

Most frequent first name of murderer: Paul, as in Hanlon ("The Most Crucial Game" (#10)), Galesko ("Negative Reaction" (#25)) and Gerard ("Murder Under Glass" (#40))

Most frequent first name of victim: Roger, as in Dutton ("Dead Weight"

(#3)), Haversham ("Dagger of the Mind" (#11)) and White (Double Exposure #19))

Male victims: 62

Female victims: 22

Nights of the week on which episodes originally aired

Sunday (36): second to sixth seasons [31]; "Columbo Goes to College" (#54); "Death Hits the Jackpot" (#57); "No Time to Die" (#58); "A Bird in the Hand" (#59); "It's All in the Game" (#60)

Monday (13): *Ransom for a Dead Man* (pilot B); "Try and Catch Me" (#39); "Murder Under Glass" (#40); all of season 8 [4]; "Murder in Malibu" (#53); "Columbo and the Murder of a Rock Star" (#56); "Butterfly in Shades of Grey" (#61); "Undercover" (#62); "Strange Bedfellows" (#63); "Murder With Too Many Notes" (#66)

Tuesday (1): *Prescription: Murder* (pilot A)

Wednesday (8): first season [7]; "Caution: Murder Can Be Hazardous to Your Health" (#55)

Thursday (3): "A Trace of Murder" (#64); "Ashes to Ashes" (#65); "Columbo Likes the Nightlife" (#67)

Friday: none

Saturday (8): "Make Me a Perfect Murder" (#41); "How to Dial a Murder" (#42); "The Conspirators" (#43); ninth season minus "Murder in Malibu" (#53) [5]

Episodes by length

1960s-70s: 16 two-hour episodes, 2 two-hour pilots and 27 ninety-minute episodes

1990s and beyond: 24 two-hour episodes

Total: 42 two-hour installments, 27 ninety-minute installments

Episodes by type of ending credits

Fade in/fade out style (24): first three seasons [23]; "Rest in Peace, Mrs. Columbo" (#51)

Man with flashlight shot (15): seasons 4-6

Individual shot ending (16): seasons 7-9 (except Rest in Peace); "Columbo Goes to College" (#54); "No Time to Die" (#58)

Multiple shots but not fade in (10): "Caution: Murder Can Be Hazardous to Your Health" (#55); "Death Hits the Jackpot" (#57); "A Bird in the Hand" (#59); "It's All in the Game" (#60); "Butterfly in Shades of Grey" (#61); "Undercover" (#62); "Strange Bedfellows" (#63); "A Trace of Murder" (#64); "Ashes to Ashes" (#65); "Murder With Too Many Notes" (#66)

Music video of Columbo: "Columbo and the Murder of a Rock Star" (#56)

Credits on black screen: "Columbo Likes the Nightlife" (#67)

Printed in Great Britain
by Amazon